JIMMY PAGE

JIMMY
PAGE

THE DEFINITIVE BIOGRAPHY

CHRIS SALEWICZ

HarperCollins*Publishers*

HarperCollins*Publishers*
1 London Bridge Street
London SE1 9GF

www.harpercollins.co.uk

First published by HarperCollins*Publishers* 2018

1 3 5 7 9 10 8 6 4 2

© Chris Salewicz 2018

Chris Salewicz asserts the moral right to be
identified as the author of this work

Extract from *I'm With the Band: Confessions of a Groupie* by
Pamela Des Barres published by Omnibus Press © Pamela Des Barres

Plate-section images courtesy of the following: Art Zelin/Getty Images (p5, bottom left);
Dick Barnatt/Redferns/Getty Images (p2, middle); BBC Motion Gallery/Getty Images
(p1, top); Charles Bonnay/The LIFE Images Collection/Getty Images (p6, middle);
Henry Diltz/Corbis via Getty Images (p8); FG/Bauer-Griffin/Michael Ochs Archive/Getty
Images (p6, bottom right); Gijsbert Hanekroot/Redferns/Getty Images (p3, top left);
Koh Hasebe/Shinko Music/Hulton Archive/Getty Images (p6, bottom left); Keystone/Hulton
Archive/Getty Images (p7, bottom left); Terry O'Neill/Iconic Images/Getty Images
(p2, bottom right); Jan Persson/Redferns/Getty Images (p3, top right); Pictorial Press Ltd/
Alamy Stock Photo (p1, bottom right); Robin Platzer/The LIFE Images Collection/Getty
Images (p5, bottom right); Michael Putland/Getty Images (p5, top); © Joe Stevens
(p3, bottom; p7, bottom right); Tracksimages.com/Alamy Stock Photo (p1, bottom left);
Trinity Mirror/Mirrorpix/Alamy Stock Photo (p2, top); Chris Walter/WireImage/Getty
Images (p2, bottom left); Graham Wiltshire/Hulton Archive/Getty Images (p4); ZUMA
Press, Inc./Alamy Stock Photo (p6, top)

While every effort has been made to trace the owners of copyright
material reproduced herein and secure permissions, the publishers
would like to apologise for any omissions and will be pleased to
incorporate missing acknowledgements in any future
edition of this book.

A catalogue record of this book is
available from the British Library

HB ISBN 978-0-00-814929-1
PB ISBN 978-0-00-814931-4

Printed and bound in Great Britain by
CPI Group (UK) Ltd, Croydon, CR0 4YY

MIX
Paper from
responsible sources
FSC www.fsc.org **FSC C007454**

For Alex and Cole

CONTENTS

PREFACE

One chilly February evening in 1975, Jimmy Page journeyed in a black Cadillac limousine to David Bowie's rented house on 20th Street in Manhattan. The Led Zeppelin leader and Bowie had known each other since the mid-sixties, Page having played on several of Bowie's early records.

The pair were also linked through Lori Mattix, Page's Los Angeles-based underage lover and a cause of considerable concern in the Zeppelin camp, thanks to the criminal complications this could create for the Biggest Band in the World. What few knew was that Bowie had taken Mattix's virginity when she was just 14.

With the superstar pair having been reintroduced by Mick Jagger, Bowie had invited Page over to his place for an evening's entertainment largely comprising lines of cocaine and glasses of red wine, along with Ava Cherry, Bowie's girlfriend.

Mired in his *Cracked Actor* phase, Bowie was known to be living on milk and cocaine, and on the edge of madness. He had been inspired to devour the writings of Aleister Crowley, whose philosophy he had first dabbled in during the late 1960s: Bowie believed that Page's deep knowledge of Crowley had enhanced the guitarist's aura until it was rock hard and ringing with power.

But despite being intrigued, Bowie was extremely wary of Page. Conversation was somewhat stiff, although there was brief talk about Page's progress, or lack of it, on the soundtrack to filmmaker Kenneth Anger's occult masterpiece *Lucifer Rising*. Attempting to inquire how Page had developed his extreme aura, Bowie found his questions were never answered: Page would simply smile mysteriously.

'It seemed that he did believe he had the power to control the universe,' wrote Tony Zanetta, the head of Bowie's management organisation MainMan, in his book *Stardust*. Besides, Page was only too aware that Bowie was picking his brain, endeavouring to crack a magician's tricks.

At one point Bowie disappeared out of the room, and Page accidentally spilled red wine on a satin cushion. When the singer returned, Page tried to blame Ava Cherry, who wasn't in the room.

His guest's inscrutable behaviour had already rankled Bowie, and now he knew that Page was lying. 'I'd like you to leave,' he said.

Page's response was simply to smile at Bowie. The window was open, and Bowie pointed at it, snapping his words out furiously: 'Why don't you leave by the window?'

Page remained sitting there, maintaining his enigmatic rictus smile, gazing through Bowie. Finally, the Led Zeppelin leader stood up silently, stepped towards the front door and left, shutting the door forcefully behind him.

Bowie was terrified. Immediately afterwards he ordered that the house be exorcised. A sensitive soul whose perceptions were addled by drugs, Bowie believed 'it had become overrun with satanic demons whom Crowley's disciples had summoned straight from hell'.

When he later ran into Page at a party, Bowie straightaway fled the event.

INTRODUCTION

John Bindon, Led Zeppelin's security guard, had stagehand Jim Matzorkis pinned to the floor of a backstage trailer at Oakland Coliseum. Bindon, a sometime actor and London gangland heavy who had reputedly once bitten off a man's testicles and would stab another man to death the following year, was viciously pummelling Matzorkis with his fists and feet. But it was only when Bindon started trying to gouge out the stagehand's eyes that Matzorkis fully appreciated the danger he was in.

For much of this day of Saturday 23 July 1977 the possibility of such a grim outcome had been building. Many of Zeppelin and their crew seemed in a state of permanent rage, as if they had surrendered control to the large quantities of drugs consumed during the course of a 51-date tour that had begun on 1 April.

Later, Jimmy Page would be obliged to deny to me that what happened that day was karmic recompense for his flirtations with the occult. 'I don't think we were doing anything ... evil,' he said, two years later.

It was especially ironic that what happened at Oakland Coliseum that day, which would utterly transform the fortunes and career trajectory of Led Zeppelin, should be on the turf of Bill Graham, whose Fillmore West had been a temple of popularity for the Yardbirds, Page's previous group, and, along with Graham's New York showcase the Fillmore East, the scene of early break-out triumphs for Led Zeppelin. Although the confluence of the interests of Bill Graham and Peter Grant, Led Zeppelin's manager, had proved mutually advantageous in the past, it was always a disaster waiting to happen. Graham was the most powerful music promoter in the United States; Grant had reinvented the relationship between managers and promoters in the United States, often through heavy-handed behaviour. And as much as Grant terrified people, Graham also possessed a fierce temper.

The previous evening, Graham, who was promoting Day on the Green, as this event was billed, for an audience of 65,000, had been summoned to Led Zeppelin's hotel, the San Francisco Hilton, to honour a sudden demand for a $25,000 cash advance against their fee for the shows. Entering their suite, Graham noticed a cowboy-hat-wearing local dealer of hard drugs; in a flash he realised what the money was needed for.

Arriving only 20 minutes before the start of the gig, Page was so evidently befuddled from his drug consumption, by that stage largely heroin, that Graham could only watch as the Led Zeppelin leader set off for the stage in entirely the wrong direction; he was rescued by an aide who stopped him and despatched him on the correct course. Midway through the set Bindon crawled out onto the stage on his hands and knees and licked Page's boots.

As the wheezing, out-of-shape man-mountain that was Peter Grant lumbered up to the stage, Jim Downey, a member of the stage crew, commiserated with him about the excessively steep climb. For this presumption Bindon, who was accompanying Grant, punched Downey with such force that he slammed him into a concrete pillar and knocked him out.

'What happened? The fuck did I do?' wondered the victim as he came to. Downey was clearly unaware of an extraordinary management edict – egregiously pathetic in its arrogance – on what would become the final Led Zeppelin American tour: no one was permitted to speak to any member of the act, or to

Grant, unless they were first spoken to. (Flying on the group's plane, journalist Steven Rosen had been made fully aware of this. He was startled when the normally benign bass player, John Paul Jones, had verbally assaulted him, demanding all of his interview tapes – a response to an apparently unfavourable comparison of Zeppelin to the Jeff Beck Group that Rosen had made years previously. This incident was indicative of the prevailing mood on the tour.)

'What I didn't like about Led Zeppelin was that they came with force,' Graham wrote later. 'I had heard stories from other cities about how they had muscled promoters to get better deals. How they had shaken them down for money … I had heard about the ugliness of their security.'

But far worse was to come. Midway through Led Zeppelin's show, during Page's acoustic set, Matzorkis noticed a young boy removing wooden plaques from the doors of the dressing-room trailers: plaques that had the names of the artists on them, and which would be required for the repeat show the following day. Also on the bill, as support acts, were Judas Priest and Rick Derringer. Matzorkis told the kid to put them back. The kid was insistent that he would be taking them. So Matzorkis took them from him – allegedly cuffing him round the back of the head, although Matzorkis has always denied this – and wandered over to the storage trailer to lock them away. Unbeknown to Matzorkis, the boy was Warren Grant, the 11-year-old son of Peter Grant.

A few minutes later Matzorkis was still in the storage trailer when John Bonham, Led Zeppelin's drummer – surplus to requirements during Page's acoustic set – called to him from the bottom of the short flight of steps outside it. Peter Grant was with him.

'You don't talk to *my* kid that way,' Grant said, as Matzorkis stood in the trailer's doorway. The burly Bonham, an effigy of muscle and blubbery booze-fat, simply stood there, as though he was Grant's security wingman. Then Grant escalated matters, like the barrack-room lawyer and bully he could be: 'You don't talk to *my* kid that way. Nobody does. I can have your job.' Grant continued in this vein, accusing Matzorkis of 'roughing this kid up. I heard you hit this child.'

Stepping up the stairs, Bonham then kicked Matzorkis between the legs, sending the stagehand flying back into the trailer. Bonham followed him in, while a pair of bodyguards endeavoured to restrain the drummer, shouting at Matzorkis to get out of there. He did, through a rear door.

When he learned of the incident, Graham went to find Grant in his trailer. For 20 minutes Graham put up a spirited defence of Matzorkis, yet Grant refused to budge from his thinking: 'Your man put his hands on *my* people. On my *son*. How could you let this happen? How could you hire these people? I'm very disappointed in you.'

'Let me speak to this man,' Grant repeatedly demanded. When Grant finally insisted that all he wanted was to meet again with 'the man' who had caused these problems to 'make my peace with him', Graham somewhat reluctantly agreed to the manager's request.

Walking over to find Matzorkis in another trailer, Graham observed that Grant was now flanked by a pair of other men; one of them was Bindon.

When Graham introduced Grant to Matzorkis, Led Zeppelin's manager seized the stagehand, yanked him towards him and smashed him full in the face with a ring-covered fist, knocking him back into his seat. When Graham lunged at Grant, one of the security men picked up the promoter, threw him down the steps and shut the door of the trailer, standing guard in front of it.

Inside the trailer Bindon held Matzorkis from behind, while Grant started to work him over, punching him ceaselessly in the face, knocking out a tooth and kicking him in the balls.

Somehow, Matzorkis, who was screaming for help, broke free of Bindon. He managed to manoeuvre himelf to the rear of the trailer, but this was when Bindon leapt upon him and went for his eyes. Fuelled by adrenaline, Matzorkis finally twisted away and got to the door.

Despite the security man guarding it, Matzorkis managed to get out of the trailer and run off across the backstage area.

Meanwhile, tour manager Richard Cole, armed with a chunk of metal pipe, had been attempting to enter the trailer. Bob Barsotti, who with his brother served as Bill Graham's creative director, had prevented him, so he then turned on him. Realising that Cole was demented from the drugs he had seen him consuming during the day, Barsotti ran off, leading him on a merry dance down into the car park, where Cole ran out of steam.

By now several of Graham's security men had gone to retrieve their 'pieces' from where they were stashed in their cars' boots, but a seasoned member of the backstage crew reminded all concerned that the next day there would be another Led Zeppelin show: if the group did not play, 65,000 fans might very well riot. Yet the Graham crew consensus was that some-how the next day they would 'deal' with Zeppelin and their team. The promoter agreed with this thinking. He also made an offer: if they couldn't 'do' Led Zeppelin and their cohorts the next day, then he would personally fly 25 of his men to New Orleans, the next date on the tour, and they could mete out revenge there.

At Graham's home that evening, where the promoter had taken Matzorkis for protection following his release from hospital, he received a call from Led Zeppelin's US lawyer: he demanded that Matzorkis sign an indemnity waiver, giving Led Zeppelin protection against being sued over what he referred to as a 'minor altercation'. Unless this was received, Led Zeppelin 'would find it difficult to play' the next day.

Graham agreed to sign; his own lawyer told him that as he was acting under duress, it would not be legally binding. Besides, Graham had a plan. Knowing that Led Zeppelin would be staying in San Francisco for a further night following the Sunday show in Oakland, he had arranged with the local district attorney to arrest those culpable on the Monday morning.

At the Sunday concert the loathing of Graham's entire crew towards Led Zeppelin was palpable: they glowered at the band and anyone connected with them. Page played most of the show seated, and he and Jones both looked bored. Robert Plant, however, sang very well indeed, dropping occasional words of commiseration in the direction of Graham; bootlegs indicate that it was a far better show than the previous day, partly because Led Zeppelin appeared drug-free. Still, it was a tense affair, and many in the audience were drunk and rowdy. Rumours were running round that a murder had been committed the previous day.

The next day, Bonham, Grant, Bindon and Cole were arrested at the San Francisco Hilton and taken, hands cuffed behind their backs, across the bay to Oakland to be booked, where they were held in a cell for three hours. There was a very real chance that if the case went to a criminal court, all involved would be deported and never be able to work again in the United States, a serious financial worry.

Bonham was charged with a single count of battery, as was Grant; Cole and Bindon were each charged with two counts of battery. The news of their arrest and the incident at Oakland Coliseum made the news all around the world. When they were eventually released they were bailed at $250 on each charge.

As the arrests at the hotel were taking place, Jones was exiting the Hilton through a rear door. He climbed into a camper van with his family and drove out of San Francisco towards Oregon and Washington state, on a planned holiday before Led Zeppelin's next date, in New Orleans, at the city's Louisiana

Superdome. He was set to rejoin the band there on 30 July, in time for the show that night.

'As far as I was concerned, every one of those guys in the band was absolutely 100 per cent accountable for that shit. Because they allowed it to go on,' said Bob Barsotti. 'And we weren't the only ones it happened to. We were just the *last* ones. We were the only ones who stood up and said something. When we started looking into it, there were incidents like that all across the country on that tour. Trashed hotel rooms. Trashed restaurants. Literally like twenty-thousand dollars' worth of damages at some restaurant in Pennsylvania. Really outrageous stuff. Like where they physically abused waiters and people in the restaurant, and then just bought them off.'

'They would do things after the show,' said Peter Barsotti. 'The traditional "go get chicks out of the audience for the band". I remember standing by the ramp and seeing these guys get girls to come over. It was like no other feeling I'd ever experienced. It was like these girls were going to be *sacrificed*. I wanted to go out and grab these girls and say, "Don't do it, honey. Don't do it." I'm as hardcore as the next guy. But I was afraid for these girls.'

If it could be possible, worse was to come. Arriving on 26 July at the Royal Orleans Hotel in New Orleans, Plant received a phone call from his wife in England: she told her husband that Karac, their five-year-old son, was seriously ill and had been taken to hospital.

Then came another call from her. Karac had died.

A devastated Plant flew back to England. All remaining dates on that eleventh Led Zeppelin tour of the United States were cancelled.

At the funeral of Karac, Plant was joined by Bonham and Cole. But there was no Page, who had flown instead to Cairo, where he was ensconced by the pyramids in the luxurious Mena House Hotel. Jones, for his part, had simply resumed his family holiday. And Grant had also remained in the US. Plant would not forget this.

On 26 July Graham received a call from the Zeppelin manager. 'I hope you're happy,' Grant muttered down the line.

'What are you talking about?' Graham asked.

'Thanks to you, Robert Plant's kid died today.'

That one absurd assessment by Grant captured everything that had gone wrong with Jimmy Page's Led Zeppelin project.

Just considering the death of Karac Plant sets off an inescapable collision of images of those nude blond children crawling up the boulders on the *Houses of the Holy* sleeve, and of the child being held aloft, as though for sacrifice. You can't help but feel that this might have crossed the mind of the bereft Robert Plant on his wretched plane ride home.

The Oakland incident, and the death of his singer's son, marked an extraordinary, certainly hubristic fall for Jimmy Page, who since the beginning of Led Zeppelin in 1968 had become the greatest archetype of a globally successful rock star that Britain has ever seen.

'Jimmy Page grew up in the hypocrisy of the United Kingdom in the 1950s and found three chords that saved him,' said his friend Michael Des Barres. 'As Led Zeppelin developed, heroin was obviously the fuel of that mad coach ride through the countryside. And inevitable.'

The mystery of Led Zeppelin had been established almost entirely through the endless enigma that is Page; later, as the apprentice matured, Plant would offer a separate sort of leadership within the group. In tandem with their extraordinarily lyrical atmospherics, Zeppelin's complex beats were the dominant soundtrack for popular culture for nigh on a decade. But the music was only one part of it; without Page's extremely pure comprehension of the intangibles of rock 'n' roll – the perfect manner in which to exit a limousine, for example – Led Zeppelin would not have been granted their place in the pantheon of rock 'n' roll gods.

From the very start – those first publicity pictures with his fluttering eyelashes and choirboy's face – Page displayed a slightly smirking look of utter confidence and haughty control, with a hidden promise of something sinister cloaked beneath it. There is that very early photograph of the four Led Zeppelin musicians in 1968 clustered around the bonnet of a Jaguar Mk 2 3.8, which had a reputation as a bank robber's car. Page is encased in a then fashionable double-breasted overcoat, its collar pulled rakishly up; he stares at the camera from between those curtains of crimped black hair, smouldering with self-assurance and poise. It is an image maintained in the first official promotional shot of the band, issued by Atlantic Records: the utter Capricorn control of Page leaning over the other three members – his string-pulling hands resting on the shoulders of the two Midlands neophytes, drummer John Bonham and Plant, who resembles a frightened faun caught in the headlights.

Their look – especially that of Page – is like that of Charles I's cavaliers, perhaps especially of *Lord John Stuart and His Brother, Lord Bernard Stuart*, Anthony van Dyck's 1638 painting of two teenagers who would be killed in the English Civil War.

Half an inch under six foot tall, permanently clad in sensuous velvet and sexy ruffled shirts, his jawline frequently dusted with five o'clock shadow, and always with that aura of androgynous otherness, Page looked to many women – and plenty of men too – like dirty sex on a stick. This image was as integral to his art as the 20-minute guitar solos with which he would blast his audience's eardrums – the violin bow he would employ when performing 'Dazed and Confused' clearly doubled as a wizard's wand to manipulate concertgoers.

And it only gets better: this romantic dandy lives in a castle with a moat. Jimmy Page does very bad drugs seemingly forever and – unlike Keith Richards, a mere also-ran in the greatest ever UK rock star stakes – never gets busted … at least until Zeppelin is over. Moreover, he is held responsible for an entire genre of music – heavy metal! – with which his group is only tangentially involved, his true focus being a blending of UK and US folk traditions with a garage band sense of hard rock.

In his renowned isolation he is like a rock 'n' roll version of Howard Hughes. But in many ways, the very idea of Jimmy Page is as much a construct as any of David Bowie's personae. And – lest we take this too seriously – it is worth considering that when his own persona is deconstructed, Page is sometimes little more than a high-art version of Screaming Lord Sutch, the plumber rock 'n' roll showman on whose attractively kitsch shock-rock records he played session guitar.

'Everyone I worked with in the 1960s thought that rock 'n' roll was really an aspect of showbiz,' said Dave Ambrose, who played bass in Shotgun Express (with Rod Stewart) and the Brian Auger Trinity, who supported Led Zeppelin in San Francisco in April 1969. Later, as an A&R man, Ambrose signed the Sex Pistols, Duran Duran and the Pet Shop Boys, among others.

Many of Page's expenditures – the palatial residences, the vintage cars he was unable to drive (he never passed his test), the enormous collection of rare guitars – seemed designed to garner respect and support among the world's wealthy and influential, to make people aware of him, to elevate his extraordinarily inscrutable profile, and to establish himself as one of the principal men about whichever town he found himself in.

But at the same time, here was a rebel cocking a snook at the Establishment, having what he knew he wasn't meant to have. With Led Zeppelin there always was that sense of being resolutely 'underground', a card played with perfect panache by the band for most of their career: hardly ever on television, with no singles released in their homeland, Zeppelin existed from the very beginning as their own outsider identity. In a sense the damning review of their first album by John Mendelsohn in *Rolling Stone*, a magazine Page came to loathe, was perfect for them; it set in motion the 'us against them' agenda from which Led Zeppelin's success soared.

By 1977, the year their myth savagely unravelled, they would come to be seen as the embodiment of behemoth rock, all that the new punk movement stood against, but when Led Zeppelin started out in 1968 their anti-Establishment stance was about as punk as it could be.

'The big question today is, Why hasn't he done new music?' said Michael Des Barres. 'Well, why does he have to? Jimmy Page is his own art piece, a performance artist, and he's busy curating his legacy. There is nobody else whose roadie was Aleister Crowley. And it worked. Led Zeppelin were not a band; they were a cult.

'Led Zeppelin brought together all those kids who otherwise would just hang around parking lots in two-bit American cities, kids for whom the obvious decadence of the Rolling Stones didn't really connect. Instead, Led Zeppelin were their cult; they became a focus for and brought together all those disaffected, lost souls who would take the fantasy world of the group and its subject matter and project onto it their own interpretation of what they were.'

The world was ready for just such a package. Around the time the Rolling Stones were writing 1968's 'Sympathy for the Devil', Mick Jagger and Keith Richards had dabbled in a friendship with the Californian film director and occultist Kenneth Anger, but – as though proof that in such areas they were distinctly lightweight – fled his company the next year after the debacle of Altamont. Instead it was Led Zeppelin, driven by Page's assiduous academic interest in altered states and realities, that provided the soundtrack to the building public interest in the occult. In 1972 *TIME* magazine ran a cover story bearing the strapline 'Satan Returns'. Colin Wilson's mammoth ground-breaking study simply titled *The Occult* had been published in 1971. More populist was the *Man, Myth and Magic* partwork series, which commenced in 1970, providing highly readable accounts of a secret world that was exciting to the newly stoned with their now-opened third eyes. As was the manner of part-works, *Man, Myth and Magic* was extensively plugged in television adverts, featuring an image of a demonic figure, painted by Austin Osman Spare. Spare had been close to Aleister Crowley and was sometimes described as 'Britain's greatest unknown artist'; Page would become the world's leading collector of Spare's work.

By then there was something frightening about the very notion of Led Zeppelin. After I interviewed Page in 1979 in a relatively forthright manner for the *NME*, a senior editorial member asked me if I wasn't nervous of any potential repercussions. When I told casual acquaintances I was writing this book, I was met with similar responses: 'Jimmy Page? Black magic?'

For some years – a decade or so – this was the prevailing view of Page. But of course time is a healer, so it should be no great surprise that by the end of the first decade of the twenty-first century, and in his own seventh and eighth decades, Page had redeemed himself to become the most loved and revered of all classic rock stars.

This redemption was fitting, given that this is the man who almost singlehandedly established the notion of the guitar hero as part of contemporary culture. 'What about Eric Clapton?' you may ask. No: Clapton was too diverse in the paths he trod. It was the singularity of Page's work with his vehicle Led Zeppelin, underpinned by his extraordinarily startling and sinisterly attractive appearance, that awarded him the guitar hero crown. Guitar hero? Guitar god, more like.

His is an extraordinary story that has taken him to the very darkest of areas – but always driven by the search for his art.

You might not approve of the methods employed to unleash and liberate his creativity, and you can't avoid the impression that Page was vain, arrogant, fanatical and power-hungry, and indulged in a scandalous private life – much, of course, to the adoration of his fans. Yet many of the accusations against him were probably fabricated or at least exaggerated by his numerous enemies – though many of these, in the timbre of the times, were no more than cosmic spivs.

Certainly, Page was a man of his age – ambitious, worldly and pleasure-loving – but the demonic caricature of evil is mostly an elaborate myth. Not that he didn't gladly play it himself, of course. By mentioning in a very matter-of-fact manner how the congregation of the original church at Boleskine House, a home of Crowley, had burned to death, Page was positioning himself as being metaphysically hard, a cosmically tough motherfucker with complex connections to ghoulish gangs of strange spirits. It was, of course, a good way to attract impressionable women, a variant on those college student 'astrologers' who would take girls back to their rooms to read their charts and then shag them.

For a time Page was fascinated with – to give it its full title – the Isis-Urania Temple of the Hermetic Order of the Golden Dawn, a late-19th-century group of occultists whose members had included the Irish poet W. B. Yeats and Crowley, who – unsurprisingly – considered his poetry superior to that of Yeats and had a bitter falling out with the Irishman.

'Much of the Golden Dawn magic,' wrote Gary Lachman in his biography of Crowley, 'as well as Crowley's, has to do with what is called the "assumption of the god form", when the magician imagines he has become the particular god he wants to invoke by visualising his form enveloping his own.' Except you might feel that the 'particular god' Page wished to invoke was none other than himself: Jimmy Page, rock god.

And this stance was carried through to every aspect of his existence, including his appearances on stage.

'On the surface,' writes the American cultural commentator Erik Davis, 'Page's live performances present typical rockist values of spontaneity, virtuosity and sweaty abandon. But Page adds a novel element to the figure of the guitar hero, an element ... of mystery. So even as Page bares his cock rock before tens of thousands of fans, the Zoso doodle emblazoned on his clothes, he reminds us that he knows something that we don't. There is a gap between the hero whose performance we consume and the sage behind the curtain, who remains concealed, literally occult. This mystique makes Page far creepier than Ozzy Osbourne, who is hiding nothing, except maybe his debt to *The Munsters.*'

A balanced appreciation of Page's character reveals traits both admirable and detestable, but claims of his ethical failings have sometimes overshadowed an appreciation of his keen creative mind. Besides, his flamboyantly dissolute lifestyle was hardly different from that of many other rock stars of his age – such as David Bowie, or Mick Jagger, or Rod Stewart.

But Page had a longstanding relationship with the art of destruction, and had been preparing for a career of hotel-wrecking since early in his life. At the rear of the secondary school he went to, on Epsom's Danetree Road, there was a bomb shelter left over from the war. Although efforts to destroy it had been made on several occasions by his fellow pupils, it was a 14-year-old Jimmy Page who finally succeeded.

In what seems less an example of urban terrorism and more like a yarn from one of Richmal Crompton's *Just William* stories, an older boy had combined sodium sulphate, weed killer and icing sugar to make several miniature bombs. A couple of these had exploded in the school grounds, with the blame always attributed to the rough kids from the neighbouring council estate.

But then this arms race escalated. Another boy constructed a pipe bomb and placed it inside the bomb shelter. Once lit, however, the fuse on the bomb burned interminably slowly. After some 20 minutes without much progress, one of boys offered a solution: he had a fuse taken from a Jetex, a motor for model aircraft that was popular at the time, which they put in the pipe bomb.

'But nobody dared light it,' remembered Page's friend Rod Wyatt. 'So Jimmy said, "I'll do it." So he goes in the entrance of the shelter, and then he comes running out. As he runs out it goes off: *P-F-O-O-F! B-R-A-MMM!* And the whole corner, which was thick concrete, flies up in the air, bricks following it. And Jimmy is running out, laughing his head off into the playground.

'Reflecting on this, I thought, "Was that a sign of the times? That he was going to be part of the loudest rock 'n' roll band ever?" This gentlemanly young guitar player says, "I'll light the jet engine. I don't mind." It fits Led Zeppelin perfectly.'

1

SPANISH GUITAR IN SURREY

Born at 4 a.m. on 9 January 1944 in Heston, Middlesex, on the far fringes of London's western suburbs, James Patrick Page was the son of an industrial personnel manager, also called James, and Patricia, a doctor's secretary. The future superstar musician's name was a combination of both of his parents', who had been married at Epsom Register Office on 22 April 1941.

According to the mythology of his rock-star legend, Jimmy Page was 'born on a full moon', with all the occult, mystical weight that that phrase carries. Yet this is not precisely true. He was in fact born 31 hours before the full moon of 10 January 1944. While the baby boy and his mother might have felt the powerful energy of the rising Cancer full moon as he was born, the earth's only natural satellite was not yet at its peak. In time Page would become a student of astrology; he would learn that in his astrological chart his moon was in moody Cancer, his sun sign was determinedly ambitious Capricorn, and he had Scorpio rising, with its suggestion of powerful sexuality and interest in arcane areas of life.

To an extent this only child – until he started school at the age of five he hardly knew any other children – was always self-educated, manifesting a strong sense of self-fulfilment, even destiny – though there is often something fixed and inflexible about the self-taught. 'That early isolation probably had a lot to do with the way I turned out,' he said later. 'Isolation doesn't bother me at all. It gives me a sense of security.'

Heston, his birthplace, has a distinct sense of J. G. Ballard-like suburban anonymity, the net curtains firmly drawn on all manner of potential darkness. Heston lies on the direct flight-path into Heathrow Airport, less than three miles away, and today is a place blighted by the ever-present roaring reverse thrust of descending jet airliners. It was the beginnings of this noise pollution that led the Page family to move first to nearby Feltham, a distance of some four miles, where unfortunately the noise from aeroplanes was even more acute, and then the ten miles or so to the south-east, to 34 Miles Road in Epsom, Surrey, in 1952. (In 1965 Page would, with Eric Clapton, record a song entitled 'Miles Road'.)

Eight-year-old Jimmy Page was enrolled at Epsom County Pound Lane Primary School, and at the age of eleven he moved on to Ewell County Secondary School, on Danetree Road in adjacent West Ewell. His headmaster, Len Bradbury, who took over in 1958 when Page was in year three, had played football for Manchester United, and Bradbury's arrival at the school was only a few months after his former team had been decimated in the Munich air disaster. (Many years later Bradbury would be a guest of honour at Manchester United's ground, with pictures of him taken with the team's captain, Roy Keane, and Ryan Giggs.) Page was in the proximity of celebrity – and he could see that such individuals were sort of ordinary people.

At 34 Miles Road, Page discovered a Spanish guitar that had been left behind, presumably by the previous occupiers. Had it ever been played? Perhaps not. In the 1950s a Spanish guitar as an *objet d'art* in the home was considered a sign of sophistica-tion. 'Nobody seemed to know why it was there,' he told the *Sunday Times*. 'It was sitting around our living room for weeks and weeks. I wasn't interested. Then I heard a couple of records that really turned me on, the main one being Elvis's "Baby Let's Play House", and I wanted to play it. I wanted to know what it was all about. This other guy at school showed me a few chords and I just went on from there.'

'This other guy' was called Rod Wyatt. Although fascinated by the Spanish guitar, Page all the same had been flummoxed by how to play the instrument. During a lunch break at secondary school, he came across Wyatt, who was in a class a couple of years above him. The owner of an acoustic guitar of his own, Wyatt was running through a version of 'Rock Island Line', a chart hit by the revered Lonnie Donegan, when he met Page. In response to the younger boy's query, Wyatt instructed him to bring his Spanish acoustic to school and he would show him how to tune the instrument. From then on the pair became firm friends.

'My mate Pete Calvert and I were always at Jimmy's house bashing out our guitars for a couple of hours on a Saturday afternoon,' said Wyatt. 'Sometimes I'd go round to Jimmy's and his mum would say, "No, he's practising." When he suddenly realised he had it, he spent a lot of time practising. Sometimes six or seven hours a day. He told me he needed to improve his technique. And he eventually became the all-round perfect guitarist. Practice is what it's all about.'

What had really turned Page on in Elvis Presley's rockabilly song 'Baby Let's Play House', released in the UK six days before Christmas 1955, was the guitar playing of Scotty Moore, who served as Presley's guitarist from 1954 to 1958. On 5 July 1954 Moore had, with bassist Bill Black and Elvis himself, mutated the original arrangement of 'That's All Right' by bluesman Arthur Crudup into a version that combined blues and country music, creating one of the foundations of rock 'n' roll.

'Scotty Moore had been a major inspiration in my early transitory days from acoustic to electric guitar. His character guitar playing on those early Elvis Sun recordings, and later at RCA, was monumental. It was during the fifties that these types of song-shaping guitar parts helped me see the importance of the electric guitar approach to music,' said Page.

On 'Baby Let's Play House' Moore played a burnished rock-abilly rhythm. Page's love of the tune would not leave him, even after almost 20 years: about nine minutes into the live version of 'Whole Lotta Love' in the Led Zeppelin film *The Song Remains the Same* he breaks into a close simulacrum of Moore's licks. But that was a long way in the future: for now the 12-year-old Page assiduously studied and copied Moore's parts. There could hardly be a purer, more perfect example of this brand new musical form, an ideal introduction to what his life would become. Every day he would take his guitar to school on Danetree Road.

'When I grew up there weren't many other guitarists,' he told America's National Public Radio in 2003. 'There was one other guitarist in my school who actually showed me the first chords that I learned and I went on from there. I was bored so I taught myself the guitar from listening to records. So obviously it was a very personal thing.'

But he also had a seemingly separate life as a choirboy. Each Sunday, wearing the appropriate surplice and cassock, he would sing hymns at Epsom's St Barnabas Anglican Church. The first image in his 2010 photographic autobiography is of him in this mode – clearly he is being ironic. As so often in the life of Jimmy Page, cold realism lay behind the impetus for his choirboy stints.

'In those days it was difficult to access rock 'n' roll music,' he said to the *Sunday Times* in 2010, 'because after all the riots happened in the cinemas, when people heard "Rock Around the Clock" in the film *Blackboard Jungle*, the authorities tried to lock it all down. So you needed to tune in to the radio or go to places where you could hear it. It just so happened that in youth clubs they would play records and you'd get to hear Elvis, Jerry Lee Lewis and Ricky Nelson – but you had to either go to church or be a member of the choir to go to the youth club.'

Page had many of the characteristics of the only child, burying himself in books and, almost the ultimate cliché, collecting overseas postage stamps. But more and more since discovering that Spanish guitar at Miles Road, he immersed himself in becoming adept on the instrument. 'The choirmaster at St Barnabas remembered that I used to take my guitar to choir practice,' he said, 'and ask if I could tune it up to the organ.'

In Epsom there is a prominent motorcar showroom named Page Motors. It has often been claimed, even by myself, that this business is owned by members of Page's family. But this is not the case at all. His relatives on his father's side came from Grimsbury in Northamptonshire, and his paternal grandfather had been a nurseryman, tending to plants. (An irony that would not be lost on Page, who later had a Plant of his own to deal with, of course.) On his father's side there was Irish blood.

At 122 Miles Road, at the far end of the street from the Page family home at number 34, lived a boy of similar age to Page called David Williams. According to Williams, Miles Road, which lay to the west of Epsom, was distinctly the wrong side of the high street. To the east lay the plush property in which affluent commuters to London were ensconced. The Page house backed onto the railway line that transported these people to the capital, less than 20 miles away, and was identical to the Williams home, having a downstairs living room and dining room and a pair of bedrooms upstairs. Downstairs, beyond the kitchen, was an outside toilet. Although most of these houses, including the Pages', later had this feature adapted into a full bathroom, there is no getting away from the fact that these were distinctly basic homes.

Page's father worked in nearby Chessington, a personnel manager at a plastic-coating factory, and his mother was the secretary at a local doctor's practice. Despite the impeccable 'BBC English' – as such received pronunciation was known at the time – with which rock star Jimmy Page would express himself, his background was no more than lower middle-class, almost jumped-up working-class.

Another good friend, Peter Neal, lived on Miles Road. Page, Peter Neal and David Williams would hang out at each other's houses. Gradually Page's home – without any brothers or sisters to get in the way – became a focal point. He also had the advantage of enjoying both parents – although Wyatt mentions some growing tension between his mother and father. When Williams was just 13, his own mother had died: 'I am certain that Jim's mother was the initial driving force behind his musical progression. She was a petite, dark-haired woman with a strong personality, a glint in her eye and wicked sense of humour. She liked to tease me in a good-natured way, but let me hang out endlessly in their front room with Jim. I think she must have known my mother and, given the new circumstances I found myself in, I guess she felt sorry for me. Although I didn't realise it at the time, I can now appreciate her kindness and tolerance, for I must have been a fairly constant presence in her house.'

After hearing Chuck Berry, the black poet of rock 'n' roll sensibility, on American Forces Network radio broadcasting fuzzily from Germany in 1956, Williams acquired a UK EP that gathered together the songs 'Maybellene', 'Thirty Days (To Come Back Home)', 'Wee Wee Hours' and 'Together (We Will Always Be)'. He and Page played it incessantly, the latter being especially taken with 'Maybellene' and its tale of amorous automobile class struggle, and with 'Thirty Days'.

From the equipment Page quickly began to amass, it seems that this only child was a little spoilt – or, at least, certainly lucky. He was the first of his friends to acquire a reel-to-reel tape recorder, which he soon replaced with a newer model, selling the older one to Williams so he could then pass on the tapes of songs he would diligently record off the radio.

Discerning in their taste, certainly to their own minds, these boys truly cared for only a handful of artists: Elvis Presley, Gene Vincent, Little Richard, Chuck Berry and Jerry Lee Lewis – the eccentric and wild Jerry Lee, with his 13-year-old bride, being Page's especial preference. Eddie Cochran would soon emerge to join this pantheon.

They would visit and revisit their local cinemas to watch such films as *The Girl Can't Help It*, a minor triumph in 1956 that featured Little Richard, Fats Domino, Eddie Cochran, Julie London and the Platters. Also released that year was the more pedestrian *Rock, Rock, Rock!*, which had a highlight performance of 'You Can't Catch Me' by Chuck Berry, his patent-leather pompadour and sneering grin permanently lending him the appearance of one of those black pimps whose look Elvis Presley had tried so hard to emulate. One Saturday afternoon in 1960 Page and Williams would hitchhike 50 miles to Bognor Regis to catch Berry performing a solitary tune in the classic film *Jazz on a Summer's Day*.

In the record department of Rogers, an electrical goods shop on Epsom High Street, the three boys ingratiated themselves with the girl behind the counter. This ally would provide them with glimpses of record-company schedules of forthcoming releases. The boys would search out the most interesting names. 'Frankie Avalon and Bobby Rydell were clearly to be overlooked in favour of the likes of Screamin' Jay Hawkins or Big "T" Tyler,' recalled Williams. 'Also, song titles could often be a good indication of something a little stronger. The dreaded "A White Sport Coat (and a Pink Carnation)" was hardly going to evoke the sort of enthusiasm and anticipation we would have for titles such as "Rumble", "I Put a Spell on You" or "Voodoo Voodoo", was it?'

Soon appreciating the limitations of his Spanish acoustic instrument, Page worked for some weeks during the school summer holidays on a milk round, until he had saved up enough money to buy a Höfner President acoustic guitar. 'It was a hollow-bodied acoustic model with a simple pickup,' said Williams, 'but when he attached it to a very small amplifier, it made something like the sound we all admired. I can recall that Saturday morning when I was summoned to his house to first feast eyes on it. Jim was like the cat with the cream. Pete and I were allowed a strum, but by now we realised that any aspirations we might have had in that direction were going to be dwarfed by Jim's talent, desire and progress.'

After Page had acquired his Höfner President, his parents paid for lessons from a guitar tutor. But the teenager, anxious to play the hits of the day, found himself mired in learning to sight-read; soon he abandoned the lessons, preferring to attempt to learn to play by ear. Later he would appreciate that his impatience had been an error, finally picking up the skill of reading music in the mid-1960s.

'Rock Island Line', the tune that Wyatt had been playing when Page approached him, was a Top 10 hit in 1956 for Lonnie Donegan on both sides of the Atlantic – in the UK alone the record sold over a million copies. The song was an interpretation of the great bluesman Leadbelly's own version, and it became the flagship for skiffle music.

Skiffle, a peculiarly British grassroots companion movement to rock 'n' roll that required no expensive equipment, was played on guitars but also on homemade and 'found' instruments. Donegan, a member of Ken Colyer's Jazzmen, would play with a guitar, washboard and tea-chest bass during intervals at Colyer's traditional jazz sets. In 1957 the BBC launched its first 'youth' programme, *Six-Five Special*, with a skiffle title song. The craze swept Britain at an astonishing rate: it was estimated that in the UK there was a minimum of 30,000 youngsters – maybe almost twice that – playing the musical form. Across the country groups were created: John Lennon's Quarrymen were a skiffle group that would lead to the formation of the Beatles.

In accord with this spirit of the age, Page formed such a skiffle group, which his parents permitted to rehearse in their home. Really, this 'group' was little more than a set of likeminded friends, sharing their small amounts of knowledge about this new upstart form. Yet they seemed bestowed with a measure of blessing: in 1957, with Page just 13 years old, the James Page Skiffle Group, following an initial audition, won a spot on an early Sunday evening children's BBC television show, *All Your Own*, hosted by Huw Wheldon, a 41-year-old rising star (11 years later Wheldon would become director of BBC television). The slot in which they were to be featured was one hinged around 'unusual hobbies'. How did they get this television slot? By chance, runs part of their appearance's myth: the show was looking for a skiffle act, and someone working on it was from Epsom and had heard of Page's band. But there is also a suggestion that Page's ever-supportive mother wrote a letter to the programme, suggesting her son's group.

Unfortunately, the membership of the James Page Skiffle Group has largely been lost in time. For the television appearance, a boy named David Hassall, or perhaps Housego, was involved. Not only did his family own a car, but his father possessed a full set of drums, which David endeavoured to play.

On a day during the school holidays when the show was to be recorded, Page and Williams caught a train up to London to the BBC studio. Page's mother had phoned William's father to ask if his son would accompany him to the recording. 'The electric guitar itself was already heavy enough for him to carry, but the amplifier was like a little lead box and he clearly could not carry both.'

At around 4 p.m. Huw Wheldon appeared, fresh from a boozy media lunch, and asked: 'Where are these fucking kids then?'

His hair Brylcreemed into a rock 'n' roller's quiff and his shirt collar crisply fitted in the crew-neck of his sweater, Page – his

Höfner President guitar almost bigger than himself – led his musical cohorts through a pair of songs, 'Mama Don't Want to Skiffle Anymore' and 'In Them Old Cottonfields Back Home'. (Page had also prepared an adaptation of Bill Doggett's 'Honky Tonk', but he was – rightly – doubtful he would get to play it, as he felt certain they would need him to sing.) After the performance, he was interviewed by Wheldon, and, with an irony now all too evident, Page declared to the avuncular presenter that his intention was to make his career in the field of 'biological research', modestly declaring himself not sufficiently intelligent to become a doctor. His 'biological research' remark certainly was not glib; Page wanted, he told Wheldon, to find a cure for 'cancer, if it isn't discovered by then'. Clearly this was a serious, thoughtful young man.

You can only imagine the confidence that this TV appearance must have engendered in the boy who had just become a teenager: in 1957 no one knew anyone who had appeared on the magical new medium of television.

Having been watched by an audience of hundreds of thousands at the age of 13, why not carry on as he had begun? Success might not have been instant, but within four years Jimmy Page would become a professional musician.

In the meantime, BBC television had finally begun to give limited exposure to rock 'n' roll, and Buddy Holly appeared on its solitary television channel. 'When he was killed in a plane crash in 1959,' said David Williams, 'I recall that Pete, Jim and I put on black ties and went to the local paper shop to buy all the newspapers that carried photos and obituaries of one of our heroes.'

In his woodwork class Page carved a reasonable simulacrum of a Fender Jazz Bass, modelling it on the instrument used by Jerry Lee Lewis's bassist in the film *Disc Jockey Jamboree*. 'It sounded good enough,' said Williams.

'To say Jim was dedicated would be an understatement. I hardly ever saw him when he wasn't strapped to his guitar trying to figure out some new licks.' Williams noted that Page's principal inspiration was no longer Elvis Presley or the anguished Gene Vincent, but the ostensibly more wholesome Ricky Nelson. This should not be a surprise: Nelson's upbeat rockabilly tunes featured the acclaimed James Burton on guitar, as much an inspiration to Page as Scotty Moore. Ten years later Burton would be leader of Elvis Presley's TCB band, playing with the King until Elvis's death in 1977.

'Those old Nelson records might seem pretty tame now, but back then the guitar solos (including the ones played by Joe Maphis) were cutting-edge stuff and greatly impressed my pal,' said Williams. 'I remember that he struggled for a long time with the instrumental break of "It's Late", but eventually someone showed him the fingerings he was after and he happily moved on.'

Now Page set about forming a group that played more than skiffle. He found a boy who played rhythm guitar – though with little of the feel of rock 'n' roll – in nearby Banstead, and then he found a pianist.

Although lacking either a drummer or a name, the trio were, after a number of practice sessions, deemed sufficiently ready by Page to play their first show at the Comrades Club, a drinking establishment for war veterans in Epsom town centre.

The gig was not a colossal success. In fact, Williams said it was 'a complete shambles'. Certainly, it didn't help that the three musicians lacked a drummer to propel the tempo; later in his career Page would ensure he played with the very best drummer he could find.

'As rock 'n' roll progressed,' said Wyatt, 'Jimmy and I added pickups to our guitars; we were going electric. Pete Calvert, a left-handed guitarist and friend of Jimmy's and mine, had a small early Watkins amplifier and I had a Selmer. Jimmy had a bigger Selmer, a sign of what was to come? All three of us were always around each other's houses banging rock 'n' roll. Tommy Steele was making headlines as Britain's first rock 'n' roller, and although that was cool we preferred the grittier sound of the American artists such as Eddie Cochran, Gene Vincent and the Blue Caps and, of course, Elvis. And for Jimmy and me, the sound made by Gene Vincent's lead guitarist, Cliff Gallup: that was the style and guitar sound we loved the best in those days.'

Page knew something had to change. At an electronics trade fair at London's Earls Court Exhibition Centre, he watched a young schoolboy called Laurie London stand up to sing on one of the stands. (Soon London would be at the top of the charts, in both the UK and USA, with his interpretation of the gospel song 'He's Got the Whole World in His Hands'.) Page noticed that the guitarist in London's backing group was playing a Fender Telecaster, the solid-body guitar he truly coveted that he had seen Buddy Holly playing on television. After the performance, Page spoke with London's guitarist, took the Telecaster in his hands and played 'Go Go Go (Down The Line)', a Roy Orbison tune covered by Ricky Nelson, with Page's idol James Burton on the guitar parts.

Fender Telecasters, made in the United States, were extremely pricey. Far more affordable, and on sale in London's musical-instrument shops, was the Futurama Grazioso, a Fender copy replete with tremolo arm, manufactured in Czechoslovakia. Page acquired a second-hand version of this instrument.

Concert venues across the United Kingdom were responding to the new youth market for rock 'n' roll. By 1958 Epsom's Ebbisham Hall, little more than a church-hall-type building, had been renamed the 'Contemporary Club' for the rock 'n' roll events it put on each Friday night.

But with another group with whom he briefly played, Page would not even get as far as the Contemporary Club. At around the age of 14, Page briefly became a member of a fledgling local act called Malcolm Austin and the Whirlwinds. On lead vocals was the aforementioned Austin. Tony Busson played bass; Stuart Cockett was on rhythm guitar; there was a drummer named Tom whose surname has evaporated with time; and 'James Page', as he was billed, played lead guitar. It was Wyatt who had introduced the various musicians to each other. In 1958 Malcolm Austin and the Whirlwinds played at Busson's school Christmas concert, a set largely consisting of covers of Chuck Berry and Jerry Lee Lewis tunes; they played no more than another couple of dates.

Busson, who was two years older than the group's guitarist, said that 'James' Page was 'very trendy: Italian jackets and Italian shoes – very pointed. Very cool in his tight jeans and trousers, but very baby-faced. We would go round to his house with our acoustic guitars and listen to his 45s and albums. His mum was always very receptive. She'd give us soft drinks. All we really talked about were guitars and pop music. When I first met Jimmy he only had a semi-acoustic Höfner. Then he got a solid electric, a Futurama Grazioso. He was a great fan of Gene Vincent and the Bluecaps, and also of Scotty Moore. I think he liked anything that was a bit complicated and a bit different.'

The guitarist's home, remembered Busson, was 'very lower middle-class.' But Page struck him as 'very arty: I thought if he didn't have a career as a musician he'd be an artist. He left school at 15. I thought he would make it. But I also wondered, "How are you going to support yourself in the interim?"' Soon Busson would receive an answer.

For Epsom also had larger venues in which more prestigious acts would perform. Wyatt recalled the buzz when a genuine professional rock 'n' roll show came to Epsom – creating an atmosphere like that of a circus or fair arriving in town. The concert was held at the local swimming baths. 'Top of the bill,' said Wyatt, 'was a singer, one Danny Storm, whose claim to

fame was being Cliff Richard's double. He was a dead ringer.
The second headliner was the Buddy Britten Trio. Buddy was a
Buddy Holly lookalike. Both Jimmy and I went along to the
show, which was very exciting at the time. Halfway through,
the compère announced an open-mike talent show; Jimmy and
I entered. We both got to play a guitar. I did "Mean Woman
Blues" and Jimmy did an instrumental, either "Peter Gunn" or
"Guitar Boogie Shuffle".'

Undaunted by the experience of his show at the Comrades
Club, Page had persevered and found a drummer and come up
with a name: the Paramounts. And at the end of the summer of
1959 he had a show booked for the Paramounts at the
Contemporary Club, supporting Red E. Lewis and the Redcaps,
a London group modelled largely on the act, antics and material
of Gene Vincent and His Bluecaps.

Although the Paramounts even had a vocalist of sorts, their
material that night largely consisted – in the manner of the time
– of an instrumental set; Page's strident guitar playing on
Johnny and the Hurricanes' recent hit 'Red River Rock' was
notable, impressing Red E. Lewis. Lewis informed his group's
manager, one Chris Tidmarsh, of this guitarist's prowess: at the
end of the Red E. Lewis and the Red Caps' set, Page came out
onstage, borrowed the solid-body guitar of Red Caps guitarist
Bobby Oats and played a few guitar parts, including some
Chuck Berry solos.

From the rear of the hall Page was watched by his parents.
Did they believe he would grow out of this silly interest? He
told me: 'No. Actually they were very encouraging. They may
not have understood a lot of what I was doing, but nevertheless
they had enough confidence that I knew what I was doing: that
I wasn't just a nut or something ...'

Also watching the Paramounts that night, from nearer the
stage than his parents, was Sally Anne Upwood, Page's girlfriend at school, a relationship that lasted for a couple of years.

Older than her boyfriend, Sally Anne was in Wyatt's class and able to observe Page's musical development.

Jimmy Page and the Paramounts played further shows at the Contemporary Club; they supported such acts as the Freddie Heath Combo, who would later be known as Johnny Kidd & the Pirates, one of the greatest English rock 'n' roll groups. And when Bobby Oats left Red E. Lewis and the Redcaps at Easter 1959, Chris Tidmarsh invited 15-year-old Page to audition, above a pub in Shoreditch, East London. He got the gig, at £20 a week.

Clearly Page's life was expanding – philosophically, as well as musically. 'My interest in the occult started when I was about 15,' he told me in 1977. At this time in his life, when still at school, he read Aleister Crowley's *Magick in Theory and Practice*, a lengthy treatise on Crowley's system of Western occult practice; not an easy book to first comprehend, and a clear indication of the full extent of Page's precocious intelligence. The book struck into his core, and he said to himself, 'Yes, that's it. My thing: I've found it.' From that age he was on his course.

2

FROM NELSON STORM TO SESSION PLAYER

At first Jimmy Page could only play with Red E. Lewis and the Redcaps at weekends; he was, after all, still at school.

In fact, at first his father had nixed the idea of his playing with the group. Chris Tidmarsh had needed to come down to 34 Miles Road to see him; it was only when he explained that almost all of the Redcaps' dates were at the weekend and would hardly interfere with his son's schooling that Jimmy's dad agreed. 'Oh, okay then,' said the elder James Page.

Yet soon Page had a major contretemps with Miss Nicholson, the deputy headmistress. When he informed her that he intended to be a pop star when he left school, this martinet was utterly dismissive of him. The minimum school-leaving age was 15 at the time, so he walked out of the school with his four GCE O levels and never looked back.

'Jimmy's playing was constantly evolving,' recalled Rod Wyatt. 'After he left school he could play lead and pick like Chet Atkins; he was a real prodigy. We still jammed at each other's houses, but not so frequently. The thing about Jimmy was that, unlike most guitarists of those early days, he could play many styles and genres of music.'

Chris Farlowe and the Thunderbirds were an emerging act on the R&B circuit in 1960. Page had first seen Farlowe perform three years before, at the British Skiffle Group Championship at Tottenham Royal in north London.

Farlowe's throaty soul vocals fronted the outfit, but it was his guitarist Bobby Taylor who Page would assiduously study. 'He would sit there and watch Bobby playing. Then he'd come backstage and say, "Oh man, what a great guitar player you are." So Bobby influenced him a great deal,' Farlowe told writer Chris Welch. 'Jimmy was very keen to meet him as he thought he was the coolest guitarist he'd ever seen. Bobby Taylor was a very handsome bloke and always dressed in black … Jimmy used to come to our gigs at places like the Flamingo. Then one day he walked up to us at some hall in Epsom, where he lived, and said, "I'd like to finance an album of you and the band."'

Clearly the 16-year-old Page, who was the same age as Farlowe, had a lucid eye on his future, as he had saved the money, aware that this creative investment would eventually repay him handsomely. And he also declared that he would be the producer of this album, a pronouncement of almost shocking confidence and self-possession from one so young.

The album was recorded at R. G. Jones Studios in Morden, Surrey. Page, observed Farlowe, seemed thoroughly *au fait* with the workings of a recording studio: 'He knew what to do and just plugged the guitar directly into the system without using any amplifiers. He didn't play any guitar himself. He didn't want to, not with Bobby Taylor playing in the studio.'

The songs included a powerhouse version of Carl Perkins's 'Matchbox' and a hard rendition of Barrett Strong's 'Money', driven by a thundering Bo Diddley beat. But the LP would not be released until 2017, on Page's own label.

Not content with working his way to becoming the greatest rock guitarist, Page's intuition had clearly told him to study the art of record production too. Did he have a glimmer that he would bring all this together in the not-too-distant future?

In 1960 Red E. Lewis and the Red Caps were introduced to the beat poet Royston Ellis, who was looking for musicians to back him at a series of readings.

Ellis was born in 1941, three years before Jimmy Page, in Pinner, north-west London, an outer suburb, like Heston in far west London, where Page first lived. Leaving school at 16, he was determined to become a writer, and at the age of 18 he had his first book published, *Jiving to Gyp*, a collection of his poetry. Ellis was immediately taken with rock 'n' roll; he would supplement his meagre earnings from poetry by writing biographies of the likes of Cliff Richard and the Shadows and James Dean. In 1961 he published his account of UK pop music, *The Big Beat Scene*.

Ellis referred to his live events, mixing beat music and poetry, as 'Rocketry'. At first he had been supported by Cliff Richards's backing group, the Drifters, who, upon changing their name to the Shadows to avoid confusion with the American R&B vocal group, almost immediately had a number one hit with 'Apache' and could no longer fulfil this function for the poet.

Determinedly bisexual and looking for someone to pick up, in 1960 Ellis had encountered George Harrison in the Jacaranda coffee bar in Liverpool. Although Harrison managed to avoid the poet's advances, the Beetles – as they were then known – ended up backing his poetry reading in the city. Ellis always claimed it was he who suggested they substitute the second 'e' in their name for an 'a'. Lennon later said he saw Ellis as 'the converging point of rock 'n' roll and literature'; the song 'Paperback Writer' was said to have been inspired by him.

Through Red E. Lewis and the Redcaps, Ellis had learned of the stimulant effects of chewing the Benzedrine-covered cardboard strip inside a Vick's inhaler, useful for the increasing array of late-night shows the group needed to play in far-flung parts of Britain. The poet turned the Beatles on to this, staying up talking to them until nine o'clock the next morning.

When it came to his backing music, Ellis decided he did not require the entire musical combo of Red E. Lewis and the Red Caps. Instead he settled on only one musician: Jimmy Page.

Between late 1960 and July 1961 Page played several stints backing Ellis. One of the most significant dates they played was a television broadcast, on ITV's Southern Television, recorded in Southampton with Julian Pettifer. Ellis would later claim that he had secured Page his first TV appearance, though this was manifestly not the case.

Page was still playing his second-hand Futurama Grazioso; soon it would be replaced with a genuine Fender Telecaster. On 4 March 1961 he and Ellis played together at Cambridge University, at the Heretics Society. And on 23 July 1961, having played in assorted coffee bars and small halls, the pair were faced with a bigger challenge. Twenty-year-old Ellis, accompanied by seventeen-year-old Page, was part of the Mermaid Festival at the newly opened experimental Mermaid Theatre, by London's Blackfriars Bridge. Such illustrious names as Louis MacNeice, Ralph Richardson, Flora Robson and William Empson were also giving readings at the festival.

'Jimmy Page was very dedicated to my poetry, understood it, and we worked well together, producing a dramatic presentation that was well received both on TV and stage,' said Ellis.

'Jimmy composed his own music to back my poems – usually ones from *Jiving to Gyp*, although I might have been performing the one with the line "Easy, easy, break me in easy" from my subsequent book *Rave*. The Mermaid show was the peak – and possibly the final one – of our stage performances.'

'Royston had a particularly powerful impact on me,' said the musician of the poet's work. 'It was nothing like I had ever read before and it conjured the essence and energy of its time. He had the same spirit and openness that the beat poets in America had.

'When I was offered the chance to back Royston I jumped at the opportunity, particularly when we appeared at the Mermaid Theatre in London in 1961. It was truly remarkable how we were breaking new ground with each reading.

'We knew that American jazz musicians had been backing poets during their readings. Jack Kerouac was using piano to accompany his readings, Lawrence Ferlinghetti teamed with Stan Getz to bring poetry and jazz together.'

These arty events with Royston Ellis were, however, rare and unusual for Page. More commonly he simply toured incessantly with Red E. Lewis and the Redcaps – and then Neil Christian and the Crusaders.

Red E. Lewis and the Redcaps' manager Chris Tidmarsh had decided that he would become the group's singer, renaming himself Neil Christian. In accordance with his own change of identity, Tidmarsh/Christian gave the group the moniker the Crusaders, and Page became 'Nelson Storm'. Rhythm guitarist John Spicer was henceforth known as 'Jumbo', while drummer Jim Evans was given the sobriquet of 'Tornado'.

Playing the same circuit, with Screaming Lord Sutch and the Savages, was a guitarist who had also grown up in Heston. His name was Ritchie Blackmore, and he had a bright future as a founding member of Deep Purple and celebrated guitar hero in his own right.

'I met Jimmy Page in 1962. I was 16, 17,' he recalled of their first meeting, at a time when 'Nelson Storm' had acquired a new instrument. 'We played with Neil Christian and the Crusaders. Jimmy Page was playing his Gretsch guitar. I knew he was going to be somebody then. Not only was he a good guitar player, he had that star quality. There was something about him. He was very poised and confident. So I thought, "He's going to go somewhere, that guy – he knows what he's doing." But he was way ahead of most guitar players. He knew he was good too. He was the type of guy, who … he wasn't arrogant, but he was very comfortable within himself.'

After two years of life on the road, Page came down several times with glandular fever, a lingering virus that was a consequence of exhaustion and a bad diet – and possibly too regular an ingestion of the Vick's Benzedrine strip. In October 1962, when he was only 18, 'Nelson Storm' quit the Neil Christian outfit.

Almost immediately he enrolled at Sutton Art College in Surrey to study painting, a love almost as great as the guitar. Needless to say, Page's love of music was undimmed, and he had extremely broad taste, eagerly lapping up classical music, both old and new, especially the groundbreaking work of Krzysztof Penderecki, the Polish composer whose 1960 work *Threnody to the Victims of Hiroshima* conveyed the devastation wrought on 6 August 1945 on the Japanese city. Page's study of Penderecki's work would be reflected much later in his use of the violin bow on his guitar.

'I was travelling around all the time in a bus,' he told Cameron Crowe in *Rolling Stone* in 1975. 'I did that for two years after I left school, to the point where I was starting to get really good bread. But I was getting ill. So I went back to art college. And that was a total change in direction ... As dedicated as I was to playing the guitar, I knew doing it that way was doing me in forever. Every two months I had glandular fever. So for the next eighteen months I was living on ten dollars a week and getting my strength up. But I was still playing.'

Only days after Jimmy Page left Neil Christian and the Crusaders he experienced something of an epiphany. For the very first time a package tour of American blues artists was scheduled to play in the United Kingdom. Following concerts in Germany, Switzerland, Austria and France, the American Folk Blues Festival had a date scheduled on 22 October 1962 at Manchester's Free Trade Hall, with both afternoon and evening performances. On the bill were Memphis Slim, Sonny Terry and Brownie McGhee, Helen Humes, Shakey Jake Harris, T-Bone Walker and John Lee Hooker.

Page arranged to go with his friend David Williams, but opted to catch the train and meet him in Manchester rather than travel together by road. By now he seemed to have registered that one of the causes of his ill health had been squeezing into an uncomfortable van to travel those long distances across Britain with the Crusaders.

David Williams travelled with a trio of companions he had met at Alexis Korner's Ealing Jazz Club, in reality no more than a room in a basement off Ealing Broadway in West London. Fellow aficionados of this music, these companions had recently formed a group. Its name? The Rolling Stones. These new friends were called Mick Jagger, Keith Richards and Brian Jones.

Although the first set of the American Folk Blues Festival rather failed to fire, perhaps an expression of the wet Manchester afternoon that it was, the evening house more than lived up to their expectations. Especially when John Lee Hooker closed the show with a brief, three-song set, accompanied only by his guitar. 'It may have been a damp and grey Manchester outside, but we thought we were sweltering down on the Delta,' said Williams. Hooker had been preceded by T-Bone Walker, the 'absolute personification of cool', according to Williams. 'He performed his famous "Stormy Monday" on his light-coloured Gibson. His playing seemed effortless, and his set just got better and better as he dropped the guitar between his legs and then swung it up behind his head for a solo. I did not look at Jim, Keith or any of the others while this was all going on, but I can tell you that afterwards they were full of praise and mightily impressed.'

Page, Jagger, Richards, Jones and Williams then drove back to London through the night, Jones nervous about the rate of knots at which they were travelling. In 1962 the M1, Britain's only motorway, extended no further from London than to the outskirts of Birmingham, a hundred miles north of the capital. 'Eventually we made it to the motorway and came across an all-night service station. Again, for most of us this was a real novelty. However, Jim was a seasoned night-traveller by now and he clearly enjoyed talking me through the delights of the fry-up menu. After a feed we resumed our journey, and it was still dark when we reached the outskirts of London.'

Early on in his time at Sutton Art College, Page encountered a fellow student called Annetta Beck. Annetta had a younger brother called Jeff, who had recently quit his own course at Wimbledon Art College for a job spray-painting cars. Hot-rod-type motors would become an obsession for Beck.

In a 1985 radio interview on California's KMET, Beck told host Cynthia Foxx: 'My older sister, as I remember it, came home raving about this guy who played electric guitar. I mean she was always the first to say, "Shut that racket up! Stop playing that horrible noise!" And then when she went to art school the whole thing changed. The recognition of somebody else doing the same thing must have changed her mind. She comes home screaming back into the house saying, "I know a guy who does what you do." And I was really interested because I thought I was the only mad person around. But she told me where this guy lived and said that it was okay to go around and visit. And to see someone else with these strange-looking electric guitars was great. And I went in there, into Jimmy's front room ... and he got his little acoustic guitar out and started playing away – it was great. He sang Buddy Holly songs. From then on we were just really close. His mum bought him a tape recorder and we used to make home recordings together. I think he sold them for a great sum of money to Immediate Records.'

Beck and Page began to spend afternoons and evenings at Page's parents' home, playing together and bouncing ideas off each other. Page would be playing a Gretsch Country Gentleman, running through songs like Ricky Nelson's 'My Babe' and 'It's

Late', inspired by Nelson's guitarist James Burton – 'so great', according to Beck. They would play back and listen to their jams on Page's two-track tape recorder. The microphone would be smothered under one of the sofa's cushions when they played. 'I used to bash it, and it would make the best bass drum sound you ever heard!' said Beck.

But this extra-curricular musical experimentation was not necessarily in opposition to what Page was doing on his art course at Sutton Art College: rather, these two aspects of himself complemented each other. Many years later, when asking Page about his career with Led Zeppelin, Brad Tolinski suggested that 'the idea of having a grand vision and sticking to it is more characteristic of the fine arts than of rock music: did your having attended art school influence your thinking?'

'No doubt about it,' Page replied. 'One thing I discovered was that most of the abstract painters that I admired were also very good technical draftsmen. Each had spent long periods of time being an apprentice and learning the fundamentals of classical composition and painting before they went off to do their own thing.

'This made an impact on me because I could see I was running on a parallel path with my music. Playing in my early bands, working as a studio musician, producing and going to art school was, in retrospect, my apprenticeship. I was learning and creating a solid foundation of ideas, but I wasn't really playing music. Then I joined the Yardbirds, and suddenly – bang! – all that I had learned began to fall into place, and I was off and ready to do something interesting. I had a voracious appetite for this new feeling of confidence.'

Despite starting his studies at Sutton, Page would, from time to time, step in during evening sessions with Cyril Davies's and Alexis Korner's R&B All-Stars at the Marquee Club and other London venues, such as Richmond's Crawdaddy Club or at nearby Eel Pie Island. Soon he was offered a permanent gig as the guitarist with the R&B All-Stars, but he turned it down, worried that his illness might recur.

There was another guitar player on the scene at the time, a callow youth nicknamed Plimsolls, on account of his footwear. Although at first Plimsolls could hardly play at all, he was known to have a reasonably moneyed background that enabled him to own a new Kay guitar. He had another sobriquet, Eric the Mod, a reflection of his stylish dress sense, and he would shortly enjoy greater success when, rather like his idol Robert Johnson, he seemed to suddenly master his instrument, and he reverted to his full name: Eric Clapton.

Page recalled that one night after he had sat in with the R&B All-Stars, 'Eric came up and said he'd seen some of the sets we'd done and told me, "You play like Matt Murphy," Memphis Slim's guitarist, and I said I really liked Matt Murphy and actually he was one of the ones that I'd followed quite heavily.'

Eric Clapton was not the only one to note Page's expertise. Soon came an approach from John Gibb of the Silhouettes, a group from Mitcham, on the furthest extremes of south London. Gibb asked Page to help record some singles for EMI, starting off with a tune called 'The Worryin' Kind'.

The Silhouettes would later occasionally feature Page's new friend Jeff Beck on guitar. What has always been a fascinating psychogeographical truth is that Jimmy Page, Eric Clapton and Jeff Beck, Britain's greatest and most creative rock guitarists of the 1960s, grew up within a radius of about 12 miles of each other.

Having witnessed Page's guitar skills with the R&B All-Stars at the Marquee Club, Mike Leander, a young arranger and producer, pulled him into a studio for a stint as rhythm guitarist in late 1962. Page was moonlighting from art school – something that would become a pattern.

Leander had been alerted to go and check out Page by Glyn Johns, another Epsom boy, a couple of years older than Page who had watched him play years before and was now a tape operator. Of that first meeting, years before, Johns said: 'One evening we had a talent night. I remember a boy in his early teens no one had seen before, who sat with his legs swinging over the front edge of the stage and played an acoustic guitar. He was pretty good, he may have even won, but I don't think anyone in the hall that night had any idea that he was to become such an innovative force in modern music.'

'I was really surprised,' Page told *Beat Instrumental* magazine in 1965 about Leander asking him to play. 'Before that I thought session work was a "closed shop".

'Mike was an independent producer then. And he wanted me to play on "Your Momma's Out of Town" by the Carter-Lewis group. The record was released and I believe it helped him considerably in joining Decca full time.'

Soon Mike Leander had another, more prestigious session gig for Page. This studio date was with Shadows expatriates Jet Harris, a bass player, and drummer Tony Meehan. The resulting tune, 'Diamonds', was a number one smash, the first of a run of hits for the duo. Later, Harris and Meehan hired one John Baldwin to accompany their act on the road. Already there were glimmers of some kind of destiny at work; soon John Baldwin would metamorphose into John Paul Jones, so renamed for a solo single by Rolling Stones manager Andrew Loog Oldham; Baldwin's new moniker was derived from the film *John Paul Jones*, a popular 1959 movie about the famed US naval commander.

Even though Harris and Meehan had departed the Shadows, it was a huge honour for the 18-year-old Page to play with the alumni of the group that, prior to the Beatles, was the biggest in the UK, largely due to the skill and charisma of Hank Marvin, their bespectacled guitarist.

'When did I first discover Hank Marvin? When I was about 14, because in those days it was really skiffle for young kids who wanted to learn three chords and have a good time,' Page told John Sugar on BBC Radio 4 in 2011. 'But going past that, more into the world of the American rockabilly and rock 'n' roll was starting to seduce us all as kids. Then you had Cliff Richard and the Drifters [as the Shadows were first known] at that time, putting forward a really, really damned good rendition of it, but it still had that sort of grit identity to it.

'So really it was a question of seeing Hank playing with Cliff as a kid, looking at Hank on the television. He was good, but he came alive with the Shadows. I mean it was such a really, really good band and Hank was such a stylist ... I mean, he was so cool. He was and still is. He had this image ... He was such a fluent player ... In those early years, all of us – Jeff Beck, myself, Eric Clapton – we all played things like "Apache", "Man of Mystery", "F.B.I.", those sort of [Shadows] hits ...

'Hank managed to come up with this unique sound, and that sound is just so recognisable. He inspired so many guitarists in those days as kids, kids who had no idea they may even be rock stars themselves one day.'

Playing guitar with Jet Harris and Tony Meehan on live dates, along with John Baldwin, was one John McLaughlin, who had given Page some guitar lessons when McLaughlin was working in a guitar shop. 'I would say he was the best jazz guitarist in England then, in the traditional mode of Johnny Smith and Tal Farlow,' said Page. 'He certainly taught me a lot about chord progressions and things like that. He was so fluent and so far ahead, way out there, and I learned a hell of a lot.'

The 'Diamonds' session kick-started a new career for Page, one in which he would play up to ten sessions a week, although he was still officially at Sutton Art College. For the next three and a half years, again while officially still a student, he became one of the UK's top two guitar session players: the other was Big Jim Sullivan, and for a time the boy from Epsom, where he continued to live at his parents' house, became known as 'Little

Jim'. Working with all manner of artists and styles, he honed his guitar playing during this period. In his early sessions he largely used a black Les Paul Custom he had played with Neil Christian. Known as 'the fretless wonder', and with a trio of pickups, it gave Page great tonal flexibility. When required, he also used a 1937 Cromwell archtop acoustic guitar and a Burns amplifier, or from time to time a Fender Telecaster.

In June 1963 Page was interviewed on Channel Television, ITV's smallest franchise, broadcasting only to the 60,000 inhabitants of the Channel Islands. With his hair immaculately swept back, Page certainly looked the rocking part, yet his accent and precise, formal speech constructions suggested someone from a rather more middle-class background than his actually was. Noted for the duty-free alcohol and tobacco on offer in this UK tax haven, Jersey and Guernsey enjoyed a certain hip cachet as a holiday location: was that why Page was there?

The interview was filmed on an outdoor quayside. The first question was the set-up:

What is a session guitarist?
'A guitarist who's brought in to make records, not necessarily doing one-night stands, hoping they'll get into the hit parade – only getting an ordinary fee.'

He doesn't work for any particular singer all the time?
'Not necessarily.'

I gather there are only a few young session guitarists like yourself: why is that?
'Well, it seems to be quite a closed shop. The Musicians' Union have their own chaps in and they don't really like to get the young people in because the old boys need the work.'

So how did you become a session guitarist?
'I don't know. Perhaps it was because I had the feel for it.'

How long have you been playing the guitar?
'Four years.'

Have you always been a session guitarist?
'No, no. For the last 18 months.'

Do you play for a regular group yourself?
'Yes: Neil Christian and the Crusaders.' [By now Page was no longer playing with them.]

And what sort of things do you do with this group?
'Well, we do one-night stands all over England.'

What are the big names that you have backed on disc?
'Jet Harris and Tony Meehan, Eden Kane, Duffy Power.'

What is it like working with some of the really big names of show business?
'Disappointing.'

Why is that?
'Well, they don't come up to how you expect them to be. Rather disappointing on the whole, I would say.'

That's probably bad news for some record fans. What is your professional ambition? Do you want to be a guitarist all the time? Do you want to make your own records?
'No, not necessarily. I'm very interested in art. I think I'd like to become an accomplished artist.'

Rather than a guitarist?
'Yes, possibly.'

Is this a means to an end for you? Are you hoping to earn
enough money through your guitar playing?
'Yes. Yes. I'm hoping to finance my art by the guitar.'

The quality of the acts Page worked with built steadily. Carter-Lewis and the Southerners' 'Your Momma's Out of Town' was an early example. 'He was a fast player, he knew his rock 'n' roll and he added to that,' said John Carter. 'He was also quiet and a bit of an intellectual.'

John Carter and Ken Lewis were essentially songwriters, with a sub-career as backing singers: the first hit they wrote was 'Will I What?', the number eighteen follow-up to Mike Sarne's 1962 novelty number one hit 'Come Outside'. They had been persuaded to form Carter-Lewis and the Southerners to promote their material. As a session musician Page played guitar on 'That's What I Want', a Carter-Lewis song that became a Top 40 hit in 1964 for the Marauders, a group from Stoke-on-Trent. Then Page briefly became an actual member of the group. Viv Prince, later drummer with the Pretty Things, played with the group while Page was with them, along with Big Jim Sullivan and drummer Bobby Graham. By 1964 Carter-Lewis and the Southerners would become the Ivy League and then magically transform into the Flower Pot Men, who in 1967 hit the UK number four slot with 'Let's Go to San Francisco'.

Page also played on records as diverse as 'Walk Tall' by Val Doonican, a kind of Irish Perry Como, and – on 6 November 1964 – with another Irish singer, Them vocalist Van Morrison, on the Belfast group's 'Baby, Please Don't Go', its B-side 'Gloria', and follow-up single 'Here Comes the Night'.

The twin pillars of Them were Van Morrison and guitarist Billy Harrison. 'We were brought over,' said Harrison, 'in the middle of 1964 and stuck in Decca's West Hampstead studio to see what we had. We did "Baby, Please Don't Go", "Gloria" and "Don't Stop Crying Now", which was released as the first single and died a death.'

The sessions were produced by Bert Berns, a streetwise New Yorker who had become a songwriter and record producer of some significance; a crucial figure at Atlantic Records – he revived the career of the Drifters and brought Solomon Burke to the label – he would later run Atlantic's BANG label, kick-starting the solo careers of Van Morrison and Neil Diamond. At first, influenced by Jerry Leiber and Mike Stoller, the white songwriting team from Los Angeles who via their cartoon-like wit transformed the subject matter of rhythm and blues, Bert Berns had been a composer of considerable success, subtly lacing his tunes with hypnotic Latin influences, especially mambo. Installed in New York's famous Brill Building, the endlessly and effortlessly enthusiastic Berns co-wrote the Isley Brothers' 'Twist and Shout', Solomon Burke's 'Everybody Needs Somebody to Love', The Exciters' 'Tell Him', Them's 'Here Comes the Night' and the McCoys' 'Hang On Sloopy', among many others. (As befitted the sometimes sleazy, occasionally Mob-affiliated world of New York popular music, Bert Berns, who everyone found a fabulous human being, attractive and glamorous to those with a fondness for boho chic, was allegedly 'connected', and possibly even a 'made man'. From his rarefied perspective he would have given Page interesting instruction about the US music business. At their first sessions Led Zeppelin recorded a song about him, 'Baby Come On Home', subtitled 'Tribute to Bert Berns', an exceptionally beautiful soul tune of precisely the type Berns would have produced for Atlantic, which was not released until 1993. In Page's guitar playing on this 1968 recording you can hear his love for Bert Berns.)

* * *

It was Bert Berns's writing of the song 'Twist and Shout' that had first brought him to London. Covered by the Beatles, with John Lennon's extraordinary, searing performance taking the song to a show-stopping further level, 'Twist and Shout' closed *Please Please Me*, the Liverpool group's first album, the number one LP in the UK for 30 weeks in 1963. Although the Beatles meant nothing in America at that time, Berns's first royalty cheque for his song on the album was for $90,000. In October 1963 he came over to London to see what was going on, producing a handful of no-hoper acts.

Already working in the British capital was Shel Talmy. A Los Angeleno who had worked with Capitol Records, he had been hired as staff producer by Dick Rowe, the Decca head of A&R – the man who famously turned down the Beatles but redeemed himself somewhat by signing the Rolling Stones. Rowe now decided that Bert Berns might fit as producer with the Belfast act he had signed named Them.

'Twist and Shout' had been covered yet again, by Brian Poole and the Tremeloes, who turned it into a Top 10 UK hit for Decca Records. It was something of a revenge release, as the act had been signed by Dick Rowe in preference to the Beatles – Brian Poole and the Tremeloes were, after all, from Essex, which was far more geographically convenient for a Londoner like Rowe than Liverpool.

In London, where he and Talmy were the only American producers working, Bert Berns had secured work through Decca Records, taking on 'Little Jimmy' Page as his principal session guitarist, recognising his talent and befriending him. 'With the new breed of British producers such as Mickie Most or Andrew Loog Oldham trying as hard as they could to make records that sounded American,' wrote Berns's biographer Joel Selvin, 'Berns was the first American producer trying to make records that sounded British.'

The sessions with Them for Decca proved as much, the

resulting recorded songs utterly unique in the resounding clarity of their sound. 'Bert Berns was inveigled into producing the session,' said Billy Harrison. 'And he brought in Jimmy Page, and Bobby Graham on drums. There was much grumbling, mostly from me, because I felt we could play without these guys. Jimmy Page played the same riff as the bass, chugging along. I played the lead: I wrote the riff.

'Bert Berns had arguments with us about the sound. I thought we were playing it okay: if someone brought in session men you took it as a bit of a sleight. I was very volatile in those days.

'There were various rows. Jimmy Page didn't really seem to want to talk to anybody. Just a stuck-up prick who thought he was better than the rest of the world. Sat there in silence. No conversation out of the guy. No response.'

Possibly Billy Harrison was misinterpreting the shyness that other musicians felt characterised the quiet Jimmy Page. And he may have been projecting his personal prejudices. 'He seemed above everybody, above these Paddies. That was the days when guest houses would have a sign up: "No salesmen, no coloured, no Irish". Page had that sort of sneering attitude, as though he was looking down on everybody. He's a fabulous technician, but there's nothing wrong with a bit of friendliness.'

'Their lead vocalist, Van Morrison, was really hostile as he didn't want session men on his recordings,' said drummer Bobby Graham. 'I remember the MD, Arthur Greenslade, telling him that we were only there to help. He calmed down but he didn't like it.'

'Whatever Morrison's reservations, they worked well together, and Graham's frenzied drumming at the end of "Gloria" is one of rock's great moments,' wrote Spencer Leigh in his *Independent* obituary of Graham.

And the opening guitar riff on 'Baby Please Don't Go' is one of the defining moments of popular music in the sixties. This was all Billy Harrison's own work. 'What annoyed me later,' he said, 'was that you would start to see how it was being said that Jimmy Page had played a blinding solo on "Baby Please Don't Go". I got narked about that: he never said he did it, but he never denied it.'

'For a long time,' said Jackie McAuley, who joined Them the next year, 'Jimmy Page got credit for Billy Harrison's guitar part. But he's owned up about it.'

Bert Berns also pulled Page in for 'Shout', a cover of the Isley Brothers' classic that was the debut hit for Glasgow's Lulu & The Luvvers. And he had him add his guitar parts to her version of 'Here Comes the Night', a majestic version that was released prior to Them's effort, but spent only one week in the UK charts.

Shel Talmy, a former classmate of Phil Spector at Fairfax High School in Los Angeles, also loved Page's playing, and the guitarist was equally taken with him: a studio innovator, Shel Talmy would play with separation and recording levels, techniques that Page would assiduously study.

Soon after he had arrived in London and started working for Decca, Talmy came across the guitarist: 'Somebody mentioned that they'd heard this 17-year-old kid who was really terrific, and I went and checked him out and I used him. We got along great and he was fabulous. I thought, "This kid is really gonna go somewhere," and I only regret that he didn't call me when he formed Led Zeppelin. It's a shame! I would like to have done that.

'He got it. I mean, he was original. At that time in London there were very few really current musicians: a lot of good musicians, but kind of mired slightly in the past. There were, like, one or two good rhythm sections and that was it. I originally started using Big Jim Sullivan, who was the only other one, and then I found Jimmy, who I thought was even better because he was more with it. He was doing what I thought should be done and certainly what was being done in the States, so it was a no-brainer.'

Fitting Page together with drummer Bobby Graham, and from time to time John Baldwin on bass, the producer had a team that was highly resourceful and fast. Talmy has described Graham as 'the greatest drummer the UK has ever produced'. While playing with Joe Brown and the Bruvvers, Graham had been approached by Brian Epstein at a gig at the Tower Ballroom in New Brighton, in June 1962. Would he care to replace Pete Best in the Beatles? Epstein asked him. Graham turned down the offer, leaving the way clear for Ringo Starr.

Graham first met Page when the guitarist was playing with Neil Christian and the Crusaders; they had supported Joe Brown at a show in Aylesbury, Buckinghamshire. 'I was so impressed. We became very good friends, and when I became a producer I always used Jimmy. We started a publishing company called Jimbo Music, for stuff we wrote. Jimmy wasn't one of the most way-out and weirdest characters I ever met: he was very quiet, very shy. Jimmy had a slightly dirtier sound than Big Jim Sullivan – they used to alternate a lot. Unless the arranger wanted a certain thing they'd fight it out amongst themselves.'

Neither Page nor Bobby could sight-read music – though the guitarist would learn how to do so over the next couple of years. 'I had to rely on what felt right,' said Graham, who estimated that he played on 15,000 tunes in the course of his career. 'I was loud. My trick was, if the singer took a breath, fill in. I was one of the first of the new generation coming in. Jim Sullivan was already in. Jimmy Page – same thing, couldn't read a note but had a great feel.'

Playing sessions paid good money, £9 a time when the average working man earned little more than that a week. And, as befitted the rules of the Musicians' Union, there would be three sessions a day: 10 a.m. until 1 p.m.; 2 till 5; and 7 until 10 p.m. During each session the musicians were expected to finish four songs, and afterwards they would be handed small brown envelopes containing their fees in cash. If you worked all three sessions, you'd come away with almost £30 for a day's work. At the end of each evening, Page, Big Jim Sullivan and Graham would adjourn to such fashionable *boîtes* of the day as the Cromwellian and Annie's Room.

'The weirdest thing I ever did with Jimmy was *Gonks Go Beat*,' reflected Graham. 'Charlie Katz had booked us into Decca number three studio, the cathedral where they did all the classical recordings. I wasn't supposed to be at that session – it was the only time at the wrong place. My part looked like a map of the London Underground. Jimmy came over and said, "I think we're in the wrong place. I can't read my part." The musical director said, "Are you ready, gentlemen?" and there was complete silence. He looked vaguely in my direction, and I thought he was talking to somebody behind me. He said, "Bob, you're in at the start," and I struggled. Finally he put the baton down and came over and ran it through with me. During the session I looked across and Jimmy was thundering away. At the end of the session I said, "You looked all right, Jim." He said, "I turned my amp off."'

With Shel Talmy, the trio of the two Jims and Bobby worked with a seemingly endless list of aspirant acts and tunes, such as the Lancastrians' 'We'll Sing in the Sunshine', Wayne Gibson's 'See You Later Alligator' and the First Gear's 'Leave My Kitten Alone', a cover of a Little Willie John tune and the B-side of 'A Certain Girl'. 'Leave My Kitten Alone' was deemed 'Page's most outstanding solo prior to "Whole Lotta Love"' by US rock critic Greg Shaw.

On 15 January 1965, again for Talmy, Page worked with 17-year-old David Jones, the leader of the Manish Boys, on 'I Pity the Fool', a cover of the Bobby Bland tune, backed with 'Take My Tip'. So as not to be mistaken for Davy Jones of the Monkees, David Jones would soon change his name to David Bowie. (In 1964 Page had been a 'member' of Jones/Bowie's Society for the Prevention of Cruelty to Long-Haired Men, a

clear publicity gimmick that succeeded in getting Jones on television news. And Page had already played with a pair of earlier
David Bowie line-ups, Davy Jones' Locker and Davy Jones and
the Lower Third, both with Shel Talmy producing. And he
worked on David Bowie's first, eponymous album, for Deram
Records, produced by Mike Vernon.)

'That "I Pity the Fool" session was phenomenal,' said Wayne
Bardell, then working in Francis, Day and Hunter, a record
shop on London's Charing Cross Road, but soon to become a
successful manager. 'I was at the session at IBC as a guest of the
not-yet Bowie, with Shel Talmy producing, Glyn Johns the engineer and Jimmy Page on guitar.'

'Well, it's definitely not going to be a hit,' Page said, correctly,
of the tune that day – it sold no more than 500 copies. But
during the Manish Boys' sessions he gave David Jones a guitar
riff that the young singer didn't yet know how to use: as David
Bowie he fitted this riff into two separate songs, first on 1970's
'The Supermen' on his *The Man Who Sold the World* album,
and again on 'Dead Man Walking' in 1997. 'When I was a
baby,' said David Bowie later, 'I did a rock session with one of
the bands, one of the millions of bands that I had in the sixties
– it was the Manish Boys, that's what it was – and the session
guitar player doing the solo was this young kid who'd just
come out of art school and was already a top session man,
Jimmy Page.'

And 'this young kid' had every right to be very excited about
the part he played on 'I Pity the Fool', which, despite his
misgivings, was a sensationally great record that should have
been a hit; this was thanks in no small part to Jimmy Page
adding searing, hard-rock guitar, like something Mick Green
could have provided for the Pirates.

'I Pity the Fool' might have flopped, but Talmy produced
breakthrough singles from a pair of acts that would become
two of the biggest UK groups of the 1960s: 'You Really Got

Me', the Kinks' third 45, and the Who's 'I Can't Explain'. Page played rhythm guitar on a version of the latter track.

'Because Shel wasn't sure I could play a solo, he asked his favourite session guitarist, Jimmy Page, to sit in,' wrote Pete Townshend in his autobiography. 'And because our band had rehearsed the song with backing vocals in Beach Boys style, but not very skilfully, Shel arranged for three male session singers, the Ivy League, to chirp away in our place. Shel Talmy got a good sound, tight and commercial, and although there was no guitar feedback, I was willing to compromise to get a hit.'

In *Guitar Masters: Intimate Portraits* by Alan DiPerna, Townshend referred to Page as 'a friend of mine'. The guitarists certainly had something in common: a fling with Anya Butler, the beautiful – and older – assistant to Who co-manager Chris Stamp. Townshend was initially puzzled by Page's presence at the session: 'I said to Jimmy, "Well, what are you doing here?" He said, "I'm here to give some weight to the rhythm guitar. I'm going to do the guitar on the overdubs." And I said, "Oh, great." And he said, "What are you going to play?" "A Rick 12," I told him. And he said, "I'll play a ..." Whatever it was. It was all very friendly. It was all very convivial.'

And on 'Bald Headed Woman', the B-side of 'I Can't Explain', it was Page who played the fuzzbox licks. On the liner notes to the Who's *Two's Missing* compilation album, Who bassist John Entwistle said: 'The fuzz guitar droning throughout is played by Jimmy Page. The reason being, he owned the only fuzzbox in the country at that time.'

Entwistle was not exactly correct. Gibson guitars had put a fuzz-tone pedal into production in 1962, giving it the brand name of 'Maestro Fuzz-Tone FZ-1'. Although in limited supply, the devices, imported from the US, could be found from time to time in London's more select musical equipment stores, and it was from one of these that Page had acquired his gadget.

Like many technological developments, the origins of the

fuzzbox and the dirty edge it added to a guitar's sound – which Page would employ to his maximum advantage and could be heard to its defining fullest when played by Keith Richards on the Rolling Stones' 'Satisfaction' – were accidental. In 1951 Jackie Brenston and his Delta Cats – actually Ike Turner's Kings of Rhythm – had hit the number one slot in the US rhythm and blues chart with 'Rocket 88'. A distinctive feature of 'Rocket 88' was the growling sound of Willie Kizart's guitar. On his way from Clarksdale, Mississippi, to Sam Phillips's Sun Studio in Memphis in 1951 to record the tune, Kizart's amplifier had fallen from his car while a tyre was being replaced. Endeavouring to repair the resulting damage to the speaker cone, the guitarist stuffed it with paper: the marginally distorted sound that resulted became a feature of the 'Rocket 88' single, which is often cited as one of the first rock 'n' roll records. From then on, guitarists sought out the means to deliver a similar grimy sound, the likes of Link Wray – who would poke holes in his loud-speaker – and Buddy Guy consciously damaging their amps to replicate such a tone. And in 1961 the great country singer Marty Robbins's 'Don't Worry' single hit number three in the US national charts, largely courtesy of his guitarist Grady Martin's muttering instrument being played through a faulty amplifier. Martin soon put out his own single, 'The Fuzz', thus bestowing the malfunction with a semi-official term.

In Los Angeles a radio-station technician developed an electronic device to create such an effect for producer Lee Hazelwood, who employed it on Sanford Clark's 'Go On Home' 45 in 1960. And in the same city, super session player Orville 'Red' Rhodes, who would become a member of the celebrated Wrecking Crew and was also an electronics whizz, developed a similar device, which was utilised by fellow Wrecking Crew guitarist Billy Strange on Ann Margret's 'I Just Don't Understand'. In turn this led to Strange employing Rhodes's invention with the instrumental surf band the Ventures, a kind of US version of the Shadows, on their late-1962 release 'The 2,000 Pound Bee'. It was this tune especially that had come to the attention of Page; anxious to replicate its juddering sound, he had purchased his own Maestro Fuzz-Tone.

Yet it was not entirely to his satisfaction. Luckily, he already knew someone who could assist him with this. Roger Mayer was a friend from the Epsom music scene. By 1964 he was working for the Admiralty Research Laboratory in Teddington, in the Acoustical Analysis section, having developed into something of an electronics boffin. And their friendship persisted: Page and Mayer would visit each other's homes to listen to American records. 'Jimmy came to me,' said Mayer, 'when he got hold of the Maestro Fuzz and said, "It's good but it doesn't have enough sustain … it's a bit staccato." I said, "Well, I'm sure we can improve on that." That conversation spurred me to design my first fuzzbox.'

'I suggested that Roger should try to make something that would improve upon the distortion heard on "The 2,000 Pound Bee" by the Ventures,' said Page. 'He went away and came up with the first real good fuzzbox … the first thing that really generated this wonderful sustain.'

Running off a 6-volt battery, Mayer's fuzzbox was constructed within a custom-made casing, which contained controls for gain and biasing along with a switch that would modify the tonal output. 'Right from square one,' said Mayer, 'Pagey and I wanted something that sustained a lot, but then didn't start jittering as it went away. One of the things that became very, very apparent early on was that you didn't want nasty artefacts. It's very easy to design a fuzzbox – anybody can do it – but to make one sound nice and retain articulation in notes, now that's something else.'

* * *

Page's part in the Kinks' career is more cloudy. Although it has often been claimed that he played the iconic solo on 'You Really Got Me', this is not the case. 'Jimmy did play rhythm on the first Kinks LP, and certainly did not play lead on "You Really Got Me", which preceded the LP by several weeks, or anything else for that matter. I only brought him in to play rhythm because at the time Ray wanted to concentrate on his singing,' said Shel Talmy. In fact, Page had already played acoustic 12-string guitar on 'I've Been Driving on Bald Mountain' and 'I'm a Lover Not a Fighter', on the Kinks' eponymously titled debut album. (In 1965 Page played the solo on an instrumental version of 'You Really Got Me'; almost identical to Dave Davies's original guitar part, it was included on an instrumental album by the Larry Page Orchestra entitled *Kinky Music*.)

'My presence at their sessions was to enable Ray Davies to wander around and virtually maintain control of everything, without having to be down in the studio all the time,' said Page later. 'Ray was producing those songs as much as Shel Talmy was ... more so, actually, because Ray was directing them and everything. At one point, there were even three guitars playing the same riff.'

'I'll tell you something about Jimmy Page,' Ray Davies told *Creem* magazine. 'Jimmy Page thinks he was the first person in the world to ever put a B string where a G string should be. And for me, that's his only claim to fame. Other than that, I think he's an asshole ... Jimmy Page and a lot of other people subsequently came to our sessions when we became hot, and I think he played rhythm 12-string on "I'm a Lover Not a Fighter", and he played tambourine on "Long Tall Shorty".'

In fact, Page did not 'put a B string where a G string should be'. He told *Melody Maker* that he would substitute the B string with a top E. Rather than the conventional E string he would swap it for a banjo octave string, either tuned to G or A: 'You'll get a raving, authentic blues sound that you hear on most pop records with that string-bending sound.'

'I didn't really do that much on the Kinks records,' Page later admitted. 'I know I managed to get a couple of riffs in on their album, but I can't really remember. I know that Ray didn't really approve of my presence. The Kinks just didn't want me around when they were recording. It was Shel Talmy's idea. One aspect of being in the studio while potential hits were being made was the press – too many writers were making a big fuss about the use of session men. Obviously I wasn't saying anything to the press but it just leaked out ... and that sort of thing often led to considerable bad feeling.'

For most of these sessions Page employed a Gibson Les Paul Custom, with the frets filed down 'to produce a very smooth playing action ... it just sounded so pure and fantastic,' he told John Tobler and Stuart Grundy for BBC's Radio 1.

Despite the griping of Ray Davies and Billy Harrison, Page played on a number of records that were significant cornerstones of mid-sixties British pop – outright classics, some of them. These included Shirley Bassey's theme song for *Goldfinger*, the third James Bond film, on which he played with Big Jim Sullivan and Vic Flick, another renowned UK session guitarist – the tune was a Top 10 US hit. Then there was Tom Jones's 'It's Not Unusual', number one in the UK and Top Ten in the US; Petula Clark's 'Downtown', a US number one; Kathy Kirby's 'Secret Love'; Marianne Faithfull's 'As Tears Go By'; P. J. Proby's 'Hold Me'; the Merseys' 'Sorrow', covered by David Bowie on his *Pin Ups* album; the Nashville Teens' 'Tobacco Road'; Brian Poole and the Tremeloes' 'Candy Man'; Twinkle's 'Terry', a motorcycle-death record in the tradition of the Shangri-Las' 'Leader of the Pack' that was number four in the UK charts at Christmas 1964 and banned by the BBC for being in 'poor taste'; 'Baby What's Wrong' and its B-side 'Be a Sect Maniac', the first single from the Downliners Sect, a wild

R&B outfit who made the Pretty Things seem like Cliff Richard.

As it had been with Bert Berns, much of Page's session work was for the Decca label, at their studios in Broadhurst Gardens, West Hampstead, a plain, nondescript building, built like an office block.

He worked extensively with Dave Berry, a Decca solo star from Sheffield whose first hit had been a cover of his namesake Chuck Berry's 'Memphis Tennessee'. He was one of British rock 'n' roll's first anti-heroes, a true original. 'I noticed how strippers used to tease the audience in Hamburg,' he said of his time playing the circuit in the German port. So almost an entire Dave Berry set might consist of him singing his songs from behind the stage curtain, with only his microphone and hand tantalisingly visible.

When Elvis Presley covered Arthur Crudup's 'My Baby Left Me', Scotty Moore's guitar licks had proved such an inspiration for the teenage Jimmy Page. Now Page took the lead guitar part himself on Dave Berry's sensational version of the song, with – as was customary – Big Jim Sullivan on rhythm.

Berry's 'My Baby Left Me' only grazed the Top 40, but his sultry 'The Crying Game' was a Top 5 tune when it was released in July 1964. However, this time it was Big Jim Sullivan who took the lead part, with Page providing rhythm; on drums, as per usual, was Bobby Graham. There was a picture in the music press, recalled Berry, of Page standing next to him, along with the engineer Glyn Johns, listening to a playback of 'The Crying Game'. 'Many of the session musicians would have left as soon as they had done their part,' said Berry. 'But Jimmy Page, being a proper player, would listen to his own part. He would sometimes want to do it again. Mind you, at the time Jimmy was in Carter-Lewis and the Southerners: by 5 p.m. he'd be gone to do a gig.'

The specific session players he used, said Berry, 'were really into it. I must have done a quarter of my career with Decca with that line-up: 25 to 30 songs. Mike Smith would call me with the studio booked. But if Big Jim and Jimmy Page were not available we'd cancel it and wait.' There were at least four tracks on which Page played harmonica: 'C.C. Rider', for example, and Buster Brown's 'Fannie Mae', which relies on a harmonica riff. Meanwhile, Page played both lead guitar and the harmonica part on 'Don't Gimme No Lip Child', the B-side of 'The Crying Game'.

Was Page, who was only 20 years old, anxious to impose his personality in the studio? Not at all, said Berry: 'He was very quiet. The true professional players don't have any edge to them anyway. The bigger the artist, the less edge they have to them. These two guitarists were really great players. And they didn't stick to how this stuff was written out. Big Jim would be improvising his solo. You could hear him doing a vocal counter-melody. We'd say, "Leave that in, it's real." You could work with these guys and suggest things. In 2010, when I met him again, Jimmy seemed exactly the same – a normal and quiet person. I was very proud of my output: it had a vast range. So when Jimmy Page was in the biggest band in the world I was very proud of my association with them. When I'd meet up with him I'd feel very proud, like a child.'

On 27 March 1964 Page played heavy fuzz-tone guitar on Carter and Lewis's 'Skinny Minnie'.

By now this was becoming customary practice for the guitar-ist. Again, in early 1964, on a session for Screaming Lord Sutch and the Savages, Page augmented his guitar with his Gibson Maestro Fuzz-Tone on a single that was released in October that year, 'Dracula's Daughter', and its B-side 'Come Back Baby', a studio date engineered by the legendary Joe Meek in his tiny Holloway Road set-up. (David Sutch, as his name was regis-tered at birth, was an eccentric English rocker who appeared onstage in a coffin, sometimes dressed as Jack the Ripper – also the title of an earlier Decca single on which Page played – and based his act on the American Screamin' Jay Hawkins, who had written and recorded 'I Put a Spell on You'. Sutch's Savages proved a fertile training ground, employing – among many others – guitarists Jeff Beck and Ritchie Blackmore and drummer Carlo Little, who had played briefly with the Rolling Stones prior to Charlie Watts. In 1963 Sutch stood as a candidate in a UK by-election, representing the Monster Raving Loony Party, the beginning of a career as a perennially unsuccessful Parliamentary candidate. Later, in 1964, Sutch founded Radio Sutch, a pirate broadcaster based in a wartime fort near the Thames estuary. Before the decade was out, Lord Sutch would reappear in the life of Jimmy Page.)

In September 1964 Decca Records paid for the dynamic, soulful American singer Brenda Lee, who was signed to the label, to come to London to record at Broadhurst Gardens. 'She said to me, "I've come here to make a record with the British sound." She felt she wouldn't get the same sound in Nashville because they're only just catching up on the British beat group sound of about six months ago,' said producer Mickie Most to *Rolling Stone* mágazine.

The tune chosen to acquaint Little Miss Dynamite with the zeitgeist was 'Is It True', another song written by Page's musical allies John Carter and Ken Lewis. The guitarist used an early wah-wah pedal on the record, which hit the same number 17 spot on both sides of the Atlantic.

By now Pete Calvert, Page and Rod Wyatt's guitar-playing buddy from Epsom, had rented a London flat, 4 Neate House in Pimlico. Page would drop in and sometimes stay over if he had an early gig the next day. Soon Chris Dreja of the Yardbirds moved in to one of the rooms.

A desire to improve upon and expand his natural abilities seemed second nature to Page. Having bought a sitar almost as soon as he learned of the instrument's existence, he became one of its earliest exponents in the UK. 'Let's put it this way,' he said.

'I had a sitar before George Harrison. I wouldn't say I played it as well as he did, though. I think George used it well … I actually went to see a Ravi Shankar concert one time, and to show you how far back this was, there were no young people in the audience at all – just a lot of older people from the Indian embassy. This girl I knew was a friend of his and she took me to see him after the concert. She introduced him to me and I explained that I had a sitar, but did not know how to tune it. He was very nice to me and wrote down the tunings on a piece of paper.' On 7 May 1966 *Melody Maker*, the weekly British music paper that considered itself intellectually superior to the rest of the pop press, ran an article entitled 'How About a Tune on the Old Sitar?', with much of its information taken from Page.

This questing side of him surfaced again in his efforts to improve his abilities on the acoustic guitar. 'Most great guitarists are either great on electric or great on acoustic,' said Alan Callan, who first met Page in 1968 and in 1975 became UK vice president of Swan Song Records, Led Zeppelin's label. 'But Jim is equally great on both, because he is always faithful to the nature of the instrument. He told me that, quite early on, he'd gone to a session and the producer had said, "Can you do it on acoustic rather than electric?" And he said he came out of that session thinking he hadn't nailed it, so he went home and practised acoustic for two months.'

The first half of the 1960s was a boom period for UK folk music, with several emerging virtuosos, revered by young men learning the guitar or – in Page's case – always eager to improve. John Renbourn, Davey Graham – who incorporated Eastern scales into his guitar playing – and Bert Jansch were the holy triumvirate of these players; Page was especially turned on by Jansch, who introduced him to 'the alternate guitar tunings and finger-style techniques he made his own in future Zeppelin classics such as "Black Mountain Side" and "Bron-Y-Aur

Stomp",' according to Brad Tolinski in his book *Light and Shade*.

'He was, without a doubt, the one who crystallised so many things,' Page said. 'As much as Hendrix had done on the electric, I really think he's done on the acoustic.' Al Stewart, a folk guitarist and singer, and, like Jansch, a Glaswegian, explained to Page that Jansch's guitar was tuned to D-A-G-G-A-D – open tuning, as it was known. Page started to employ this himself.

3

SHE JUST SATISFIES

While much of Jimmy Page's work consisted of bread-and-butter pop sessions, from time to time he would be offered the opportunity to indulge his creative side. On the morning of 28 January 1965, for example, half a dozen of Britain's most accomplished musicians met at IBC Recording Studios at 35 Portland Place in London for the morning session slot. Page was on guitar, Brian Auger on organ, Rick Brown played the bass and Mickey Waller was the drummer, with Joe Harriott and Alan Skidmore on saxophones. They were assembled to record an album with the American blues legend Sonny Boy Williamson. 'We started at 10 a.m. and it was all done by 1 p.m.,' recalled Waller. 'Also, it was done completely live: there were no overdubs. We all sat in a circle and played.' After Williamson grew progressively more drunk, his skewed sense of timing made the session increasingly difficult.

Page later recalled: 'Sonny Boy was living in [Yardbirds' manager] Giorgio Gomelsky's flat. Somebody told me once that they went to the house and they heard Sonny Boy plucking a live chicken. I don't know how true that was. That didn't happen when I was there. Sonny Boy and I rehearsed these numbers in the manager's flat, and by the time we got into the studio a couple of days later Sonny Boy had forgotten all of the arrangements. It was cool. Good music comes out of that.' (During Sonny Boy Williamson's time in Britain, the bluesman performed at Birmingham Town Hall: there, a 16-year-old

Robert Plant, stunned almost breathless from watching his performance, didn't permit his awe to prevent him from sneaking backstage and stealing one of the blues master's harmonicas – revenge, apparently, for the legendarily acerbic Williamson having told Plant to 'fuck off' when the teenager attempted to greet him while standing side by side at a urinal.)

When the Sonny Boy Williamson album session took place, Page had just become involved with another American – one who was blonde and female. Jackie DeShannon, hailing from Kentucky, was a beautiful singer-songwriter and a musical prodigy from an early age. By the time she was 11 she had her own radio show. In her early teens she had become a recording artist, at first singing country music. Her records 'Buddy' and 'Trouble' came to the attention of the great American early rocker Eddie Cochran. With Chuck Berry and Buddy Holly, Cochran was a rock 'n' roll singer-songwriter; by a measure of synchronicity he was also a hero of Page – Led Zeppelin would sometimes feature covers of some of Cochran's greatest songs: 'C'mon Everybody', 'Summertime Blues', 'Nervous Breakdown' (which effectively was what 'Communication Breakdown' was) and 'Somethin' Else'. 'You know, you look like a California girl,' Eddie said to her. 'I think that you should be in California if you want to have a great career.'

DeShannon moved to Los Angeles, where Cochran was based, and he teamed her up with singer-songwriter Sharon Sheeley, his girlfriend, who wrote 'Poor Little Fool' for Ricky Nelson. The two girls started to write songs together, resulting in 'Dum Dum', a hit for Brenda Lee, and 'I Love Anastasia', which scored for the Fleetwoods. (Along with Gene Vincent, Sharon Sheeley was injured in the car crash in England that took Eddie Cochran's life on 17 April 1960.)

At the age of 15 DeShannon became a girlfriend of Elvis Presley, which became part of her myth; she also had a relationship with Ricky Nelson. Although she failed to have

big chart hits of her own in the United States, her version of
Sonny Bono and Jack Nitzsche's 'Needles and Pins' was a
number one record in Canada before the Searchers covered it
in the UK, where it also topped the charts. The Searchers soon
covered DeShannon's own song 'When You Walk in the Room',
releasing it in September 1964, when it reached number three
in the UK charts. In August and September of 1964 she was
also one of the support acts on the Beatles' first tour of the USA
– her backing musicians on those dates included a young Ry
Cooder.

Sniffing the cultural wind, as Shel Talmy, Bert Berns and
Brenda Lee had done, Jackie DeShannon arrived in the UK to
record at the EMI Studios on Abbey Road at the end of 1964.
'I was very used to working with people like Glen Campbell
and James Burton and Tommy Tedesco – all these great, great
guitar players,' she recalled. 'So when I was there I said, "Who's
an amazing acoustic guitar player that I can have on my
sessions?" and they all said that Jimmy Page was the guy,
because he had played on a lot of different hit records at the
time and was one of the guys on the "A list" of studio musicians
to call.

'So I said, "Great, let's have him," and they said, "Well, you
can't get him here because he's in art school." I said, "What?"
He showed up ... with paint on his jeans and he was the youngest player in the room. I went over to him to play a few of my
piddling chords, and when he played them back to me I was
almost knocked out of the room. Even then, he was spectacular.
I knew right then that he was an amazing talent, so he played
on a song of mine called "Don't Turn Your Back on Me" and
we did some writing together.'

There was, however, an attraction beyond his guitar-playing
skills and Jackie DeShannon's own musical abilities. 'We got
together afterwards,' Page said in an interview in 1977 when he
revealed how she enticed him with a very attractive proposi-

tion: 'She said, "I've got a copy of Bob Dylan's new album if you'd like to hear it," and I said, "Would I like to hear it?"'

For most of 1965 Page and Jackie DeShannon were an item, and this almost-eminent American songwriter took him under her wing; together they wrote the song 'Dream Boy', a rocking single, like Ronnie Spector handling a surf tune. At the time Marianne Faithfull felt that Page was 'rather dull'. She saw his relationship with DeShannon as his way of 'undulling himself'. Tony Calder, her manager and close associate of Rolling Stones manager Andrew Loog Oldham, recalled that 'One night I couldn't get into our hotel room because Jimmy and Jackie DeShannon were in there shagging, so I yelled, "When you've finished could you write a song for Marianne?"'

The result was Marianne Faithfull's second hit, 'Come and Stay with Me', which reached number four. 'In My Time of Sorrow', an album track for Marianne, also emerged from this partnership.

'We wrote a few songs together, and they ended up getting done by Marianne, P. J. Proby and Esther Phillips or one of those coloured artists ... I started receiving royalty statements, which was very unusual for the time, seeing the names of different people who'd covered your songs,' said Page.

But how must it have felt for Page to be having sex with someone who had been to bed with two of his idols, Elvis Presley and Ricky Nelson? No doubt it considerably boosted his sense of himself and who he could be, given his increasing belief in psychic connections and the powerful, allegedly transcendent energies of Aleister Crowley's 'sex magick'.

Page was always financially astute. Early in 1965 he had set up his own publishing company, and soon, urged on creatively and emotionally by Jackie DeShannon, he was making his first solo record. 'She Just Satisfies' was a Kinks-style rocker, released on the Fontana label, on which he sang; its B-side was another Page–DeShannon tune, 'Keep Moving'. Hearing it now, 'She

Just Satisfies' sounds like it could have been a likely chart contender.

'"She Just Satisfies" and "Keep Moving" were a joke,' Page later said, dismissing the record with an element of false modesty. 'Should anyone hear them now and have a good laugh, the only justification I can offer is that I played all the instruments myself except the drums.'

In his 1965 interview with *Beat Instrumental* magazine, Page was asked about the possibility of a follow-up to 'She Just Satisfies'. He rejected the notion saying, 'If the public didn't like my first record, I shouldn't think they'll want another.'

In March 1965 DeShannon took Page on his first trip to the United States, first to New York and then to Los Angeles. For the guitarist, who later admitted his first impressions of the USA came from the glamour of Chuck Berry's witty, lyrically descriptive songs, life was suddenly opened up almost unimaginably.

In New York, Page crashed in the spare room of Bert Berns's sumptuous Manhattan penthouse apartment, with the producer, who was in town, and his Great Dane and pair of Siamese cats. While Page was in the Big Apple, the ever-dynamic Berns produced Barbara Lewis's 'Stop That Girl', a song written by Page and DeShannon; this mid-tempo heartbreak ballad was included on the Michigan soul songstress's *Baby, I'm Yours* LP, released on Atlantic that year. Through Berns, Page met Ahmet Ertegun and Jerry Wexler, the head honchos of Atlantic Records; it was a connection that would prove exceptionally valuable. Berns also 'took him to an Atlantic session, where he strummed along uncredited because of the union and immigration'.

Then Page flew to the West Coast. With its warm whisper of fecund possibility, Los Angeles in the mid-1960s seemed like a mythical setting. Almost all knowledge of the city was informed by its portrayal in movies, with Hollywood almost like the Holy Grail. With many of its inhabitants drawn from across the globe by the hope of stardom, LA housed some of the most beautiful individuals, of either sex, that any urban conurbation could boast.

The perfect weather of Los Angeles, its motorised modernity, gorgeous landscapes and fascination with alternative, free-thinking lifestyles – since the 1920s the city had been known for its practitioners of the more arcane, esoteric arts – made for an attractive package.

But its air of affluence could be illusory. In August 1965, when the foreign press went looking for the riots in the south Los Angeles district of Watts, many newshounds famously drove straight through the neighbourhood. Searching for a 'black ghetto', they were unable to believe that this place, with its palm trees and neat bungalows, could be the scene of murder-ous urban discontent.

The Watts riots were in stark contrast to the received wisdom about Los Angeles and southern California in general. But they were also a metaphor for the darkness that lay at its heart, always ready to erupt, like the city's ever-present threat of earthquake.

It was already apparent that Page had a nose for the zeitgeist, and here he was ahead of the times: for shortly Los Angeles would become the world's popular-music capital. 'I first came here in 1965 when I was a studio musician,' he told the *Los Angeles Times* in 2014. 'Bert Berns brought me out. He invited me to stay at his place. I met Jackie DeShannon, I saw the Byrds play at Ciro's [the Byrds debuted at Ciro's on 26 March 1965], which I think is now the Comedy Store. It was a magical time to be here. It was really happening.'

One morning he walked into the coffee shop at the Hyatt House on Sunset Boulevard. Seated there, having his breakfast, was Kim Fowley, a veteran of the Hollywood music scene who had been involved with the Hollywood Argyles, B. Bumble and the Stingers, and the Rivingtons; in London, where he had met

Page, Fowley had worked with P. J. Proby. 'In he comes, Mister boyish, dressed in crushed velvet. He spotted me, and came and sat down. He told me he'd just had the most insane, disturbing experience.

'A well-known singer-songwriter of the time, a pretty blonde, had asked him over to her house. When he got there, she'd detained him. He said she'd used restraints. I asked if he meant handcuffs and he said yes, but also whips – for three days and nights. He said it was scary but also fun. They say there's always an incident that triggers later behaviour. I contend that this was it for Jimmy Page. Because being in control – that became his deal.'

After a few months this early example of a rock 'n' roll couple went their separate ways. 'He wanted to split from the music world because he was getting disillusioned,' said Jackie DeShannon. 'Jimmy wanted to go to Cornwall or the Channel Islands and sell pottery. He couldn't stand the business, the strain, and I couldn't stand his dream of quietness, so we split, but I guess he's changed a lot since then.'

The song 'Tangerine' on *Led Zeppelin III* is said to have been inspired by Jackie DeShannon.

In May 1965 Bert Berns was back in London, producing tracks for Them's first album, this time at Regent Sounds Studio on Denmark Street. Clearly uninfluenced by the protests of Billy Harrison, Berns again brought in Jimmy Page, who provided a 'vibrato flourish' on an interpretation of the Josh White folk song 'I Gave My Love a Diamond'.

Prior to the arrival in October 1962 of the Beatles with 'Love Me Do', their first Parlophone single, and their subsequent phenomenon, not just as performers but supreme songwriters, British pop music was dominated by material that traditional 'Tin Pan Alley' publishers touted to acts. Despite the Liverpool quartet's success, which led to so many emergent acts writing their own material, by 1965 the Beatles had by no means over-thrown this system. The Yardbirds, a group largely from the extremes of south-west London, were an act that demonstrated the severe disparity between their singles, chosen by such a method, and the material in the five-piece group's live sets – essentially another version of the harmonica-wailing, thunder-ously paced and mutated rhythm 'n' blues sound that the Rolling Stones and Pretty Things and other lesser UK groups like the Downliners Sect were somewhat histrionically howling.

The Yardbirds had formed after Chris Dreja, Anthony 'Top' Topham and Eric Clapton met at Surbiton Art College. 'It was through Top Topham's father,' said Chris Dreja, 'who had this amazing collection of 78s from America [that was] not available to anybody. It was black blues music, and that was the initial turn-on, of course. Discovering that music was like the genie coming out of the bottle, really. We had really rather kitsch pop music with no free fall and very little emotion back in the depressing post-war fifties and sixties.

'And poor old Anthony Topham gets left out, doesn't he? He was quite pivotal, actually. The band was made up of two halves originally. One half was Top and me at art college, and Clapton was in the same art stream. In Surbiton, Surrey, of all places.

'At that stage Top Topham was perhaps as agile and skilled a guitar player as Eric Clapton. He was only 16, however, and his career with the Yardbirds was stymied when his parents insisted that he must remain in full-time education.

'Topham is still a great guitar player. He went on to play for Chicken Shack. Out of all us he was actually the most talented artist around. Clapton and I were all into music, but he got dropped at Kingston Art School because his attentions were elsewhere. But Top's parents, when we were getting wages from it, grounded him, unfortunately, and that is when we got

Clapton. He was really the only professional player we knew out there who had any background in the music we were doing.'

Keith Relf, the group's singer, knew Eric Clapton better than the pair of students who were at college with him, so he went and 'tracked him down', as Dreja remembered. Clapton had already moved on to Kingston College of Art, but had been dismissed after his first year; it was considered by his instructors that he was focused on music and not on art.

By the end of 1964 the Yardbirds had a blossoming reputation and were considered one of the coolest UK acts, clearly on the cusp of breaking out from being a cult attraction, not least because of their by now revered guitarist. The Yardbirds – who otherwise consisted of flaxen-haired vocalist Keith Relf, second guitarist Chris Dreja, bass player Paul Samwell-Smith and drummer Jim McCarty – were managed by Giorgio Gomelsky, who had had the Rolling Stones stolen from him by Andrew Loog Oldham and Eric Easton.

The song that would pull the Yardbirds up to full pop stardom was 'For Your Love'. One of the first two tunes written by Manchester's Graham Gouldman, later of 10cc, 'For Your Love' had been intended for his group the Mockingbirds, until they turned it down, as did Herman's Hermits, who in Harvey Lisberg had the same management as Gouldman. Undaunted by this negative response, Lisberg, who was very impressed by 'For Your Love', then offered it to the Beatles when they played a season of Christmas shows at the Hammersmith Odeon in 1964. Unsurprisingly, the Fab Four, who had their own abundant source of material, displayed no interest. But supporting the Beatles on these Hammersmith shows were the Yardbirds, and they recognised its chart potential and recorded it.

A good call: the single, released in March 1965, was a big hit. Yet 'For Your Love' was at considerable odds with the rest of the band's previous material. The Yardbirds had already put out a pair of what might be considered more characteristic tunes: 'I

Wish You Would', a version of the 1955 Billy Boy Arnold Chicago blues tune; and 'Good Morning, School Girl', an adaptation of the 1937 Sonny Boy Williamson song, often titled 'Good Morning Little Schoolgirl' – a title that in later years would have guaranteed zero radio airtime. On the live version of 'Good Morning, School Girl', on the Yardbirds' first live album, *Five Live Yardbirds*, the vocal duties on the song were taken by bass player Paul Samwell-Smith and Eric Clapton rather than singer Keith Relf.

He might have been underestimated in his days at the Ealing Jazz Club, but by now Clapton was showing that he was very much his own man, utterly singular in his purist vision of the kind of music he should be playing: he was determined that the next Yardbirds single should be an Otis Redding cover. His stance, and clear supreme abilities on the guitar, were beginning to transform him into a hero for his fans. And in March 1965 the *Melody Maker* headline told the story: Clapton Quits Yardbirds – 'too commercial'.

'I thought it was a bit silly, really,' said Clapton of 'For Your Love'. 'I thought it would be good for a group like Hedgehoppers Anonymous. It didn't make any sense in terms of what we were supposed to be playing. I thought, "This is the thin end of the wedge."'

In the story that accompanied the *Melody Maker* headline, Keith Relf gave his version of what had taken place. 'It's very sad because we are all friends. There is no bad feeling at all, but Eric did not get on well with the business. He does not like commercialisation. He loves the blues so much I suppose he does not like it being played badly by a white shower like us! Eric did not like our new record "For Your Love". He should have been featured but did not want to sing or anything, and he only did a boogie bit in the middle. His leaving is bound to be a blow to the group's image at first because Eric was very popular.'

Chris Dreja put the problem more succinctly: 'We had this massive record and we had no lead guitar player.'

Within two weeks Clapton had joined John Mayall's Bluesbreakers. After a couple of months graffiti began to appear around London: 'Clapton is God'. John Mayall, a bohemian Mancunian who rivalled Alexis Korner as the godfather of the UK blues scene, had already offered Page the job with the Bluesbreakers, but he had turned it down, clearing the way for Clapton.

Page was clearly in demand. The Yardbirds and their manager Giorgio Gomelsky, at the suggestion of Eric Clapton himself, first approached Page to be the guitarist's replacement.

'It was thought,' remembered Jim McCarty, 'that maybe we could get Jimmy Page because Jimmy was the hottest session player, and Giorgio knew Jimmy. He asked Jimmy if he'd join the band but at that time Jimmy was so busy playing sessions that he wasn't into joining a live band. He said why don't you try one of my understudies, a guy called Jeff Beck. So we went down to see Jeff and asked him to join the band.'

Page's friend Jeff Beck was playing with the Tridents, a rocking blues group he had joined in August 1964, never missing their weekly residence at Eel Pie Island, which would draw up to 1,500 people. Beck accepted the offer.

Page was still shadowed by the ill health that had dogged him during his time with Neil Christian and the Crusaders, and was also aware of the large amounts of money he continued to earn as a session player. But his main reason for turning down the offer, he said, was because of his growing friendship with Clapton. 'If I hadn't known Eric, or hadn't liked him, I might have joined. As it was, I didn't want any part of it. I liked Eric quite a bit and I didn't want him to think I'd gone behind his back.'

(This was not the only act of generosity that Page displayed towards his friend Jeff Beck. When, in 1962, he announced he would be leaving Neil Christian and the Crusaders, Page had suggested Beck as a replacement for himself.)

Jeff Beck played his first show with the Yardbirds on Friday 5 March 1965 at Fairfield Halls in Croydon, south London, only two days after Eric Clapton quit the group. They were second on the bill to the Moody Blues, flying high for the first time with their hit 'Go Now'.

Beck was so grateful that Page had recommended him as Clapton's replacement that he went round to Page's parents' house in Epsom and presented his friend with his 1959 Fender Telecaster. 'A beautiful gesture,' said Page later. But Beck's gratitude was realistic: although distinguished in his blues guitar band the Tridents, it was not until he joined the Yardbirds, whom he enriched with his fuzz-soaked solos, that he found the vessel for his upward flight into the guitar stratosphere. In fact, he soon borrowed a quite specific vehicle from Page: his Roger Mayer fuzzbox, on which Beck worked out the Eastern-flavoured riff for 'Heart Full of Soul', the first Yardbirds' single he was involved in. 'I still remember the time Jeff came over to my house when he was in the Yardbirds and played me "Shapes of Things". It was just so good – so out there and ahead of its time. And I seem to have the same reaction whenever I hear anything he does,' recalled Page.

'The great thing about Jeff,' said Chris Dreja, 'is that his roots were also the blues and rock 'n' roll, but he was also much wider in his musical tastes. And he had a mind and a talent that wanted to go much further than playing rock 'n' roll and blues riffs, which was perfect for us because we were about to enter a phase of all sorts of experimentation. In retrospect we put Jeff under a lot of pressure. We would work on stuff and then bring Jeff in. Like, for example, the sitar sound he got on "Heart Full of Soul". We brought in a sitar player ... but it sounded thin and weedy. We said to Jeff, "Can you do it?" And he came in and created this incredible sound. Jeff Beck became a prototype of late-sixties psychedelia. He got chords from Stax and Motown records. The locked-up sound in the band gave it that sound.'

4

BECK'S BOLERO

It was in 'the latter years of the first half of the 1960s' that Jeff Dexter first encountered Jimmy Page. Dexter was a Mod scenemaker, the DJ at Tiles who, as a 15-year-old, famously demonstrated the Twist on BBC television; he had hung around the 2i's Coffee Bar in London's Old Compton Street, the seed-ground of British rock 'n' roll, where Cliff Richard, among others, had been discovered, and would be instrumental in founding the Middle Earth venue, out of which sprang UK underground rock. 'Jimmy was running around town at that time. But we really became friends about 1965 or 66. We both had an eye for a nice suit and a nice shirt.'

Page and Dexter would meet up in Soho to rummage through the wares of the area's assorted rag-trade specialists, sometimes seeking cloth for jackets and trousers, more often looking for potential shirt fabric. An especial temple of suitably exotic material was found at Liberty, the Tudor-fronted department store on Great Marlborough Street. Armed with their cloth, they would then make their way to Star Shirtmakers on Wardour Street, two doors from the Whisky A Go Go. Star Shirtmakers was run by a Hungarian husband-and-wife tailoring team; they would knock up the fabric into shirts styled precisely as their customers desired, for – even then – the ludicrously cheap price of 11 shillings, the equivalent of 55 pence. (After the Beatles had been to their tailor, Dougie Millings, Dexter took them to nearby Star Shirtmakers, beginning a flood of celebrity shoppers at the place.)

One day, when they were leaving Liberty, Page and Dexter found themselves strolling down Kingly Street, which ran off the west end of the store. There they discovered an art gallery called 26 Kingly Street, with extraordinary lighting, sheets of Perspex and glittery screens. London's first psychedelic gallery, 26 Kingly Street was run by Keith Albarn (whose son Damon is the singer in Blur). 'We'd just discovered acid,' said Dexter. 'I tripped in Jimmy's house but never tripped with him – I sought refuge with him a few times. I went to a Yardbirds rehearsal when I'd dropped acid. And he looked after me.'

Contrary to Billy Harrison's dismissal of Page, Dexter insists that his friend was highly regarded on the London music scene, not simply for his musical accomplishments but as an empathetic human being. 'He was a lovely chap. One of the boys. You'd see him at record launches, and the odd club – though he didn't go to the Speakeasy as much as many others – and stuff like that. When I was running the Implosion shows Jimmy would come along. Ian Knight, my cohort on those events, went from Middle Earth to becoming the Yardbirds' staging and lighting guy, and went on to have the same job with Led Zeppelin. We hung out at some of those crazy happenings, like the 14 Hour Technicolor Dream at Alexandra Palace.'

Page had moved up from Epsom and was living in a flat off Holland Road in west London, a thoroughfare that ran from Shepherd's Bush to Kensington High Street; it was an area in which it seemed every single one of its myriad bedsits contained a hippie hash-dealer. In 1966 Dexter was invited to Deià in Majorca, home to a bohemian community, by Lady June, an artist and *éminence grise* of the psychedelic scene. In Deià he encountered an especially louche breed of Portobello Road-style hippie chick, some of whom relocated back to London, becoming habitués of Blaises, a nightclub in South Kensington:

'Jimmy and one of these dodgy birds used to get really stoned and play Buffalo Springfield again and again and again. "This is the direction I want to go in," he would say. "I want to have a band that does magical things."'

The folk scene, to which Page was always drawn, remained a prominent feature of Swinging London. 'I used to go to Les Cousins,' Dexter said of London's dominant folk venue. 'I was best friends with Beverley and John Martyn. Nick Drake only felt comfortable at their flat in Hampstead.'

Dexter was always impressed with Page's phenomenal knowledge of art: 'He was a collector. Of everything. He's kept every piece of clothing he's had since he was a child. His mother was incredibly neat and tidy. And so is he.'

Dexter also became friends with another woman who would have a significant impact on Page: a French model called Charlotte Martin. She was 20 when they first met, Dexter 19. 'I first clapped eyes on her in a place called Westaway and Westaway, a fantastic shop near the British Museum that sold Scottish knitwear. All the young birds would gather there or at the Scotch House. She was a fabulous model who did it all: magazine level, and then once people saw how gorgeous she was she was employed all over the place. She did all the modelling with the Fool, for their collection. She was great friends with them because they all hung out at Eric's place in the Pheasantry.' 'Eric', of course, was Eric Clapton, and he and Charlotte Martin were an item.

By now Page had effectively dropped out of art college. Even though he would later acquire a considerable reputation for financial canniness, it is somewhat cheap to suggest that it was only his considerable earnings from session playing that continued to attract him to the craft. In fact, for him the art of recording, and coming to as full an understanding of it as possible, appears to have held far more attraction than treading the rock 'n' roll boards. And in the most select quarters his skills were being further recognised. In August 1965 came the press announcement about the formation of Immediate Records, an independent label that was the pet project of Andrew Loog Oldham, Rolling Stones manager and wunderkind of UK pop, and his business partner Tony Calder. 'Immediate will operate in the same way as any good, small independent label in America,' said Oldham. 'We will be bringing in new producers, while our main hope lies with the pop session guitarist turned producer Jimmy Page and my two friends, Stones Mick and Keith.'

Page had first worked with Andrew Loog Oldham in 1964, on one of Oldham's versions of the Stones' songs, performed by the Andrew Oldham Orchestra, part of his endeavour to become the UK's Phil Spector. That session was at Kingsway Studios in Holborn, London; the producer was John 'Paul Jones' Baldwin.

Page then went on the road with Marianne Faithfull, who that summer had hit the Top 10 with her first release, 'As Tears Go By', written by Mick Jagger and Keith Richards, and on which Page had played.

Page had been recommended to Oldham by Charlie Katz, who booked musicians for his sessions. 'He said to me one day, "There's this young lad, Jimmy, we are trying him out. Why don't you give him a go? He doesn't read but Big Jim Sullivan will take him under his wing." And so Jimmy started playing on my sessions,' said Loog Oldham. 'One of the first was Marianne Faithfull's "As Tears Go By". He was a bright spark. It was nice having him on the floor … All smiles and not much talk.'

Soon Page found himself playing on the Rolling Stones' 'Heart of Stone', though it was a version that would not be released until the Stones' *Metamorphosis* album, in 1975.

'Jimmy was like a wisp,' said Loog Oldham. 'I don't really know what kind of a person he was, because the great ones keep it hidden and metamorphose on us, so that the room works.'

Andrew Loog Oldham decided to take their relationship up a level, hiring Page as Immediate's producer and A&R man. 'In those days if you got on with people you tried to work with them. It seemed logical and Jimmy liked the idea ... I thought he was very good. What he went on to do kind of proves it, doesn't it?'

As for sessions with the Rolling Stones, Loog Oldham recalled: 'He played on some of the demos Mick, Keith and I did that ended up on the album released in 1975 called *Metamorphosis*. The Stones did not play on that. I think he was on a Bobby Jameson single that Keith and I wrote and produced ... I only considered people the way they considered themselves. Jimmy was a player, an occasional writer at that time with me and with Jackie DeShannon. I never considered him as a solo artist and I don't think he did either.'

Page worked on a trio of demos for the Stones themselves: 'Blue Turns to Grey', 'Some Things Just Stick in Your Mind' and the aforementioned 'Heart of Stone'. Although the version of 'Blue Turns to Grey' on which Page played was never released, a later edition of the song was included on the Stones' 1965 US album *December's Children (And Everybody's)*, and Cliff Richard's cover of the song was a number 15 hit in 1966. 'Some Things Just Stick in Your Mind' and 'Heart of Stone' were included on *Metamorphosis*, the first song being covered by Vashti Bunyan for an unsuccessful release on Immediate.

What had specifically drawn Page to the Immediate production gig was the chance to work with his old mucker Eric Clapton, now with John Mayall and the Bluesbreakers, who had formed an arrangement with the label.

In June 1965 John Mayall and the Bluesbreakers went into Pye Studios at Great Cumberland Place in London's West End. Page was at the production helm for what would turn out to be a landmark session in the history of contemporary music.

'I'm Your Witchdoctor' and 'Telephone Blues' were the tunes involved. They featured John Mayall on keyboards, Hughie Flint on drums, John McVie on bass and Eric Clapton on guitar – the John Mayall's Bluesbreakers line-up that had recorded the celebrated *Beano*-cover album. 'When "Witchdoctor" came to be overdubbed, Eric had this idea to put this feedback wail over the top,' said Page. 'I was with him in the studio as he set this up, then I got back into the control room and told the engineer to record the overdub. About two thirds of the way through he pulled the faders down and said: "This guitarist is impossible to record." I guess his technical ethics were compromised by the signal that was putting the meters into the red. I suggested that he got on with his job and leave that decision to me! Eric's solo on "Telephone Blues" was just superb.'

It was Page who intuited how Clapton's solos could be enhanced by pouring reverb onto them, bringing out the flames in his playing, characterised by Clapton's overdriven one-note sustain.

But – as Page noted – Clapton's plangent, lyrical playing on 'Telephone Blues', the B-side, is perhaps even more distinguished, the first time that he gets to really stretch out with a beautiful, mature stream of notes. You are struck by the clarity of the separation – and simultaneous harmony – of the instruments. Clearly Page had learned much from his countless hours in recording studios, learning to appreciate how the very best rock 'n' roll records were assiduously constructed, put together piece by piece.

Tellingly, for his first go in the control seat for Immediate, the subject matter of the single's title track alluded to the kind of dark material with which Page would later be associated, perhaps even tarnished by. The opening couplet ran:

'I'm your witchdoctor, got the evil eye
Got the power of the devil, I'm the conjurer guy.'

On one hand this was no more than the stock imagery that peppered blues music; yet, in the bigger picture, it holds an interesting subtext. It was as though Page was toying with – giving a test run to, really – the entire mysterious and dark philosophy that would form the aura of Led Zeppelin.

'The significance of this session cannot be emphasised enough, for it represented the birth of the modern guitar sound. And while Clapton did the playing, it was Page who made it possible for his work to be captured properly on tape,' wrote Brad Tolinski.

That year Page also worked with the distinguished American composer Burt Bacharach on his album *Hit Maker! Burt Bacharach Plays the Burt Bacharach Hits*. 'Page respected Bacharach's meticulous approach to rehearsing and recording,' wrote George Case in *Jimmy Page: Magus, Musician, Man*. Again, it was part of Page's learning curve. 'Bacharach, in turn, admired the young Briton's politeness and polish.'

As part of his deal with Immediate, Page played guitar with Nico, a German actress, model and singer based in France whom Andrew Loog Oldham had met in London, where she was soaking up the scene. Loog Oldham and Page co-wrote a song for her, 'The Last Mile', and Page arranged, conducted, produced and played on the tune. It was relegated to the role of B-side, however, to the Gordon Lightfoot number 'I'm Not Saying' – again, Page played guitar on this track.

'Brian Jones brought Nico to my attention,' said Loog Oldham, 'and Jimmy and I wrote a song, which we recorded with her as a B-side. It might have been better than the A-side. It should have been the A-side, because that was fucking awful. It really was stiff as Britain. Then he went on the road with Marianne Faithfull. We were all impressed by this new wave of women who were coming in.'

Page's friendship with Eric Clapton continued to blossom, and soon Slowhand, as Clapton ironically became nicknamed, would often be accompanied by his beautiful French girlfriend, Charlotte 'Charly' Martin, who was friends with Jeff Dexter. Clapton met her in the Speakeasy nightclub in the summer of 1966, while he was forming his next group, Cream.

Problems with Immediate Records, however, almost created a rupture in the camaraderie between the two guitarists. Without informing Clapton, the label released some tunes that he had recorded onto Page's Simon tape recorder when Clapton had stayed at his house – which led to Clapton mistrusting Page for a time. Yet this suspicion was misplaced. 'I argued that they couldn't put them out, because they were just variations of blues structures, and in the end we dubbed some other instruments over some of them and they came out, with liner notes attributed to me ... though I didn't have anything to do with writing them. I didn't get a penny out of it, anyway,' Page said, revealing what was for him generally a key subtext to any endeavour. (The musicians who overdubbed these instruments onto Clapton's basic tracks were Bill Wyman, Charlie Watts and Mick Jagger, on harmonica.)

Born in 1939 in west London, Simon Napier-Bell was the son of a documentary filmmaker. After attempting to become a jazz musician in the United States, he drifted into music supervision for movies in Canada; eventually he returned to London, where he continued in the same line of work, including on the 1965 screwball comedy *What's New Pussycat?* He expanded into the production of records and demos, and he would use popular London studios such as Advision on Bond Street and Cine-Tele Sounds Studios, popularly known as CTS, in Kensington Gardens Square, the top film-music studio in London. He would employ session musicians recommended by Dick Katz, who booked all the top players in London.

Highly intelligent and witty, Napier-Bell became something of an archetypal character of Swinging London, a gay man who was known for driving around in an imported Ford Thunderbird, a cigar clenched between his teeth. His best friend was Vicki Wickham, the producer of *Ready Steady Go!*, the hip pop music show broadcast every Friday night on ITV. Almost as a jape, he and Wickham co-wrote the English lyrics for the Italian ballad 'Io Che Non Vivo (Senza Te)', which had been featured at the 1965 San Remo Festival; their friend Dusty Springfield sang at the event and had been moved to tears by the song's music and melody. Knocking up their set of English lyrics to match the music in an hour so that they could head out to a London night-club, Wickham and Napier-Bell gave the tune its title, 'You Don't Have to Say You Love Me'. Recorded by Dusty Springfield, the song was a number one hit in the UK and number four in the United States; in subsequent years it would be a hit again many times over, across the globe, with even Elvis Presley doing a version of it in 1970.

By the time Napier-Bell wrote the 'You Don't Have to Say You Love Me' lyrics, he was manager of the Yardbirds, having replaced Giorgio Gomelsky. That the talented and fascinating Gomelsky had been fired was perhaps not surprising; later he declared, 'I should never have been a manager: I need someone to manage me.' Though there were no suggestions of impropriety, the Yardbirds had dismissed him because of his inability to turn a profit for the group. All the same, Gomelsky had been an inspirational figure for the Yardbirds, under whose auspices they had become a hit recording act. During their first US tour in 1965 he had even secured a recording session at Sun Studio in Memphis with Sam Phillips, who had mentored Elvis Presley early in his career. The tune they recorded? The Tiny Bradshaw 1951 jump-blues classic 'Train Kept A-Rollin'', reworked in a rockabilly style by the Johnny Burnette Trio in 1956, and included on the Yardbirds' US album release *Having a Rave Up*. 'Train Kept A-Rollin'' was a song that would replay significantly in the Yardbirds' career.

'Some time around the end of 1965 or the beginning of 1966,' recalled Napier-Bell, 'Paul Samwell-Smith, who played bass with the Yardbirds, called me. His girlfriend, later his wife, was Vicki Wickham's secretary. I went to a gig the Yardbirds played in Paris. I quickly realised that a manager's job was to keep the group together.'

Behind Napier-Bell's management of the Yardbirds lay a continuous awkward subtext: 'The Yardbirds were blokes in a pub talking about football. I was gay and couldn't really enter into that world.'

During his time working in recording studios Napier-Bell had always employed session musicians. 'You never think session players aren't playing well: they know they are in the top league, the best in the world. They can play next to the guys in LA who would play with Sinatra.'

Napier-Bell's first choice for guitarist was 'always Big Jim Sullivan'. Even though, he says, 'these guys were all infuriating. They'd put you through it. Big Jim Sullivan would always have a paperback book with him that he would read as you did a take: it would be balanced on his music stand. He would even read it halfway through the take until it came to his moment – he would be doing it to show off.'

If an additional guitarist was required, it would invariably be Page. 'He and Big Jim would work out their parts between them. I talked to Jimmy Page enough to know he was a real session player. I knew he was a brilliant technician and admired by others. We'd also use John Paul Jones, who did all the arrangements for Herman's Hermits. But I never really liked Jimmy Page. He had a sneer about him. At school the people who bullied me had this terrible, frightening sneer and Jimmy Page reminded me of those people. People who sneer have usually had unhappy childhoods.'

On 16 and 17 May 1966, at IBC Studios in London's West End, Jeff Beck and Page were involved in what in retrospect can be seen as one of the very first super-sessions.

The tune was 'Beck's Bolero'. Maurice Ravel's *Boléro*, which was first performed in 1928 at the Paris Opera, provided the basis for 'Beck's Bolero'; the Russian ballet dancer Ida Rubinstein had commissioned Ravel to write the work, an undulating, insistently repetitive piece based around the Spanish music and dance known as bolero.

By 1965, largely influenced by the tastes of the likes of Paul McCartney, always an assiduous culture vulture, assorted classical composers had become fashionable among fans of what formerly would have been known as 'pop'. These composers included Bach, Sibelius, Stravinsky, Prokofiev, Gershwin, Debussy and Ravel, whose *Boléro* was relatively well known in 1966. The song's structure is considerably amended in such a way that it could be interpreted as the first blow of the hard-rock sound that Led Zeppelin would very soon develop.

'Beck's Bolero' employed a formidable cast: Beck on lead guitar, Page on acoustic, revered session pianist Nicky Hopkins, the Who's Keith Moon on drums and John Paul Jones on bass. The Who's John Entwistle, Moon's bass-playing rhythm part-ner, had originally agreed to do the session, but when he failed to turn up John Paul Jones was called in.

'I heard rumours that Jimmy was talking with Keith Moon about joining his supergroup,' said Napier-Bell. 'I don't think the name Led Zeppelin was in the air at that time, though it may have been mentioned between them. Cream was being formed at the same time. Whether that had much influence on Beck, Page and Moon, I don't know. The Who's managers, Kit Lambert and Chris Stamp, were in the same building as Clapton's manager, Robert Stigwood. So when he was putting Cream together, they would have known all about it, as I did too. Keith Moon would have heard from Kit and Chris as to what was going on too. From my point of view, I was thinking only of keeping Jeff in the group [the Yardbirds]. Jimmy, I think, was thinking of a new group, which would be a blend of all their talents.'

'I always try to do things wholeheartedly or not at all,' said Beck, offering a slight rewrite of history, 'so I tried to imagine what my ideal band would be. We had the right producer, Keith Moon on drums, Jimmy on guitar and John Paul Jones on bass. You could feel the excitement in the studio, even though we didn't know what we were going to play. I thought, "This is it! What a line-up!" But afterwards nothing really happened because Moony couldn't leave the Who. He arrived at the studio in disguise so no one would know he was playing with another band.'

'Jim Page and I arranged a session with Keith Moon in secret, just to see what would happen,' said Beck. 'But we had to have something to play in the studio because Keith only had a limited time – he could only give us like three hours before his roadies would start looking for him. I went over to Jim's house a few days before the session and he was strumming away on this 12-string Fender electric that had a really big sound. It was the sound of that Fender 12-string that really inspired the melody. And I don't care what he says, I invented that melody. He hit these Amaj7 chords and the Em7 chords, and I just started playing over the top of it … He was playing the bolero rhythm and I played the melody on top of it, but then I said: "Jim, you've got to break away from the bolero beat – you can't go on like that for ever!" So we stopped it dead in the middle of the song – like the Yardbirds would do on "For Your Love" – then we stuck that riff into the middle. And I went home and worked out the other bit [the uptempo section].'

'Even though he said he wrote it, I wrote it,' said Page, presenting an argument that would become somewhat familiar.

'Moon did this amazing fill around the kit, and a U47 mic just left its stand and went flying across the room; he just cracked it one,' said John Paul Jones.

'I remember Jimmy at the studio yelling at us and calling us fucking hooligans,' said Beck. 'Everyone had prior commitments. That session that day, it was one day that really started my head turning – we were almost doing it.'

That band, claimed Beck, was the original Led Zeppelin – 'not called "Led Zeppelin", but that was still the earliest embryo of the band'.

'It was going to be me and Beck on guitars, Moon on drums, maybe Nicky Hopkins on piano. The only one from the session who wasn't going to be in it was Jonesy, who played bass,' said Page. 'It would have been the first of all those bands, sort of like Cream and everything. Instead, it didn't happen – apart from the "Bolero". That's the closest it got … The idea sort of fell apart. We just said, "Let's forget about the whole thing, quick." Instead of being more positive about it and looking for another singer, we just let it slip by. Then the Who began a tour, the Yardbirds began a tour, and that was it.'

In fact, there had been some efforts by Page and Beck to find an appropriate vocalist to transmogrify the 'Beck's Bolero' studio line-up into a working outfit, as Page told *Guitar World*'s Steve Rosen: 'Well, it was going to be either Steve Marriott from the Small Faces or Steve Winwood.' Marriott was managed by Don Arden, the self-styled 'Al Capone of pop'. 'In the end, the reply came back from his office: "How would you like to have a group with no fingers, boys?" Or words to that effect.' Sufficiently warned off, the pair never even approached the Spencer Davis Group's Steve Winwood.

There was even controversy over the 'Beck's Bolero' production credit. Mickie Most claimed it, part of a contractual issue between him and Beck, his managerial client. Simon Napier-Bell would insist it was his, and Jimmy Page claimed that he had done the record's production, staying behind in the studio long after Napier-Bell had gone home.

'The track was done and then the producer just disappeared,'

Page told Steve Rosen in September 1977. 'He was never seen again: he simply didn't come back. Napier-Bell, he just sort of left me and Jeff to it. Jeff was playing and I was in the box [studio]. And even though he says he wrote it, I'm playing the electric 12-string on it. Beck's doing the slide bits, and I'm basically playing around the chords.'

Simon Napier-Bell has a different point of view. 'Jimmy Page was being demeaning when we were making the record: he was sneering. Later, when Beck and Page were discussing how the mix should be, I went away to leave them to it. The purpose of a producer is so that the record ends up as it should. That's why I went away – to leave them to it. As for Mickie Most, my agreement with him over the management of the Yardbirds was that all product reverted to him. I just said, "What the hell, I don't need it." I didn't really – but that track became a rock milestone.'

When Pete Townshend discovered that Keith Moon had played on the session, he was furious. He began to refer to Beck and Page as 'flashy little guitarists of very little brain'. Page's response? 'Townshend got into feedback because he couldn't play single notes.' Townshend later commented: 'The thing is, when Keith did "Beck's Bolero", that wasn't just a session, it was a political move. It was at a point when the group was very close to breaking up. Keith was very paranoid and going through a heavy pills thing. He wanted to make the group plead for him because he'd joined Beck.'

Later, it was claimed that Moon had declared that if the studio line-up became an actual band, it would go down 'like a lead balloon'. According to Peter Grant, Entwistle then added, 'like a lead zeppelin'. (Entwistle was always adamant that he came up with the Lead Zeppelin name all on his own; and also that he had the idea of a flaming Zeppelin as an album cover.)

When writing his Keith Moon biography *Dear Boy*, Tony Fletcher interviewed Jeff Beck about the 'Beck's Bolero' session.

Fletcher asked Beck if Moon had been using him to pressure the Who for his own ends. Beck replied that that wasn't the case at all: the subtext to the 'Beck's Bolero' session was the relationship between Jimmy Page and himself: 'No, it was something to do with Jimmy and me. I had done sessions for Jimmy. He used to get me to do all the shit he didn't want to do. He used to get me to pick him up in my car and pay for the petrol, and I'd find out he was on the session anyway. When he heard what I was doing on the sessions … he started taking an interest in my style, and then we went from there. And then the Yardbirds got in the way – I can't remember the sequence of events. I remember thinking, "Why can't I have what I want instead of what I've got?" That's always the way. To have someone who's so musically aware and talented as Jim alongside me was something I could really do with. But that wasn't to be until later on in the Yardbirds. Meanwhile, I'm watching the Who going from strength to strength with a fantastic powerful drummer and knowing that that was what I really needed to get myself going. So it was a guiding light in one sense and fragmented what I already had. I was never content being in the Yardbirds, and I left Jim to paddle his canoe in the Yardbirds.'

The Yardbirds' rhythm-guitar player Chris Dreja was yet another denizen of the Surrey Deep South from which Page, Clapton and Beck hailed. Brought up in Surbiton, where he continued to live, he would from time to time run into Page while the guitarist was studying at Sutton Art College. On more than one occasion he came across him in nearby Tolworth, outside the tropical-fish shop: Page was a tropical-fish enthusiast. 'Hello, Chris, I've just bought a nice thermometer for my fish,' he once greeted him.

On 18 June 1966 Page travelled up to Oxford in the passenger seat of Jeff Beck's maroon Ford Zephyr Six to watch his friend play with Chris Dreja and the other Yardbirds at the May Ball at Queen's College. They were on the same bill as seasoned Manchester hitmakers the Hollies. Not that that 'seasoned hitmaker' rubric couldn't also have been applied to the Yardbirds. Since Beck had joined the band it seemed like they were never out of the UK charts – and increasingly the US hit lists were also welcoming the group's 45s: 'Heart Full of Soul', 'Evil Hearted You', 'Shapes of Things' and 'Over Under Sideways Down' had all been hit singles. Meanwhile, their critically acclaimed *Yardbirds* album – more generally known as *Roger the Engineer* – was about to be released in the middle of July 1966.

Although events such as the May Ball paid well, they were formal, black-tie occasions, in the main quite uptight and, as defined in the new underground vocabulary, extremely 'straight'. Becoming increasingly drunk as the evening progressed, Keith Relf, the Yardbirds' singer, took exception to this prevalent social posture, and he began to harangue and berate his audience of bright young things. It was a stance that Page, notwithstanding his fondness for tropical fish, always a rebel and in tune with the more esoteric minutiae of pop culture, admired greatly: he thought Relf put on 'a magnificent rock 'n' roll performance'. Paul Samwell-Smith, the Yardbirds' bass player, was so appalled by Relf's stance, however, that as soon as their show was over he quit.

With further dates coming up, the Yardbirds were concerned about how they could play them without a bass player. On the spot, Page volunteered his services. 'They had a show at the Marquee Club, and Paul was not coming back. So I foolishly said, "Yeah, I'll play bass." Jim McCarty says I was so desperate to get out of the studio that I'd have played drums.'

For some time Page had harboured doubts about whether he could continue working as a session player. 'My session work was invaluable. At one point I was playing at least three sessions a day, six days a week. And I rarely ever knew in advance what

I was going to be playing. But I learned things even on my worst sessions – and believe me, I played on some horrendous things. I finally called it quits after I started getting calls to do Muzak. I decided I couldn't live that life any more; it was getting too silly.'

'I remember the May Ball,' said Beck. 'Jimmy Page actually came to that gig. He came to see the band and I told him things were not running very smoothly. There were these hello-yah Princess Di types around. Trays with drinks with sticks. And as soon as we started Keith fell over back into Jim's drums. After, I said, "Oh sorry, Jim, I suppose you're not interested in joining the band?" He said it was the best thing ever when Keith fell back into the drums. It wasn't going to put him off that easily.'

And so, slightly oddly, Jimmy Page joined the Yardbirds. That Marquee show took place three days later, on 21 June. How was Page's performance? Terrible, according to Beck. 'Absolute disaster. He couldn't play the bass for toffee. He was running all over the neck. Four fat strings instead of six thin ones.'

Whatever. As soon as Page became a part of the group, he changed his look entirely: he presented himself as a highly stylised, very chic rock star, someone of ineffable good taste and class. And very quickly, with his characteristic diligence, he became adept on the bass guitar.

Before Page formally joined the Yardbirds, he went round to Simon Napier-Bell's flat in Bressenden Place, near Buckingham Palace, for a meeting with the group and their manager. 'When he arrived,' said Napier-Bell, 'he had an enormous swollen lip. Nobody knew who'd done it. He said some people had stopped him in the street and hit him. I remember thinking that if you're Jimmy Page that could happen to you because of your sneering. Jimmy's superciliousness was hard to take. When Jimmy Page looked as nice as he does, maybe he thought he could get away with it.

'He came into the group. I said, "We don't really get on." "You're my manager: I want to see the contract," he said. I said, "You won't. I'll take my percentage off four-fifths of the money, and I won't manage you." Because I knew he would want to pull a stunt and say the contract was terrible.

'I always thought Jimmy Page was partially gay. He didn't have a great childhood: because he was such a cunt, you knew he didn't have a great childhood. And later he got into transvestism. Which meant he thought he was straight.

'I said to Jeff Beck, "Jimmy Page is coming in to the Yardbirds and you will leave." He said, "No, I won't."'

Although 'Jeffman' had been proprietorially spray-painted onto the rear of the Telecaster Beck had gifted him, Page customised the instrument, giving it a psychedelic colour-wash, adding a silver plate to catch stage lighting and reflect it back at the audience, a simple but extraordinarily effective trick. For some time this Telecaster became identified with Page.

Yet before he could graduate to playing this guitar with the Yardbirds, Page remained the group's bass player. It must have been a baptism of fire: vocalist Keith Relf, an asthmatic, would drink all day, the singer's inner turmoil perhaps exacerbated by the fact that, oddly, the Yardbirds' tour manager was his own father. Between the Marquee show and the end of July, the Yardbirds played 24 dates, all over the UK. For Page it must have been like getting back on the gruelling road with Neil Christian and the Crusaders. There was a show with the Small Faces in Paris on 27 June, and a set of dates in Scotland early in July; at one of these Beck and Page were spat at for wearing the German Iron Cross. Couldn't these former art students have explained that they were simply indulging in a spot of street-level conceptual art? (Or perhaps it was an indication of chronic immaturity? A decade later comparable attempts at shock would be made by the likes of punk stars Sid Vicious and Siouxsie Sioux, similarly employing Nazi regalia. As with the

Yardbirds' efforts, wouldn't you consider this to be comparable to naughty ten-year-olds drawing such images on their school exercise books?)

Although he had his flat off Holland Road in west London, Page was still frequently staying at his parents' house in Epsom. But in the mid-sixties his parents separated and then divorced. This brought great pain to their son. Moreover, shockingly, his father had been living a double life: he had created a separate family with another woman. This would have been devastating news. 'You would never trust anyone again, especially intimate people,' commented Nanette Greenblatt, a renowned London life coach. 'In any relationship you were in, you would be worrying, "This is okay for now, but how will it turn out?" Accordingly, you would want to control people. There would be a strong distrust of male figures. And Aleister Crowley would fit in nicely as an unreliable father figure.'

The kind of trauma to which Page and his mother were subjected by this egregious information about his father must have been almost overwhelming. But, just as a new birth is said to bring good luck, so a figurative death in the shape of divorce can sometimes offer the opportunity for a phoenix-like rise to escape the grief of the event. Something like that happened to Page. Some constraints fell away, to expose a desire for the ultimate promulgation of who he could be, and how far he could take it. You can have this fantasy image of yourself, which, if you work hard enough at it, is what you become. In other words, find your true will: who you are meant to be in this existence and what you are here for – the meaning of Crowley's 'Do what thou wilt', appropriated almost predictably from a freemasonry text. Once upon a time, 'Jimmy Page' was a construct in Page's own mind. But because he meant it, and, more importantly, needed it, it became him, and he it. With some assistance from his beliefs, of course.

5

BLOW-UPS

Jimmy Page finally moved away from his childhood home. First, he took the flat off Holland Road in Kensington. But part of the mood of the age was the need to connect communally with the essence of the earth, a need that would later be expressed by the likes of the Band, who creatively isolated themselves in Woodstock in upstate New York, and the English group Traffic, fronted by Page's friend Steve Winwood, who wanted to 'get it together' in a cottage in rural Berkshire.

And it was to that same verdant county of Berkshire that Page now moved. Kenneth Grahame, author of the children's classic *The Wind in the Willows*, had retired to Pangbourne, situated on the River Pang four miles west of Reading, in later life, and now Page made the village his home, buying a former boathouse on the river, water frequently being close to the homes he would purchase, solace for his Scorpio rising. Later, he would develop a reputation for being to some extent a recluse; it was here that such an existence was first nurtured, one he found creatively beneficial. 'I really enjoyed that bachelor existence – working and creating music, and going out on my boat at night on my own; switching off the engine and just coasting in the twilight. I liked all that,' he told the *Sunday Times*. His tank of tropical fish survived the journey from west London, although his long absences away on the road eventually obliged him to give up this hobby.

And anyway, Page was almost straightaway off on the road again. This time it was to the United States.

That same month, June 1966, someone else demonstrated an intriguing element of experimental good taste – unsurprisingly, given that the record was produced by Shel Talmy, Page's long-time studio champion, a master of innovation. 'Making Time', the stunning, sneering tune in question, was released by a Hertfordshire group called the Creation; Eddie Phillips, the guitarist, would at times play his instrument with a violin bow. It has long been alleged that Page took note of this and copied the effect. 'Eddie Phillips deserves to be up there as one of the great rock 'n' roll guitarists of our time, and he's hardly ever mentioned,' said Talmy. 'He was one of the most innovative guitarists I've ever run across. Jimmy Page stole the bowing bit of the guitar from Eddie. Eddie was phenomenal.'

However, Page claims another source for the inspiration. At the Burt Bacharach session he played on, David McCallum, Sr., another session player, who played violin with both the London Philharmonic and Royal Philharmonic orchestras and was father of the co-star of the hit television series *The Man from U.N.C.L.E.*, asked the guitarist if he had tried to bow his instrument as though it were a violin. Page borrowed the violinist's bow – a wand finding its own wizard – and had a go, in front of McCallum. 'Whatever squeaks I made sort of intrigued me. I didn't really start developing the technique for quite some time later, but he was the guy who turned me on to the idea.'

The summer months of 1966 were a pivotal time for much of 'Swinging London', as *Time* magazine had dubbed the city. In May, at the *NME* Poll Winners' Concert at Wembley's Empire Pool, the Beatles played what would prove to be their last ever live show in Britain. However, as far as viewers of the televised broadcast of the *NME* poll were concerned, the Yardbirds closed the concert. Acting on a perverse whim, Andrew Loog

Oldham decided that the Rolling Stones' segment should not be broadcast. When Beatles manager Brian Epstein learned of this, he also demanded – for anxious reasons of 'cool' status – that the Beatles be kept off the TV, thereby depriving viewers of the Beatles' last scheduled live performance in the UK.

Only a few weeks after Page joined the Yardbirds came the debut performance of an act that would seismically shift the entire music scene. On 29 July 1966 Cream – which Clapton had formed with drummer Ginger Baker and bassist and vocalist Jack Bruce – performed their first ever stage show, at Manchester's Twisted Wheel, a venue more accustomed to hosting pill-popping Mod all-nighters, itself an indicator of changing times. Within a year Cream would be touring the United States to enormous acclaim, and, in a new twist, long-haired and stoned American audiences would reverently sit cross-legged on ballroom floors as Clapton tore through epic, frequently self-indulgent, guitar solos.

The day after the first Cream gig, on 30 July 1966, England won the football World Cup for the first time, on home soil, and national confidence surged. And by the end of the year another power trio, the Jimi Hendrix Experience, were ferociously tearing up and down the UK's venues and charts, with their first hit 'Hey Joe' and sensational live performances.

Following that Wembley *NME* date, the Rolling Stones were on something of a hiatus. Anita Pallenberg, Brian Jones's girlfriend, had bought a flat at 1 Courtfield Road, behind Gloucester Road tube station, and the Rolling Stone had moved in with her. Like several women in this rarefied bohemian milieu, Anita had about her an intriguing high-priestess aspect; she was attracted to the occult and was rarely without a bag containing rolling papers, tarot cards and occasionally the odd bone. Christopher Gibbs, a fashionable Chelsea art and antiques dealer, had insisted to Anita that she must buy the property, which only had one room and a set of stairs leading to a minstrel's gallery that formed a bedroom of sorts.

Page had been friendly with the Rolling Stones, especially Brian Jones, since he first saw them at Ealing Jazz Club four years earlier. Now, in those first months with the Yardbirds, he was an occasional visitor to the Courtfield Road flat, along with Keith Richards and Tara Browne, the Guinness heir who would be dead by the end of the year, crashing his Lotus Elan after leaving the flat, his death celebrated in the Beatles' 'A Day in the Life'. It was at 1 Courtfield Road that Jones and Pallenberg began to regularly ingest LSD, soon introducing Richards to its glimpses of another reality. It is unlikely that Page, who developed a fondness for psychedelic drugs and was no longer confined by the rigidity of session work's time constraints, did not also enter this arcane coterie.

Through Robert Fraser, a Mayfair art dealer and major player in the Swinging London scene, the trio of Jones, Pallenberg and Richards became friends with the revered independent filmmaker and occultist Kenneth Anger, a disciple of Aleister Crowley. Anger's very beautiful short movies, marinaded in metaphysical matters, were like visual poems. Anger's use of pop music to tell the story in his films would prove to be hugely influential. Martin Scorsese would replicate it in his breakthrough film *Mean Streets*, and Anger used Bobby Vinton's 'Blue Velvet' in his 1963 movie *Scorpio Rising*, 23 years before David Lynch's film *Blue Velvet*. Anger considered Pallenberg to be 'a witch' – in turn she claimed that everything she knew about witchcraft had been learned from the filmmaker – and Brian Jones too, and that 'the occult unit within the Stones was Keith and Anita and Brian'. Keith had been turned on to such matters by Anita, and the pair would soon become lovers. A principal consequence of such out-on-the-edge thinking was the writing and recording of the Rolling Stones' 'Sympathy for the Devil', a song that – as Altamont would suggest – may not have been without its consequences. Page was yet to meet Kenneth Anger. But when he finally did, some years later, it began a relationship also not without penalties.

At the beginning of August 1966 the Yardbirds went into IBC Studios to record a new single, with Simon Napier-Bell at the production helm. Although 'Happenings Ten Years Time Ago', as the song was titled, came from the germ of an idea that Page and Keith Relf had come up with, the composing credits for the song would be attributed to all five group members. 'Happenings Ten Years Time Ago' would be the most psychedelic of all the Yardbirds' singles. Like a pointer to the future there were dual lead guitars on the record, Page and Jeff Beck, and so Page once more brought in his friend John Paul Jones to play bass. Beck, who had been suffering from ill health, added his own guitar parts later, along with a piece of spoken-word absurdism based on his experiences in a sexual health clinic. Aside from this whimsy, the lyrics themselves had considerable poignancy, relating to experiences of déjà vu or even of past-life existences – appropriately complex subject matter as the pop-based first half of the 1960s gave way to the rockier second half.

'It was a compressed pop-art explosion, with a ferocious staccato guitar figure, a massive descending riff and rolling instrumental break and LSD-inspired lyrics that questioned the construction of reality and the nature of time,' wrote Jon Savage in 1966: *The Year the Decade Exploded*. But by some it was seen as wilfully clever clogs. Penny Valentine, *Disc and Music Echo*'s reliable record reviewer, was extremely dismissive: 'I have had enough of this sort of excuse for music. It is not clever, it is not entertaining, it is not informative. It is boring and pretentious. I am tired of people like the Yardbirds thinking this sort of thing is clever when people like the Spoonful and Beach Boys are putting real thought into their music. And if I hear the word psychedelic mentioned again I will go nuts.'

In fact, in the UK 'Happenings Ten Years Time Ago' only stuttered to the edge of the Top 30. As far as Britain was concerned, the Yardbirds were – in the jargon of the time – on their way out.

On 5 August 1966 Page played bass with the Yardbirds in the eighth-floor Auditorium of Dayton's Department Store in Minneapolis, Minnesota, a regular gig venue. Although he had visited the United States twice before, this was the very first American show that he ever performed. This, the Yardbirds' third US tour, had been scheduled to kick off a week earlier, but Beck was bedridden with tonsillitis, which was why he had not been present at the initial 'Happenings Ten Years Time Ago' session. At Dayton's Department Store there were two concerts, one at 1 p.m., the other at 4. 'The surroundings felt quite surreal,' Page remarked on his website many years later. For the show he was clad in a purple jumpsuit.

'Shapes of Things' had been a US hit when it was released in February that year, reaching the number 11 slot; it was followed by 'Over Under Sideways Down', out in June and two months later still in the US charts, where it would peak at number 10, the group's biggest-ever American hit. The *Roger the Engineer* album had been released in July in the USA as *Over Under Sideways Down*, and that esteemed LP would get to number 52, not bad for a group starting its career in the USA.

The tour trundled through the Midwest – Chicago, Detroit, dates in Indiana – and down into Texas and assorted Bible Belt areas, playing the same sort of state fairs that had so irritated the Rolling Stones on their early US tours – unaware perhaps that these sort of shows were where Elvis Presley first honed his live act. Jeff Beck had not fully recovered from his illness, and would frequently take out his ire on the inadequate amplifiers at the venues. 'If he didn't get his sound right, he'd just kick the amps offstage,' recalled drummer Jim McCarty.

Not that the shows weren't without a modicum of glamour. Due to a national airline strike, Simon Napier-Bell had been obliged to charter a small private plane. After Beck had smashed his own Marshall amp, he insisted that he would not carry on without an identical replacement. According to Napier-Bell, Page used the dilemma to undermine him: '"Simon is our manager," he said, "so it is on him to find a replacement." There were hardly any Marshall amps at all in the USA at that time – probably no more than 20 – so when I finally tracked one down we had to send the plane to pick it up, which cost an absolute fortune, far more than the amp cost. But that kept Jeff Beck happy, and allowed Jimmy Page to feel he'd got one over on me.'

On 23 August 1966 the Yardbirds played Santa Catalina Island, a resort 22 miles from Los Angeles in the Pacific Ocean. The group arrived on a boat from Long Beach filled with competition winners from radio station KFWB, and one of these fans noticed that Beck seemed in a 'difficult' mood. He had been in this 'mood' for the entire tour: his tonsillitis had never fully gone away and now seemed to be on the offensive once again.

For Simon Napier-Bell, however, this show at the island's Casino Ballroom was the best he had ever seen by the group. Beck played a solo, he said, that seemed to last for ever. During it he interplayed with Page's thundering bass guitar, and their sonic concoction drifted off into the soundscapes of what already was becoming known – and dreaded by Penny Valentine – as 'psychedelia'.

By the time the Yardbirds returned to Long Beach, it was clear that Beck was not in good shape. Although he retired for the night to the arms of Mary Hughes, his Los Angeles girl-friend, he was so sick the next day that that night's show, at Monterey County Fairgrounds, was cancelled.

Beck's health was bad enough for him to have to drop out of the rest of the tour, a cause of considerable controversy within the group, but a decision of huge significance for Page. For the remaining 12 dates, beginning on 25 August at San Francisco's Carousel Ballroom, Chris Dreja switched from rhythm guitar to bass, and Page, wearing the newly fashionable wide-flared trousers, took over as lead guitarist. 'It was really nerve-wracking,' he said, 'because this was the height of the Yardbirds' concert reputation and I wasn't exactly ready to roar off on lead guitar. But it went all right, and after that night we stayed that way. When Jeff recovered, it was two lead guitars from then on.'

During the tour Page would hear his own guitar work on the radio, on a single from a recent session he had played in London produced by Mickie Most. Now 'Sunshine Superman' by Donovan, an innovative and definitive sound of the summer of 1966 that heralded a golden period and shift of style for the former folk singer, was rising up and up the US charts, reaching the number one slot for a week. Although not released in the UK until December that year, it would almost emulate its US chart position, reaching number two.

Jimmy Page and Donovan Leitch were like-minded musical souls, each with their own interest in metaphysics. Playing on 'Sunshine Superman' with Page was – yet again – John Paul Jones on bass. At those same sessions Page played the haunting guitar on Donovan's equally memorable 'Season of the Witch', which was on the *Sunshine Superman* album. Built around a D ninth chord shown to Donovan by master guitarist John Renbourn, 'Season of the Witch' was ideal for extended versions and would be frequently employed as soundcheck material by Led Zeppelin.

Back in the UK, Jeff Beck's health returned, and he drove over to Page's Pangbourne home, its interior design already beginning to reflect the prevailing rock-star rococo style. The two guitarists worked out a stage routine that would allow each to play lead guitar, intertwining with one other and mutually strengthening their playing and that of the group. Among the songs they developed was a version of Freddie King's 'Goin' Down' – though this was never recorded.

They needed to work fast. On 23 September the Yardbirds again hit the road, supporting the Rolling Stones and the Ike and Tina Turner Revue on a 12-date tour of the UK, two shows a night, ending on 9 October 1966.

The tour kicked off at London's Royal Albert Hall, where the Yardbirds allegedly blew the Rolling Stones off the stage. Yet the review they received from the *NME*, especially for Jeff Beck, was extremely sniffy; it irritated him that he was described as 'a guitar gymnast'. Simon Napier-Bell utterly disagreed with such an assessment: 'They were really fantastic. What Jeff and Jimmy were doing was playing Jeff Beck's solos, but in harmony. It was astonishing to hear, and to watch.'

Difficulties soon arose, however. According to Chris Welch in *Led Zeppelin: The Book*: 'One problem was that Jeff couldn't handle the competition and would try to blow Jimmy off the stage. Page was always on the ball, but Jeff's returning fire in guitar exchanges would be unpredictable and relied on volume when accuracy failed.' Napier-Bell was in agreement in an interview he did with Jim Green in the October 1981 edition of *Trouser Press*: 'Jimmy deliberately upstaged Jeff, Jeff got moody and walked out towards the end, fortunately we finished it.'

Quickly forgiven, Beck was admitted back into the Yardbirds fold. This was a necessity, as they were about to join the winter leg of Dick Clark's Caravan of Stars – a regular feature of the American popular music calendar organised by the legendary DJ. But before that there was another avenue to explore.

An exaggerated, dramatised version of the high-end hippiedom found at Anita Pallenberg and Brian Jones's home was expressed in the party scene in the classic – yet occasionally extremely pretentious – metaphysical thriller *Blow-Up*, which Italian director Michelangelo Antonioni started filming in London in April 1966. (The scene was actually shot in Christopher Gibbs's Cheyne Walk house.) In the film a fashion photographer, played by David Hemmings and clearly based on *enfant terrible* David Bailey, thinks he has witnessed a murder.

After completing the London shoot in June, Antonioni decided that to fully represent the capital's glamorous, swinging spirit he should shoot a sequence in a rock 'n' roll club. In September he returned to London and booked a meeting with Kit Lambert, manager of the Who. The day before the meeting, Lambert had lunch with Napier-Bell at the Beachcomber restaurant in London's Mayfair Hotel; the two men were close friends and Lambert wanted to pick Napier-Bell's brain about how to approach Antonioni. Napier-Bell decided to set him up to the advantage of his own group: 'I told him to ask for £10,000 and insist that the Who had final edit on their sequence. Antonioni kicked him out after about a minute.

'Then I went to see Antonioni: "We don't want money. This is art. Of course I don't want to edit it."' (In fact the Yardbirds received £3,000 for their part in *Blow-Up*: car-freak Jeff Beck immediately spent his share on a second-hand Corvette Stingray.)

Napier-Bell had scored. The Yardbirds' *Blow-Up* sequence was filmed at Elstree Studios in Borehamwood, north of London, doubling for Windsor's hip Ricky-Tick Club, in the week beginning 6 October 1966. The band played 'Stroll On', as it was called in the film's credits, the lyrics having been rewritten the previous night by Keith Relf for copyright reasons – in other words, so he could snatch the credit. But it was better known by fans who had experienced the song when rivetingly performed by the Johnny Burnette Trio as 'Train Kept A-Rollin'' – the same song that the Yardbirds had recorded at Sun Studio in Memphis the previous year. (Howlin' Wolf's 'Smokestack Lighting', a Yardbirds live favourite, had been first choice, but the idea was shelved when Antonioni decided it lacked the relentless pace he needed for the scene.)

'Train Kept A-Rollin' would be the very first number that Led Zeppelin would play in their initial rehearsal; in *Blow-Up* the Yardbirds essay an angry, explosive version of the song before a consciously static audience, which includes a young Michael Palin and a dancing, silver-coated Janet Street-Porter. Page stands stage-right to Beck's stage-left and, rather in the manner of the Kinks' Dave Davies, his hair is parted in the centre, his mutton-chop sideburns kissing his jawline and peeking out beneath the twin tonsorial curtains waterfalling from his head. He wears an open black jacket, a trio of badges balanced symmetrically on each lapel. In the sequence Beck freaks out over a malfunctioning amp, smashing his guitar to splintered pieces in a manner that only Pete Townshend would actually do in reality. Upon learning of his role, Beck had recoiled: would he have to destroy his new Gibson Les Paul? No fuckin' way!

A bunch of cheap Höfner replica guitars were brought in. 'Jeff Beck had to be coaxed into smashing the guitar. And then he did it half a dozen times,' recalled Napier-Bell. It is only after the guitar has been destroyed that the audience breaks out into a feverish response.

Smashing the guitar wasn't the only problem Beck had on the film, however. 'Antonioni was a pompous oaf. I didn't like him at all,' he said. 'The film was a bit of a joke. Crap. I thought, "Oh, that's the end of us." Because I saw the premiere in LA. But people loved it. It kept us going.'

This scene from *Blow-Up* appears to be the only filmed record of Page and Beck playing together in the Yardbirds. Though he is only briefly glimpsed in this scene, and Beck's thuggish fury unquestionably steals their joint screen time, Page's almost girlishly pretty looks – which crease momentarily into a smile – contrast powerfully with Beck's pugnacious posture, like that of a yob awaiting his borstal sentence. You can see why, for the brief time they played together, the pair proved such a potent force in the Yardbirds.

Along with the Yardbirds on the Dick Clark Caravan of Stars tour were bill-toppers Gary Lewis & the Playboys, whose singer was the son of comedian Jerry Lewis. The group – safe in a Herman's Hermits/Gerry and the Pacemakers kind of way – had seven successive US Top 10 singles. Then there were 'Wooly Bully' hitmakers Sam the Sham and the Pharaohs; the Distant Cousins; Bobby Hebb, high in the US charts that summer with his sophisticated, sexy 'Sunny'; and early sixties vocal star Brian Hyland, purveyor of puppy-love pop. Soon, as album rock became the principal market force, several of those acts would see their careers nosedive forever.

The tour wound through the south, the Midwest and East Coast before winding up in Huntington, West Virginia, on 27 November. 'Thirty-three dates, I think, and of those twenty-five were doubles, two shows in one night,' said Page. 'You'd think a double would be played in the same town, but it wasn't – it was two different towns. The show was in two halves. When the first half finished, and there was an interval … the performers would get on the coach driving to the next venue, while the second half carried on. Then, they in turn carried on to the next place, where the others had by then finished. It was the worst tour I'd ever been on, as far as fatigue is concerned. We didn't know where we were or what we were doing.'

Travelling conditions were abysmal, the artists being driven 600 miles or so a day in a pair of converted Greyhound buses to play four songs each at every show. 'The other acts had little or nothing in common with us,' said Jim McCarty. 'Sam the Sham and his Pharoahs, Brian Hyland. I mean, they were just so different, though Sam the Sham had his moments. Anyway, when they let us off the bus, we'd go onstage and they'd shout, "Turn the guitars down!" Jimmy was getting through it because he was a professional. Chris and I stood up to it because we were creating humour from all sorts. Keith was drinking his way along. But Jeff ...'

Jeff Beck was becoming a specialist in crossing the United States in a bad mood: 'The bus was supposed to have air-conditioning, but didn't seem to. And all the American groups on the bus played their guitars non-stop, and were always singing. Could you imagine? Cooped up on a stuffy bus with everyone around you singing Beatles songs in an American accent?'

His technique honed on the set of *Blow-Up*, Beck cut a destructive swathe through the tour's initial dates: amps thrown out of windows, instruments smashed. 'Jeff Beck had to be coaxed into smashing his guitar for the *Blow-Up* scene,' said Napier-Bell. 'And then he fell in love with doing it and with smashing his amp. I'm sure Jimmy Page was counting the nights, because then Jeff Beck left.'

The frustration within the group began to mount, and, as Beck would admit in hindsight: 'I was quite messed up. At 21 I was really on my last legs. I just couldn't handle it.'

'One time in the dressing room,' recalled Page, 'Beck had his guitar up over his head, about to bring it down on Keith Relf, but instead smashed it to the floor. Relf looked at him with total astonishment, and Beck said, "Why did you make me do that?"'

In the middle of the tour, in Harlington, Texas, Beck caught a taxi to the airport and flew to Los Angeles – where, of course, Mary Hughes awaited him. Beck's explanation for his departure? A return of his chronic tonsillitis. He was going to have treatment and would soon return, he said.

The day after Beck disappeared, Napier-Bell was obliged to appear on a local television show to announce that the next Yardbirds concert had to be cancelled. Showing that they were perfectly adaptable under stress, Relf and Page scoured the area for a joke shop. When Napier-Bell took a lengthy pull on the cigar his pair of charges had presented to him, he had to jump back as it exploded in his mouth – in the middle of the live television broadcast. At the time there was a term for such behaviour among UK groups: looning. Page's part in this moment clearly showed that he was not above indulging in this, although, given the complicated relationship he had with his manager, was there a subconscious maliciousness in the very notion of this deed?

Once again, Page took over as the sole lead guitarist. 'Jimmy was always a real pro,' said Chris Dreja, 'whereas Jeff was a man of emotion. I think Jeff always found it harder than Jimmy because he was prone to playing according to how he felt, whereas Jimmy's idea was always, "We're professional entertainers."'

'I didn't like my territory being encroached upon, and I wanted to be it, to do all the guitar playing,' admitted Beck. 'And when it got to the point when I was exhausted, we then embarked on a six-week Dick Clark tour. Six hours in that thing was enough for me. To be faced with those kind of travel problems and emotional tear-ups, and you'd get to the end and play a toilet gig with music you didn't feel comfortable with, was a recipe for disaster. Things just got on top of me and I cracked up, basically. I wanted to do something other than travelling … So it's not important whether I was kicked out or I left – it just happened.'

After a period of reflection in Los Angeles, Beck attempted to return to the Yardbirds. He realised that he had essentially been suffering from a minor nervous breakdown. But when word got back to the Yardbirds that their AWOL guitarist had been seen enjoying himself in LA nightclubs, they voted Beck out of the group.

'That was the point at which I gave up on trying to manage the Yardbirds,' said Napier-Bell. 'I thought it was too difficult and the only person I really liked in the group – apart from

Chris Dreja, who is a nice guy, a good person – was Jeff Beck. So I kept the management of Jeff Beck. I found Jimmy very difficult to deal with. Always narky.'

Page, however, felt it was unsurprising he was considered awkward: 'Bloody right. We did four weeks with the Rolling Stones and then an American tour and all we got was £112 each!'

One aspect of Page that Napier-Bell had observed was the guitarist's tendency to be tucked away in a corner reading yet another esoteric volume by Aleister Crowley. 'People would ask him about it, and he would reply something along the lines of, "Oh, you wouldn't understand it. You're not intelligent enough."'

6

'YOU'RE GOING TO KILL ME FOR
A THOUSAND DOLLARS?'

If Aleister Crowley performed a role as a kind of absent meta-physical father figure to Jimmy Page, the fastidiously loyal Peter Grant would prove to be a very physical manifestation of one.

Born into considerable poverty on 5 April 1935 in London's South Norwood, Peter James Grant was the illegitimate son of a secretary. He never met his father, who was rumoured to have left his mother because she was Jewish – even though she was employed as a typist for the Church of England Pensions Board.

Soon Grant and his mother moved to a tiny terraced house in down-at-heel Battersea, on the edge of the Thames. During the Second World War his school was evacuated, and he was sent to Godalming in Surrey, where he was educated at posh public school Charterhouse. Bullied by resentful incumbents, he developed an abiding loathing of the upper classes that would remain with him all his life. Emotionally distraught at being torn from his mother and home, meagre though it was, Grant began to put on the excessive weight that would characterise him.

'This boy will never make anything of his life,' read the final report by the headmaster of the south London school where Grant finished his education.

The first few weeks of Peter Grant's working life were spent labouring in a sheet-metal factory. At six feet, five inches tall and on his way to being just as wide, he certainly had the physique for physical work, but he quickly changed course, first becoming a messenger delivering photographs on Fleet Street for the Reuters news agency, and then a stagehand at the Croydon Empire Theatre.

After National Service in the Royal Army Ordnance Corps, where he attained the rank of corporal, he became doorman – bouncer, really – at the 2i's Coffee Bar on Old Compton Street, the birthplace of British rock 'n' roll and the venue from which sprang Cliff Richard, Tommy Steele and Adam Faith, among others. It was during this time that he met Mickie Most, who had recently returned to London after finding success as a pop star in his wife's native South Africa.

Through connections he made with Most, Grant was swept up into the newly popular world of televised professional wrestling, appearing as both Count Massimo and Count Bruno Alassio of Milan. From this springboard Grant secured bit parts in a number of films – among them *A Night to Remember*, *The Guns of Navarone* and the epic *Cleopatra* – and television shows – *The Saint*, *Dixon of Dock Green* and *The Benny Hill Show*, among others.

Grant pulled together his 2i's connections, bought a minibus and started a business transporting rock 'n' roll musicians to their gigs. He started off with the Shadows, before he was approached by Don Arden, who gave Grant the task of road-managing American acts he brought over for tours – the Everly Brothers, Chuck Berry, Bo Diddley, Little Richard, Gene Vincent and Brian Hyland – a role he performed with alacrity, personally ensuring the artists were paid every penny owed, in cash.

Arden had a very nasty reputation: he was rumoured to have held Steve Marriott, of the Small Faces, out of a third-floor office window by his ankles when the diminutive singer requested an accurate accounting of his earnings. Grant learned from such behaviour. 'When he was with Led Zeppelin he was a batterer of people,' said Napier-Bell. 'Although that was probably because of the drugs. When he had cleaned up he became a very nice person.'

But that was all yet to come. Grant also acted as road manager for the Animals and the New Vaudeville Band, and began sharing an office with Mickie Most at 155 Oxford Street, on the border of then sleazy Soho in London. When Most took over the management of the Yardbirds from Napier-Bell, Grant became their de facto manager and Most's partner in RAK Management.

'They needed someone like Peter Grant,' said Napier-Bell. 'He wouldn't stand for Jimmy Page's sneering.'

The group was losing traction in the UK, but in America they still carried considerable cachet. Grant travelled with the band on the road in the US, and, for the first time, they returned to England with money in their pockets. 'He was a great manager for the time,' said Chris Dreja. 'He was hands-on, nuts and bolts. He travelled with the band. He made sure they didn't get screwed. He loved his artists. He changed the music scene. He was responsible, especially with Zeppelin, of course, because they had such a huge audience, for changing the percentage points around between the record companies and the artists and the promoters. He was just a fantastic manager.'

On a date in a snowbound northern American state, the bad weather caused the Yardbirds to arrive late, almost missing their call time. Furious at being so put out, the pair of Mafia promoters refused to pay the group's fee, one of them pulling a gun. Peter Grant walked his considerable girth up to the man: 'What? You're going to kill me for a thousand dollars? I don't think so.' He got the Yardbirds their money.

Grant became close to Page, who, he noted, seemed in control of himself and intelligent, far more businesslike than the other Yardbirds and apparently much older than his 22 years. In this odd-couple relationship, Grant expressed his 'utter faith' in the young but extremely seasoned guitarist. 'It was funny how well

Jimmy and Peter got on because Jimmy was a very softly spoken, gentle guy and Peter was from a very different background and education,' said Napier-Bell. Among other things, the pair shared an interest in antiques, and they would go shopping for them together on tour.

'"Peter, there's only one problem with the band,"' Grant had been told by Napier-Bell. '"There's a guy there who's a real smart arse, a real wise guy." I said, "Who's that?" He said, "Jimmy Page." I was a bit puzzled. I thought, he must know I've known Jimmy since 1962/63. Apart from Neil Christian, when I was in business with Mickie Most, he did all the Herman's Hermits and Donovan. So when I met Jimmy I said, "I hear you're a bit of troublemaker and I should get rid of you. What have you been up to?" He said, "We did a four-week tour of the UK with the Stones and an American tour and we got £112 each." And he was the only one who had the balls or savvy to say something. By then Mickie Most was recording them. Mickie Most is a pop producer, an excellent pop producer. And there was always a bit of friction there. The way I saw the band going, the way they wanted to carry on, was against the pop thing.'

Yet Mickie Most appeared unaware of the cultural wind of change. 'The intention,' he said, 'was to try and resuscitate their pop career.'

In October 1967 Most insisted that a new Yardbirds 45 was released in the United States: 'Ten Little Indians', a song penned by Harry Nilsson and included on his second album *Pandemonium Shadow Show*. A truly dreadful record, it climbed no higher in the American charts than number 96, although Page had attempted to save the song, which featured a cloying brass section, by turning this into a feature after it had been subjected to what became known as 'reverse echo'.

That 'Ten Little Indians' was only released in America was a testament to how out of touch Mickie Most had become. Both

Page and Grant were well aware of the emerging new under-ground scene in America, the more reflective, less materialistic outlook of the hippie audiences at Bill Graham's Fillmore West auditorium in San Francisco, which became almost a temple to the Yardbirds. The soundtrack to this counter-culture was provided by the advent of FM radio and its new 'progressive rock' stations like San Francisco's KSAN, New York's WNEW and Orlando's WORJ, which were prepared to play an entire album with no commentary from a DJ (in the UK this was mirrored to an extent by John Peel's late-night *The Perfumed Garden* show on the pirate-ship Radio London).

The 'Season of the Witch' was upon us. There was a new generation of American music-makers with very strange, surreal and hitherto unimaginable names that suggested copious drug consumption: Strawberry Alarm Clock, Captain Beefheart, Love, the Doors, Iron Butterfly, Jefferson Airplane, Moby Grape, Quicksilver Messenger Service, the Grateful Dead. They were all allied to the burgeoning 'rock' album audience, a devel-opment spurred by the arrival in late 1965 of the first relatively cheap stereo systems. Long-haired, free-loving, pot-smoking and acid-dropping, this new market was cemented together by the considerable schism in American society brought about by the ceaselessly expanding war in Vietnam. Crisscrossing the United States with the Yardbirds, Page and Grant witnessed the success of first Cream and then the Jimi Hendrix Experience, seeing how they fitted perfectly into this new world. It was a musical and cultural sea change.

Another of these novel new acts, the Velvet Underground, championed in New York City by the artist Andy Warhol, supported the Yardbirds on several shows in the winter of 1966, most notably a show at Michigan State Fairgrounds. Soon the Yardbirds started dropping a snatch of the Velvet Underground's 'I'm Waiting for the Man', the group's paean to heroin dealers, into the middle section of an extended version of their own tune

'I'm a Man'. Page had heard the Velvets' first album while touring the USA with the Yardbirds. 'I'm pretty certain we were the first people to cover the Velvet Underground,' he said. At one of those Manhattan parties at which Andy Warhol was ubiquitous, the artist asked the guitarist to take part in a screen test for him for a movie he had in mind.

As the sole guitarist with the now four-piece Yardbirds, Page spent much of 1967 and the first half of the next year on long, gruelling tours in far-flung places. It was relentless. There were five American tours, a UK tour, a European tour and in January 1967 an Australasian tour with Roy Orbison and the Walker Brothers, playing two shows a night. But it was not without its rewards. 'When Jeff left and we carried on,' he said, 'the pure nature of the band was that they had a lot of numbers you could really stretch out on.'

Back in Britain from Australia during February 1967, Page worked with Brian Jones at IBC Studios on the soundtrack for *A Degree of Murder*. Directed by German New Wave filmmaker Volker Schlöndorff and starring Jones's girlfriend Anita Pallenberg, the film was entered for competition at the 1967 Cannes Film Festival. Although both Page and Nicky Hopkins, the celebrated session pianist, played on the soundtrack, along with Small Faces drummer Kenney Jones, with Glyn Johns engineering, there was never an official release for Brian Jones's music. 'Brian knew what he was doing,' said Page to *Rolling Stone*. 'It was quite beautiful. Some of it was made up at the time; some of it was stuff I was augmenting with him. I was definitely playing with the violin bow. Brian had this guitar that had a volume pedal – he could get gunshots with it. There was a Mellotron there. He was moving forward with ideas.'

'I don't remember much about the sessions other than we got Jimmy Page to come and play some amazing guitar during the murder scene and that the German director was thrilled with the end result,' recalled Glyn Johns.

Page still had time to play the occasional session. For the past couple of years, Johns had produced Johnny Hallyday's records, a Gallic Elvis who was indubitably the biggest music star in France. Hallyday would often record in London, and a distinct attraction for anyone working on his sessions was that he always paid in cash. But on this occasion he decided to work in Paris, with his own band, which included Mick Jones, later of Spooky Tooth and then Foreigner. 'I took Jimmy Page,' recalled Johns. 'He was nothing short of brilliant.'

On the tune 'À Tout Casser' Page performed one of his greatest session moments. And on 'Psychedelic' he employed a bluesy, Albert King-like bending riff that would resurface a couple of years later on Led Zeppelin's 'Whole Lotta Love'. The tune has a classic freak-out section as Hallyday repeats the word 'psychedelic' over and over to blasts of Jimmy Page guitar.

During this period in early 1967 Page became briefly involved with 19-year-old model Heather Taylor. A friend of New York photographer Linda Eastman, Taylor had run the fan club for Monkee Davy Jones and briefly been his girlfriend; she had also been a lover of Jimi Hendrix – 'Foxy Lady' was allegedly written for her – and Jeff Beck.

After Page met her at Ondine, the fashionable Manhattan nightclub, she had followed him to London. But he quickly told her they were 'seeing too much of each other' – after only three dates in London. Taylor was later introduced to the Who's Roger Daltrey by her Californian friend Catherine James, who was living in London with former Moody Blue Denny Laine. Taylor would go on to marry Daltrey, while Catherine James would crop up again in Page's future.

Fresh from his experience on the *A Degree of Murder* soundtrack, which was very much part of the 'progressive' new musical order in his eyes, Page was keen on leading the Yardbirds in a similar heavier and more experimental direction. Later in

1967, this would include the group's rendition of a new song, sometimes known as 'I'm Confused', but more reliably as 'Dazed and Confused'.

On 25 August 1967, the peak of the year's alleged Summer of Love, the Yardbirds played two shows at the Village Theater in downtown Manhattan. They were supported by the Youngbloods and by Jake Holmes, a singer-songwriter who spun a twist on the folk tradition by working with a guitar and two bass instruments but no drums. Watching from the wings, Jim McCarty was impressed by Holmes's song 'Dazed and Confused', with its descending riff, as was Page. The next day they went and bought *The Above Ground Sound of Jake Holmes*, his debut album, on which 'Dazed and Confused' was featured. Adapting the song, but only to an extent, with Keith Relf altering the lyrics, 'Dazed and Confused' became a stand-out performance in Yardbirds live shows for the last ten months of the group; Page's dramatic and highly effective flourishing of a violin bow on his guitar during the performance was an undoubted highlight. 'Dazed and Confused' became a showcase tune on the first Led Zeppelin album.

In the UK the Yardbirds were beginning to seem increasingly irrelevant, but in the United States they remained a substantial concert attraction. Yet even there, the hits didn't keep coming, largely because – as with 'Ten Little Indians', which would be released later that year in the US – their selection made almost no sense.

The Yardbirds' Greatest Hits was released in March 1967 in America, and made number 28, their biggest-selling US album. But whereas the Yardbirds' three biggest singles had been written by group members, from now on Mickie Most brought in – as he had done with their first hit 'For Your Love' – songs by established hit-making teams.

Accordingly, the choice of some of the 45s released seemed baffling. Written by Harold Spiro and Phil Wainman, 'Little

Games' was released in March 1967 in the US and a month later in the UK. It only reached number 51 in America and didn't even chart in the UK. As the title track of the next Yardbirds album, released in mid-July only in the United States – a mark of their dwindling UK status – the single was intended as a trailer for the LP.

There were further odd decisions. 'Ha Ha Said the Clown', for example, had been a Top 5 hit in the UK for Manfred Mann, but had failed to gain any chart movement whatsoever in America. Most persuaded the Yardbirds – or, more accurately, Keith Relf plus session musicians, including John Paul Jones, who arranged much of Most's material – to record the song and release it in the States. In July 1967 'Ha Ha Said the Clown', not featured on *Little Games*, staggered up to the number 45 slot in America. The breezy pop tune was an extraordinary choice for the Yardbirds to release, utterly inappropriate for the market they were trying to build in the States. But the B-side was another matter altogether: the explosive 'Tinker, Tailor, Soldier, Sailor', written by Page and Jim McCarty, with a bass-line like a relentless train rolling, featured the first recorded instance of Page using a violin bow on his guitar.

The *Little Games* album – derided by Page as 'horrible' – did contain some interesting moments: 'Tinker, Tailor, Soldier, Sailor' itself, and 'Glimpses', a suggestion of the way Page's compositional mind was developing. 'It featured the violin bow, and when it was played in concert I had tapes that played all this stuff – the Staten Island Ferry, locomotives, shock sounds – with textures from the bow. But we didn't get a chance, with the Yardbirds, to take it far enough,' he told *Rolling Stone*'s David Fricke; and 'White Summer', a mesmerising instrumental piece that he would perform live, both with the Yardbirds and Led Zeppelin, on his 1961 Danelectro 3021 or his 1967 Vox Phantom XII 12-string guitar.

'Goodnight Sweet Josephine' was the Yardbirds' last single, released in March 1968. Written by Tony Hazzard, who had also composed 'Ha Ha Said the Clown', it was about a man-eating groupie who lived in Clapham in south London – where Hazzard himself was based. Uncertain whether to commemorate its clear music-hall origins or celebrate its implied cultural comment, it did neither and ended up truly awful – a shockingly bad record. First recorded at the end of 1967 at Advision Studios in London, with Mickie Most producing, the Yardbirds disliked the final result so much that they insisted on doing a further version, on 6 February, at De Lane Lea Studios. It was no help, however; the single was the worst they ever released, and the group quickly asked for it to be recalled, reissuing a further version in the United States and Australasia. On the other hand, the single's B-side 'Think About It' had much more going for it – a shredding solo midway through that Page would take in all its glory into Led Zeppelin's version of 'Dazed and Confused'. With his assiduous thoroughness, the guitarist had grabbed the production of the B-side from Mickie Most.

On 6 March 1968 Page gamely went to plug 'Goodnight Sweet Josephine' on the long-running BBC radio show *Saturday Club* – the show had been a Saturday morning feature of the Light Programme before the station was transformed into Radio 1 the previous autumn, a supposed substitute for the now-banned pirate stations. Interviewed by the ever-avuncular Brian Matthew, the self-styled 'old mate' of his audience, Page described the troubles around making the record in his boyish, accentless voice and concluded, 'It's quite a good product now.'

However, Jeff Beck's summary was more to the point. 'When I heard "Goodnight Sweet Josephine" I thought, Thank God I left the Yardbirds.'

* * *

Three days after that *Saturday Club* performance the Yardbirds were in Paris. They played at the Assas Faculte du Droit, supported by the Brian Auger Trinity, featuring Julie Driscoll, and recorded the *Bouton Rouge* television show, performing 'Train Kept A-Rollin'', 'Dazed and Confused' and 'Goodnight Sweet Josephine'.

The next day, 10 March, the Yardbirds played at Paris's legendary Olympia venue. Afterwards the group moved on to a private party thrown by Eddie Barclay, who ran the renowned Barclay Records. Among the celebrated guests was Brigitte Bardot, dressed in leather motorcycle gear. She looked 'hot', noted Page.

Back in London on 15 March, Page played a session for Joe Cocker, for his 'Marjorine' single and its B-side, 'The New Age of the Lily'. (Later in the summer he would play on Cocker's epochal version of Lennon and McCartney's 'With a Little Help from My Friends', the song that made Cocker's career.) The next day he was again in Paris with the Yardbirds for a show.

A week later, following a concert at Retford College in Nottinghamshire on 23 March, the Yardbirds flew to New York for the start of their American tour. The opening date, 160 miles from Manhattan, was at the Aerodrome in Schenectady in New York state, a venue with a famously tremendous sound system, the kind favoured by Page for the more complex sound he was developing on tunes like 'Think About It', 'White Summer' and 'Dazed and Confused'. But such aural developments would not be employed for much longer with the Yardbirds, as the band knew before they even set off that this was to be their final ever tour.

Inspired by the prevailing softer sounds of the likes of – curiously – the Turtles and Simon & Garfunkel, and by LSD, Keith Relf and Jim McCarty had concluded that they no longer wanted to be part of the Yardbirds and would form a more folk-influenced outfit instead.

Two nights later, at Manhattan's Anderson Theater, the Yardbirds played a pair of shows that Epic Records recorded for a live album, which would eventually be released in January 1971 but quickly withdrawn after Page protested that it was a cash-in on the success of Led Zeppelin. 'We knew the American tour was going to be the last one, and all the pressure was off,' said the guitarist. 'We played well and had a really good time. We even managed to play consistently good venues; it was almost entirely universities and psychedelic ballrooms. The only low point was the Andersen Theater gig in New York, which was recorded for a live album. The rats at Epic had got wind of the break-up and decided to get the last drop of potential profit out of us. It was pure convenience for them, being based in New York, where we didn't like playing anyway. It should have been done at somewhere like the Shrine in LA, or the Fillmore. The Anderson Theater was a horrible place, very cold and unfriendly, and it didn't help that the Vanilla Fudge, currently local heroes, were playing across town at the Fillmore East. To cap it all, the Epic sound team had no idea how to record us. They were really straight and they just draped a few mikes around. It was pathetic. When they discovered the inadequacies of the recording, they dubbed on all those ridiculous bullfight cheers.'

As the tour headed into the American heartland, the audiences noted that the group seemed in tune with the prevailing psychedelic currents. 'I was a real Yardbirds fan,' posted John B on Facebook on 18 May 2015 of their show at Chicago's Blue Village, 'and was a bit high at the time. The band, especially Relf and Jimmy, seemed a bit higher than me. I didn't feel they were "drunk", but perhaps tripping. All of that aside, they practically melted the place, and most of the audience (me included) weren't really sure how to process the event – it was jaw-dropping. Page played the Tele with a bow and a wah-wah. I remember seeing broken strands of the bow hair trailing as he sawed away. The fellows were dressed very "psychedelically" and Relf was sporting a long moustache. I specifically recall "Over Under Sideways Down" as being a highlight and thinking, Oh my god, this guy can actually play this stuff!'

'I was there that night at the Cellar club,' posted Don Dawson on Facebook, 7 March 2015, of the show at the Cellar club in Arlington Heights, Illinois, on 20 April. 'Page was really wasted but managed to pull himself back together after rallying with a brilliant solo rendition of "White Summer" played seated. Then the rest of the band got back in gear to finish their set.'

Moving over to California on 10 May, the Yardbirds played the Earl Warren Showgrounds in Santa Barbara, a venue with a growing underground reputation. The British group Dave Dee, Dozy, Beaky, Mick & Tich had been scheduled as support, along with Turquoise. But the UK outfit was not there, replaced by Three Dog Night. In the audience was a Londoner called Paul Reeves, a former dancer on *Ready Steady Go!* and a fashion designer of some reputation who was visiting California to sniff the wind. 'After the Yardbirds' set I decided to go backstage and introduce myself, as Englishmen did in those days in California because we were a relative rarity,' said Reeves. 'We got on like a house on fire and I travelled with Jimmy and the band for the rest of the tour, even sleeping on his hotel-room floor in New York.'

The pair, who remain close friends to this day, bonded over their art-school backgrounds and mutual interest in design and fashion: they had both bought clothes at John Stephen's first shop on Carnaby Street; they both loved the garments you could buy at Granny Takes a Trip, Hung on You, and Emmerton & Lambert in the Chelsea Antiques Market – where they stocked some of the shirts Reeves designed. The pair also shared a love of the Arts and Crafts movement, and of the then very fashionable Pre-Raphaelites – from whom Page appeared to have gleaned much of his very being.

Back in London that year Paul Reeves would launch Alkasura, a high-end, futuristic clothes shop on the Kings Road frequented by the likes of the Beatles, the Rolling Stones, the Faces, David Bowie and later – naturally – Led Zeppelin. Together, Page and Reeves drove down to the famed Costa's in Tooting Bec, south London, a Greek Cypriot shoemaker who made them buckled snakeskin boots, the inspiration for which derived from an image in *East of the Sun and West of the Moon*, a book by the early 20th-century illustrator Kay Nielson. (Page's pair eventually became part of the Victoria and Albert Museum's collection, and in 2008 Paul Reeves curated an exhibition at the museum called *The Best of British*, dedicated to 19th- and 20th-century design from these islands. Page contributed several pieces, including the superb Edward Burne-Jones Pre-Raphaelite tapestry *The Quest for the Holy Grail: The Achievement*, worth at that point around £1 million.)

Paul Reeves was not the only person Page met on this return to southern California. Catherine James had left Denny Laine and moved back to her birthplace of Los Angeles, bringing her baby son home with her.

Moving into a house in Bronson Canyon, on the edge of the Hollywood Hills, she took a job in the ticket office of Thee Experience, a cutting-edge rock venue on the Sunset Strip. After the Yardbirds' date in Santa Barbara, they had a further show in southern California – on 11 May 1968 they played in Anaheim, south of Los Angeles – and two days later recorded a television interview that heavily featured Page.

During this time Page visited Thee Experience and linked up with Catherine James. 'I had plenty of handsome suitors, but no one really had my heart until I encountered the ethereal Jimmy Page,' Catherine James wrote in her autobiography. 'Heather had given me a pretty accurate description, but there were no real words to describe his seductive allure and painful charm. It wasn't just his lithe, elegant, rock-and-roll mien, or his

Pre-Raphaelite angelic face and soft, long curls. He had an inde-scribable smouldering look in his eyes, like he had a secret he might share with you one day. When we kissed he inhaled my breath like he was savouring my soul. I'd never felt anything quite as dark or sensuous as James Patrick Page. He captivated me with stories of the English countryside and his lone manor in Pangbourne … He always made me feel like we were some-where off in the mists of Avalon.

'Although he hadn't exactly spoken the words, he did some heavy alluding. I had illusive visions of being the blithe young maiden of the manor; we'd give life to a band of seraphim and be eternally happy. Little did I know several other girls were under the same identical spell.'

Would Catherine James have been more nervous if she had learned what other members of the Yardbirds knew of their guitarist's liaisons? 'Jimmy Page used to show us Polaroids of often blurred close-up parts of female anatomy, often featuring fruit, I seem to remember,' recalled Chris Dreja.

What Catherine was aware of was that her lover was making plans for the future: 'Jimmy was still playing guitar with the Yardbirds, but he was also working on putting his own group together in England. He said he was hoping to come back to California soon. If the band did well, then they'd do a West Coast tour.'

Although both Page and Peter Grant were thoroughly cognisant of the shifts in the music scene in the United States, other members of the Yardbirds were not as clued up. 'We weren't aware that the market was changing into an album market,' said Jim McCarty. 'We thought that maybe an updated *Roger the Engineer* would have worked for us. At this time we'd all wear kaftans … The thing about Keith and I was that we were so tired of travelling around and playing "Smokestack Lightning". And we couldn't see any future for it. Jimmy had been in the band a year or so. And was fresh.'

In fact, Page had been in the Yardbirds for almost two years. But his steely determination remained undimmed: 'When the band finally folded and I wanted to try something new, I just wanted to carry on rocking. I had this great stockpile of material in my mind and songs and riffs I had written down on tape at the time. So it was really handy. I knew which way I wanted the group to go if I could get a group together. Thankfully I did.'

However, Grant hadn't only discussed the shifting American sands with Page. The guitarist's old sparring partner Jeff Beck – himself a client of RAK Management, Simon Napier-Bell having finally decided to absent himself from Beck's career – also benefitted from this information, as he told *Uncut* magazine: 'Peter was fantastic. What he realised, long before the others, was that there was a sizeable audience for an underground scene away from the Top 40. We'd been playing shitholes in England and then he took us to America ...'

The Yardbirds' last show was at Luton Technical College on 7 July 1968. With the band to all intents dead and buried, Grant went on the road in the US with Beck, who – having turned down the task of replacing Syd Barrett in Pink Floyd – had formed the Jeff Beck Group, with former Steampacket and Shotgun Express singer Rod Stewart, bass player Ron Wood and drummer Micky Waller.

The Jeff Beck Group's US debut was on 14 June 1968 in New York, at Bill Graham's recently opened Fillmore East, where they played four shows, the opening salvo of a six-week tour. Thanks to the headliners, the Grateful Dead, the 3,000-strong venue was sold out. And although Rod Stewart suffered from such extreme stage fright that he at first delivered his raspy, soulful vocals from behind the amps, the act's performance was a colossal success, described by Robert Shelton the next day in the *New York Times* as 'wild and visionary', the writer declaring that the British group had upstaged the Grateful Dead. The Jeff Beck Group's burgeoning reputation was only enhanced when, four days later, they began a week's residency at Manhattan's Scene Club, during which both Jimi Hendrix and Eric Clapton regularly got up onstage to jam with the four-piece. And, as a consequence of the wildly successful Fillmore East shows, they were booked to play six nights at San Francisco's Fillmore West.

What was most extraordinary about this groundbreaking tour was that the Jeff Beck Group did not have an album in the stores in the United States. Mickie Most's hit-singles-factory ethos meant he was indifferent to Beck's blues inklings and to his group as a whole. He was also dismissive of Rod Stewart's singing strengths, making Beck take the lead vocals on 'Hi Ho Silver Lining', a Top 20 UK hit in the early spring of 1967, a song more suited for pub sing-along choruses than as a flagship single for a pioneering British guitarist. 'Hi Ho Silver Lining' did, however, have the redeeming feature of including 'Beck's Bolero' as its B-side.

Bolstered by Robert Shelton's *New York Times* review, Grant contacted the head of Epic Records in New York and Beck's *Truth* album, already recorded during several long, stretched-out sessions, was rush-released in August 1968, quickly climbing to number 15 in the US charts. Among the varied tracks, which included a reworking of the Yardbirds' 'Shapes of Things', Jerome Kern and Oscar Hammerstein's 'Ol' Man River' and Howlin' Wolf's 'I Ain't Superstitious', was a version of Muddy Waters' 1962 classic 'You Shook Me'. Jimmy Page pricked up his ears.

7

'LIKE A LEAD ZEPPELIN'

You know that inner sensation when you can almost touch the several directions your life might take, when you know the decision you are about to make will probably be final and there will be no return to what was there before? It can be troublesome and worrying. Or it can be enlightening and energising and exciting. For Jimmy Page it was certainly the latter.

Although the Yardbirds had split up, they were still contracted to undertake a Scandinavian tour in September 1968. Keith Relf and Jim McCarty left the band during the summer and were in the process of putting together Renaissance, their folk-influenced art-rock project, but they licensed Page to use the Yardbirds name on the Scandinavian dates only.

The idea of forming a very specific type of band had been gestating gradually in Page's mind ever since the 'Beck's Bolero' session in 1966. The singer, he had then hoped, might be Steve Marriott of the Small Faces, or Stevie Winwood of the Spencer Davis Group. In the summer of 1968 he was still searching for that kind of white soul singer.

Page had been working at Immediate on sessions with his old friend Chris Farlowe, whose first, unreleased solo album he had produced and paid for. Farlowe was a possibility for Page's 'the New Yardbirds', the working title for the band, as he possessed a similar vocal style to those blue-eyed soul stalwarts, but unfortunately little of their charisma. 'Jimmy liked me,' Farlowe told *Record Collector* in 2017. 'But I was an established artist and a bit of a mod.' (Later, after Led Zeppelin, Farlowe would be called back into service by Page, singing on three tracks on his 1988 solo album *Outrider*.)

Page moved on to another emerging singer, like himself another teenage prodigy: Terry Reid, conveniently managed by Mickie Most, and – even though he was still only 19 – the handsome former vocalist with UK dancehall favourites Peter Jay and the Jaywalkers. Attempting to reinvent himself as an 'underground' artist, Reid had released a critically acclaimed album, *Bang, Bang You're Terry Reid*. But Reid had just accepted the task of opening for Cream on their final US tour and was obliged to turn down Page's approach. However, he recommended that Page check out another vocalist he had heard in the Midlands, one Robert Plant. Reid had played on the same bill as Plant's outfit Band of Joy, and mentioned that the group also had a remarkable drummer – John Bonham.

By now Robert Plant had been somewhat taken under the wing of Alexis Korner, who would let him stay at his Bayswater flat, sleeping on the same couch that had – something Korner would always point out – once been used for the same purpose by Muddy Waters.

Playing blues music with Alexis Korner appealed greatly to Plant, and at first he failed to respond to the phone messages Peter Grant left for him at the Three Men in a Boat pub in Bloxwich, where Plant had rented a room.

On 20 July 1968 the shockingly named Obs-Tweedle – the latest group Plant was singing in – played a show at the West Midlands College of Education. There was only a small crowd, but in it were Page, Grant and Chris Dreja. 'This big guy with a University of Toronto sweatshirt let us in backstage,' said Grant, 'and I remember Jimmy saying, "Crikey, they've got a big roadie!" It turned out to be Robert Plant! Jimmy loved Robert straight away.'

Although they were singularly unimpressed by Obs-Tweedle, Plant's clear vocal magic shook Page. How on earth, he wondered, had this singer not yet been discovered? Page was utterly unaware that Plant had already had a pair of flop singles released by CBS, or of his work with Alexis Korner, or that Move manager Tony Secunda was fluttering around him. Instead he worried that the vocalist might have some worrying hidden character defect that had so far kept him from the stellar heights he clearly deserved.

All the same, a few days later Plant received a telegram: 'Priority – Robert Plant. Tried phoning you several times. Please call if you are interested in joining the Yardbirds. Peter Grant.'

At the end of July 1968 Page invited Plant to his Pangbourne home. Arriving off the train, Plant, who was still only 19, was extremely impressed by the house, which was stuffed with dazzling antiques and was an audiophile's dream, with Tannoy speakers and Fischer amplifier, on which Page would excitedly play the Beatles' *Magical Mystery Tour* double EP. Of course, these possessions were thanks to Page's session work rather than from his relatively brief career with the Yardbirds; later Plant would discover that Page was extremely shrewd financially. And it wasn't just the house that impressed the young singer: 'He was so charismatic,' thought Plant.

Page, however, was not so sure about Plant: 'I liked Robert. He obviously had a great voice and a lot of enthusiasm. But I wasn't sure yet how he was going to be on stage: what he'd be like once we actually got together as a band and started playing.' He also told Mick Wall: 'I didn't know what he'd be like yet as a songwriter. When I first saw him he was a singer first and foremost.'

Nevertheless, Plant stayed at Page's Pangbourne home for an entire week. The singer was already especially taken by the West Coast sounds of acts like Buffalo Springfield, a particular favourite of Page's, Jefferson Airplane, Moby Grape and Love.

However, he also had a thorough grounding in relatively esoteric blues music. And Page's musical library not only included all these favourites, but extended far beyond them.

Plant shared Page's adoration of the early work of Elvis Presley, as well as such blues staples as Sonny Boy Williamson, Solomon Burke, Howlin' Wolf, Muddy Waters – whose 'You Shook Me' was on the Pangbourne playlist – and Robert Johnson, as well as rock 'n' roll greats like Jerry Lee Lewis, Chuck Berry and Eddie Cochran. And such arcane curios as Don and Dewey's sensational 'Justine'.

They listened to the folk-rock sound of Fairport Convention's 'If I Had a Ribbon Bow', and the joy on Plant's face was writ large when he discovered that Page owned a copy of Joan Baez singing 'Babe I'm Gonna Leave You', written in the 1950s by Anne Bredon. Page had already decided, he told the infectiously enthusiastic Midlands Mod-turned-hippie, that the group he was planning would play an electric version of the song. He had played an acoustic 'Babe I'm Gonna Leave You' while touring with Marianne Faithfull.

Plant's position in the group was sealed when Page asked him if he knew any good drummers. Having been unable to prise Keith Moon away from the Who, Page had had his eye out for a drummer of similar stature and talent, but he'd been turned down by the one he liked most: B. J. Wilson, who played with Procol Harum, riding high on their year-old mega-hit 'Whiter Shade of Pale'. Page had also checked out Mitch Mitchell, who was believed to be dissatisfied in the Jimi Hendrix Experience; Aynsley Dunbar, a Liverpudlian who had played with John Mayall's Bluesbreakers and Jeff Beck; and Clem Cattini, a super-session drummer and friend of Page's who refused to be parted from his regular and substantial session pay.

Naturally Plant suggested his old mucker John Bonham, but this was definitely no old-mates act. Plant knew that Bonham was almost certainly the finest drummer he had ever encountered, an opinion shared by most musicians who came across him.

Bonham was lengthily touring Britain with Tim Rose, a gruff-sounding American singer-songwriter who had acquired kudos on the 'underground' scene in London. And when Page went to see them play on 31 July 1968 at the Country Club in Belsize Park, he immediately knew who his drummer would be.

This would prove important for Plant's place within Led Zeppelin, providing him with a certain subconscious strength. Like a neophyte offering sacrifice, he had brought someone into the group. He had helped form Led Zeppelin. Bonham's presence also meant that he immediately had an ally in the group.

Noisy and boisterous, determinedly non-Londoners, Plant and Bonham were the antithesis of the quiet, rather shy but sophisticated Page; in some ways, of course, they permitted him to present a more fully formed variant of himself, round him off as he vicariously lived out fantasies through them.

Page needed a new bass player too, as Chris Dreja had finally decided to bow out and become a photographer. His replacement – after Page had been unable to get John Entwistle as part of a failed raid on the ever-fractious Who's rhythm section – was someone with whom Page was already well acquainted.

Born on 3 January 1946 – like Page he was a Capricorn – and brought up in Kent, the boarding-school-educated John Paul Jones came from a family of professional musicians. He first met Page at a Decca session in West Hampstead in 1964.

'He was very passionate about music, which is why I immediately took to him,' John Paul Jones told *Uncut* magazine. 'Very knowledgeable about music too. About old records. He was always very interested in recording. We were kind of geeks in those days, in a way. At the end of a session, most of the musicians would sit back and read their golf magazines, but we would always go into the control room to listen to playbacks and watch the engineers and producers. We both wanted to know how things were done. He was quiet, and he was reserved ...

'He was the youngest session musician until I came along. We were always really glad to see each other on the sessions, because it meant that you had a young, hip rhythm section. The drummer would be older, I suppose, and Big Jim Sullivan was older, but we were relatively young compared with all the other session musicians. In those days, to be a session musician was considered the pinnacle of your professional music career. If you got a foot in, at that early age, you kind of held on to it.'

Jones was already aware of Page when they met: 'I remember him having a reputation almost before I turned professional in early 1963, when he was with Neil Christian and the Crusaders. It was always, "You've got to hear this guy." In fact, I never actually heard him before we worked together, but yes, I knew of his reputation.'

When the four musicians rehearsed together for the first time in the middle of August 1968 in a tiny rehearsal room on Gerrard Street in London's Chinatown, their amps almost falling on top of them, the tune they immediately worked on was 'Train Kept A-Rollin'', straight out of recent Yardbirds live sets.

Jones thought their performance was 'stunning'. And Page was equally as enthusiastic: 'It was there immediately. It was so powerful that I don't remember what we played after that. For me it was just like, "Crikey!" I mean, I'd had moments of elation with groups before, but nothing as intense as that. It was like a thunderbolt, a lightning flash – boosh! Everyone sort of went, "Wow."'

'He had this whole thing about a dynamic rock band ... a whole light-and-shade thing,' said Jones, 'which was pivotal, and it informed every musical decision that he made. I mean, there weren't dynamic rock bands in those days. Everything was either a soft, folky-rock type thing, or just blasting all the time. It was very important to him.'

At the end of that first rehearsal, Page organised baked beans on toast for his three hungry new musical compatriots – then diligently collected from each of them the few pence that the food cost. With his accountancy training, Plant looked on approvingly.

Before they could even get out on the road as 'the New Yardbirds', fulfilling dates already booked, the four musicians found themselves in the recording studio. There was another previous booking to honour: Jones was scheduled to record an entire album with P. J. Proby, the American *enfant terrible* of British pop music. Proby had earned tremendous media appro-bation for having split his trousers on several dates on a 1965 package tour. But he had a powerful, almost operatic voice, reminiscent of Elvis Presley's deep baritone register; in fact, like Ral Donner, with whom Plant was always taken, Proby had sung demo records of songwriters' tunes for Elvis.

There were some definite financial upsides to the obligation, which Jones – listed as 'producer' – could not get out of: 'I was committed to doing all the arrangements for the album. As we were talking about rehearsing at the time, I thought it would be a handy source of income. I had to book a band anyway, so I thought I'd book everybody I knew.'

Page had already worked with P. J. Proby, on his 'Hold Me' single and his first album, *I Am P. J. Proby*, in 1964, playing rhythm guitar to Big Jim Sullivan's lead. The two days of sessions for the album that would be known as *Three Week Hero* began on 25 August 1968, and without vocal duties to perform Plant played harmonica on the LP.

Proby was so impressed with the results that he asked the four musicians if they would back him on an American tour. Unable to entirely forget his old session-playing ways, Page half-agreed to do it, though with the proviso that they were planning an exploratory set of dates on their own in the United States. So could he make a decision after those shows?

Proby said, 'Look, from what I've heard and the way you boys played tonight, not only are you not going to be my backing band, I'm going to say goodbye right now, because I don't think I'm ever going to see you again. That's how successful you're going to be. You're exactly what they want; you play all that psychedelic stuff and everything. You're going to go over there and go down so great I don't think you're ever going to come home.'

A Scandinavian tour had been booked in for the Yardbirds that had to be honoured, and it offered an opportunity to iron out the new group's set. Out of sight of the UK media, the New Yardbirds played their first-ever show at Denmark's Gladsaxe Teen Club, a gymnasium complex a few miles out of Copenhagen, on 7 September 1968.

There was a healthy turnout, some 1,200 strong. 'It was only a short while before the concert that we realised it wouldn't be the "real" Yardbirds that were going to play,' said Jorgen Angel, who was 17 and photographed the performance. Page wore a white ruffled shirt over white trousers. Both Plant and Bonham chose floral shirts, Plant's unbuttoned to the waist. Jones wore a long satin coat.

The set included a number of Yardbirds staples – 'For Your Love', 'White Summer', 'You Shook Me', 'Dazed and Confused' and 'Train Kept A-Rollin''. But they also played 'Communication Breakdown', 'I Can't Quit You Baby', 'How Many More Times' and a cover of Garnet Mimms's 'As Long As I Have You'.

A subsequent newsletter issued by the Gladsaxe Teen Club assessed this first Led Zeppelin show in a most positive light: 'Their performance and their music were absolutely flawless, and the music continued to ring nicely in the ears for some time after the curtains were drawn after their show. Let me in particular give my praise to Jimmy Page, who has made a great job with the three new men. They really succeeded and in particular the guitar solo by Page created huge applause ... We can therefore conclude that the new Yardbirds are at least as good as the old ones were.'

The gig was followed by another that evening, at the Brondby Pop-Club in the south of Copenhagen, and the next day the New Yardbirds played three more shows. Then they had three days off before crossing the border into Sweden, where they played five concerts, many at outdoor amusement parks. The Swedish crowd adored them, pounding their feet into the floor, demanding more.

Just over two weeks after the end of that Scandinavian tour, on 27 September 1968, the four musicians went into Olympic Sound Studios in Barnes, which had an eight-track set-up that was becoming popular with other 'underground' acts – that summer the Rolling Stones had made *Beggars Banquet* there – to record the first Led Zeppelin album.

Page was in charge of the sessions, booked on weekend nights' downtime, and he was personally footing the bill. He played the Fender Telecaster that Jeff Beck had given him as thanks for getting him the job in the Yardbirds: by now the guitar had received its psychedelic paint job. As he would be on all Led Zeppelin records, Page was producer, with the in-house engineer Glyn Johns ably assisting him.

'I wanted artistic control in a vice-like grip, because I knew exactly what I wanted to do with the band. That first record sounded so good because I had gotten so much experience in the recording studio. I knew precisely what I was after and how to get it.'

All his experience and mastery in studio sessions came to the fore. 'Certainly on the first album I had a very good idea of what I wanted to try and get with the band. Because at that stage I was extremely instrumental in the total direction of it. Obviously there was a definite concept of what one was trying to achieve there, and it was done. But we were definitely right out there on a limb, weren't we? Doing what we believed in. And it didn't really follow any sort of trend that was going on at all – or certainly nothing relative to any other band.'

Employing natural room ambience, Page enhanced the reverb and recording texture on the record. In addition to placing a microphone in front of the drums and amplifiers, he put an additional microphone some 20 feet from the amplifier, recording the time-lag balance between the two. 'Everything leaked into everything else. Which was part of the sound,' said Jones.

'Backwards echo was a technique that I invented at the time,' Page said. 'The engineer said it couldn't be done but I knew it could because I'd already suggested it earlier on a Yardbirds track. You reverse the tape, record the echo, then put it around the right way again so that the echo precedes the signal. It created a fantastic sound, but it was really only employed in the first album, on the end of "You Shook Me".'

In total there were 30 hours of sessions, costing £1,782. A high point was 'Babe I'm Gonna Leave You', over which Page and Plant had bonded at Pangbourne. And there was a clutch of further great songs: 'Dazed and Confused', 'Communication Breakdown', 'Good Times Bad Times', 'Your Time Is Gonna Come' and a pair of Willie Dixon tunes, 'I Can't Quit You Baby' and 'You Shook Me'.

By personally financing the first Led Zeppelin album, Page displayed his knowledge of the music business. Almost the only other successful British artist to own the master tapes of his songs was Dave Clark, leader of the phenomenally successful Dave Clark Five, who had rivalled the Beatles in the USA and was famously financially astute. Page knew that Clark's fortune was a great deal larger than the Beatles' simply because he had always owned his own recordings.

'I was up for it,' said Glyn Johns of his engineering work on *Led Zeppelin*, 'as Jimmy and I grew up in the same town and had been pals since the early sixties, and John had been the number-one session bass player in London for years. When I was an engineer I would see him almost every day, and a nicer guy you could not wish to meet.

'Knowing that anything these two put together was bound to be pretty good, I turned up at Olympic a couple of weeks later, not having any real idea of what I was walking into. I was blown off my feet. The album that we made in the next nine days was a landmark in rock and roll history, taking it to another level altogether.

'The sound they created, the arrangements they came up with, and the standard of musicianship were equally astonishing. Each session seemed to be more exciting than the last, as what they had prepared unravelled in front of me. All I had to do was press record, sit back and try to contain the excitement of being in the same room as what was going on.

'The stereo mix of this record is certainly one of the best sounding that I ever made, but the credit has to go to the band, as all I did was try to faithfully put down on tape what they were giving me, adding a little echo here and there to enhance the mood.'

Johns took the LP's acetate to a production meeting for *The Rolling Stones Rock and Roll Circus* television film. He played it to Mick Jagger, hoping to persuade the Stones singer to include Led Zeppelin on the show: 'I felt the band was going to be huge and therefore we should have them on the show, as it would be an enormous coup. My suggestion fell on deaf ears, as Mick did not get it at all.'

Mick Jagger's was not the only stellar testimonial that Glyn Johns sought: 'A couple of months later I dragged George Harrison to Olympic on the way home from a Beatles session and played him the master tape with the same result – he didn't get it either. I found this slightly disconcerting, as I could not understand why they did not get what was so exciting to me ...

Jimmy and John Paul Jones were from the same era with the same influences, and yet Mick and George openly disliked what they had done, seeing no value in it at all. In any event, they were perfectly entitled to their opinion, and fortunately a large proportion of the record-buying population disagreed with them.'

There were those who did get it, however. A little later, on Christmas Eve, Johns played the album again, to another guitarist, Peter Frampton, his house guest. 'My jaw dropped,' remembered Frampton. Then the phone rang. It was Steve Marriott on the line from Paris, where the Small Faces had just played a show. 'He said, "I've left: can I join your band?"' And so was formed Humble Pie, who from time to time would become something of a simulacrum of Led Zeppelin. When the second record, *Led Zeppelin II*, was released, however, Steve Marriott would find reasons to seriously dislike Jimmy Page's group.

Exciting new album or not in the works, there was still the small matter of the Yardbirds' schedule to fulfil. To Page's concern, these shows were often only half-full at best.

The UK debut of the New Yardbirds came on 4 October 1968, at Newcastle's Mayfair Ballroom, an established venue on the rock circuit – but only a few dozen people turned up. 'We originally thought that by calling ourselves the New Yardbirds we would be able to keep a sort of continuity from the early days of the old group,' explained Page. Yet on finding a group onstage that lacked Keith Relf, a few audience members asked for their money back. 'We realised we were working under false pretences. The thing had quickly gone beyond where the Yardbirds left off. We all agreed there was no point in retaining the "New Yardbirds" tag, so that was when we decided to change the band's name.'

Ironically, Terry Reid, who had been considered for the new line-up by Page and had recommended Plant, was supposed to be on the bill and featured on the early promotional posters, but his support-act slot on Cream's farewell tour of the United States meant he'd had to pull out of the Newcastle show. He was replaced, at a week's notice, by New York Public Library. 'We'd met Jimmy Page years before, when he was in Neil Christian's Crusaders,' said Tez Stokes, the New York Public Library's guitarist. 'He was a very well-respected guitar player, but very quiet, reserved and shy. John Paul Jones I met when he was the bass player with the Tony Meehan band.'

'Before the gig, either the band or their roadie asked if they could borrow our organ,' said Charlie Harcourt, guitarist with the Junco Partners, also on the bill. 'They didn't seem very well prepared. We told them no, they should have brought their own.'

'I stood right at the front and watched,' said Tez Stokes. 'There was hardly anyone there. Some people were sitting in the balcony, looking down.'

The Mayfair had a revolving stage, on which the next act would set up while the group preceding them were playing. 'Zeppelin weren't playing when the stage came round – they were farting around. Jones was on the left side in front of a silver-fronted Fender Bassman amp,' said Charlie Foskett, who was in the audience that night. 'He hit a note and the cloth on the front of the amp wobbled, which I thought was cool. Page posed about with his Les Paul. They weren't using monitors, all of that came later. The riser, which had the amps, waiting for someone to go: "One, two, three, four." That came pretty quickly.

'A lot of the audience went: "Where's the Yardbirds? Who's this?" It wasn't the Yardbirds, it was another band. After five minutes it was: "This is great!" Everybody had forgotten about the Yardbirds. Nobody knew the name Led Zeppelin then, of course, so it was: "Yeah, this is the New Yardbirds!"

'I thought the band were terrific. The first thing was the energy. Everything was a bunch of riffs. Page's guitar was ripping away. I've heard better soloists, but he was a great showman, a walking skeleton with skin-tight bell-bottom jeans, the hair and tons of posing.

'I was very much into their overall noise and energy, along with the visual thing. They really had their chops together. It was as loud as the gear would allow it to be at that point, and full throttle, including the couple of Yardbirds hits they did. The discerning music lovers were glued to it.'

'I wasn't very impressed with Robert Plant. He was a bit fey,' thought Ray Laidlaw, the drummer with Downtown Faction, also on the bill, who would evolve into Lindisfarne. 'I was more interested in the mechanics of the band. Bonham was pretty damn good. John Paul Jones kept himself in the background, and Jimmy Page was a fantastic player. But the band wasn't finely tuned.

'Page was basing it on the Jeff Beck Group. He knew how successful they'd been in the US, and was using that as his model. I wouldn't be surprised if after each gig he'd go through it with the band: a little more of this, a bit less of that, polish that, drop this number, bring that one in. Like managing a football team.'

'There was a track on *Truth* called "You Shook Me", with Rod Stewart singing,' recalled Bob Sargeant, the keyboard player with the Junco Partners. 'The New Yardbirds did that number at the Mayfair. They also did "Shapes of Things", the old Yardbirds hit. And they played "Communication Breakdown" and a couple of other songs that turned up on the first Zeppelin album.'

Fourteen days later, the New Yardbirds performed their second UK show, at London's Marquee Club. They were observed to play at what would become their characteristic phenomenal volume. Although the club wasn't entirely full, there was a disproportionate percentage of male drummers making up the audience. John Bonham's reputation preceded him.

The next night they played at Liverpool University. As they entered the building, two students, John Bold and his friend Chris Wallis, offered to carry in Page's guitar and other equipment, thereby guaranteeing free entry to the hall. Meanwhile, Wallis sold Plant a lump of hash. 'The group was sensational,' said Bold. 'Phenomenally loud. And very dramatic as Jimmy Page waved his violin bow about during "Dazed and Confused".'

By the next show, six days later, at the University of Surrey in Guildford, the 'Lead Zeppelin' name had been decided upon, though the group were already billed as the New Yardbirds. Always with a keen eye on things over the Atlantic, Peter Grant was concerned that US record buyers might think the name was pronounced 'Leed' Zeppelin, so he made an executive decision to drop the 'a' in 'Lead', transmogrifying the name to Led Zeppelin.

The group were paid £300 for the show, with an audience of no more than 200. During their soundcheck they played a pair of Creation songs, 'Painter Man' and 'Making Time', as they did regularly at this time. Creation's Eddie Phillips was, of course, a primary source for Page's appropriation of the violin bow during 'Dazed and Confused'.

Glen Colson was a drum roadie for the first couple of months of Led Zeppelin's life: 'Guildford was one of the first gigs I did with them. I set the drums up. And I used to sit behind John Bonham and hand him sticks. Why was he so good? Because he was incredibly technically brilliant. Musically, he was the driving force in Led Zeppelin.

'They were only playing the first album, slow and arranged blues songs. They were so heavy and good that it was obvious there was something going on: I was into music but I had no idea what they were up to. They were heavy and positive, louder and flashier than anyone else. Their angle was that they'd found this incredibly heavy drummer, like the heaviest session man you've ever seen. It was all very professional. A foregone conclusion they would be massive.'

Yet even this early in their career, the extraordinarily talented drummer seemed to come with a difficult subtext. 'Bonham behaved like someone who might be a gypsy. He nicked everything he could out of the dressing room: not only the rug, which he just rolled up, but also the tannoy speakers. Then he smashed the place up. The others were just sitting there, watching. Robert Plant was the PR guy, saying hello to everyone, very polite. The other two just sat there looking at me. I was embarrassed to be in the dressing room. Page sat there, saying nothing, like a voyeur. John Paul Jones never said a word: you could mistake him for a road-sweeper. Occasionally they would snigger about something to each other.' In fairness, it must be said that often the last thing a performer requires before going onstage is a cosy chat with the staff. They are focusing on delivering a performance, their opening lines or notes ready in their heads.

What surprised Colson was when his friend Kenny Pickett told him that the four musicians knew he was *au fait* with modern music and asked if he could provide a list of records they could use as inspirational reference points. 'Although Page and Jones had worked in studios on sessions for years, they had never really written any music. They weren't sure if they could do it consistently: they were looking for ideas. So I gave them a list of stuff, including Spirit and Moby Grape, I recall – though Plant may have already been familiar with those.'

In the British provinces, audiences remained hard to find, while in London it was easier: on 9 November Led Zeppelin topped the bill at the Roundhouse in Chalk Farm, already established as the premier underground venue in the capital. Their fee was

£150; when they played Bath Pavilion five weeks later, they received only £75.

The morning before the Roundhouse date, at West Bromwich register office, 19-year-old Robert Plant married Maureen Wilson, his girlfriend since 1966. Their daughter Carmen was born shortly before, on 21 October, and being the well-brought-up, socially responsible Midlander, Plant was legitimising Carmen and making an honest woman of Maureen, a qualified nurse whose father, once head of Calcutta's mounted police, owned a steel factory in the West Midlands. During the previous couple of years of struggle, Maureen had often kept them financially afloat.

Driving down to London in time for the Roundhouse sound-check, Plant and his new wife celebrated their marriage following the show.

Although on occasions Plant was considered by some to be trying a little too hard in his live performances, he and John Bonham – the raw recruits – were settling in well with the pair of seasoned session players. 'Jimmy was a member of the Yardbirds and he was a session musician, so he was successful,' said the singer. 'Jonesy was much more the backroom boy ... So their sort of positions and previous roles weren't really that daunting.

'But how they handled themselves with us was important. Jonesy was a bit ... not withdrawn, but he stands back a little and shoots the odd bit of dialogue into the air. It's good stuff but an acquired taste really. And Jimmy's personality initially was ... I don't think I'd ever come across a personality like it before. He had a demeanour that you had to adjust to; certainly it wasn't very casual to start with. But then again, the music was so intense that everything was intense.

'The ambition was intense and the delivery was intense, and where we were going was intense. Nobody knew where the fuck it was, but we all knew that this power was ridiculous from the beginning. So it was very hard to relax, sit down and have a beer and be the guys from the Black Country. Bonzo and I were much more basic in every respect, in how to deal with everything – including Jimmy. Because he had to be dealt with.'

8

AMERICAN ADVANCES

The first person to whom Peter Grant offered the Led Zeppelin album was Chris Blackwell, who owned Island Records, the premier underground label in the UK. Island's publishing division occupied another floor in the same building as Grant's at 155 Oxford Street. Blackwell almost bit. 'I knew Peter and really liked what I heard. I almost signed them. In the end, after all that happened, I was glad I didn't. I thought they treated women very badly. Jimmy Page was already very rich before he even started Led Zeppelin. But he was always kinda cheap,' said Blackwell.

But Blackwell did offer Grant a $25,000 per album deal for world rights, excluding the US and Canada. Blackwell later told Robert Greenfield in *The Last Sultan*: 'It was a handshake deal, but I was dealing with Grant and so it wasn't a deal until it really was a deal.' Accordingly, armed with Blackwell's offer, Grant and Page flew to New York at the end of November 1968. Grant went straight to Atlantic Records, originally formed as a jazz and R&B label in 1948, a beacon for soulful black music of every kind. He had already befriended Ahmet Ertegun and his wife Mica, an established interior designer who restyled Atlantic's London offices, and of course Page had connected with both Ertegun and his partner at Atlantic, Jerry Wexler, when he had visited New York at the behest of Bert Berns.

Back in June 1966, Ertegun had flown up to Los Angeles from Mexico City, where he had watched Tottenham Hotspur defeat the Mexican national football team in a friendly fixture by a single goal, in a 1–0 result. Ertegun had been urged to take the trip to LA by Wexler, as there was a group in the city who were attracting plenty of interest from other labels, but Wexler, who was only really interested in black music, needed Ertegun's opinion. The band was Buffalo Springfield, and the Atlantic Records founder was knocked out. 'First of all, the songs they wrote didn't resemble anything that anybody else was doing,' he said in Greenfield's *The Last Sultan*. 'They also had three outstanding lead singers who were also great guitar players – Neil Young, Stephen Stills, and Richie Furay ... The power in Buffalo Springfield was too incredible. They were one of the greatest rock 'n' roll bands I've ever heard in my life.'

So rapidly did Buffalo Springfield become the sensation of first the Sunset Strip and then the entire American recording industry that you can almost taste their nearly inevitable rapid disintegration less than a year later, after they played their final gig at the Long Beach Arena in California.

Shortly before Buffalo Springfield split up, Neil Young mentioned an act called Iron Butterfly to Ertegun that he thought Atlantic should sign. Young's management team – very soon to be his ex-management team – went to see them. 'I thought they were shit, actually,' said Brian Stone, one of Young's managers, in *The Last Sultan*. 'Cacophonous. Out of tune. Awful. I called Ahmet and I said we had a new band, and he saw them at the Purple Onion or some crazy place on Sunset Strip and signed them. Iron Butterfly became such a giant act that it made Jerry Wexler go out and sign Led Zeppelin.'

Iron Butterfly's first album was almost not even released by Atlantic: Ertegun considered each potential single to be 'shit'. But then there was a twist of fate that was a kind of zeitgeist moment in the history of the rise of underground rock: the new college FM stations began playing Iron Butterfly's album's title track, 'In-A-Gadda-Da-Vida', itself a twist on 'In the Garden of

Eden'. As a consequence Iron Butterfly's *In-A-Gadda-Da-Vida* album became the number two album in the US charts for the next two years.

And Atlantic's diversification didn't stop with Iron Butterfly; they had signed several other white rock groups and enjoyed considerable success with them, including Vanilla Fudge and – the most famous of all, part of Page's template for Led Zeppelin – Cream. Clapton's act, who had been signed by Ertegun, were at that time on their final tour of the United States, having announced they were to split up.

In late 1968 Jerry Wexler was producing *Dusty in Memphis* for another Springfield – Dusty this time – an LP that would seal her reputation. 'The story,' recalled Grant, 'is that she was down at Jerry Wexler's house and he told her about this new group that was in the offing with Jimmy Page and John Paul Jones. She said she'd worked with Jonesy on arrangements and such like, and Jerry was knocked out.'

Not only was Wexler acquainted with Page's assiduous approach to his art, he had somehow also learned of John Bonham being 'a hell of a drummer' – though he had never heard of Robert Plant.

So when Grant arrived in New York with Page that November with the tapes of Led Zeppelin's first album, the timing was perfect. Wexler was up for signing an act that would keep him at the vanguard of this new 'underground' world, while Grant used the Chris Blackwell offer as a bargaining chip to push up the Atlantic figure. Wexler offered Grant and Page $75,000 per album for American and Canadian rights for five albums over five years.

Wexler was then offered Led Zeppelin's remaining world rights for $35,000. After the UK head of Polydor Records turned down Wexler's tentative offer of $20,000 for the UK rights to Led Zeppelin, the Atlantic man bought those remaining world rights for the suggested $35,000. For Wexler and

Atlantic Records it would prove to be an extraordinary financial coup.

'To tell you the truth,' said Blackwell, 'I'm glad I didn't get them because it wouldn't have worked for us at Island. Too dark: I couldn't have dealt with it.'

After some wrangling, Wexler gave Grant a cheque for over $100,000, the highest advance paid for any act at that time. The deal included a promise – insisted upon by Page – that the group would appear on the Atlantic label itself, not on Atco, the subsidiary label on which the white rock acts so far had appeared. Page had also made it clear to Grant what his deal would be with Led Zeppelin: he would receive 50 per cent of all earnings, the rest to be shared among the other three musicians and Grant.

Once Wexler signed Led Zeppelin, he had almost nothing more to do with them, passing everyday control of the group over to Ertegun. Aware that Led Zeppelin were Page's group, the ever-diplomatic Ertegun focused on building a relationship with the guitarist and his manager, somewhat to the detriment of the perpetually charming Plant.

Notwithstanding the group's on-the-road excesses, Ahmet Ertegun would accompany them on tour, turning up unexpectedly in their dressing rooms at some backwoods venue to wish them well before they went onstage. Although he became good friends with Grant, there were also constant arguments with the manager over album costs or record release dates. The efforts Ertegun made to keep Led Zeppelin happy would pay off a thousand-fold. 'Ahmet was the guy who went to the concerts and dealt with the managers,' said Wexler. 'He plunged into it heart and soul. He became their friend and it was those efforts that made Atlantic a monster company.'

However, Led Zeppelin never formally signed to Atlantic itself. Having set up publishing and production companies for his protégés, Grant was able to cut a deal from a different angle than normal: 'We didn't sign direct to the label, we had a production company called Superhype. The title came from Jimmy, who was aware of the hype surrounding us at the time. So I did a tongue-in-cheek number and called it Superhype Music Inc. We sold off the publishing company some years later. The whole deal with Atlantic gave us various clauses that we were able to use in our favour.'

This was a difficult age when it came to expressing personal ambition, artistic, financial or otherwise. In the underground it was 'uncool' to value possessions of any sort – despite the evident wealth of the Rolling Stones and the Beatles, who were the true figureheads of the new hippie counter-culture. Led Zeppelin's huge advance from Atlantic Records was interpreted as evidence of their moral laxity and greed; you may feel that overlooking the conceptual irony of calling your production company Superhype said it all. Superhype? With its tongue firmly in its cheek, the company's name was utterly of its satirical time, like the Great American Disaster, the fashionable Fulham Road purveyors of genuine US-style hamburgers in London, where the walls were decorated with front pages of the *New York Times*, reporting such national traumas as the Wall Street Crash and the assassination of JFK; or Mr Freedom, which opened in 1969 at 430 Kings Road, peddling pop-art fashion by Tommy Roberts, Page's good friend. Didn't anyone notice the almost Ionesco-like absurdity of their name, Led Zeppelin?

Interestingly, Grant never had a formal contract with the four musicians in Zeppelin. 'That was a very strange thing,' said John Paul Jones. 'In fact, when Atlantic eventually found out, they nearly went mad. They said, "You can't be serious." But we just had a gentlemen's agreement ... We were signed to Atlantic, but we weren't signed to Peter. We never had a management contract. He got the normal management fees and royalties from the records as executive producer.'

Grant himself had an extremely liberal, rather evolved philosophy of what his role as manager should be, which belied his reputation for controversy. 'In the old days everybody thought the artist worked for the manager,' he said. 'In America they'd say: "Oh, so and so owns those people." You don't own artists. They hire you and give you a percentage of their money to do the very best for them.'

According to Jones, the four musicians' relationship with Grant was extremely satisfactory: 'All pretty above board and as a result it was a really happy band. We could never believe how other bands got on. They never spoke to each other and travelled in separate cars. Why did they play together if it was that bad? Everybody thought we were the prima donnas, yet there was hardly an ounce of attitude in the whole band. Page and I had seen it all before. We just didn't want to make the obvious mistakes.'

Jeff Beck was in New York, and he encountered Page and Grant, fresh from securing their deal. 'Page said, "Listen to this. Listen to Bonzo, this guy called John Bonham that I've got." And so I said I would, and my heart just sank when I heard "You Shook Me". I looked at him and said, "Jim, what?" and the tears were coming out with anger. I thought, "This is a piss-take – it's got to be." I mean, there's *Truth* still spinning on everybody's turntable, and this turkey's come out with another version. Oh boy … then I realised it was serious, and he did have this heavyweight drummer, and I thought, Here we go again – pipped at the post kind of thing.'

In the United States Beck was signed to Epic, a division of CBS Records, to whom the Yardbirds had also been signed. However, Page himself had never signed a contract with CBS. All the same, Clive Davis, the legendary head of CBS, assumed that his label would have the first offer on Page's new band. When Grant, accompanied by his attorney Steve Weiss, paid a courtesy call on Davis, the CBS honcho assumed it was to discuss the new Jimmy Page act. When Grant informed him that Led Zeppelin had already signed to Atlantic, Davis became apoplectic with rage. Grant and Weiss soon left the building. Later, Epic would release the live Yardbirds' album recorded in New York, and Page immediately would cancel its release with an injunction. 'I never signed any contracts with Epic – they didn't want me at the time,' he said.

The *Led Zeppelin* LP was set to be released in the USA on 12 January 1969, three days after Jimmy Page's twenty-fifth birthday. By then Led Zeppelin would be into the third week of their first tour of America, promoted by Frank Barsalona's Premier Talent agency, the first to concentrate exclusively on rock music; Premier Talent had already blazed forward with a pair of acts with similar power line-ups to Page's group: the Who and the Jimi Hendrix Experience.

Page, Plant and Bonham flew to Los Angeles on 24 December 1968. At the airport they were met by Richard Cole, their newly appointed tour manager, who, according to Grant's wishes, had the three ensconced in bungalows in the legendary Chateau Marmont on Sunset Boulevard.

Cole, a former roofing scaffolder and old Mod, had pulled himself up by his boot straps and transformed himself into a respected road manager known for his dedication to the acts he worked with. On his first job, with popular soul roadshow Herbie Goins and the Night-Timers, he met Jones, who was playing with the act on live dates. After Cole had worked with Unit 4 + 2, an act managed by Don Arden – useful for all sorts of nefarious tips, one imagines – in quick succession he was employed by the Who, the Yardbirds (where he became acquainted with Page), Jeff Beck, Vanilla Fudge, the Rascals, the Searchers and the New Vaudeville Band. Most recently he had been working with Terry Reid on Cream's farewell tour of America, an irony, all things considered.

Jones was to meet them in Denver, Colorado, on 26 December for their first-ever US date. With his wife Mo accompanying him, he had disgorged himself into New York as their plane from Heathrow landed at JFK, leaving the other three musicians to catch a connecting flight to Los Angeles; spending Christmas at the New Jersey home of Madeline Bell, a largely UK-based black American singer, he then made his own way to Denver for the Boxing Day concert. Jones's act of independence became a characteristic of his behaviour in the group, an early statement of his need to create 'my own space within the band'.

One assumes that the classy Chateau Marmont had been intelligently chosen for its luxurious essence, a psychological boost for the new troops; this was what they could look forward to paying for themselves in the hopefully not-so-distant future. But it was pricey, and for once Page was happy to go along with this. It was Page, Jones and Grant who bankrolled this first US tour, on which everything else was trimmed to the minimum; this was long before the days of record companies offering 'tour support': in other words underwriting the cost of their acts going out to play live dates. Mickie Most had put up £1,000 for amps and speakers, and in return took 1 per cent of Led Zeppelin's income in perpetuity.

'We didn't do a tour budget,' said Cole. 'In those days, it was like: Okay, the hotels are going to cost us this much, the air fares this. It wasn't even worked out, the job had to be done. We haven't got that much money, we've got to make it as economical as possible without it being too uncomfortable. As there was more money coming in for shows, things were escalating.

'TWA used to have a thing called Discover America, where you'd buy your airline tickets, you would work out the route of an entire tour, and as long as it went in a circle so you flew into New York and ended up back in New York and didn't go back to the same city twice, you'd get 50 per cent off. The only problem with that was if dates come in or fall out, you'd have to redo all the tickets again. They'd hate it when you took the tickets into the Hilton, where TWA had a desk, because everything was written by hand in those days. And each ticket had maybe 20 stops on it, but everything was economically worked out, even the 707 jets. With a jet like that, you didn't need to order room service because it was supplied, so most of the times we ate on the plane.'

At the Chateau Marmont, which had catering facilities in each bungalow, Bonham cooked Christmas dinner: turkey with all the trimmings. Yet everyone – especially Plant – was so nervous they could barely eat a mouthful. Crippled by the jetlag from the eight-hour time difference that hits most people travelling to the West Coast for the first time, both Bonzo and Plant were freaked out about leaving their families behind at Christmas. 'It's a sacrifice,' said Page, 'but there's going to be a pay-off. This band has a lot going for it. Let's make the best of it.' As befitted his position in the band, Page was then able to retire to his own bungalow at the hotel. While the others shared accommodation – Plant and Bonham together, Jones with Cole – Page never did.

Bright and early on 26 December, Cole roused his three charges at the Chateau Marmont, drove them out to LAX Airport and caught a flight to Denver for Led Zeppelin's debut live performance in the United States.

Linking up with Jones in the mile-high city, the tension among the four musicians was palpable. How would American audiences respond to them? Would they be as lukewarm as so many of the UK crowds had been?

Their worries were not without foundation. They had been added late to the bill and were not even included on the posters for a show at the Auditorium Arena headlined by Vanilla Fudge and with Zephyr, a local blues-based hard-rock outfit, on before them. To make matters more complex, Led Zeppelin had only snagged the concert after the Jeff Beck Group pulled out of this and several subsequent shows. Vanilla Fudge had toured with Beck's outfit as support, and had already become friendly with Cole and Grant. The Fudge were hardcore: their moody, keyboard-dominated interpretations of classic tunes such as the Beatles' 'Eleanor Rigby' and the Supremes' 'You Keep Me Hangin' On' had won them a substantial audience; as Led Zeppelin hoped they would do with them, Vanilla Fudge had won their status by playing second fiddle to such acts as Cream, the Doors, the Who and Jimi Hendrix, and frequently blowing these headliners off the stage.

As the four nervously chain-smoked their way through Zephyr's set, the youngest of them all – Robert Plant – was undergoing a deep personal crisis. *How on earth would America take to him?*

'Ladies and gentlemen, for their first American appearance, from London, England, please welcome … Led Zeppelin!' Then for Plant, problems were exacerbated even further. The stage on which they were playing was constantly revolving: every time he tried to establish eye contact with someone in the audience, the stage would shift yet again and he'd find himself staring out into space, disconcertingly searching for the last connection he had made. 'Good Times Bad Times', 'Dazed and Confused' with Page on his violin bow, 'Communication Breakdown' were all stormed through … Then Plant had a sudden realisation: matters were proceeding exceedingly well – the audience loved them.

And with that acknowledgement from the crowd's cheers, the four-piece hit their stride: a 40-minute set was extended to just over an hour, concluding with deafening applause.

Led Zeppelin's first show in the United States was a hit. With their music from the distant future and ancient past, and its fragmented and jagged dominance of the instant present, Led Zeppelin punched their audience in their third eye, coring into their startled beings. They would not leave you alone, like primaeval pterodactyls snatching at your clothing and dragging you towards them; entrancing you with the visual double-act of cherubic Jimmy Page and primal Robert Plant – even as early as this, cock-rocker Plant paradoxically squealing like a bitch on heat, like a 12-year-old who had lived for a thousand years, drawing out the androgynous, screamingly libidinous nature of both frontmen, interweaving with the musical dramatics.

In the eyes of Atlantic Records, Led Zeppelin were a replacement for Cream. But Page's band were far more precise and measured – certainly more calculating – than Cream, whose sprawling self-indulgence had only increased on their final tour. And at first, judging them only on the sound of their first album, Led Zeppelin seemed to stand in stark contrast to the increasingly soft rock emerging from LA's Laurel Canyon.

There were 25 shows in all, and a week supporting Vanilla Fudge, whom Led Zeppelin successfully went out of their way to upstage on each occasion. There were four more dates in 1968, in Seattle, Vancouver, Portland – where they were billed as 'Led Zeppilen featuring Jimmy Page' – and Spokane – where the poster advertised an appearance by 'Len Zefflin'. Following these shows in the chilly northern regions of the West Coast, Led Zeppelin were set to move down to southern California and the warmer climes of Los Angeles.

However, a fierce snowstorm descended on the Spokane region and the airport was closed. But 200 miles away in Seattle planes were still taking off and landing. Despite the ever-thickening snow, Richard Cole made the decision to drive the highway to Seattle, slipping and slithering all the way. Even when state police ordered them off the dangerous route, Cole simply returned to it at the first opportunity. In the rear of the car, Page was wrapped up in every item of clothing he could find, as he sweated out a case of Hong Kong flu, his temperature rising to over 40 degrees. Accordingly, the guitarist 'didn't have much energy to complain about anything', said Cole.

The Whisky a Go Go on the Sunset Strip, where Led Zeppelin were booked to play four consecutive nights starting on 2 January 1969, was a perfect setting for the group, who were supported by a new act called Alice Cooper. Page already loved LA, and for Plant it – along with San Francisco – was a power-point temple, a land where acts beloved to him such as Buffalo Springfield, the Doors and Love had formed.

Originally Led Zeppelin had been scheduled to play two shows a night at the Whisky, but Page's flu meant he was only capable of playing the first house on each evening. He still managed to be driven down to Hollywood's tiny Mirror Sound, where Bobby Fuller and Ritchie Valens had once recorded: he was deeply impressed with the energy palpable in the very walls of the studio. Efforts to employ the city's Gold Star Studios, from whence Phil Spector had driven his Wall of Sound around the world, were less successful, the building's 'vibes' disappointing.

Once he had again checked into the Chateau Marmont, however, Page resisted permitting his fever to interfere with his fun. 'Led Zeppelin hit Los Angeles like napalm,' wrote Catherine James. 'After their dazzling debut at the Whisky a Go Go, Led Zeppelin became the new rock-and-roll gods. Jimmy stayed at my house for the first two luminous nights, then the band went up to San Francisco for more accolades at the Fillmore.

'The next thing I knew Jimmy had disappeared. I heard he was holed up at the Hyatt House on Sunset with … Hollywood's chief groupie, Miss Pamela. My romantic teenage heart was shattered. I agonised, longed and generally stirred myself into a state.'

Soon after, Catherine James fell into the arms of a new singer-songwriter called Jackson Browne, and her soul was comforted.

From Los Angeles, Page, his health marginally improved, and the rest of Led Zeppelin flew the 350 miles up to San Francisco. Such was the kudos around the city's by now legendary Fillmore

West that the three nights they were about to play there promised to be key in breaking the band in the USA.

In San Francisco, Peter Grant was waiting for them. As was Maureen Plant, permitted to fly out for this stretch of the road primarily because Grant was aware of her husband's insecurities about playing the Fillmore. 'Robert did lack a bit of confidence,' Grant admitted later.

The Fillmores West and East were the personal suzerainty of Bill Graham, the legendary – and sometimes legendarily difficult – promoter who would transform concert promotion in the United States, for much of the time carrying Zeppelin in his wake. Graham had long been a supporter of the Yardbirds, for whom the Fillmore West had always proved a shrine.

For this first show, on 9 January, Page's 25th birthday, the headliners were the ragtag political act Country Joe and the Fish, with the iconoclastic and innovative Taj Mahal opening the evening's music. Led Zeppelin's set blew both these acts out of everyone's memories. Page said: 'The early interest was partly caused by the fact that I'd been in the Yardbirds and a lot of Americans had liked that group and wanted to see what Jimmy Page had moved on to. But then when they saw what we had to offer … I mean, Led Zeppelin was frightening stuff! The concept of psychedelic music was about roaming and roving but never actually coming together. That's why Zeppelin succeeded: there was a real urgency about how we played. Everyone would be getting laid-back and we'd come on and hit 'em like an express train. Playing the Fillmore West was the moment when I knew we'd broken through. There were other gigs, like the Boston Tea Party and the Kinetic Circus in Chicago … where the response was so incredible we knew we'd made our impression. But after the San Francisco gig it was just – bang!'

The subsequent Fillmore shows were as kinetically powerful, astounding the audiences with their light and shade, the extremities of the set's tensions – Plant again squealing like a bitch on heat as he hit his vocal stride.

On 12 January the album *Led Zeppelin* was released in the US – the day after the last of the group's three nights at the Fillmore. The LP would not be released in the UK until March.

The record sleeve was created by George Hardie. Page rejected his first effort – a zeppelin largely shrouded by clouds – and instead the chosen image was of the *Hindenburg* disaster in 1937, in which the airship caught fire and 35 of its 97 passengers were killed. Hardie received £60 for his design. The rear picture, of the four musicians, was taken by Chris Dreja – proof of the continuity of their bond.

While the record-buying population voted with their cash, Mick Jagger and George Harrison's inability to comprehend Led Zeppelin's oeuvre was a reflection of how establishment thinking would respond to the act.

This was the age when CBS Records was running ads in *Rolling Stone* magazine declaring 'The Man Can't Bust Our Music'. It was as though the company hippies had scaled the ramparts and won the revolution. But that wasn't the case at *Rolling Stone* itself. They were having no truck whatsoever with these po-faced, pretty-boy Limeys. The media often imagines it is utterly in touch with the zeitgeist when, most often, it is at least six months behind: across the nation, fans were already going gaga for Led Zeppelin at their live shows. Yet here, in *Rolling Stone*'s dismissive review of Led Zeppelin's first album by LA-based writer John Mendelsohn, was an unalloyed example of someone who needed to get out more, preferably to those Whisky shows he had clearly missed. The review was especially damning in its comparison of Zeppelin to Jeff Beck: 'In their willingness to waste their considerable talent, the Zeppelin has produced an album which is sadly reminiscent of *Truth*.' Page was characterised as 'a very limited producer and a writer of weak, unimaginative songs, and the Zeppelin album suffers from him having produced and written most of it (alone or in combination with his accomplices in the group)'.

Mendelsohn's sneering review would signal the start of years of animosity between Led Zeppelin and the highly influential *Rolling Stone*. Page, who could be described as sometimes over-sensitive to press criticism, would not forget what Mendelsohn had written.

Mind you, Ritchie Yorke, writing in the Toronto *Globe and Mail*, clearly got it: 'Led Zeppelin will be the next super group in the US ... they have merged with a positive, driving, distinctive sound ... Page's guitar work skims across the melody with pure joy ... Jones's bass and organ rhythms are forceful and invigorating ... unlike many groups, Led Zeppelin has managed to maintain simplicity while striving for depth ... the best debut album by any group since *Are You Experienced* by the Jimi Hendrix Experience.'

When the LP was released two months later in the UK, there were only a pair of positive notices: in the satirical magazine *Punch* Chris Welch described the record as 'the definitive recorded rock performance of the year'; and Felix Dennis, writing in the underground *OZ* magazine, declared it to be 'a turning point in rock'.

Following San Francisco, there was a date in San Diego, down on the Mexican border. Then, via a show in Iowa, it was over to the other side of the country for gigs in rapid succession in Baltimore, followed by three nights in rock'n'roll-loving Detroit – also considered a potential break-out city for Led Zeppelin. In New York City they played the Fillmore East, blowing the headlining Iron Butterfly off the stage. 'The audience was still going "Zeppelin, Zeppelin" when Iron Butterfly had started their set!' said Peter Grant. 'Good band, not a bad band ... but no match for Zeppelin.'

'Led Zeppelin landed at Fillmore East and in the first of four weekend shows, the British quartet showed it could develop into the next big super group,' wrote Fred Kirby in *Billboard*. 'Page, a former member of the Yardbirds, ranks with the top pop guitarists in the world and his performance substantiated his reputation. Plant is a blues-style screamer and wailer, whose vocalising was wild. Iron Butterfly had a tough assignment in following Led Zeppelin.'

But after the Fillmore West, the tour's greatest triumph occurred in Boston, Massachusetts. There they played the 400-seater Boston Tea Party for three nights on 24–26 January 1969, legendary performances in which their 90-minute set was extended to four-and-a-half hours, the material effectively being performed twice, with mass encores including Beatles and Rolling Stones songs. 'A laughing, sweating Page could only cough into his cigarette and beg the others: "What songs do you know?"' said Mick Wall. If ever there was an East Coast break-through moment for Led Zeppelin, this was it.

Slipping across the border to Toronto in Canada for another triumphant show, the band met Ritchie Yorke, the Australian writer who had given the *Led Zeppelin* album such a prescient and positive review. A good man, Ritchie Yorke would prove a stout ally of Zeppelin over the years.

There then followed shows at Chicago's Kinetic Playground, an archetypal 'head' venue. A guitarist named Joe Wright was at the first gig, on 7 February 1969: he organised the Tuesday-night jam sessions at the Playground and would always be let in for free, with backstage access; having played for the US Olympic ice hockey team, he was possessed of a measure of self-belief. That night at the venue he had with him his 1964 Les Paul Standard, a rare and beautiful guitar. As soon as Page saw the instrument, he made Wright an offer: 'Oh, this is a lovely guitar. I'll give you $800 for it.'

'I'll give you $950,' said Bonham.

'I'll give you $1,300,' butted in Plant.

'I found out later,' said Wright, 'that they did this a lot. They had to be one up on the other. But you always had to let Pagey win. It was always building up to that. He was in charge. For example, they loved that South-west turquoise Native American jewellery. Robert would get a ring, Bonzo would get a little piece, but Pagey would get the crème de la crème. So you could never top Jimmy. But I wouldn't sell him my guitar. And that's when I met Zeppelin, that moment.

'Then they played. My jaw hit the floor. I fell in love with that superpower that they presented with the jamming, with the blues on steroids. You never saw any of that before with white people. I fell in love with them.'

After the show, Joe Wright went backstage again. He had a task to fulfil: one of his friends had formed a group and was searching for a name for it. Joe decided to ask Page if he had any ideas. 'Call them the Wankers,' suggested the guitarist. Unaware of English slang, Wright relayed this suggestion to his mate, who acted upon it, touring for the next few months as a member of the Wankers. Until Wright took a job roadying with the Who and discovered what the name meant.

After Chicago, Led Zeppelin moved on to Memphis, where the group went on a pilgrimage to Graceland and failed to utilise the facilities at the legendary Sun Studio. 'By the time of our second album, it wasn't the original Sun Studio anymore,' said Page, recalling how *Led Zeppelin II* was recorded on the hop, during the brief lulls between live work. They played the Thee Image in Miami, Florida, before Led Zeppelin's triumphant and musically revolutionary first tour of the USA concluded at Baltimore's Civic Center on 16 February 1969.

The day before, *Rolling Stone* had published its 27th edition, which would become notorious as the 'Groupie' issue, as much of the magazine was given over to the study of a social group most people had never heard of. The lengthy article was credited to a trio of writers: John Burks, Jerry Hopkins and Paul Nelson.

The words were accompanied by Baron Wolman's portrait pictures of the likes of the GTOs (Girls Together Outrageously) and the Plaster Casters of Chicago; the Plaster Casters' speciality was to take plaster-of-Paris moulds of rock stars' penises. With exceptions like the Sanchez twins, Judy and Karen, and Catherine James, you were struck by how unattractive, unglamorous and rather sad looking so many of these girls were.

'The phenomenon of the groupie – it exists because of glamour and power,' commented life coach Nanette Greenblatt. 'It emerges from old paradigm culture originating in the perception of women as virgins, wives, mothers, whores and under the control/ownership of the bigger primate. The rock and roll lifestyle seemed to make it easy to find willing people, sufficiently glamourised, to seduce.'

The *Rolling Stone* review of the *Led Zeppelin* album did not appear until 15 March. Otherwise, would Page have been so ready to offer the magazine his thoughts on these self-styled rock 'n' roll girls? The guitarist was remarkably forthcoming when he was interviewed – though he was no doubt aware that by appearing in such an article he would help secure his reputation as a deeply sexual figure, a powerful element of Led Zeppelin's attraction. Asked whether he found more or fewer groupies during this first American tour with his new group than he did during the eight tours of the country he undertook with the Yardbirds, he was characteristically equivocal: 'By now I've got friends I look up, or they call me, in nearly every city. But the other boys in the band who've not been here before – I kind of prepare mental lists in my mind to try to predict who they'll pair off with. I know which chicks are going to come out and the kind of fellows they go for, and I know the taste of the guys in the band, and so I try to make my predictions, girl by girl. I can come pretty close.'

In Page's opinion, the most beautiful groupies were in New York. Yet he found the girls in San Francisco more likely to develop 'personal relations in depth with the musicians'. But, he added, 'You take each as they come, though. And they're all over the world. We even found them in Singapore.'

As they stepped aboard a plane to return to the UK, the *Led Zeppelin* album had risen to number 90 in the US Billboard album charts. It would leap upwards until, three weeks later, it was in the Top 20, rising to as high as number 10. It would spend literally years in the charts.

Page was reluctant to depart America. He felt they should stay and push on with more dates. They would be heading back very shortly, Peter Grant advised his client. First, they had a set of UK shows to play.

9

'WHOLE LOTTA LOVE'

Led Zeppelin's homecoming was not a triumphant one, playing dates at the likes of Plymouth's Van Dyke Club or Hornsey's Wood Tavern, often for no more than a flat fee of £140.

In the UK, the band were viewed as a capitalist act whose only purpose was to milk the United States for as much money as possible. 'We just couldn't seem to do anything right as far as the critics were concerned,' complained Jimmy Page. 'At which point I think we all just sort of gave up on the idea of ever pleasing them.'

On another brief Scandinavian jaunt, however, things were a bit more like it for them. In Denmark, Led Zeppelin performed a full set in front of television cameras, the first time they had ever done so. The audience sat cross-legged on the floor in front of them. 'They don't cheer too madly there, you know?' said Page. 'It was sort of an experimental concert to see if we were any good, I guess.'

What was on his mind was the need for new material. The group were buzzing – they couldn't come down from the US tour – with adrenaline running round and round their jetlagged and exhausted but exhilarated beings.

That year Led Zeppelin played four live sessions – concerts more like – for the BBC, beginning with a show at London's Playhouse Theatre, essentially a BBC venue, on 3 March. This was especially aimed at offering material for John Peel's *Top Gear* show.

The radio performances were a reflection of Led Zeppelin's seemingly overnight success in America. Their US fame had washed across the Atlantic, picked up by fans, if not by dismissive doyens of the underground. Led Zeppelin went out of their way in these BBC sessions to emphasise the improvisational skills with which they enhanced their album material during live performances. Really, there was no other way to get this across to the very many who still had not seen Led Zeppelin live. (More than 20 years later these live versions would finally be released, as *BBC Sessions*.)

Apart from their Danish experience, and a mimed Swedish version of 'Communication Breakdown', Led Zeppelin hardly ever appeared on television. Like releasing singles, TV was uncool, and, like their later bêtes noires, the Clash, Led Zeppelin never once performed on *Top of the Pops*, a show that almost guaranteed chart success. Like some twist of karmic victory for such a stance, a version of 'Whole Lotta Love' by Alexis Korner's CCS became the show's weekly theme tune. (On 21 March the group did make their UK television debut, performing 'Communication Breakdown' on *How Late It Is*, a BBC 2 arts show.)

This was quite a statement. Everyone else was saying singles were lower-status artefacts and that they were now serious album artists. Ever since *Pet Sounds* and *Sgt. Pepper*, this had been the thinking.

But everyone else continued to release them: the Who's 'Pinball Wizard', Cream, Jimi Hendrix seemingly ad infinitum, Traffic, the Beatles and Stones inevitably.

Now the supposedly hyped Led Zeppelin were at the vanguard of insurrectionist thinking as virtually the only act to stand by their principles and not release singles. Of course, doing so only increased exponentially the level of mystique that began to build around the group; it provided them with an image of distant power, as though they were puppet-masters –

which in a way they were. After all, they were telling the man, which now included their record company, that no one could bust their music.

From time to time singles leaked out, a consequence of over-enthusiastic record company thinking. 'Good Times Bad Times', coupled with 'Communication Breakdown', was pressed up for DJ copies by Atlantic in the US – and quickly nixed by Peter Grant. There were efforts to release 'Whole Lotta Love' as a 45 in the UK, another idea shot down in flames by the manager. But the lack of a single made radio promotion awkward, almost hopeless. Hence the BBC sessions.

History can make it seem all part of a master plan. Although Page and Grant had a strategy, there was much more reacting to events as they happened on a day-to-day basis. Still, Page's vision remained clear. Interviewed by Nick Logan of the *NME*, he showed no doubts: 'I can't see the heavy thing going out. Ever since the underground thing happened a couple of years ago, people's tastes have been broadening. You can have a group … who are into a light, folky thing on the one hand, and us on the other. The whole scene is broad enough to take us all in, and I don't see why that situation shouldn't continue.'

There are a trio of Led Zeppelin songs that have transcended their catalogue of material to become aural calling cards for the group: 'Whole Lotta Love', 'Stairway to Heaven' and 'Kashmir'.

Despite the stratospheric success of 'Stairway to Heaven', it is the insidious five-note riff of 'Whole Lotta Love', the first hard-rock standard and a tune that radically altered expectations of the sound of the electric guitar and rock vocal, that has most insinuated itself into global popular culture.

Yet the origins of 'Whole Lotta Love', which would open the second Led Zeppelin LP, are less straightforward. The song is by no means a Page–Plant original, as the composing credits attest. 'Whole Lotta Love' is a reworking of Muddy Waters'

'You Need Love', which had been taken up by the Small Faces, retitled as 'You Need Loving' and featured on their first album, but credited to Small Faces singer Steve Marriott and bass-player Ronnie Lane. The song was a high point of the Small Faces' live sets.

Steve Marriott told Paolo Hewitt in his book *Small Faces: The Young Mods' Forgotten Story* that Plant was a regular at their shows. '"Whole Lotta Love" by Led Zeppelin was nicked off that album. Percy Plant was a big fan. He used to be at all the Small Faces gigs. We did a gig with the Yardbirds which he was at, and Jimmy Page asked me what that number was we did. "'You Need Loving'," I said, "it's a Muddy Waters thing," which it really is, so they both knew it, and Percy used to come to the gigs whenever we played in Kidderminster or Stowbridge, where he came from. He was always saying he was going to get this group together. He was another nuisance. He kept coming into the dressing room, just another little Mod kid. We used to say, "That kid's here again." Anyway, we used to play this number and it became a stock opener after that album. After we broke up they took it and revamped it. Good luck to them. It was only old Percy who'd had his eyes on it. He sang it the same, phrased it the same, even the stops at the end were the same; they just put a different rhythm to it.'

Plant's vocals – the breathing, the intonations, the inflexions – on 'Whole Lotta Love' were directly modelled on Steve Marriott's performance of 'You Need Loving'. But there is a fundamental flaw in any complaint made by Steve Marriott: it's that Marriott–Lane credit on the first Small Faces album. For it certainly was not written by the duo; Muddy Waters' 'You Need Loving' was written by Willie Dixon, the extraordinarily influential performer, songwriter and producer who had shaped the sound of post-Second World War Chicago blues music.

When, many years later, Willie Dixon's daughter Shirley brought 'Whole Lotta Love' to her father's attention, he realised that it was his tune. A lawsuit followed, in 1985, and Dixon ultimately received a substantial out-of-court settlement. 'Some people said later that "Whole Lotta Love" was based on Willie Dixon's "You Need Love" and the Small Faces' "You Need Loving",' Page said in his defence to Marc Myers, author of *Anatomy of a Song*. 'My riff – the basis for the entire song – sounds nothing like either of them. Robert had referenced the Dixon lyrics because with my riff, they felt right. This eventually forced us to give Dixon a co-credit on our song. But if you take Robert's vocal out, there's no musical reference to either song.'

(All the same, Dixon also received further substantial financial compensation when a further song on *Led Zeppelin II*, 'Bring It On Home', which closed the LP, was revealed as being another of his compositions. Despite the settlement, writer Gavin Martin was asked by Dixon's daughter not to mention Led Zeppelin when he went to interview her father, who was still extremely distressed about the entire matter. And the charges of copyright theft did not end there. 'The Lemon Song', with its coyly prurient, schoolboy-like reference to lemon-squeezing, itself a direct lift from Robert Johnson's 'Travelling Riverside Blues', was revealed as the bastard son of Howlin' Wolf's 'Killing Floor'. Sued in the early 1970s by Arc Music, Wolf's songwriting publisher, Zeppelin again settled out of court.)

'Wherever it comes from,' Plant told Ritchie Yorke, 'it was all about that riff. Any tribute that flows in must go to Jimmy and his riffs. They were mostly in the key of E and you could really play around with them. Since I've been playing guitar myself, I've realised more than ever that the whole thing, the whole band really, came straight from the blues. Everything.'

'Just a basic rock tune, using some electronic sounds in the middle section,' Page said as he made his characteristically equivocal and modest case to Yorke. 'It does sound great on headphones. It reminds me of a sort of Rolling Stones feel.'

The reference to headphones that Page made is significant. With the cheaper stereo systems readily available, especially in the United States, headphones – 'cans', as they were known – had become integral to underground culture. Some radicals had dispensed altogether with their pair of stereo speakers and only had headphones. The backward psychedelic section of 'Whole Lotta Love' was perfect for stoned listening in such a manner, the song's arrant sexuality bouncing backwards and forwards within your skull. Headphones culture, as useful for listening to the newly popular FM radio as to a record playing in your room, was yet another reason for the growing popularity of Led Zeppelin in the USA.

'John Paul and I knew our way around a recording studio,' explained Page to Marc Myers in *Anatomy of a Song*, 'so we weren't going to waste studio time or produce something that wasn't cohesive. More important, I wanted to expand our approach to ensure that our album wouldn't be chopped up into singles for AM radio. To make sure that didn't happen, I produced "Whole Lotta Love" – and our entire second album – as an uneditable expression, a work that had to be aired on stereo FM to make sense.'

Page had first come up with the famous five-note riff during the summer of 1968, while doodling around with his guitar on the deck of his Pangbourne boathouse. 'I suppose my early love for big intros by rockabilly guitarists was an inspiration, but as soon as I developed the riff, I knew it was strong enough to drive the entire song, not just open it. When I played the riff for the band in my living room several weeks later, during rehearsals for our first album, the excitement was immediate and collective. We felt the riff was addictive, like a forbidden thing.'

At rehearsals for *Led Zeppelin II* Page decided that of all their material, 'Whole Lotta Love' was so uniquely strong that it should be the album opener. 'So I wanted to record the song first,' he said.

On 10 April 1969 Led Zeppelin went into Olympic Sound Studios with engineer George Chkiantz, who had worked with Jimi Hendrix in the same studio on *Axis: Bold as Love*. Chkiantz noted that Page had brought a theremin with him to the studio. Its 'eerie sound', as Page described it, encouraged further unorthodox approaches; he would detune his guitar and tug on the strings, searching for sounds. To boost the drums, Chkiantz made a significant alteration to the studio's set-up: a platform was erected so the drums were some 18 inches off the wooden floor, which stopped the rumble transmitting to the other microphones. Page wanted the listener to precisely feel every drum stroke, the song's foundations for what he envisaged as a panoramic audio experience. Above the drums Chkiantz set up a stereo microphone on a boom.

'I was playing a sunburst 1958 Les Paul Standard guitar I had bought from Joe Walsh in San Francisco when we were out there on tour,' said Page. 'The Standard had this tonal versatility, allowing me to get a blistering high pitch.'

Energised and empowered thanks to Led Zeppelin's success in the US, Plant had fully overcome the nervousness and uncertainty he had felt on those first American dates. Now he was in a new creative phase. First recording his vocals in the studio itself, he soon retired to the cocooned privacy of the vocal booth. 'Robert's vocal was just as extreme,' said Page. 'He kept gaining confidence during the session and gave it everything he had. His vocals, like my solos, were about performance. He was pushing to see what he could get out of himself. We were performing for each other, almost competitively.'

When *Led Zeppelin II* was mixed at Atlantic's studio in Manhattan late that June, engineer Eddie Kramer – who had first worked with Page in 1964 on the Kinks' debut album and had worked on several of the second Zeppelin album's songs at Olympic – discovered that the original tape contained 'bleed-through of a previously recorded vocal in the recording of

"Whole Lotta Love". It was the middle part where Robert screams, "Woman. You need it." Since we couldn't re-record at that point, I just threw some echo on it to see how it would sound and Jimmy said, "Great! Just leave it."'

'I hadn't heard anything like that before, and I loved it,' Page told Marc Myers. 'I was always looking for things like that when I recorded. That's the beauty of old recording equipment. Robert's faraway voice sounded otherworldly, like a spirit anticipating the vocal he was about to deliver.'

Kramer also flung Page's guitar parts about between the speakers, increasing the song's sense of sexual frenzy, splashing on reverb. 'Because Jimmy was a studio brat, he really understood how we could push the limits,' said Kramer to Marc Myers of the Zeppelin leader's electronic animism. 'When you have limitations in the studio, you go for it and stretch your imagination.'

'I knew what I wanted, and I knew how to go about it,' Page told *Guitar World*. 'It was just a matter of doing it. I created most of the sounds with a theremin and my guitar. The theremin generates most of the higher pitches and my Les Paul makes the lower sounds.'

'I detuned it radically and just basically pulled on the strings to make an assortment of growling noises,' he said. 'Evil sounds that you're not supposed to hear on commercial radio. I might've detuned it to a chord, but really I'm just pulling on strings and making them howl! And then, during the mix, with the aid of Eddie Kramer, we did all the panning and added the effects, including using low-frequency oscillators on the tape machine to really pull the whole thing down and lift it back up so the sound is moving in rhythm. It was something no one had ever done before in that context, let alone in the middle of a song. That's how forward thinking we were, that's how avant-garde it was, and that's how much fun we were having.'

* * *

In April 1969 Page gave an interview to *Record Mirror*. He was extremely pleased, he remarked, that Led Zeppelin had now become accepted in the United Kingdom: the first album was already high in the charts. Yet he was only too aware where the principal market for the group lay: 'We're working every day here now – but before we went to the States nobody wanted to know. And it's not just London – it's all over the country. Very pleasing reaction. I still reckon the States is our main market, though.'

There was hardly time for more BBC sessions anyway. Another American tour had been rapidly booked by Peter Grant for the end of April. And for this second tour, they were far higher up the bill, co-headlining with Vanilla Fudge on some shows; it would depend on the popularity of each act in the individual city as to who closed the night. They were also earning approximately four times the $1,500 they had earned per concert on the first set of dates.

They also variously toured with the Brian Auger Trinity, featuring 'face of 68' Julie Driscoll, Three Dog Night, and Delaney and Bonnie. On certain shows Led Zeppelin performed as the only act on the bill, setting a template for the future.

The tour kicked off at the Fillmore West, switching – because of the large ticket demand – to Bill Graham's Winterland Ballroom for two nights, then returning to the Fillmore for a final San Francisco show; on all four of these San Francisco dates they were supported by the Brian Auger Trinity. Then it was straight down to LA for two nights at the Whisky a Go Go.

When they arrived in Los Angeles an earthquake erupted in the nearby desert, a 5.6 on the Richter scale. Believing that the safest place to be in an earthquake was in a bathtub – because the piping would keep the bath in place, so the myth ran – Page insisted that only he should be able to use the bath in the two-bedroom suite at the Chateau Marmont he was sharing with Richard Cole. The tour manager was obliged to find other facilities for his ablutions.

During these dates Page shifted professional tack. He no longer appeared onstage with the psychedelic 1958 Telecaster he had used on early UK dates. Returning to Pangbourne after Zeppelin's first American tour, he discovered that a friend had 'thoughtfully' removed all of his customising, returning the instrument to its original, innocent state. Page was flabbergasted by this misjudged act of kindness; paint had seeped into the guitar itself, even into the pickups, destroying the instrument utterly. From here on it would be the Gibson Les Paul slung low, almost to his knees, in a stance that would be copied by countless other guitar players, a boon to osteopaths and chiropractors everywhere.

A different sort of story began to emerge about Led Zeppelin on this tour, of an act whose libidinous pursuits were elevated sometimes to the level of art form. Not least when Page, covered in offal, was wheeled on a hospital trolley by John Bonham into a Los Angeles hotel room filled with groupies, who proceeded to devour him.

On 29 April Led Zeppelin played the Whisky a Go Go. At the first show that night, Pamela Miller and Miss Mercy, members of Frank Zappa's Girls Together Outrageously, the GTOs, went along. Pamela, known as Miss Pamela, was 20 years old. 'I got sticky thighs over the very naughty Jimmy Page while I watched him reinvent guitar playing,' she wrote in her book *I'm With the Band: Confessions of a Groupie*. 'He was wearing a pink velvet suit and his long black curls stuck damply to his pink-velvet cheeks. At the end of the set he collapsed to the floor, and was carried up the stairs by two roadies, one of them stopping to retrieve Jimmy's cherry-red patent-leather slipper.'

Later, at the after-party at Thee Charming Experience, Miss Pamela observed Richard Cole carrying a girl upside down, her panties spinning around one of her ankles; Cole's face was buried in her crotch. Another girl was being fucked on a table. She could not help but notice that Page, who personally inclined to a light, gentle manner with women, was sat rather aside from this bacchanalia, 'observing the scene as if he had imagined it: overseer, creator, impossibly gorgeous pop star'.

At Mystic Studios in Los Angeles the next day, Led Zeppelin recorded 'Moby Dick' and 'The Lemon Song'. Page had discovered the studio the previous month, when assisting his old friend Screaming Lord Sutch. Temporarily based in the city, the indomitable, eccentric David Sutch had persuaded a ragtag assortment of newly stellar names who had performed in his group the Savages to play on what Page had first thought were no more than demo sessions. John Bonham came along for the ride, although drummer stalwart Carlo Little was there already, along with Jeff Beck, Noel Redding and pianist Nicky Hopkins. When the scrappy consequences of these sessions were released the following February as *Lord Sutch and Heavy Friends*, Page's ire was hard to ignore.

After playing the hip Whisky, Led Zeppelin stormed southern California with a series of shows in more conventional venues, notably two nights at the 3,000-seater Santa Monica Civic Center on 4 and 5 May, a university show in Irvine and at the Rose Palace in Pasadena; and then in Santa Barbara, 90 miles up the coast from LA. They concluded this leg of the tour in their favoured US region, joining Lord Sutch's show at Thee Experience on 8 May. For the encore all four members of Led Zeppelin carried Sutch onstage in a coffin.

Then it was time to head north, up over the border into Canada for shows in Edmonton and Vancouver. 'The hottest new rock band from Britain stalked onstage at the Gardens Friday night and let loose an earthquake of sound and frenzy,' wrote Bob Harvey in the *Edmonton Journal*. 'Their music's loud, almost to the point of pain, but they don't use volume to cover up deficiencies. The volume is part of their attack. They don't titillate or tease audiences to share their inspiration. Instead, they blast out with raw, jagged power, enough to bust a new door into your brain. They use their instruments like a brush and palette, creating frenzied visions that tumble through space and time.'

The group thundered back down the West Coast to Seattle, where they topped the bill with Three Dog Night, to whom the local reviewer awarded the trophy of best act.

After a break in the sun of Honolulu for a show at the Civic Auditorium they headed for another city where Zeppelin would always reign supreme: Detroit and its legendary venue the Grande Ballroom, with its reputation for rock 'n' roll rowdiness. On their pair of shows they were supported by the remarkable cosmic jazz artist Sun Ra and Dutch hard-rockers Golden Earring.

In Detroit they were joined by the cultural journalist Ellen Sander, assigned by the prestigious *Life* magazine to cover the group.

Later she would assess Page as 'ethereal, effeminate, pale and frail'. When she asked about the already evident on-the-road abuse of women by his group, Page answered, revealingly, with the social grace of a car salesman: 'Girls come around and pose like starlets, teasing and acting haughty. If you humiliate them a bit, they tend to come on all right after that. Everyone knows what they come for.'

On 25 May, following shows in Athens, Ohio, and two nights at Chicago's Kinetic Playground, the four-piece hit Columbia, Maryland, midway between Washington, DC and Baltimore, where they shared the bill with the Who, the only time the two groups would ever play together; Led Zeppelin accepted playing second on the bill. When they ran over time, Zeppelin had their amps unplugged by the Who's crew, a cause of considerable brouhaha from Cole. 'We played together only once,' said Pete Townshend. 'I think it must have been the last gig they did playing before another group on the bill … and we just about got it together, we just about topped what they'd done … you get this ideology thing happening for the ideal rock guitarist – like the B.B. King syndrome, the Eric Clapton thing, the Jimmy Page trip – and I think Jimmy Page has been right in it and probably invented it.'

Up to Massachusetts, Page and his boys played three nights at their stronghold the Boston Tea Party before winding up this second US tour with two nights at Bill Graham's Fillmore East, on 30 and 31 May, supported by Woody Herman and His Orchestra, and Delaney and Bonnie and Friends, an act that had been championed by George Harrison and which frequently included his old friend Eric Clapton. In keeping with Fillmore East policy, there were two shows a night: one at 8, the next at 11.30. Led Zeppelin 'left the audience paralysed', wrote Denise Kelly in *World Countdown*.

Ellen Sander stayed with the group until the end of the tour. In the Fillmore East dressing room she claimed she was attacked by a pair of Led Zeppelin members, notably John Bonham: 'Shrieking and grabbing at my clothes, totally over the edge.' Although Peter Grant stepped forward to save her, it was not until Sander's assailants had ripped the rear of her dress.

Later, Page would be asked about Sander's disparaging reaction to his group. 'That's not a false picture,' he admitted. 'But that side of touring isn't the be all and end all. The worst part is the period of waiting before going on. I always get very edgy, not knowing what to do with myself. It's the build-up where you reach a point almost like self-hypnosis. There's a climax at the end of the show and the audience goes away, but you're still buzzing and you don't really come down. That's when you get a sort of restlessness and insomnia, but it doesn't bother you too much if there's a creative stream coming through. Maybe it's necessary to that creative stream. What's bad is that it's not always a release. You build yourself to that pitch and the release doesn't come. There are different ways of releasing that surplus adrenaline. You can smash up hotel rooms – it can get to that state. I think we've learnt to come to terms with it. I've learnt to enjoy it and achieve something creative from it too.'

Following that second show at the Fillmore, Ahmet Ertegun and Atlantic Records threw a reception for their hot act at New York's swish Plaza Hotel. Each member was presented with a gold record for sales of their first album. 'We were touring until the day we were presented with a gold record. I thought, "My goodness! A gold record!"' Page said, keenly aware that it was less than a year since the group had formed. At the party, however, it was impressed on him how urgently the next Zeppelin LP was required, to catch the Christmas sales boost. Straight after the party he took Led Zeppelin back into the studio to continue their work on the album.

Their glittering gold discs were symbolic of the tremendous breakthrough that had taken place. Whereas the first tour had lost money, now their earnings were very different: they would be divvying up somewhere in the region of $150,000 from these shows.

10

LED ZEPPELIN II

In June 1969 Led Zeppelin went into Morgan Studios in north-west London. 'Ramble On' was concluded; 'Living Loving Maid', a rockabilly song for which Jimmy Page never professed any fondness, was written by himself and Plant and knocked off in an afternoon; as was their version of Ben E. King's 'We're Gonna Groove', a frequent addition to the live set during the encore finale of other artists' songs. But, just like in the US, these studio dates were snatched between further live dates.

On the quasi-art nouveau poster for the first Bath Festival of Blues, scheduled for 28 June 1969, Led Zeppelin were ranked fourth, beneath headliners Fleetwood Mac, John Mayall's Bluesbreakers and Ten Years After – all stalwarts, in different ways, of 'British blues'. It is worth recalling that, subsequent to the demise of Cream, the always creative and exciting Fleetwood Mac, led by John Mayall alumnus Peter Green, were deservedly the most credible act in the UK. Before his sad demise, due to psychological problems, Green was one of the most revered guitarists Britain had ever produced.

As for Ten Years After, in less than two months' time Alvin Lee's machine-gun-like approach to guitar playing at the Woodstock festival – and therefore in the *Woodstock* movie released the following year – would transform him briefly into a serious contender for Jimmy Page's role as king of guitar heroes. In the late 1960s it seemed that everywhere you looked there was a new gunslinger, vying for the title of fastest guitar player in the West.

Led Zeppelin performed at Bath in the middle of the afternoon, and Page's violin-bow routine on 'Dazed and Confused' caused jaws to drop. 'Nobody had coerced the youth of England into becoming Zep fans, but there they were, cheering Page, Jones, Bonham and Plant, as the drums thundered and the guitars roared,' wrote Chris Welch in *Melody Maker*.

The next night was two shows at the 'Pop Proms' at London's Royal Albert Hall, the most prestigious venue in the British capital at the time, with a capacity of some 4,500. Zeppelin were supported by Blodwyn Pig, founded by former Jethro Tull guitarist Mick Abrahams, and Liverpool Scene, a semi-satirical trio comprised of the poets Adrian Henri, Mike Evans and Andy Roberts. Individuals from each act came onstage to perform with Led Zeppelin on their final encore, 'Long Tall Sally', Little Richard's 12-bar blues. 'When the group returned to the stage, they found the power had been switched off. "Hey, put the power on," demanded singer Robert Plant as the group stood bewildered. Stalemate: Plant took up a harmonica and let fly on that and all the others could do was clap until a few minutes later the flow of juice was resumed. With the first few bars of "Long Tall Sally", the audience was on its feet, dancing in the aisles and in the boxes, and there was incredible mayhem happening on and around the stage. The saxists from Blodwyn Pig and Liverpool Scene added their support to the Zeppelin's rock,' ran Nick Logan's review in the *NME*.

Then it was back to America, for their third US tour.

On the first of these dates, at the first Atlanta International Pop Festival on 5 July 1969, Jimmy Page was in an introverted frame of mind. In London that afternoon, the Rolling Stones had played a free concert in Hyde Park with their new guitarist Mick Taylor, and their set was dedicated to Brian Jones, the group's founder and Page's friend, who had died two days previously.

The 16th annual Newport Jazz Festival on Rhode Island ran from 3–6 July 1969. In contrast to such acts on the bill as Miles Davis, Dave Brubeck and the Sun Ra Space Arkestra, the Friday night of 4 July was given over entirely to rival rockers to Led Zeppelin, such as the Jeff Beck Group and Ten Years After, as well as the more pastoral sounds of Jethro Tull. Led Zeppelin were set to play the closing show on Sunday night. Such had been the excitement generated by the Friday night acts, the local authorities demanded that Led Zeppelin be thrown off the bill, the festival promoter releasing a specious tale of Page being sick and unable to perform.

Joe Wright had driven over to Newport from Chicago with his 'hippy girlfriends'. 'Those were the days when all you needed was a little bit of long hair and a guitar, and you were instantly backstage. So on the Saturday afternoon I go for a little walk, along with my guitar, and I never came back. I go backstage: "I'm with Led Zeppelin." Then here comes Jimmy Page, walking all by himself.

'I walked straight up to him and I said, "Hey, asshole: remember me? Joe Wright? From Chicago?" And he takes a couple of steps back: "Oh, I'm all alone: there's no bodyguards." "You're the guy who told me to tell my buddy to call his band the Wankers." Then he burst out laughing.

'So the ice was broken. Then Clive Coulson, the head roadie, came over, who I knew from the Kinetic. He said, "What are you doing here?" I said, "I've just come to give shit to Jimmy Page. Which I've done." He said, "You're kidding?" But I explained and we all started laughing. Then Clive starts moaning about his assistant roadie: "I wish I had someone to replace him." I said, "I'm in!" So he went off to talk to Jimmy and to Peter, and I was hired on the spot.'

Despite the story having been put out that Page was too sick to close the festival, and the alleged ban by the local authorities, the guitarist and his group paid no heed, taking to the stage at 1 a.m. and playing a sensational 90-minute set to close the festival.

Before taking the boards, Page had been having a conversation with Joe Wright. 'I didn't know about black American music,' said Wright, 'which is where everything Zeppelin did came from. "We're all very happy to have you here, but why are you not back in Chicago?" Jimmy Page asked me. Back in Chicago, though, I got into the black blues clubs, where I would be the only white boy. I really got into it, heavy.'

Newport was only the second date of this summer tour. When Joe Wright joined up, there were another 45 to go. 'They paid me really well. Peter Grant paid me the same as Robert Plant and John Bonham: I was getting $500 a week. They were on salary. Bonzo almost got fired, because he was so drunk and so stoned. He ran the risk of being fired several times. I remember the meetings: "We've got to get rid of him, we've got to get rid of him." "No, no," insisted Jimmy. Absolutely. They didn't call him "the Beast" for nothing.

'I think Bonzo, like so many people in show business, didn't know how ugly it could be. He was a Gemini, and you can't get more schizo than that. He was a lovely guy but I don't think he knew how much bullshit was coming with that kind of success. The heavy pressure of the fans, of the idiots chasing you, of the death threats, of the marriage proposals, the endless dates. Jimmy knew that was coming because of the Yardbirds, but I don't think Bonzo had a clue. I want to be rich and famous, think all those kids, but they don't realise what they have to do to get it.'

At this stage Led Zeppelin were short on songs to play live.

'Zeppelin used to do a little bit of cover material,' recalled Joe. 'They'd do "Fresh Garbage" by Spirit.

'Zeppelin never played their own material the same way twice; Jimi Hendrix didn't either. They were overwhelmed by Hendrix. But Jimi was a singing guitar player, which Page and Jeff Beck were not. As a pure player they always envied his fluidity.'

Joe Wright quickly discovered that his job had far more to it than merely humping equipment. And Page gifted him with a new name. 'Jimmy would always be late for rehearsals. I was like his understudy and would play the guitar while everyone was waiting for him at the soundchecks. Robert would be on drums and Bonham on bass, and we'd be goofing around jamming.

'But then Pagey says, "You're a guitar player: why don't you take care of my stuff?" To me that was when "guitar tech" was born.

'In every single one of those towns I would always find the nightclubs where you could go and jam. And I'd be up onstage with the local guys. So whenever Led Zep would come in from their gig they'd see me playing. At first my nickname was an insult from Pagey: "Oh, Joe the jammer: he's always jamming." But then I became "Joe Jammer".'

On 12 July, Led Zeppelin shared the bill at the Philadelphia Summer Pop Festival with Jeff Beck, Johnny Winter, Blood, Sweat and Tears, Buddy Guy's Blues Band, Al Kooper and Jethro Tull, somewhat to the chagrin of Tull's leader Ian Anderson. 'After an unfortunate occasion in Philadelphia at the Spectrum, where we followed them onstage,' said the singer in *Uncut* magazine in 2015, 'I learned it is much better to go on before Led Zeppelin. But if you are to go on after, you've got to man up and face the music – or lack of. I always felt pretty good with Zeppelin. The only awkwardness lay between Robert and me. I probably didn't do enough to make him feel that I was a relaxed co-conspirator in the world of rock music. He probably saw me as being a bit remote and aloof and unwilling to chat.

But I was intimidated, frankly. Jimmy was more at ease, a natural guy. John Paul Jones never spoke to anybody. Peter Grant was always a real gentleman with me. I used to watch Led Zeppelin and know there were things quite clearly that I could not do. In particular, Robert's performance. You'd have to put a cross in the box saying "Don't try that". In the Robert Plant department, there were a lot of crosses in my box. I was very jealous of his vocal abilities and his stage swagger.'

Although having played together for less than a year, Led Zeppelin were utterly steaming as a live act, a fact reflected in their loftier status in the bills they played. Vanilla Fudge were now regularly supporting them, while on other dates they would be billed as co-headliners. After their Vancouver show on 26 July, they earned a tremendously positive and perceptive review from J. Hesse in the *Vancouver Sun*, one that fully acknowledged the part played by the group's founder: 'Led Zeppelin exists on the genius of lead guitarist Jimmy Page, whose baby face belies his musical message, that of jarring and unnerving the listeners with a fortissimo yowl that never lets up. Never allows time for recovery … it is made up of four individual musical artists attuned to each other's whims, capable of ensemble performance as well as separate forays into the jungle of lonely escapades. How perfectly Led Zeppelin has assessed the hang-ups of their listeners is evident when Plant screams, "Do you feel all right?" And the seething mob below the platform screams back, "Yes!"'

In the late 1960s the biggest band in the United States was the Doors, led by the charismatic, histrionic Jim Morrison. At the Seattle Pop Festival, the day after the Vancouver show, Zeppelin played straight after the Doors – and wiped the stage with them. But the English group's notoriety was enhanced not by their live set, but by an episode at their hotel, the Edgewater Inn, situated on Seattle's Puget Sound, where guests were able to fish directly from their windows.

According to myth, the band tied a girl to a bed and then stuffed pieces of a mud shark into her vagina and anus, the proceedings filmed by Mark Stein, Vanilla Fudge's keyboard player. The incident was a key passage in Stephen Davis's best-selling *Hammer of the Gods*. Yet the truth is apparently far more prosaic. The principal perpetrator was not any of the group – although John Bonham was peripherally involved – but Richard Cole and possibly Carmine Appice, Vanilla Fudge's drummer. Nevertheless, when Davis's book was published it only enhanced Zeppelin's reputation for rock 'n' roll debauchery.

Whatever might have happened had nothing to do with Page. He was elsewhere, looking ahead to a show in four days' time, at Earl Warren Showgrounds in Santa Barbara, California.

On 31 July Page flew into New York on the red-eye from Salt Lake City in Utah, where he had just played two shows at the Terrace Ballroom. He went directly to A&R Studios in Manhattan. Waiting for him was Ritchie Yorke, who had been brought in by Peter Grant to listen to a mixing session of some of the new material. 'Dressed in Chelsea Kings Road-style Regency splendour – the buckled burgundy patent-leather boots, the flaming red velvet bell-bottoms, the dusty pink-brushed velvet jacket ... Page was calmly slouched behind an extensive mixing console with engineer Eddie Kramer. He looked up, munching on a prune Danish pastry, which he was coaxing down with a plastic cupful of teabag swill,' recalled Yorke in *Led Zeppelin: Led to Gold 1967–89*.

The tune Page was working on was 'Bring It On Home', which would close *Led Zeppelin II*, a record that would rocket upwards the already seemingly unstoppable career of the group.

As Page controlled the production with an iron-hard clarity, Yorke watched closely: 'Eddie Kramer, one of the finest in his field, manoeuvred the myriads of dials and faders, translating Page's notions into sounds. Occasionally Kramer tossed up a suggestion and Page listened. More often than not, he had an intuitive projection of what the outcome would be. The sound splintered into muddier and dirtier incarnations as Page pushed for the raw and heavy echo he wanted, a style of recording closer to the classic early Chess milieu.'

Eddie Kramer had worked on, among others, the Beatles' 'All You Need Is Love' and Jimi Hendrix's *Electric Ladyland*, released the previous October, a record Page was especially fond of. He had nothing but admiration for Page's abilities in the studio. 'Jimmy was an excellent producer,' said the engineer, '[who] had a very definite picture of what he wanted to capture on tape. He was very demanding, but at the same time completely open to suggestions. Jimmy's biggest asset was he knew how to draw the best performances out of the band,' Kramer later said.

Yorke was given a playback of 'Living Loving Maid', 'Heartbreaker', with its magnificent assembly and architecture, and 'What Is and What Should Never Be'. 'Like myself, Grant had yet to hear these completed mixes. We sat in stunned silence as the speakers burst forth.'

'Page seemed genuinely pleased,' wrote Yorke, 'by our natural enthusiasm for what we were hearing – it was the first reaction he'd observed outside of the four band members and engineer Eddie Kramer.'

Jerry Wexler, Atlantic Records' 'spiritual Godfather of rock and roll', as Yorke called him, felt similarly rapturous about the three tracks when they were played to him. 'I would have to say that this is the best white blues I have ever heard,' he said.

Page defined his extraordinary pace of work to Yorke: 'We've been so busy that we just weren't able to go into one studio and polish the whole album off. It's become ridiculous – we put a rhythm track down in London, add the vocals in New York, overdub harmonica in Vancouver and then come back to New York to do the mixing here at A&R. We never really expected to be as big as this. We just wanted to be able to come over to America to play some gigs a couple of times a year. It's almost gotten out of hand now.' Is he being disingenuous? Is this false modesty? Unlikely: Page was always strong on understatement.

'There are so many guitarists around who I think are better than me. Everywhere I go I hear some cat who sounds better than I do. That's the trouble: everyone's good these days. I'm a trifle disappointed with some of the guitar playing on the second album. When I'm in the studio I really miss the rapport you get with a live audience. There's only a few people there looking at you through a window: it's all very depressing really. The hardest thing in the world is to get excitement on to a piece of plastic. I really do think that we all play better on stage than we do on record.'

Later, in April 1998, Page insisted, to *Uncut*'s Nigel Williamson that he never said that.

'I do worry,' Page told Yorke, that the second album is turning out to be so different from the first – we may have overstepped the mark. But then again, I suppose there are enough Led Zeppelin trademarks in there. It's very hard rock, there's no doubt about that. There aren't many bands into hard rock these days and I think that might account for some of our success. All sorts of people are into folk and country and softer stuff. We just like to play it hard and bluesy. There aren't many exponents of real contemporary blues either. John Mayall doesn't do it any more. But there's always a market for it, I think. Taj Mahal is my idea of contemporary blues. Our stuff I think is a combination of everything.'

According to Yorke, Page harboured considerable worry over the worth of *Led Zeppelin II*: 'The album took such a long time to make ... it was all on and off. It was quite insane really. We had no time and we had to write songs in hotel rooms. By the time the album came out, I was really fed up with it. I just heard it so many times in so many different places. I really think I lost confidence in it. Even though people were saying it was great, I wasn't convinced myself.

'There was probably more attack on the second album because it was written while we were on the road and only getting into the studio when we could find an opening. I suppose that feeling of playing all the time is evident in the new album. There wasn't much time to sit back and think about it.'

After his day in the A&R studios in New York City, Page got straight on a plane to Los Angeles. In her autobiography *I'm With the Band*, Miss Pamela listed extracts from her diary entries. Mr Carlos, a member of the BTOs, the male companion group to the GTOs, had run into Page in Paris. Page had declared his intention to bed Miss Pamela. Her diary entry for 31 July 1969 read: 'Jimmy Page is coming to town today. I don't know whether I want to be with him or not, who knows what diseases I'd get? Such a sweet and lovely precious-looking cherub, why is it that he's perverted? Maybe he's not?? Perhaps I'll find out.'

Despite her trepidation, that night Miss Pamela went along to Thee Experience. There, she sat 'sipping red wine through a straw' as she waited for Zeppelin to show. 'I was feeling haughty one minute and petrified the next, trying to get a little tipsy before the demonic darling darkened the seedy doorstep.' Although Robert Plant and Richard Cole arrived, there was no sign of Page. 'Richard Cole stumbled over and handed me a scrap of paper with Jimmy's number at the Continental Hyatt House scribbled on it. He leaned into me and mumbled thickly in my ear, "He's waiting for you."'

Although the Hyatt House was only a short walk away, Miss Pamela instead sat back and watched Bo Diddley play his set.

Playing it cool seemed to work to Miss Pamela's advantage. The next day, Page called her up, asking why on earth she hadn't shown at the Hyatt the previous night. Led Zeppelin were playing that evening at the Earl Warren Showgrounds in Santa

Barbara, ninety miles north of Los Angeles, on the Pacific coast; Page asked her to join him on his journey to the venue. 'But I came down by myself to show a little more hard-to-getness ... He seems so shy and delicious, grey eyes gazing into mine, sweet sweetness, pale white skin, gentle gentleman with something to hide. What does he want from me?'

Picking up the ticket and backstage pass Page had left for her at the venue, Miss Pamela found herself escorted backstage after the show by Richard Cole to a waiting limousine. 'The long ride from Santa Barbara was one of these dream experiences that leave you glowing in the dark. From the moment Jimmy slid his small velvet-clad ass across the seat of the limo, right next to mine, until the door was thrown open in front of Thee Experience, we cooed and giggled like doves in heat. It was a hundred-mile drive, which gave him plenty of time to come out with "all the lines". He told me he had gotten my number the last time he was in town but was too nervous to use it until the last day, and he called and called but the line was constantly busy ... He said he wanted to spend time with me more than anything in the world. Tell me more. I kissed and slobbered all over the inside crease of his slim white arm until he rolled his head back against the plush seat, gasping, "Oh, Pamela, yes, yes, yes." He warned me that his previous LA girlfriend would probably be in the club and that I would have to give him the chance to "explain" to her about me. Uh-oh.

'I climbed out of the warm, dark backseat womb, full of wet kisses and flaming glazed eyes, and found myself in the precarious position of sharing this splendid divinity with Catherine James, the most gorgeous rock courtesan alive. She and I hissed at each other from a dark distance, and I beat the old hasty retreat back to my cozy pad.'

In her diary entry dated 2 August 1969, Miss Pamela describes how her friend Michelle told her that Page was astonished she had left Thee Experience the previous evening. 'He was asking everybody if they'd seen me. He looked all over the club after "explaining" to Catherine, and left alone.'

Later in the day her phone rang. She picked it up and heard a voice declare: 'Long distance, Mr Page calling.'

'He knew what to say all right; he could have given a Master's course in how to turn a fairly sane girl into a twittering ninny. No one had ever gushed over me, or given me all the lines before, and I could feel myself falling apart and turning into one of those gooey unrecognisable substances. He told me he was going to come to my door, sweep me off my feet, and take me away in his white chariot; he told me he was my knight in shining armour; he told me he didn't know what was coming over him, he had never felt like this before … He acted like he couldn't believe I ever gave him a second glance. When I told him I missed him, he came out with, "Oh Miss P. Really? Are you telling me the truth?" My melting heart wasn't ready for this guy. I swallowed it all whole, and it was fucking delicious.'

He called her from Houston, where Zeppelin had played the Music Hall on 3 August, saying he would be coming round for her the next evening. And he arrived in a white limousine, taking her to the Palomino Club, something of a country music venue, in North Hollywood. The Everly Brothers were performing. 'We got all caught up in those glorious harmonies. Jimmy's eyes misted up and he squeezed my hand on certain meaningful lyrics: "Mmmmmm: I never knew what I missed until I kissed you …" He looked hard at me with a tiny smile on his rosebud lips, making me sweat about the long night to come. He put something into my hand, and it turned out to be a silver ring with twenty pieces of turquoise embedded into it, and I wondered if I was going steady with the best guitar player in the world. He always messed with his black curls, poofing and fluffing them around his flawless face; he wore emerald velvet and white chiffon, thin little socks, and the most perfect brooch on his lapel. I couldn't wait to get back to the hotel and take it all off.'

Page, Miss Pamela noticed, was forever checking out how he looked in the mirror, 'putting perfect waves in his long black hair with a little crimping machine. He used Pantene products, and whenever I smelled them … I remembered being buried in his hair.'

When they went to bed, she wrote, 'Such a face, so gentle and soft, I'm amazed at his sadistic tendencies; they're such a part of him that I doubt if he'll ever stop. It was really frightening, he changed into another person, but all he did was chew me and slap me a little.'

When Miss Pamela noticed the set of whips in his suitcase, he promised, '"Don't worry Miss P, I'll never use those on you, I'll never hurt you like that." Then he sucked on my neck, and when I could feel the bruise being called up out of my bloodstream, he tossed me down on the bed and told me he would throw away the whips to show how much I meant to him.'

Miss Pamela described how Page had with him a test pressing of *Led Zeppelin II*, which he played again and again, taking notes. For her part, she turned him on to Nudie Cohn, who had tailored sumptuous outfits for such singing cowboy royalty as Gene Autry and Roy Rogers, as well as making Elvis Presley's $10,000 gold lamé suit. The entire group, along with Peter Grant, went to Nudie's store in North Hollywood, to be fitted out with the legendary tailor's western wear. 'We went to the Glass Farmhouse, where Jimmy got a long antique coat embroidered with a dragon and a silly velvet hat with a feather in it.'

In Las Vegas, Miss Pamela was with them to watch Elvis Presley from front-row seats at the International Hotel. Following the show, one of the King's people emerged to ask if Page would care to come backstage for an audience with Elvis. 'No, thank you,' he replied.

When Led Zeppelin left the West Coast, Miss Pamela was on her own and somewhat distraught. At the end of the month, however, the group were to play in New York, at the Singer Bowl in Queens. Page sent her a plane ticket, and she was with him in the city for three days, where he introduced her to people as 'Mrs Page'. She then travelled with him to the Texas International Pop Festival in Lewisville for their last date of this tour, where Zeppelin played to 80,000 people, before it really was goodbye, and he and the band returned to England to finish *Led Zeppelin II*.

Coming to the UK at the invitation of Page, Joe Jammer found himself with a manager, Peter Grant, who secured a record deal for him with EMI, on the Regal Zonophone label. At the instigation of Page, Joe became yet another of Screaming Lord Sutch's apprentices, playing guitar with him. But the American was aware of one of the downsides to the guitarist's character: 'I learned early that they had a nickname for Jimmy: Led Wallet. Because he would never pay for anything for anybody. And it came to a time when Zep were becoming more famous, but Jimmy would come in from Pangbourne hitchhiking. To save money. They talked him into at least taking a train. But he would only do second-class. And some hippy guy came up to him: "Jimmy, why are you here in second-class?" He told that story in the office. So Peter Grant made a decision. He hired a car to bring Jimmy Page into town. And Jimmy refused to pay for it. So the other four had to pay for Jimmy's car. He had the money. But he was very tight. Maybe there was something way back when with mum and dad and the Second World War. He knew he had to be smart, super-smart.

'Peter was hired by Jimmy and John Paul Jones. They paid him out of their own money at first. He was one of the first managers ever who didn't screw his band, the first manager ever who defended his band – to the point where everybody outside hated him for being Led Zeppelin's manager. Jimmy did call all the shots. Peter made them happen.

'Jimmy was like a musical Hitler. He had a big master plan to take over the world and he certainly did. There was no question about it. No "we're goofing around and gonna have fun"; we might have fun along the way but this was serious work.

'It may not have been that premeditated. But "we're gonna make it superbig" was certainly the position. "We're going to be the biggest band ever" – that was premeditated.

'The Led Zeppelin sound came through that last Yardbirds album, which Mickie Most produced. And Mickie Most was under the impression that he was going to be allowed to produce Led Zeppelin. But they said, "No, Jimmy's going to do it." And that had a lot to do with Mickie and Peter falling out. Mickie didn't like all the drugs: he was dead straight. Mickie was a drinker: later he went to AA. But Led Zeppelin eventually went really hardcore and Mickie didn't like that.' Joe Jammer miming injecting a syringe into his arm should make clear what he means by hardcore.

'When I was with them, it was just pot and booze. But they noticed that the pot made them hungry and they ate and got fat. So then they discovered the other thing: old Charles. And then Henry kind of came along on the heels of Charles. But not all of them: Jimmy and Bonham – Bonham was into anything, anytime, anywhere.'

John Paul Jones, however, was another kettle of fish altogether: 'He was the most serious of them all. And he was the quietest. And they always say, "The wise man is the silent man. He who speaks does not know. And he who knows does not speak." So Jonesy, while the fucking chaos was swirling around him, as a bass player was absolutely a fucking world-class master, but just wanted to do a fucking good job.

'He was like the Brian Jones of Led Zeppelin, always introducing weird new instruments, playing keyboards with his foot.

Super-musical. What he did gave them was a big advantage over any other four-piece rock band.'

Joe Jammer also quickly perceived the importance of Richard Cole to the Zeppelin operation. 'Richard Cole is the one man who knows everything about everybody. He was the key, the axle in the wheel. He knows everything about everybody. Hence his book *Stairway to Heaven*. Richard knew everything about everybody: without him none of it would have happened. He's the key man. He was third man down the chain: Jimmy Page, Peter Grant, Richard Cole. Jonesy and Jimmy were equal. Because they started it together and paid for it together. I think it was 50/50.

'The hierarchy of Led Zeppelin was like the Cosa Nostra. I was the guy who didn't get shot. I was the guy who didn't get beat up. I was the guy who didn't get abused. You've got to have one. I thought it was very brutal. When the junk started, they started losing their liking of everybody. Jimmy got real mean to me. But it was the junk doing all the talking.'

The *Led Zeppelin II* sleeve design was now ready. Page had asked David Juniper, who had studied with him at Sutton Art College, to come up with 'an interesting idea'. Juniper took a First World War photograph of German flying ace the Red Baron and his esteemed Flying Circus, and then airbrushed the faces of Led Zeppelin's four members over them – an angelically dangerous-looking Page sat in the centre of the group. Further iconic faces were added: Blind Willie Johnson, for example, and what was at first thought to be Neil Armstrong, but was in fact another astronaut, Frank Borman. There was also the actress Glynis Johns, a sly dig at engineer Glyn Johns, with whom there had been a disagreement.

To coincide with the release of *Led Zeppelin II* the group returned to America on 17 October for a brief tour. This time there were no shows in Los Angeles; instead they played three sold-out nights at San Francisco's Winterland Ballroom, with its 5,400 capacity, supported by Roland Kirk and Isaac Hayes.

For security reasons the group decided to stay in Sausalito, in hip Marin County. Miss Pamela flew up from Los Angeles, and, while taking her on a tour of the city, Page found an art gallery where he bought a number of etchings, at $500 a pop, by the Dutch graphic artist M.C. Escher; he had long loved Escher's work. 'He bought me a book of Sulamith Wülfing's ethereal paintings, and I clutched it to my chest,' she wrote.

When it came time to leave once again for London, Page said to Miss Pamela at the airport: 'P, you're such a lovely little girl. I don't deserve you. I'm such a bastard, you know.'

There were problems with the first factory pressing of *Led Zeppelin II*: due to the sound of the bass on the record being so heavy and overmodulated, the record kept skipping, necessitating Jerry Wexler to throw a hundred thousand dollars' worth of pressed albums in the bin and start all over again.

The record was finally released on 22 October 1969. Rattling and bustling with the energy of the group's live shows, around which it had been recorded, and kicking off with the very unique 'Whole Lotta Love', the album surpassed expectations. It was a major statement of Led Zeppelin's position – as a cutting-edge, zeitgeist act, endlessly inventive and exciting at an extremely primal level. It was one of the raunchiest records ever made. 'It was still blues-based but with a much more carnal approach to the music,' said Plant.

'They were the first numbers written with the band in mind,' Page told Mick Wall. 'It was music more tailor-made for the elements you've got. Like knowing that Bonzo's gonna come in hard at some point, and building that in.' Almost US garage-band punk in the simplicity of some of the songs, there is something curiously amateurish about material like 'Ramble On', indubitably part of the appeal.

Utterly contrary to what Page wanted – although he was often prepared to be pragmatic when it came to the success of his group – Atlantic, anxious for a trailer to advertise the new LP from their expensive signing, edited 'Whole Lotta Love' and released it as a single in the USA, where it hit the number four spot. Attempts to do the same in the UK had Peter Grant expressing his feelings in no uncertain terms to Phil Carson, who ran Atlantic there.

At the end of 1969, at London's prestigious Savoy Hotel, Led Zeppelin were presented with gold discs for their first album by Gwynneth Dunwoody, a minister at the Board of Trade in Prime Minister Harold Wilson's government, in honour of the group's contributions to the UK's balance of trade. Afterwards Grant took his client to the swish neighbourhood of Berkeley Square, where he bought Page a brand new Rolls-Royce – despite the guitarist not having a driving licence.

In the US there were 400,000 advance orders for *Led Zeppelin II*. It jumped straight into the Billboard chart at number 15. By Christmas it had replaced the Beatles' *Abbey Road* at the top of the US charts. It was still in that position in February 1970, when the album hit the number one spot in the UK. As it did so, Led Zeppelin were undertaking a UK tour. Called back for a fourth encore at Leeds University on 24 January, the quartet of musicians played a soul-shaking medley of Eddie Cochran songs intertwined with snippets of 'Communication Breakdown'.

On 9 January 1970, Jimmy Page's 26th birthday, Led Zeppelin had played again at London's Royal Albert Hall. When they had performed there only six months before, they were somewhat nervous. But now, having knocked the Beatles off the top of the US charts, and with no support act, their confidence was supreme. Among those at the show were John Lennon, Eric Clapton and Jeff Beck.

They kicked off with 'We're Gonna Groove'. Plant said to the audience, 'This is Jimmy Page: lead guitar,' the Led Zeppelin leader's hair dangling to his shoulder blades.

'Albert Hall was a massive gig for us, and we really wanted to do the best we could,' Page told *Guitar World* in 2003. 'It was a magic venue. It was built in Victorian times, and you are in there thinking about all the musical history that has preceded you. On top of that, it was something of a homecoming for John Paul Jones and me, because we had both grown up around there. So we were all really paying attention to what we were doing.'

Such scrutiny clearly paid off. The show, filmed by Peter Whitehead, was utterly sensational. There is something extraordinarily sexual about the sliding of Jimmy Page's violin bow during 'Dazed and Confused', and the reviews echoed the frenzied atmosphere.

'For 10 years, rock and roll had been working towards something that would combine the extraordinary capacities of electronic instruments with the anarchic energy of youth, and there in the Albert Hall on 9 January 1970, [we] found it ... the sound came up to me with a force that pummelled me breathless. No other band ever managed to make a sound like that. It was certainly loud, but it was also driving, pushing along with incredible energy,' wrote the eminent feminist Germaine Greer in the *Daily Telegraph*. Meanwhile the *NME* claimed that the show 'completely destroyed the ever-weakening argument about British reserve'.

If that colossally successful evening wasn't enough celebration for his birthday, Page received an even greater present after the show. Heather Taylor, his former flame who was by now regularly on the arm of Roger Daltrey, introduced Page to her friend, the model Charlotte Martin. In fact, it was something of a re-introduction: Page had already met her several times, when she was with Eric Clapton.

A fanatical vanity and an almost immeasurable self-adoration would appear to be important prerequisites for any aspiring rock star. But although he may have possessed these attributes, what was far more dominant in Page's case was an impulsive drive that derived much more from an almost obsessive self-knowledge, underpinned by what he had learned about himself from his studies of both art and the occult and the consequent confidence it gave him. Frail, sexually androgynous and mentally muscular, he exuded a complex iron toughness; this was someone who would not back down. When he met Charlotte Martin again he knew they had been drawn together by other forces.

Page and Martin were immediately smitten with each other. He asked Richard Cole to give them a ride to her nearby apartment. Soon she moved into his Pangbourne home. 'Charlotte was the type of girl you couldn't look at just once,' said Cole in *Stairway to Heaven*. 'Tall. Thin. Blonde. Perfect features. You had to glance a second time.' All the same, he was not necessarily taken with her. 'At least in her relationship with me, she was aloof, unfriendly and indifferent. It was my feeling that unless she really liked you, she had a "take it or leave it" attitude. Frankly, I wasn't impressed.'

Led Zeppelin's next US tour, their fifth, which ran from 21 March to 19 April, was almost entirely performed in arena-sized venues.

The group's enormous, sudden success had offered Peter Grant a battering ram with which to smash down the barriers erected by the somewhat amateurish, hit-and-miss – and often corrupt and Mob-affiliated – nature of much of American concert promotion. Led Zeppelin's earnings had jumped significantly: a pair of shows at Chicago's Kinetic Playground in February 1969 earned the four-piece $7,500. Returning in May for a similar slot, they picked up $12,500 per night.

Now Grant set about renegotiating the very structure of the deals he struck with US promoters, which would make his clients extremely rich. Zeppelin insisted on 90 per cent of the gross take of ticket sales, leaving just 10 per cent profit for the local promoter. Page could hardly disguise his approval. 'The new system is to put groups on a percentage of the gate money and we drew $37,000 from one amazing gig in Los Angeles,' he said.

Following this US tour, London's *Financial Times* declared that Led Zeppelin had now earned over $5 million in the United States. Was the story run, at the instigation of Peter Grant, to cock a snook at those stalwarts of the underground who still considered Led Zeppelin a 'capitalist' group? Quite probably.

Midway through the tour, however, there was a problem. At Winnipeg Airport in Canada a road manager noticed that something was missing: Page's 'Black Beauty' guitar, a Les Paul Keith Richards gave him that he had played on the entire tour. 'Whole Lotta Love' had been recorded with Page playing the Black Beauty. (Most of his Led Zeppelin slide work was on his Danelectro.)

Despite Led Zeppelin standing to gross a further $1 million for this tour, the guitar's loss put Page in a dark mood for much of the rest of their time on the road. 'Jimmy never seemed to fully recover from the loss,' said Richard Cole. 'We got through all 29 performances without any noticeable impact upon his playing. It really didn't matter that every show was a sellout, that it was a guaranteed million-dollar tour before it had even begun. To Jimmy, the loss of the guitar ruined everything.'

In case Led Zeppelin were beginning to take their sudden, colossal success for granted, it was on this tour that they received a severe wakeup call. On 8 April 1970, playing an arena in Raleigh, North Carolina – resolutely in the distinctly unliberal 'South' – a Zeppelin employee overheard a pair of local cops planning to plant narcotics on a member of the group. Immediately Richard Cole went into action, trying to hire security from the local Pinkerton's office. But then he gave up and called Steve Weiss, the Zeppelin lawyer, in New York. Weiss arranged for a pair of local private detectives to stand guard over the group at all times until they left Raleigh.

Were those Raleigh police officers responding to the signs of excess around Zeppelin that were everywhere evident during their spring 1970 tour of the USA? This was the first time that an unalloyed sense of decadence had begun to hover about the group: drink, drugs and excessive sexuality were omnipresent. Whereas once all four members would have been happy with a drink and a spliff, now cocaine had entered their world, as well as something even worse: when they played in Los Angeles, John Bonham was on heroin.

And the overindulgence of these dates took its toll. Suffering for much of the latter days of the tour from a bad cold, Robert Plant's vocals became increasingly ragged. Finally, following their show at the Arizona Veterans Memorial Coliseum in Phoenix on 18 April, Page startled the audience with an announcement following the end of 'Whole Lotta Love': 'You've been a fantastic audience, but there's been something happening tonight ... Robert's been very ill, and as he came off he's just collapsed and we've just called for a doctor. We'd really like to do more, but obviously it's impossible.'

The show scheduled for the next day, in Las Vegas, was cancelled. Led Zeppelin flew home to London.

11

'DO WHAT THOU WILT'

The day after Led Zeppelin returned to London, Jimmy Page appeared as a solo guest on Julie Felix's folk-lite BBC television show *Once More with Felix*, which was broadcast three days later, on 26 April. Page appearing alone was unusual, and his choice of songs was curious too. He played his medley of 'White Summer'/'Black Mountain Side' – in Phoenix the previous week he had performed the same material – for what would be the last time until it resurfaced on the group's 1977 tour. Julie Felix introduced him in a manner befitting of someone who had acquired the status of rock nobility: 'My next guest this evening is a member of certainly the most successful group to come out of Britain in the last couple of years. Led Zeppelin LPs top both the British and American charts, and the lead guitarist in that group is definitely a very talented and special musician.'

Back home in the Midlands, however, Robert Plant was not enjoying quite as warm a homecoming. His voice fully recovered, he was now employing it in arguments with his wife Maureen. In his state of semi-permanent jetlag, Plant was enduring a period of angst about his rapidly improved position in life. Returning home from a tour where he had been worshipped as a god had not readily acclimatised him to adjusting to simple domestic life. However, Plant was an intelligent man, and he felt he could come up with a solution: going on holiday with Jimmy Page and their respective 'old ladies'.

Plant had spent a summer holiday with his parents near Bron-Yr-Aur, a broad, two-storey cottage in north Wales close to the mountain Cadair Idris, which is steeped in mythology, legendarily the site of the last battle of King Arthur. And as spring began to bloom, Plant sold Page on the idea of spending time in the area. 'I had already written "Immigrant Song",' recalled Page to the *Guardian* in 2014, 'and came up with "Friends" a day or two before we got together at Robert's house in the West Midlands. I was keen to do "Gallows Pole" because I had an arrangement I wanted to try, and I had "Tangerine" from a number of years beforehand – before Led Zeppelin.'

With Clive Coulson and Sandy Macgregor, a pair of Zeppelin roadies, strapped into service by Richard Cole, the party journeyed up to north Wales, invoking the getting-away-from-it-all creative ethos of acts like the Band and Traffic. 'We had done a lot in 1969,' said Page. 'We'd done six months of solid touring in America. We'd performed all over Europe. We'd also done an album on the road. It was exhilarating, but it was nice to be able to stop. We finally had the chance to slow down, and that's reflected in our third album.'

'Whatever our physical state was at the end of *Led Zeppelin II*, there was now only one place to go: up into the misty mountains with our families,' said Plant.

It was perfect peace, a long way physically and – more importantly – culturally from the Hyatt House. So long as you didn't mind the lack of running water – it was necessary to adjourn to a nearby pub for a bath – or electricity, and the constant drizzle of the rain billowing in from nearby Snowdonia's mountains. Old hippie that he was, still regularly to be found immersed in yet another rereading of J. R. R. Tolkien's *The Lord of the Rings*, Plant loved it, bringing along his daughter Carmen and their spotted Border collie Strider – named after a *Lord of the Rings* character – as well as Maureen. You wonder how the sophisticated model Charlotte Martin took to it all.

'We were just trying to get some ideas down to bring back and work on,' said Plant. 'So there we were, up in the mountains with one of the very first Sony cassette recorders and a bunch of Eveready batteries, just sitting going: "Well, what shall we do?" Carmen was two and needed bathing. Strider needed feeding. And we needed cider.'

It was here that Page and Plant, armed with a pair of acoustic guitars, first began to actively write together. A pair of songs would immediately find their way onto the next album. The ballad 'That's the Way' – initially titled 'The First Time' – resulted from a set of chords that Plant unearthed; taking a long walk with Page's guitar and a portable cassette recorder, they hummed and sang the song – essentially an eco hymn with reflections on the negative reception they sometimes received from rednecks in the US – into completion before they had returned. '"That's the Way" came out of there as a complete song,' said Page.

'Friends' was a drone-like tune cloaked in mystic sounds that Page came up with after he'd had a severe row with Charlotte Martin. Half an hour after finishing the song, Page had make-up sex with Charlotte, conceiving their child Scarlet in the process.

'Bron-Y-Aur Stomp' was a tune that Plant composed in honour of his dog Strider; on the final recorded version Page's acoustic work revealed the influence of the British folk guitarists Bert Jansch and Davy Graham. The song was first tried out as a rocking electric tune entitled 'Jennings Farm Blues', the name of Plant's new home in the West Midlands.

There were more. 'Over the Hills and Far Away' and 'Down by the Seaside' would appear on later records, as would 'Black Country Woman' and 'The Rover'. 'Another Way to Wales' and 'I Wanna Be Her Man' never appeared on any record by the group.

Equally as important as this new material was the fact that this was the first opportunity for Page and Plant to form a genuine friendship, to come to a measure of mutual understanding. 'I really came to know Robert, actually living together at Bron-Yr-Aur, as opposed to occupying nearby hotel rooms. The songs took us into areas that changed the band. It established a standard of travelling for inspiration, which is the best thing a musician can do,' Page said later, to Cameron Crowe in *Rolling Stone* magazine.

'Jimmy was much more of a man of the world than I was,' admitted Plant to the *Guardian* in 2016. 'He'd travelled a lot with the Yardbirds, he'd done those Dick Clark tours … And he was the face, so I was master at arms at that point in the development of our relationship – it was all developing before me. It was a very easygoing and very unaffected time – miraculous really.'

There are suggestions that recording for the album then commenced at Headley Grange, a rotting 18th-century mansion house in Hampshire. But Page firmly nixes this notion.

Instead he insists that *Led Zeppelin III* was recorded at Olympic Studios and at Island Records' Basing Street Studios in Notting Hill. 'The whole thing,' confirmed Andy Johns, the engineer and younger brother of Glyn, 'was done at Studio 2 at Olympic. I remember for sure, then I got them to go to Island, where we did the mixes. And that went pretty well. They used to work very quickly.'

On 22 June there was a break from the routine of recording. The British Council asked Led Zeppelin to represent British popular music on a cultural visit to Iceland. With its ancient independent tradition celebrated in the island's sagas, Plant was stirred into writing the lyrics for the number that would kick off the new LP: 'Immigrant Song'.

Equally importantly, the gig in Iceland's capital Reykjavik, before a 5,000-strong audience, served as a warm-up date for what would be the largest UK showcase so far for the group.

On 28 June 1970 Led Zeppelin topped the bill at the second Bath Festival of Blues and Progressive Music, promoted by Frederick Bannister; the four musicians had come a long way from their mid-afternoon slot at the festival the previous year. The band cancelled a pair of shows at New York's Madison Square Garden to appear at Bath after Bannister promised Peter Grant a minimum crowd of 200,000 people. Led Zeppelin received £60,000 for their appearance at Bath, less than they would have picked up for Madison Square Garden.

The exciting festival bill featured a feast of acts, the cream of underground rock in the US – Canned Heat, the Byrds, Steppenwolf, Santana, Johnny Winter, Country Joe and the Fish, the Mothers of Invention, Jefferson Airplane, Dr John and Flock – and at home – John Mayall, Pink Floyd, the Moody Blues, Fairport Convention, Donovan and many more.

Peter Grant insisted that Led Zeppelin's set was to begin at 8.30 p.m. A week on from the summer solstice, this would ensure that the sun set a few minutes after Zeppelin began their show with the brand new 'Immigrant Song', a tune whose ironic title celebrated Viking rampages to other lands but seemed like a metaphor for Led Zeppelin itself. In the line 'Our only goal will be the western shore', Plant's lyrics clearly refer to both the documented Norse journeys to America and Led Zeppelin cutting a broad swathe across the United States to California. Yet in Plant's barked utterance 'We are your overlords' was there not a suggestion of the hubris that would finally undo Zeppelin – especially in a song where Page's guitar riff was not really as commanding as it needed to be? Really, the galloping 'Immigrant Song' seemed like a subconscious effort to replicate the power and simple complexity of 'Whole Lotta Love' – and came up wanting.

Further new songs were tried out: 'Celebration Day' and 'Since I've Been Loving You', the third song of the set and future fan favourite that featured John Paul Jones on Hammond organ. This song had been played in a different form at the Royal Albert Hall on Page's birthday.

'We've been playing America a lot recently and we really thought that coming back here we might have a dodgy time,' pronounced Plant from the stage. 'There's a lot of things going wrong in America at the moment that are getting a bit sticky. It's really nice to come to an open-air festival where there are no such bad things happening and everything's turned out beautiful.'

Mind you, there was the by now established atmosphere of 'heaviness' about Zeppelin's performance. Richard Cole and three of the group's roadies stepped onto the stage during Flock's set and aggressively pulled out the plugs so they could play no more.

'Unbeknownst to Freddy Bannister, I went down to the site and found out from the Meteorological Office what time the sun was setting,' said Peter Grant. 'It was going down right behind the stage. By the band going on at sunset, I was able to bring up the stage lights a bit at a time. It was vital we went on stage at the right time. That's why I made sure the previous band, Flock – or whoever they were – got off on time.'

Each member of Led Zeppelin was in vogue with a beard – a hangover of that time in Wales when water itself was at a premium. Page was accoutred in a tight double-breasted over-coat – the identical one he'd worn in that 1968 first publicity shot with the group posed about a 3.8 Jaguar – and a bucket-like hat, giving him the appearance of an especially spectral scarecrow. With his flowing, shoulder-length locks comple-mented by a trimmed beard and moustache, Plant now appeared like a character from the court of Louis XIV. And anyone watching might have felt that the Zeppelin singer had taken more than a hint of stagecraft from the Who's Roger Daltrey, who was similarly tonsorially styled and was the prototype of the microphone lassoist into whom Plant had evolved.

What was specifically significant about Led Zeppelin's performance at the Bath Festival, where they would perform four encores, was an alteration to the tone of the set that would remain with the group for most of the rest of their time together. Some 40 minutes in, John Paul Jones put down his bass guitar and picked up a mandolin; meanwhile, Page swapped his Gibson Les Paul for a Martin D-28 acoustic guitar. As the two musicians tuned up, Plant cracked a joke: 'This is a medley of Lonnie Donegan tunes.' Then he announced the next song: 'This is called "The Boy Next Door", for want of a better title.' And so 'That's the Way' – as the song would be renamed on the album – became the first song the group played acoustically in the UK. Suddenly an entirely new side of Led Zeppelin was revealed. Those who carped at notions of sudden change accused the four musicians of aping the styles and subject-matter of such newly popular West Coast singer-songwriters as Crosby, Stills, Nash and Young, handily omitting the wealth of evidence from their first two LPs of similarly styled material.

The rigorously rehearsed set was paced to build to a series of climaxes, ending a full three hours later, after the four encores, the final one a rock 'n' roll medley featuring 'Long Tall Sally', 'Say Mama', 'Johnny B. Goode' and, finally, 'That's All Right Mama'. Led Zeppelin came offstage after three hours, to the adoring words of Mike Raven, the Radio 1 DJ: 'Unbelievable! Led Zeppelin! You're fantastic! Led Zeppelin: England adores you!'

The show was an utter triumph. With the Beatles having announced that they were breaking up two months previously, Led Zeppelin became the kings of British rock music. Yet even so, there were 'freaks' who basked in the snobbish cool of informing you that they had left the festival site before Led Zeppelin had come onstage; among 'intelligent' fans of rock there were many who were still utterly dismissive of Page's group.

Earlier in the day Page noticed that Roy Harper was wandering around the backstage area. Harper was a gnarled, idiosyncratic artist whom the Zeppelin guitarist had first watched on the London folk circuit in the mid-sixties. Although they had never spoken before, Page approached Harper and asked to be shown how to play an instrumental track, 'Blackpool', from Harper's first LP. 'I played it for him and he said, "Thanks very much." We exchanged pleasantries and then he walked away. The only thing I thought as I watched him leave was, "That guy's pants are too short for him."'

Only when Page went onstage with Led Zeppelin did Harper appreciate who he was. 'During the second song, all the young women in the crowd started to stand up involuntarily, with tears running down their faces. It was like, "Jesus, what's happening here then?" In the end, you knew you'd seen something you were never going to forget.'

Harper and Page became close friends, a relationship celebrated in the 'Hats Off to (Roy) Harper' song on *Led Zeppelin III*, which served as an introduction to the world's record buyers of a performer whose rigorously uncommercial music had so far been understandably sidelined. Later in the year, at Led Zeppelin's office, Page gave Harper a copy of the new LP, urging him to look at it closely. When he discovered the tribute to him the folk singer was deeply moved. He became an integral feature of the Led Zeppelin scene, sometimes opening for the act.

When Zeppelin played the 1970 Bath Festival, Joe Jammer was also on the bill. Although he was no longer part of the group's technical crew, his position as a companion to Page was resoundingly confirmed when, one afternoon at Pangbourne, Charlotte Martin drew up his astrological chart: to the astonishment and then fascination of first Martin and then Page, it was revealed that Joe Jammer and Aleister Crowley shared an almost identical planetary set-up. 'Double Libra, moon in Leo,' said Jammer. 'Same natal chart as Aleister Crowley – that was the first time I had heard that name. And that really flipped Jimmy out. And Charlotte.' When they first met, Page and Jammer had almost immediately clicked; now it seemed as though this friendship had been written, almost literally, in the heavens.

'Jimmy would use me because there weren't multi-track machines then. So you could only play one part and had to imagine the other part. He'd call me into his room on that 1969 US tour, and ask me to play a little riff as he played something opposite against me. And this went on all the while after I came to London. I'd go out to Pangbourne to help him with some songs. There's a Zep song called "Black Dog". But I couldn't learn the riff. I mean, this guy is a master guitarist. He plays me this incredibly complicated riff, and says, "Play that!" I couldn't do it, so now he's kinda getting a little mad. But he was gracious: "Let's move on to something else!" So he said, "What do you like to play?" I said, "Well, I'm into funk." I taught Jimmy how to play funk on that session that day. And it emerged in that Led Zeppelin tune "The Crunge". Which is exaggerated acid-trip super-funk. Robert goes, "Where's the bridge? Can't find the bridge?"'

Again assisted by Page, Jammer considerably boosted his income by becoming a session player in the UK, playing on over 150 albums during a ten-year period. 'It was good money. I used to get union scale. But by the time he stopped doing it Jimmy had negotiated his pay up to three times union scale. He had his own Jimmy Page Music right from early on. His mum advised him on that. He also wrote an enormous amount of B-sides for singles. He was certainly a millionaire by the start of Led Zeppelin.'

* * *

Led Zeppelin returned to the recording studio to record 'Hats Off to (Roy) Harper' – 'a piece of spontaneous combustion initiated by Page late one night inspired by some frenzied slide-guitar channelling of Bukka White's "Shake 'Em on Down"', wrote Mick Wall. 'Gallows Pole' was also laid down, an interpretation of the old English folk song 'The Maid Freed from the Gallows'.

'Since I've Been Loving You' could be seen as the ancestor of the power ballads that would emerge during the 1980s. Yet again there would be questions about the inspiration for this song, which would become a *tour de force* of their live sets. The genesis of 'Since I've Been Loving You' was surely the song 'Never' by Plant favourites Moby Grape. 'Never' begins with the lines 'Working from eleven to seven every night, ought to make life a drag, yeah, and I know that ain't right'. 'Since I've Been Loving You', meanwhile, starts off with the lines 'Working from seven to eleven every night, it really makes life a drag, yeah, and I know that ain't right'. Compare and contrast, pop fans. 'There are also uncanny echoes in the music, both songs being extrapolations from a stately B.B. King-style blues, working it up into a melodramatic musical statement with beginning, middle and end where the Grape working is more content to meander forth in the one-take jam style it was intended,' considered Mick Wall.

The engineer on 'Since I've Been Loving You' was a trainee called Richard Digby Smith. In 2000 he was interviewed about the session by *Mojo* magazine: 'I can see Robert at the mike now. He was so passionate. Lived every line. What you got on the record is what happened. His only preparation was a herbal cigarette and a couple of shots of Jack Daniel's ... I remember Pagey pushing him, "Let's try the outro chorus again, improvise a bit more" ... There was a hugeness about everything Zeppelin did. I mean, look behind you and there was Peter Grant sitting on the sofa – the whole sofa.'

Although he had vowed never to repeat the process of the second album, lugging tapes around and ducking into studios while on tour, Page found history repeated itself. A US tour was scheduled to begin on 5 August 1970, although the first week's dates were cancelled when John Paul Jones's father fell seriously ill. For Page, however, the timing was fortuitous: he flew down to Memphis, linking up with his old friend Terry Manning, with whom he had toured in the Yardbirds and who now ran Ardent Studios in the city. Among other acts that Manning had worked with there were Sam and Dave, Isaac Hayes and Booker T. and the MG's – Stax Records used Ardent as a kind of overspill facility when their own studio was fully booked. Soon the legendary Big Star would make their records here.

Page worked on mixing the sound of the new album at Ardent, and finally accepted that the guide solo, both plangent and searing, that he had laid down when they first began recording 'Since I've Been Loving You' was precisely what the track needed for its conclusion. 'It's my all-time number-one favourite rock guitar solo,' said Terry Manning. 'We took three or four other takes and tried to put takes together and come up with something, and they were all great. But there's something magic about that one take he did, that stream of consciousness.'

'With "Since I've Been Loving You" we were setting the scene of something that was yet to come,' Page told Brad Tolinski. 'It was meant to push the envelope. We were playing in the spirit of blues, but trying to take it into new dimensions dictated by the mass consciousness of the four players involved.

'The same thing goes for the folk stuff as well. It's sort of, "Well, this is how it was done in the past, but it now has to move." It's got to keep moving, moving. There's no point in looking back. You've got to keep moving onwards. Another factor was that my playing was also improving, and it was developing around the band. I didn't play any of this stuff when I was doing studio work or even in the Yardbirds. I was just inspired with this energy that we had collectively. I don't think there was any way to look backwards.'

It was Page's scrupulous attention to the most minute detail that truly stood out for Manning. The apparent roughness of some of the production – Bonham calling out 'Fuck!' at the beginning of 'Celebration Day', for example – was absolutely deliberate, asserted Manning. Quickly, he realised that Page was 'a really brilliant producer'. 'Not to demean or cast any aspersions,' Manning told Mick Wall, 'but I think he harmed himself perhaps in a few ways later on. But at that particular time, the very early days, Jimmy was an incredibly insightful, true musical genius, in my opinion, and I've seen a lot of musical people. I would say that very little happened by accident. Yes, there would be the occasional take that you can't repeat so you go with that, but it did take the insight to know that. He studied everything. When it says "Produced by Jimmy Page", it seriously was.'

Discussing the Bonham expletive on 'Celebration Day', which no one seemed to notice, Page explained to Manning: 'That's not why I wanna leave it, not 'cos that's cool. I like the sonic texture of everything. I like the feel that you're really there.'

'With "Since I've Been Loving You", we wanted to do a blues track that wasn't a 12-bar, because we'd done that on the first album,' reflected Page in the *Guardian* in 2016. 'So we came up with a blues in a minor key. It wasn't something that took forever and a day: it came together very quickly and it was perfect, with its sentiment and how it was approached.

'It felt right for the album to have a rocky side and a folky side – and the rocky side clearly had to start with "Immigrant Song". With that hypnotic riff and Robert's bloodcurdling scream, I thought, "That's the way to open an album."'

'"Immigrant Song" was written after we had been to Iceland,' said Plant. 'It was a cultural exchange – although who they sent over here, I can't imagine. The song was a vignette of what it

was like being there. Of course, it ended up spawning genera-
tions of guys with crossed axes tattooed on their arms. It's
slightly funny now.

'From what little I can remember of the subsequent recording
sessions at Olympic Studios in London, it was a case of using
mike placement and the right engineers to capture the rawness,
energy and attitude of each track. Sometimes it was a bit of a
struggle, but we did things quickly and were serious about
making something pretty as well as powerful. The outro of
"Gallows Pole" is great, with all the manic singing I'd over-
cooked horrendously prior to that. It started having some
meaning. I was learning how to syncopate. I was flourishing.'

'Gallows Pole', a traditional blues tale that opened side two
of *Led Zeppelin III*, was discovered by Page on a 1962 album
titled *Twelve-String Guitar* by American acoustic performer
Fred Gerlach. Originally the song had been recorded in 1939 by
legendary bluesman Leadbelly as 'The Gallis Pole'.

'Tangerine', meanwhile, had been recorded at the final
Yardbirds recording session in April 1968; at that point it was
titled 'Knowing that I'm Losing You', a tribute to Page's
ex-girlfriend Jackie DeShannon. As to his present girlfriend
Charlotte Martin, her pregnancy was becoming visible, the
unborn child who had been conceived during their time together
at Bron-Yr-Aur.

Finally at Ardent in Memphis the new LP was ready to be
mastered. Manning was aware of the possibility of adding a
small amount of handwritten text to the run-out groove at the
end of a side of vinyl. He asked Page if there was anything he
would care to write. The musician did indeed have something.
On side one he chose the words 'So mote be it'; and on side two
'Do what thou wilt', an abbreviation of 'Do what thou wilt
shall be the whole of the law. Love is the law, love under will.
There is no law beyond do what thou wilt.' Both these aphorisms
were central tenets of Aleister Crowley's Thelemic philosophy.

Their appearance in such a central position on the first vinyl pressings of the work brought Page's interest in Crowley more firmly into the minds of Led Zeppelin's followers.

From now on rumours began to swirl of a supernatural darkness at the heart of the group, immeasurably adding to its sense of mystery and mystique, its place in an apparently impenetrable world. Now there was a cachet of sinister glamour to everything Led Zeppelin touched.

12

THE BEAST 666

*'If one were to take the bible seriously one would go mad.
But to take the bible seriously, one must be already mad.'*
Aleister Crowley

At around 1.40 p.m. on 23 December 2015, a passing driver
saw flames raging through Boleskine House, the former abode
of both Aleister Crowley, once branded 'the wickedest man in
the world', and Jimmy Page. In a 1976 interview in *Sounds*,
Page declared that 'Aleister Crowley is the great misunderstood
genius of the twentieth century'. (Others disagree. Gary
Lachman, a former member of Blondie and now a successful
author specialising in occult matters, refers to Crowley's outlook
as 'kitsch-Nietzschean ideas about a super-race'.)

After only two hours of the blaze, 60 per cent of the low-built,
broad house had been destroyed. At the time of the fire,
Boleskine, which is situated on the southern bank of Scotland's
Loch Ness, was unoccupied, its owners absent. After a seven-
hour battle by over 30 fire crews, the blaze was finally extin-
guished. But the entire building had been gutted, rendered
utterly uninhabitable.

Like many aspects of the lives of both Aleister Crowley and
Jimmy Page there seemed an extraordinary poetry about this fire,
as though it were a statement from on high. Precisely why should
this have occurred on 23 December 2015, less than 36 hours
before Christmas Day, Christianity's principal celebration?

Page bought Boleskine in 1970. Not only did the purchase satisfy his fascination – some might say obsession – with the work and life of Aleister Crowley – 'I'm attracted by the unknown,' the Zeppelin leader told the late writer Timothy White while discussing Boleskine – but the 18th-century property was intended to be a retreat where the Led Zeppelin guitarist could muster his forces and write new material.

Charles Pace, an occult artist, was commissioned to paint appropriately atmospheric magic murals in the house. Then Page called Miss Pamela to ask her to search out some rare Crowley works that he had heard were in a Hollywood bookstore; this included a copy of Crowley's sexually explicit *White Stains*, privately published in an edition of a hundred copies in 1898: almost every book had been confiscated and destroyed by Her Majesty's Customs, alerted to how variations of sodomy, pederasty, bestiality and necrophilia are interwoven into the verse. What Miss Pamela found was 'a killer-diller item: a typed manuscript with notes in the margins written by Al himself. Jimmy wired me $1,700 and I sent this treasure across the ocean, wishing I could go with it.'

As some sort of exchange for his wounded seemingly exgirlfriend, Page did send Pamela a Christmas present, a necklace bearing an antique turquoise phoenix, which contained a beautiful pearl. And there was a note: 'For my dear P. With all my love at Christmas, Jimmy. XXXXXXX' Seven kisses, in numerological terms the number of the intellectual explorer of the obscure; Page's interests in other dimensions had brought him a measure of self-knowledge.

In the end, however, despite owning the house for over 20 years before he finally sold it, Page never spent more than a total of six weeks at Boleskine. Yet he had still been observed driving in the Loch Ness area in a Land Rover, a set of stag's antlers resplendent on the vehicle's bonnet, as though he were a Scottish aristocrat.

Certainly Page's purchase of Crowley's Scottish home confirmed the musician's interest in the Beast 666, as Crowley styled himself, a nickname first bestowed on him by his mother; in consideration of this apparent parental damnation, it should never be overlooked that Crowley's extremely erudite writings reveal a man with an attractively impish sense of humour, someone who clearly didn't take himself as seriously as might first be suspected. Although Crowley had been given that damning 'wickedest man in the world' rubric by the *Daily Express* columnist John Bull in 1923, his reputation in less orthodox circles had only risen since those days. And in hip mid-sixties London Page was far from the only aficionado of the visionary that he perceived Crowley to be.

None other than the mighty Beatles had declared their allegiance to Crowley in the most public of ways: by including his image among those of the inspirational figures collated by artist Peter Blake on the cover of their *Sgt. Pepper's Lonely Hearts Club Band* LP. The record sleeve has Crowley's shaven head and bulging eyes peering from between Indian guru Sri Yukteswar Giri and actress Mae West: aptly, as mysticism and sex formed the heart of Crowley's life, his libidinous appetites apparently undiminished by his extreme heroin intake later in life. Other figures sharing space on the *Sgt. Pepper* cover with Crowley – Aldous Huxley, Carl Jung, Sri Mahavatar Babaji and Sri Paramahansa Yogananda – show that by the time the Beatles came to know about the Beast, magic, mysticism and altered states had become the seminal ideas driving the counter-culture.

Shortly before his death John Lennon gave an interview to David Sheff for *Playboy* magazine. 'The whole Beatles idea was to do what you want ... do what thou wilst, as long as it doesn't hurt anybody' – he misquoted Crowley's famous edict, 'Do what thou wilt', which, in the parlance of the time, transmogrified into the indulgent hippie mantra of 'Do your thing'. In fact,

Crowley was speaking of a need to find oneself and one's own path in life, one's purpose. As to the choice of Crowley and others on the cover of *Sgt. Pepper*, Paul McCartney commented that such individuals were 'our heroes'; Ringo Starr acknowledged that they were people 'we like and admire'. Interestingly, the album sleeve is full of masonic symbolism. There are eleven freemasons depicted: of these eleven, three are master masons – Karl Marx, H. G. Wells and Crowley. (Is it not worth bearing in mind that EMI, for whom the Beatles recorded, had always been whispered to be a hotbed of freemasonry?)

Among underground figureheads, LSD champion Timothy Leary was extremely influenced by Crowley's vision. David Bowie referred to Crowley in 'Quicksand' on his 1972 album *Hunky Dory* – he was 'immersed in Crowley's uniform', he sang. (According to Angie Bowie, for a time Bowie believed he was in a secret duel with Page to become head warlock and chief Crowley acolyte.) On the rear cover of the Doors' 1970 compilation album *13*, Jim Morrison and the other members of the group are shown posing with a bust of Crowley. In 1980, on his first solo album, Ozzy Osbourne released a tune titled 'Mr Crowley'. Iron Maiden, of course, recorded 'The Number of the Beast', also giving their 1982 album on which it featured that title. Marilyn Manson has said he is a follower of Crowley. And Manic Street Preachers feature Crowley in the video for their song 'You Love Us'.

At the peak of his interest, Jimmy Page owned Crowley's 'artefacts – books, first editions, manuscripts, hats, canes, paintings, even the robes in which Crowley had conducted rituals'. There were apparently mumblings of discontent from less well-heeled Crowleyites that the guitarist was hogging so much Crowley arcana.

Aleister Crowley was a man of considerable achievements. Not only was he a prolific writer and poet, he was also – for a while – arguably the world's finest mountaineer. The author

Somerset Maugham even declared him to be 'the best whist player of his time'. Reputedly responsible for introducing yoga to Western society, Crowley was also a prominent member of the Hermetic Order of the Golden Dawn, the late-19th and early 20th-century society dedicated to the exploration of metaphysics, headed during Crowley's membership by W. B. Yeats, the great Irish poet. Breaking away from the Golden Dawn, Aleister Crowley joined the Ordo Templi Orientis, the O.T.O., as it is more familiarly known. Although it was founded at the beginning of the 20th century by Carl Kellner and Theodor Reuss, Aleister Crowley soon became its leader, reorganising it with the Law of Thelema as its religious core.

Indeed, Crowley was most famous, or infamous, for having founded Thelema, a religion whose beliefs had been, he asserted, dictated to him while he was in Cairo, Egypt, on 8–10 April in the year 1904 by Aiwass, a mystic entity. Allegedly 'channelled' to him, the knowledge Crowley received was published as *The Book of the Law*. One of Thelema's principal tenets was a belief in the power of tantric sex, which Crowley defined as 'sex magick'. It was a reputation that lingered among its disciples, and was much of the cause behind rumours about Page.

Boleskine was built on the site of a church that had burned down during the 10th century, along with its congregation, as mass was being celebrated. The house was constructed as a hunting lodge in the late 18th century by Archibald Fraser, the son of Lieutenant General Simon Fraser, Lord Lovat, whose estate surrounded Boleskine's land. The head of an executed man – believed to be a previous Lord Lovat who fought with the English during the 1745 Jacobite Rising – allegedly could be heard rolling around the house. 'I certainly used to hear the "rolling of the head",' wrote the Beast in his autobiography, *The Confessions of Aleister Crowley*, 'but when I put in a billiard table, the old gentleman preferred it to the corridor and confined his amusements to the gunroom. Even before that, he had always stopped at the pylon of the corridor which marked off from the rest of the house the wing which was consecrated to Abramelin ... We used to listen at the door of the gunroom, and the head would roll merrily up and down the table with untiring energy. The moment we opened the door the noise would stop.'

Crowley's father was a leading figure in the Plymouth Brethren, a fundamentalist Christian sect almost guaranteed to lead to rebellion in his offspring. And his intelligent son certainly did that: while still a teenager, Crowley had come to loathe the notion of organised Christianity, viewing it as a system to control its subjects – in fact, he took this further, detesting all organised religion. Part of his belief system hinged on what he considered true Christianity, the original Gnostic church, which portrayed Christ as a rebel, entwined in a sexual relationship with Mary Magdalene – part of the inspiration for Crowley's theory of 'sex magick'.

When his father passed away Crowley was 11 years old: he came into a fortune, inheriting the wealth of the successful family brewery. Crowley bought Boleskine in 1899, when he was only 25. He had been searching for an appropriate location to carry out a series of rituals from *The Book of Abramelin*, a text central to Thelema, that would enable him to make contact with his holy guardian angel.

A secluded property was required with a north-facing door, which Boleskine had. From there Crowley would deliver the requisite words to the demons, and when they appeared on Boleskine's terrace he would banish them.

This process would take up to six months. During this time Crowley was obliged to remain in residence at Boleskine, tending to his enactments. Midway through the ritual, however, he was obliged to suddenly depart for Paris on urgent business. The consequence was that the demons were left en masse at Boleskine.

Or so the legend runs. In 1970 the house was bought by Page. Especially attractive to him was the notion of finding your true purpose in life, which Crowley's rituals could go a long way to uncovering.

In his 1975 interview with Timothy White, the guitarist said of Boleskine: 'Strange things have happened in that house which have nothing to do with Crowley. The bad vibes were already there.'

Although he bought Boleskine House as a retreat in which he intended to immerse himself in work, its remote location made this hard to achieve. Yet Page's intellectual and emotional relationship with the legacy of Crowley certainly added to the guitarist's mystique. Later, when stories emerged of – among other things – the whips he would carry with him on tour, this only intensified the dark sexual aura he already held in his very appearance, with its more than glimmer of androgyny. There were whispered tales, apocryphal no doubt, of Page, when Led Zeppelin kicked off, ensuring that all the business details were in place, with everything set to go: but, just in case, he had also sacrificed a goat. And another, equally preposterous, asserted that, in order to guarantee success, three members of Led Zeppelin each signed their recording contract in blood – John Paul Jones had demurred. There are those who do not believe this myth to be preposterous.

A suggestion of something extremely dark at the core of Led Zeppelin became part of the group's myth, even adding to its attraction, in a kind of B-movie Hammer-horror or Dennis Wheatley-novel way. But then Page was already very aware of the power of mystique in rock 'n' roll. Later, Ed Bicknell, who became the manager of Dire Straits, would report on Peter Grant telling him how he would always play the guitarist's interests in the dark arts to their advantage: 'It was really useful sometimes, especially when we went into a record company office. Sometimes I'd take Jimmy into Atlantic in New York and everybody would hide in their offices because they thought he was going to put a spell on them. He was very good at intimidating them.'

How had Crowley inserted himself back into contemporary culture with such an impact? Since his death in 1947, his reputation had certainly been bedraggled. But it was restored after the publication in Paris in 1960 of *Le Matin des Magiciens*, a kind of compendium of the occult's greatest hits, frequently brimming with inaccuracy. Translated into English and published in 1963 as *The Morning of the Magicians*, Louis Pauwels and Jacques Bergier's tome became a zeitgeist book, one of those publications found on every thinking person's bookshelf. Among other things, it reinstated Crowley as an avatar of alternative thinking; almost inevitably, he had been a proponent of 'free love'. In the October 1967 edition of *International Times*, the influential broadsheet of the underground, a lengthy article billed him as 'Aleister Crowley: the Proto-Hippie'. Although he was on tour in the United States with the Yardbirds when the magazine was published, you can be certain that Page would have read that article.

But you can also be certain that Page would have been aware of the tragic circumstances of Crowley's death: penniless, lodged in a boarding house in the end-of-the-line East Sussex town of Hastings, still chronically addicted to heroin. As Mick Brown wrote: 'An addict to his last breath, his heroin would be despatched by Heppell's the chemists in London. He was said to be taking 11 grains of heroin a day – approximately 666 milligrams.

'On 1 December 1947, Crowley died of asthma and chronic bronchitis. The nurse at his bedside reported that his penultimate words were "I'm perplexed." And his very last words? "Sometimes I hate myself ..."'

But what is Page's actual relationship to the formal aspects of being a Thelemite? He is not a member of the O.T.O. But he had very strong relationships with some members.

'The only extant thing I know of, tying him to Thelemic religion, is the brief shot of him staring at the stele in *Lucifer Rising*,' said Steve Parsons, the former singer with the Sharks and himself a Thelemite, of the Kenneth Anger film that would cause Page such controversy. 'I find it odd that after they fell out, Anger left him in the film. Jimmy has put it on record about finding the book *Magick* when he was 14 or so, and it makes perfect sense. He wouldn't have to be a member of an organisation. His internal prowess would be on another level.'

As a deeply creative individual Page takes the attitude that he will make it anew and do it himself: he will create his own cosmic theme park, which will be called Led Zeppelin, in which he will banish what he doesn't want or need.

With Led Zeppelin he built a magical universe from such thinking. And Led Zeppelin has made a serious impact in the real world. Whatever Page does on an esoteric level, exoterically there it equally is. Put on a Led Zeppelin record and the room is full of spirits. The piece of art that he titles 'Led Zeppelin' has a profound power. There is nothing at all of the rock 'n' roll dilettante about Page.

Through soaking up what their forms have encountered, voodoo and hoodoo mutate every couple of decades. Led Zeppelin had a similar ability to soak up all influences – blues, rockabilly, soul, world music, reggae, psychedelia – and throw them back at you in a radical form. It does not always work, but when it does it is with colossal majesty. It is not music to rearrange the room, like an audio piece of soft furnishing; it is too powerful for that. There is nothing cute whatsoever about Led Zeppelin.

13

ALL THAT GLITTERS

Led Zeppelin's sixth tour of the United States of America finally got underway on 15 August 1970 in New Haven, Connecticut, under a full moon. 'Lest one think that Led Zeppelin is a sedate, socially acceptable group, he may perish the thought. Led Zeppelin is the very reincarnation of the apocalyptic bad trip,' wrote P. Gionfriddo somewhat breathlessly in the *New Haven Register*. Turning this comment on its head, the writer concluded: 'With the dust lingering behind the empty bowl, the people were going home stoned on electric Kool-Aid running full tap from Led Zeppelin's keg of true rock professionalism.'

John Paul Jones's father's declining health continued to hover over the bass player, and on 26 August the show in Cleveland, Ohio, had its start time of 8.30 moved earlier to 5.30. Jones needed the extra hours to fly home for his father's funeral. Ever the professional – as you'd expect from a man who had never missed a booked studio session – Jones played the gig and departed for the local airport and his private plane before the final encores. But the audience was so insistent that the group return to the stage that the rest of the band complied: Robert Plant busking on his harp as Jimmy Page fixed a broken string, while a local girl employed by the promoter picked up Jones's bass and joined in.

The set on this tour included 'Since I've Been Loving You', 'Out on the Tiles' and 'Bron-Y-Aur Stomp'. As was their wont, it was when Led Zeppelin reached California that they really hit their stride. On 2 September at the Oakland Coliseum, across the bay from San Francisco, the four-piece played an astonishing set. By now 'Whole Lotta Love' had evolved into a rock 'n' roll blues medley, which would be set inside the original structure of the tune. At Oakland the mixture included John Lee Hooker's 'Boogie Chillen'', Carl Perkins's 'Boppin' the Blues', Lloyd Price's 'Lawdy Miss Clawdy', 'For What It's Worth' by Page and Plant's beloved Buffalo Springfield, Don Hinton's rockabilly classic 'Honey Bee', Muddy Waters' 'Long Distance Call', Hank Snow's 'I'm Moving On', Allen Toussaint's 'Fortune Teller' and Arthur Crudup's 'That's All Right Mama'; this choice of cover material gives a sense of how broad were the tastes and influences within Led Zeppelin. Similarly, the structure of 'Communication Breakdown' was broken up so that 'Good Times Bad Times' could be slipped inside it.

Moving down to the US–Mexico border the following night, they played the Sports Arena in San Diego. Suffering from malfunctioning equipment during his acoustic set, Page scrapped his intended performance of 'Bron-Y-Aur', shifting into 'Since I've Been Loving You' instead.

The next night, Friday 4 September 1970, at the Forum in Los Angeles, Led Zeppelin were at their peak. At least two bootlegged albums of the show have since appeared, most notably *Live on Blueberry Hill*, named after Fats Domino's huge 1956 hit, which Zeppelin played as an encore. Among other highlights was a rare performance of 'Out on the Tiles', both heavy-metal thunder and Beatle-like pop, and a version of 'Communication Breakdown' that segued into snatches of 'Good Times Bad Times', 'For What It's Worth' and the Beatles' 'I Saw Her Standing There'.

The group's acoustic set was also rapturously received. Immediately after the show, they headed to the celebrated Troubador on Santa Monica Boulevard in West Hollywood, where they joined Fairport Convention onstage during their second set of the evening.

UK recognition was also officially theirs when they were voted Best Group in the World in the *Melody Maker* readers' poll, usurping the now defunct Beatles. On 16 September, Zeppelin, minus Jones, attended *Melody Maker*'s awards ceremony at London's luxurious Savoy Hotel. They were photographed with Fairport Convention's Sandy Denny, who had won the Best Female Vocalist award.

The next month, at Island Studios, Page played both electric and slide guitar on 'Lady Wonder' for Mike Heron, a solo effort by this member of the extremely influential Incredible String Band; accompanying him were Fairport Convention's bass player Dave Pegg and drummer Dave Mattacks. At Abbey Road's Studio 3 that October he also played acoustic guitar on Roy Harper's 'The Same Old Rock', a song on Harper's *Harvest* LP, produced by Peter Jenner.

Earlier in the year, Page had been in touch with Richard Drew, who worked under the name of Zacron; Drew had been at Kingston College of Art, where he had become friends with Eric Clapton. Page asked him to work on the sleeve design for the new album, taking as its basic premise a rotating volvelle based on crop-rotation calendars.

So elaborate was the resulting packaging that Atlantic Records required a formal meeting to figure out where their own logo would sit. In the end it was tucked in amidst the assorted images of this most pop art of record covers. Note that the label is given as 'Atlantic Deluxe', indicating a higher cost than usual for this LP, thanks to its very expensive sleeve.

In a similar vein to the collage of images on the *Sgt. Pepper* sleeve, *Led Zeppelin III*'s was dotted with chunks of quasi-symbolism.

For example, the image of a walnut at the top of the sleeve front, above the second 'p' of Zeppelin, is 'like a thing cruising through the sky with a brain in it. A boat that can think,' said Drew. There's a vintage car crossing a bridge, with the initials 'JP' on it: the picture was shot on the humpbacked bridge coming into Pangbourne. A man who had been seated in a boat near Guildford was turned, thought Drew, into 'a sort of Mary Poppins'. The image of a screw in almost the centre of the sleeve insert was a reference to the complicated construction of the revolving cover – and perhaps to something else.

But in a way the elaborate revolving cover was a mistake: along with the inscriptions from Crowley on each side of the vinyl, it took away from the greatness of the music, almost overwhelming it and becoming the main talking point about *Led Zeppelin III*. The sleeve seemed almost like a gimmick, something Page had always hated in pop music. Wouldn't a single image on the front of a simple card sleeve have been more potent?

Led Zeppelin III was released on 5 October in the US and 18 days later in the UK. The record had advance orders – which means the number of copies ordered in by stores – of 750,000 in America and 60,000 in the UK. Accordingly, on its first day on sale in the US the record went gold.

Whereas its predecessor had been a highly successful hotch-potch of songs recorded in the unlikeliest of circumstances, *Led Zeppelin III* had been conceived in less stressful conditions, allowing time for it to be considered much more as a total work.

Yet, mystifyingly, critics were no kinder. Lester Bangs's *Rolling Stone* review began with a devastating putdown: his relationship with the group, he said, sprang from 'genuine interest and indefensible hopes, in part from the conviction that nobody that crass could be all that bad'. 'Most of the acoustic stuff,' he continued, 'sounds like standard Zep graded down decibel-wise, and the heavy blitzes could've been outtakes from *Zeppelin II*. In fact, when I first heard the album my main impression was the consistent anonymity of most of the songs.'

The *Los Angeles Times* went further, in its pseudo-analysis of the nature of the group's fans: 'Their success may be attributable at least in part to the accelerating popularity among the teenage rock 'n' roll audience of barbiturates and amphetamines, drugs that render their users most responsive to crushing volume and ferocious histrionics of the sort Zeppelin has heretofore dealt in exclusively.'

Why did Led Zeppelin draw out such intellectual snobbery among critics? It wasn't just in the US; many music writers in the UK would also snigger about Page's group. In fact, the record's contents precisely exemplified his initial concept of Led Zeppelin: that it would reflect 'light and shade'. Although I might carp at the weaknesses of 'Immigrant Song', *Led Zeppelin III* has more than stood the test of time as one of the group's very greatest works and a testament to the guitarist's creative vision.

By now Page had become a collector of classic cars: a Bentley, a Cord Sportsman, an Austin Champ and an ancient Mercedes, among others. Yet still he never learned to drive; from time to time he would head down to his garage and sit in these motorised pieces of art.

To possess a skill so prosaic as the ability to drive could have been advantageous. For he had been on the lookout for a new country property, and no such home would be accessible without a motor vehicle.

As 1970 drew to a close, Jimmy Page was moving house. His boathouse in Pangbourne had become known to fans, some of whom would attempt to pay him a visit, and, besides, with Charlotte Martin pregnant, it was too small a home in which to raise a family.

The musician had discovered a country estate for sale in East Sussex called Plumpton Place, near Brighton and within easy commuting distance of London. The cost of the house was an indication of Page's earnings in the two years that Led Zeppelin had been running: £200,000, a colossal price at the time.

A 16th-century manor house with its own moat, Plumpton Place was an archetypal example of rock-star rococo, one that only enhanced Page's increasingly distant image. In 1927 it had been bought by Edward Hudson, the founder of *Country Life* magazine. At this time Plumpton Place was in serious need of repair, and Hudson brought in his favourite architect Edwin Lutyens and garden designer Gertrude Jekyll; they set about a major restoration of the main house, the mill house and the 60 acres of land and lakes. In 1969 George and Pattie Harrison had come across the property, which was for sale, and tried to buy it. The vendor, however, disliked the notion of one of those longhaired rock 'n' roll musicians living in her delightful abode. Accordingly, she sold it to a local doctor. Who, three years later, sold Plumpton Place to Jimmy Page. In line with what would come to be seen as Page's fondness for such matters, Plumpton Place was also haunted. People interested in occult phenomena, after all, like to hone their skills; being certain of the existence of a ghost or two would be an act of rebellion against his choir-boy upbringing; it was also somewhat sensationalist proof of his occult resilience and toughness.

In November 1970, as though in conscious defiance of the negative reviews picked up by *Led Zeppelin III*, Page and Plant returned to Bron-Yr-Aur, which was now decidedly autumnal and even more damp. There they came up with further rough song ideas, including a tune called 'Going to California' and another with the working title of 'Stairway to Heaven' – although nothing became as complete as on the previous Bron-Yr-Aur stay.

In December the four musicians reconvened in Barnes at Olympic Sound Studios to work up further ideas. But then it was decided that a more creative use of time would be for the group to stay together in one place. The original idea was to use the Rolling Stones' mobile studio while staying at Stargroves, Mick Jagger's Hampshire mansion. However, when Page discovered that in addition to paying for the recording unit, they would also be charged a high fee to stay at Jagger's house, he balked at the idea and looked elsewhere. Led Zeppelin's office was set to work finding an alternative location, and came up with Headley Grange, which had been built in 1795 as a poorhouse, and more recently had been used for rehearsals by Fleetwood Mac, who lived nearby. Headley Grange is in Headley, East Hampshire, near Bordon, on the Hampshire–Surrey border.

'It was a horrible place – cold and freezing,' said Richard Cole. 'They were all staying there, though later on it'd just be Jimmy and some of the crew that kept rooms. It was too miserable for the rest of us.

'They'd all wander downstairs at different times. Jimmy would be messing around with something. Jonesy would listen in and add a little bit to it. Robert would sit there writing his lyrics. It was as informal as that.'

Unsurprisingly, Headley Grange was rumoured to be haunted. Again, you might question what it was that drew Page to buildings that contained evident spirits. As he was someone who spent so much of his time in an alternative world, might you not feel that this somehow brought him comfort? Except this doesn't seem to always have been the case. 'It was very Charles Dickens ... I'm pretty sure it was haunted,' Page told Brad Tolinski in 2002. 'I remember going up the main staircase on the way to my room one night and seeing a grey shape at the top. I double-checked to see if it was just a play of light, and it wasn't – so I turned around pretty fast, because I didn't really want to have an encounter with something like that.'

Notwithstanding such spectral visions, the miserable winter weather focused Led Zeppelin's collective mind and they worked hard. There were to be six days of rehearsals, followed by six days of recording; the Rolling Stones' mobile was brought in, Andy Johns at the controls.

Often when an artist attempts a new style – as Led Zeppelin had done with *III* – their effort is initially dismissed, until a subsequent significant work allows it to become appreciated as transitional, moving their art on to a further level.

All the same, Page had been aware of the extent to which his group was perceived as a cock-rock boys' band, one with a largely male audience. Since the spring of 1970 at his Pangbourne home he had consciously been evolving an epic work that female fans of the group would respond to. 'It begins with the concept of trying to have something that would unravel in layers as the song progressed,' he told the *Guardian*'s Michael Hann. 'You've got the fragile guitar that is going to open the whole thing, you've got the vocal over that fragile guitar, and then it moves into the more sensual wave with the twin 12-strings, and the electric piano as well.'

Although none of the group appreciated at the time what an impact the song would have, it was at Headley Grange that the writing and original recording of 'Stairway to Heaven' was completed, the beginning roughed out in Wales.

'The music came first,' said Page to Pete Frame. 'I'd written it over a long period; the intro in Bron-Yr-Aur, in the cottage, and other parts came together piece by piece.'

Most of Robert Plant's words effectively poured out of him in a stream of consciousness as he sat on the floor at Headley Grange, in front of a blazing fire with a notepad. 'When we came to record it, at Headley Grange,' said Page, 'we were so inspired by how the song could come out, with the building passages and all the possibilities, that Robert came out with the lyrics just like that … I'd say that he produced 8o per cent of the lyrics almost immediately.'

And the singer's words and the music of 'Stairway to Heaven' intertwined with perfect harmoniousness. 'Bonzo and Jonesy had gone off to the Speakeasy Club in London – to relax, I think that's a good term for it,' said Plant. 'Jimmy and I stayed in, and we got the theme and the thread of it there and then.'

By slowly speeding up, 'Stairway to Heaven' defied conventional recording rules. In fact, it was essential for Page that the song's tempo would gradually build. 'You would find that, having been a studio musician,' he observed, 'the one thing any trained musician will tell you that you don't do is speed up or slow down. This, as far as I could see, was in league with the whole concept of classical writing where everything is moving, moving, moving.'

In time 'Stairway to Heaven' would become the most played song ever on FM radio in the US, with over three million plays totted up by the year 2000 – an extraordinary achievement by any standard, but given that the song logged in at just over eight minutes, simply remarkable. Despite his ambitions for the song, Page at first saw nothing especially unique in it; but as he worked on it more and more, with John Paul Jones also working on the arrangement, he felt a growing magical quality: 'It would keep unfolding and more layers would be introduced into the equation. Keeping John Bonham on drums to come in for effect was a trick I'd used before, on things like "Ramble On". I knew that would be successful, because whenever he came in he made so much difference. And then it's two more verses before you get to the solo, with this sort of fanfare approach to it. Then everything's flying at that point.'

'There's almost a hysterical trill at the end of the solo that leads into the finale … "And as we wind on down the road …" It's like an orgasm at the end. It's whatever you want it to be,' said Plant, emphasising the ever-present sexuality in the music of Led Zeppelin.

With Jones on keyboard and Page on acoustic guitar, they structured the separate sections, working out how they would elide with each other. As the group leader had said, for maximum impact Bonham's hammering drums were to be held back. 'When John Bonham comes into it,' Page told the *Guardian* in 2014, 'you need to have the confidence that he knows there's a whole passage that's going to go by without him coming in, otherwise he's going to think, "That's a bit shambolic. I'll just come in at the beginning." It needed proper structure and proper discipline right from the beginning. And then Robert's writing his lyrics, and it's almost like he's channelled the damn thing.'

Page has always insisted that, above all else, it is Plant's words – the only Zeppelin lyrics ever printed on one of their albums, in an Arts and Crafts typeface – that make 'Stairway to Heaven' the song that it is. 'I contributed to the lyrics on the first three albums, but I was always hoping that Robert would eventually take care of that aspect of the band,' he said.

The subject of Plant's words is materialism and those who believe that possessions can lead to salvation, personified by the woman who fallaciously believes all that glitters is gold and it will buy her that stairway to heaven. Although cloaked in pastoral Romanticism, the song is a kind of blues lament against selfish gold-digger females, a grasping breed all four members of Led Zeppelin would have encountered during their treks on tour. And as the song comes to its close there is salvation, as we are shown there is another way to lead our lives. In the somewhat impenetrable maze of its mystical narrative there was a universal truth; each listener was able to interpret it according to his or her experience – which was why it held such resonance for the colossal amount of record buyers of *Led Zeppelin IV*. Like so many similar parables, its meaning was ripe for dissection – which both Plant and Page always studiously avoided.

Plant also cleverly allowed the potential for turning any interpretation of the lyrics on their head with the suggestive, ambiguous line: 'Cause you know sometimes words have two meanings ...'

Page would come to consider that 'Stairway to Heaven' 'crystallised the essence of the band. It had everything there and showed us at our best. It was a milestone. Every musician wants to do something of lasting quality, something which will hold up for a long time. We did it with "Stairway".'

14

THE LEGEND OF ZOSO

On a February afternoon in 1971, Bruno Wizard, a denizen of the very rundown Notting Hill, was walking along Portobello Road with a friend. All of a sudden a white Rolls-Royce Silver Cloud pulled up next to them. The rear window rolled down to reveal the faces of Jimmy Page and Robert Plant. 'Hey,' Page said, summoning Wizard over. 'Do you know anywhere we can get some hash?'

Bruno Wizard, who clearly looked the kind of character to whom such a question might be posed, was delighted. In his flat around the corner he had eight ounces of such a substance: recently purchased, powerful black Afghani hashish. Answering in the affirmative, he was given an address – Island Records' Basing Street Studios.

From Headley Grange Led Zeppelin had moved back to London, checking in to Island Studio 1. When Bruno and his mate delivered the goods, they were then permitted to hang out in the studio with the superstar musicians. 'What I realised,' said Bruno, 'was that just because people were huge rock stars, they still had to go out and find their drugs. They didn't magic-ally arrive in their lives.'

As Bruno and his friend lounged on one of the studio's couches, rolling joints, Page turned to Plant: 'So do you want to try out those lyrics for that song?'

Nodding, Plant stepped up to the mike. And opened his voice: 'There's a lady who's sure all that glitters is gold …'

'So I was there at an epochal moment,' recalled Bruno. Later, in the punk era, Bruno would form his own band, the Homosexuals, becoming a musical *éminence grise*, a true lyrical philosopher.

The engineer for these sessions was Phil Brown, who had worked with the group at Olympic Sound Studios on their first album. He felt there had been a distinct shift since the innocence of those days.

'It was really rough,' he told author Paul Rees. 'Peter Grant was there pretty much all the time. He used to sit either with me at the mixing desk or on this big settee behind. He unnerved me. He was like an East End hood. He was about 350 pounds then – big, sweaty and aggressive. Having him sat there with a couple of 220-pound minders, it wasn't the usual way we did things at Island.

'At that point Jimmy Page seemed really messed up. There were obviously a lot of drugs around but he was also into this Aleister Crowley thing. It just put an edge to the session. There was something unpleasant about the whole thing.

'The rest of the band were okay. Robert seemed very polite. He'd make the odd comment but more to Page than anyone else. John Paul Jones was a bit of a sweetheart, very clever music-ally. Bonham could be full-on and aggressive, though I didn't see him that much because he wasn't needed.'

'Unlike at the Grange,' writes Rees, 'the pace of work was slow and laborious. Time and again Page took a pass at his "Stairway to Heaven" solo.' 'The track was still in something of a skeletal state,' recalled Brown. 'We did take after take with Page and for days on end. Robert told me that Jimmy does a lot of experimenting, and out of all the best bits he moulds a solo. Nothing was explained to me at the time, though. I was just left to wonder what the hell was going on.'

As he had on 'Since I've Been Loving You' on the third LP, Page worked ceaselessly on his Telecaster to establish the absolutely appropriate guitar solo for the song. He had three distinctly separate examples, finally deciding almost arbitrarily late one night which one he would use; it would become the most famous solo in the history of popular music. 'I had the first phrase worked out, and a link phrase here and there, but on the whole that solo was improvised. I think I played it through a Marshall,' he told Brad Tolinski.

The layering of guitars on 'Stairway to Heaven' posed some difficulties. 'I've employed so many guitars on "Stairway" – there are two lots of 12-strings going on, there's an acoustic, there's a solo – that how am I gonna do this live? The answer to that was a double-necked guitar, so I could do the opening on the 6-string, go to the 12-string, do the solo on the 6-string, then go back to the 12-string. That seemed to make the most sense.' Page knew what he needed: a 12- and 6-stringed Gibson. He had wanted one ever since he saw bluesman Earl Hooker working with one. Although they were no longer in production, Gibson agreed to come up with the double-neck for Page, a custom-built, cherry-red EDS-1275. It would become an additional element of his onstage mystique. (To maintain the song's profundity when it was performed live, Plant was instructed by Peter Grant not to speak after the band had finished 'Stairway to Heaven'.)

'Page was all over the shop, too,' remembered Phil Brown. 'Out of tune a lot of the time. He didn't communicate with me at all. A lot of it was done in the control room, through an amp in the studio and with him sat right next to me. He would just go: "Again … Again … Again." It was all very aggressive. He seemed a dark character, that's the only way I can explain it.'

Or did Jimmy Page seem 'dark' simply because he was so immersed in his art? For ultimately this album would prove to be Led Zeppelin's defining statement, an enormous success with around 40 million copies sold.

The record itself? Well, what was it called? The truth is, no one knew. In defiance at the reception given critically to *Led Zeppelin III*, Page was adamant that what was clearly *Led Zeppelin IV* should have no title – or the name of the artist – on its cover whatsoever. That this would lead to record-company apoplexy at the removal of such a clear and useful marketing device should be no great surprise.

Visiting a second-hand shop in Reading, on the way to Headley Grange with Jimmy Page, Robert Plant unearthed a 19th-century painting of a rustic character bent low by the burden he carried on his back. This figure, Page would immediately have noted, bore a distinct resemblance to 'Old George' Pickingill, who it was believed had first instructed Aleister Crowley in the occult arts.

Is this story true? Or was the image of this fellow created specifically for the album? Furthermore, although this rustic figure is considerably older, there is a distinct resemblance to the character in the tarot card the Ten of Wands. The Ten of Wands can be interpreted as the need to rise to responsibilities and pressure, which Page certainly felt work on this new album was realising.

Whatever its provenance, this was the central image that featured on the front sleeve of Zeppelin's fourth album, affixed to a decaying house wall and overlooked by a Birmingham tower block; almost unnoticed is a poster for Oxfam that reads: 'Someone dies from hunger everyday.' Were Led Zeppelin – or more likely Page, who was heavily involved with the design of each LP sleeve – professing to be carrying the weight of the eco world on their back? That seemed the most clear reading, confirmed by the guitarist in an interview with Dave Schulps of *Trouser Press* in 1977: 'It represented the change in the balance which was going on. There was the old countryman and the blocks of flats being knocked down. It was just a way of saying that we should look after the earth, not rape and pillage it.'

'The cover was supposed to be something that was for other people to savour rather than for me to actually spell everything out, which would make the whole thing rather disappointing on that level of your own personal adventure into the music,' he told James Jackson in *The Times* in January 2010, indicating how broad the levels of creative thought were that overhung every area of Led Zeppelin, the personal suzerainty of Jimmy Page.

Each member of Led Zeppelin was represented on the sleeve by a sigil, a rune-like symbol, a clear reflection of Page's occult interests, and also of Robert Plant, even if the latter's were less obsessive: the singer's fondness for the Viking oracle method of runes had been solidified on the group's trip to Iceland.

These were not archetypal symbols but devised by each individual in the band. Both John Paul Jones and John Bonham took their sigils from Rudoph Koch's *The Book of Signs*. Jones's image was appropriately of an individual who possessed both confidence and competence. Bonham's three interlocking rings represented the man, woman and child – of his marriage, presumably; twisted upside down, much to the delight of the rest of the band, Bonham's image became the logo of Ballantine beer, his Midlands local brew. Robert Plant devised his own symbolic image, a feather within a circle, an icon that spoke very much of Native Americans but which the singer claimed was sourced from the ancient Mu civilisation.

But what of Jimmy Page's rune, the sigil that became known as Zoso, which *Led Zeppelin IV* was sometimes called before Page himself adopted it as a kind of sobriquet? (He even named his own photographic autobiography, published much later, *Zoso*.) As might be expected from the ever precise and measured Page, the origins of Zoso were considerably more arcane.

In recent years it has become known that the world's most prolific collector of paintings by Austin Osman Spare, sometimes described as Britain's greatest unknown artist, is Jimmy Page. The work he has collected includes Spare's 1907 *Portrait of the Artist*. It should not surprise you to learn that Spare was not only a visionary artist, but also a philosopher and occult musician; he was the inspiration for what is now known as chaos magic. One of Spare's specialities were his sidereal paintings, as though you were looking at a cinema screen from the side. Looking at Spare's paintings, you may receive similar impressions as you would when listening to the music of Led Zeppelin: images from the far, far past coupled with those from a distant science-fiction future – what you imagine and what you see are equally valid and interrelated.

Spare was a Clerkenwell policeman's son who became a teenage painting prodigy, celebrated in exhibitions while still at the Royal College of Art. Turned off by the commercial art world, he rebelled, downgrading himself and selling his work at what were nothing more than inebriated evenings masquerading as exhibition openings in south London pubs. Always taken with notions of mysticism and other worlds, Spare – like his mentor for a brief time, Aleister Crowley – claimed to have had direct experience of the existence of extra-terrestrial intelligence. (Around the time of the recording of *Led Zeppelin IV*, Spare was championed by Kenneth Grant, a protégé of Crowley, in the popular *Man, Myth and Magic* encyclopaedia partwork, which commenced publication in 1970.)

Among the several methods through which Spare communicated his art was his use of sigils, influenced by Egyptian hieroglyphics. He would elaborate these sigils by condensing letters of the alphabet into what have been described as 'diagrammatic glyphs of desire, which were to be integrated in postural practices' – yoga, in other words. These sigils would thereby become 'monograms of thought, for the government of energy'. Spare was endeavouring to rediscover the evangelical concept of the 'word' as a magical complex image. 'Spare's "sentient symbols" and his "alphabet of desire" situate this mediatory magic in a libidinal framework of Tantric – which is to say cosmological – proportions.'

Also a writer, in his grimoire *The Book of Pleasure* Spare spoke of the Zos Kia Cultus, a philosophy of magic he developed that focuses on one's individual universe and the influence of the magician's will on it; a way of thinking – influenced by Crowley – that was very familiar to Page.

And Zos, of course, is only one letter away from Zoso. For his part Page has often maintained that Zoso was intended purely as a representative of Saturn, the ruling planet of his Capricorn sun sign, the ruler of hard work, adamantine will and strength, and necessary strengthening restriction.

The influence of Austin Osman Spare on Page's choice of rune – or sigil – seems rather clear.

The occult elements of the sleeve were only followed through on the central gatefold image, a painting that was a reworking of the Hermit, the ninth card of the Major Arcana in the Rider-Waite tarot pack, which represents Prudence. The staff the Hermit bears is a symbol of his authority. In its archetypal sense the Hermit, a reclusive, solitary figure, shines the light of a lamp on matters, and desires to give solitary time for thought to himself, while simultaneously not permitting others to stand in his way. The Hermit represents a character who has acquired or is seeking to acquire wisdom in order to better guide others using his lantern, very much as you might imagine Page may have perceived himself at that time. As an image it evidently appealed to him: in the 1976 Led Zeppelin film *The Song Remains the Same*, he would choose such a character as a representation of himself. (Interestingly, here Page appeared to be crossing party lines: Crowley himself allegedly disapproved of the Rider-Waite tarot pack, and set about having his own set devised, the Thoth deck; Waite had been a member of the Golden Dawn at the same time as Crowley and was considered a direct rival by Page's spiritual mentor.)

It is worth bearing in mind that, as we see things coming to pass in the life of Jimmy Page, the Hermit, despite its positive and success-inspiring energies, is warning against the isolation that could be harmful to him at certain times: it is very important that he always endeavours to achieve the right balance. The Hermit invites us to discover wisdom and the progress that comes with study; the card also indicates that the Hermit is a person of integrity, but that he is scared to trust in others and completely express what he is feeling – very much as Page was, polite to the point of sometimes being a little boring. The painting of the Hermit on the inner sleeve was by a supposed friend of Page called Barrington Coleby. There is no record whatsoever of any such person, and there were those who believed the real painter was none other than Page himself.

All the same, there was something very appealing and romantic about the notion of Jimmy Page as a rock 'n' roll recluse, dabbling with potions and spells in his high tower.

There were certainly magical elements to the design of the *Led Zeppelin IV* LP sleeve; could these in any way have helped contribute to its astonishing success, both commercially and creatively?

But above that, there was the stunning music. The record drew you in straightaway with 'Black Dog', supposedly named after a literal black Labrador retriever at Headley Grange, but containing an interesting double-meaning: the 'black dog' was, of course, Winston Churchill's euphemism for the spells of depression that afflicted him from time to time. Both being intelligent men, you imagine Page and Plant were aware of this. This 'Black Dog', however, was a powerful anti-depressant, like musical cocaine. There was nothing downer whatsoever about this pounding, primal tune with one of Page's characteristic low-register fuzz riffs. Although always present, the guitarist is very restrained: holding back, nothing really flashy going on at all, punctuating the tune with perfect panache. 'Rock and Roll', the next tune, maintains the pace, charging relentlessly on, living up to its title, fresh and exciting. The combination of the two tunes is an invigorating way to start an album.

Track three, 'The Battle of Evermore', which at first seems to be returning us to the light and shade of the previous record, has a great sense of confidence and clarity about it. An old folk song, replete with additional Tolkien references in Plant's lyrics, and a determined blues-like drive.

Page wrote it on the mandolin, an instrument he'd never played before, at Headley Grange one afternoon. In 1977 he told *Guitar Player* magazine: 'On "The Battle of Evermore", a mandolin was lying around. It wasn't mine, it was Jonesey's. I just picked it up, got the chords and it sort of started happening. I did it more or less straight off. But, you see, that's fingerpicking again, going back to the studio days and developing a certain amount of technique – at least enough to be adapted and used. My fingerpicking is a sort of cross between Pete Seeger, Earl Scruggs and total incompetence.'

With Plant in the room tossing out lyrics inspired by a book on Scottish history the singer had read, appended by thoughts from Robert Graves's *The White Goddess* and Lewis Spence's *The Magic Arts in Celtic Britain*, the song emerged, fully formed, almost straightaway. As is evident from the words, they concern the battle between night and day, good and evil. There is a reference to 'Avalon'.

'The band was sitting next to the chimney in Headley, drinking tea,' recalled sound engineer Andy Johns, 'when Jimmy grabbed a mandolin and started playing. I gave him a microphone and stuck a Gibson echo on his mandolin. Jimmy had brought this stuff before and had asked me to take a look at it.

Suddenly Robert started singing and this amazing track was born from nowhere.'

As on 'Black Dog', Page again reverses into 'The Battle of Evermore' with gently rising volume, but now on the far more delicate mandolin, while the song featured something unique: a guest, Sandy Denny sharing the vocals with Plant. Page thought that the song 'sounded like an old English instrumental first off. Then it became a vocal and Robert did his bit. Finally we figured we'd bring Sandy by and do a question-and-answer-type thing.'

Erik Davis, who wrote a book about the album in the 33 1/3 series, considered that gender also played a role in the song, with Plant's Prince of Peace and Denny's Queen of Light occupying true male/female roles as opposed to the gender-blurred androgyny of Page and Plant themselves. As a reward for being the only singer to perform on a Led Zeppelin record other than Plant, Denny was given her own three-pyramid rune on the album sleeve.

Emotionally, the album's next song was very different to what Led Zeppelin had up until then offered to their audience. The closing tune on side one of the vinyl edition: 'Stairway to Heaven'.

Following 'Stairway' on the album was the extremely funky 'Misty Mountain Hop'. Inspired by Plant's visit to a 'legalise pot' rally in London's Hyde Park in July 1968, just before he joined what would become Led Zeppelin, the title refers to the Misty Mountains mentioned in J. R. R. Tolkien's *The Hobbit* – the perpetual, Leonine hippie in Robert Plant imbued Led Zeppelin with a necessary warmth, firing on top of not only Jimmy Page's Capricorn earthiness, but also that of John Paul Jones, another 'Cap'; Bonzo was the communicative Gemini, pounding out a life beat.

And with the meter shifting from 5/8 to 6/8, 'Four Sticks' – so titled because Bonham played the song with two sticks in each hand – was propelling a series of classic Page riffs around its complex time signature. 'It was supposed to be abstract,' the guitarist said of the song.

Although 'Going to California', first titled 'Guide to California', is sometimes said to have been inspired by Joni Mitchell's song 'California', this could not have been the case; Mitchell's *Blue* album, on which 'California' featured, did not hit the stores until June 1971. Instead it is more likely to have been influenced by Mitchell's 1968 tune 'I Had a King'.

Essentially a song of heartbreak, 'Going to California' is an acoustic number: behind Plant's vocals John Paul Jones is featured on mandolin and Page on guitar, with Bonham absent from the session. A hugely popular Led Zeppelin song, tucked in as the penultimate track on the album, it changes the character of the record; by the time it has finished you have forgotten the pounding openers of 'Black Dog' and 'Rock and Roll'.

But it is the album's closing track, 'When the Levee Breaks', that raises *Led Zeppelin IV* to even greater heights. The song matches 'Stairway to Heaven' in scope and stateliness: forceful, free, hypnotic and deceptively simple, with its timing manipulated in the studio, it is one of Zeppelin's greatest-ever recordings. The song is a lament over the Great Mississippi Flood of 1927, when the river broke through the protecting levees.

For Page it had always been the drum sound that was paramount in Led Zeppelin's recordings: refining Bonham's deeply skilled but deceptively simple meat-and-potatoes power-hammering until it became perfection, anything could be built on it. 'Distance equals depth' was Page's adage. And achieving that paradox so masterfully on 'When the Levee Breaks' was one of his finest production achievements. It was done by the simple expedient of putting Bonham's drums at the base of the naturally echoing stairwell at Headley Grange, and exaggerating that echo and slowing everyone down except Plant.

When *Led Zeppelin IV* was finally released, US rock critic Robert Christgau chose the song as the highpoint of a record he lauded: 'I think the triumph here is "When the Levee Breaks". As if by sorcery, the quasi-parodic overstatement and oddly cerebral mood of Led Zep's blues recastings is at once transcended (that is, this really sounds like a blues), and apotheosised (that is, it has the grandeur of a symphonic crescendo) while John Bonham, as ham-handed as ever, pounds out a contrapuntal tattoo of heavy rhythm.'

'I call it the heaviest track of all time,' blogged music critic Bob Lefsetz, 'because I remember the force pounding in my ears, like Bonzo was hitting the skins with baseball bats, like I was on DMT; this cut with absolutely no airplay entranced me, made me feel like I bonded with these madmen.'

In late February 1971 engineer Andy Johns, Jimmy Page and Peter Grant had flown to Los Angeles to mix the new album at Sunset Sound Recorders. Almost as soon as they arrived an earthquake hit LA. Was it an omen? By the time they returned to London and heard what had come out of Sunset Sound, they appreciated that it may well have been: they were bitterly disappointed with the results. 'I still don't know what happened,' said Page. 'Maybe the monitors were giving us a totally false sound picture, because Sunset Sound had these real state-of-the-art monitors that were able to reproduce a big stretch of frequencies. Who knows?'

They returned to Island Studios and restored the eight tracks to their true greatness, and then, almost immediately, they were off on tour again, this time a set of UK dates played at small venues. As much as anything, this back-to-their-roots tour was a public-relations exercise set up by Peter Grant, an effort to quell British complaints about Zeppelin spending all their time playing large arenas in the US.

'Stairway to Heaven' was first played live at Belfast's Ulster Hall on 5 March 1971, but the song, which Led Zeppelin would become even more associated with than 'Whole Lotta Love', drew little more than a smattering of applause. 'Stairway' was followed by another new song, 'Going to California', and Tony Wilson, reviewing in *Disc* magazine, deemed the show 'sensational'.

Getting back to their roots wasn't without its pitfalls, of course. Sniffing round the poky dressing room of Newcastle's Mayfair Ballroom, where they played their first-ever UK date, Page complained to Richard Cole: 'Once you've played in the big places, these small clubs are murder. It's nice to be near the audience, but you forget how small the dressing rooms are. At this point in our career, I think we're entitled to more luxury than this. This is really hard to believe.'

In Manchester, after a show at the university, the group visited Mr Smith's nightclub and returned to their hotel with some girls. They were hanging out in the room of promoter Tony Smith, when Page led one of the girls into the bathroom. There soon came the sound of running water, and after a few minutes smoke began to emerge from under the bathroom door. 'Jimmy had somehow started a fire in the middle of the sink with newspapers and towels,' wrote Cole. Robert Plant rushed to find a fire extinguisher, and he put out the fire – but filled the bathroom with foam. When the hotel manager arrived he was told that Page had been involved in a 'religious rite'.

'Incidentally,' wrote Cole, 'we never did find out what Jimmy's bathroom conflagration was all about. Of course, there was his growing preoccupation with the occult. Perhaps the fire was somehow related to that. When I asked him about it, all he said was, "I liked Percy's explanation best. Let's just say that it was an ancient rite that went up in flames."'

* * *

Led Zeppelin IV was finished and ready for release. But, unsurprisingly, Jimmy Page and Atlantic Records again found themselves at odds over how a Led Zeppelin record should be packaged. The Zeppelin leader was adamant that the new LP's sleeve would contain no indication whatsoever as to the identity of the act within it. Unsurprisingly, Atlantic Records in New York were equally insistent that this would mean commercial suicide. 'I had to go in personally and argue with the record company about it,' Page told Mick Wall. 'That's why the album took so long to come out, because they wanted to put a name on the cover. But I went in there with Peter, and I stayed in there even after Peter left, talking to them about it. Finally, it came down to, "Well, let's have a symbol on it" … I said, "You can't have one symbol, because no one's going to agree on what it should be. Let's have four symbols, and everyone can choose their own." And with the four symbols, that also made it *Zeppelin IV*, so it was a completely organic process.'

By so imposing the four runes on their audience Page had employed an elemental number through which Led Zeppelin were fused together: in other words, it was the record cover – and record – as spell.

From the sleeve inwards there is magic all over this record. You begin to wonder – comparing the success of both records – if Page had disempowered *Led Zeppelin III* with that Crowley inscription etched into the run-out groove? It had mystified people, and rather worried them, leaving the album with a strange, almost sinister taste for many.

At the very beginning of the next month, on 1 April 1971, the band appeared before an audience of 400 fans at the BBC's Paris Cinema on Lower Regent Street in central London. In consideration of the slim possibilities for many fans of getting tickets for Zeppelin's small-venues tour, Peter Grant had arranged for the band to play their set so it could be broadcast to the whole of the UK. In fact, the show had originally been scheduled for 25 March, but Robert Plant had developed laryngitis, a consequence of hanging out in draughty Northern dressing rooms, and they'd had to postpone. Page and Plant went to the BBC's editing facilities in Maida Vale the day after the performance to edit down the rock 'n' roll section of 'Whole Lotta Love'– losing 90 seconds of Page's guitar solo – and entirely removing 'Trucking Little Mama', 'For What It's Worth', 'Honey Bee' and 'The Lemon Song' for its broadcast slot on 4 April.

By now, there had been a significant development in the personal life of Jimmy Page. On 23 March Led Zeppelin played at the Marquee Club in London, the last day of their roots tour. The Marquee could pack in up to 500 people – in extremely uncomfortable circumstances. When Zeppelin played there the club was so rammed that it was not necessarily a pleasant experience.

The very next day, Charlotte Martin gave birth to the child conceived at Bron-Yr-Aur on Page and Plant's first songwriting expedition there: a daughter, Scarlet Lilith Eleida Page.

In the baby girl's names there were strong references to the thinking of Aleister Crowley. For example, Crowley always gave his girlfriends the nickname 'Scarlet Woman'. And Lilith, the name of one of Crowley's own children, in Jewish tradition was a predecessor of Eve, and an alleged wilderness spirit who was considered a figure of uncontrolled sexuality in the Talmud. In more recent times, specifically in esoteric circles during the 1960s and later, she has become a feminist icon, the representation of the 'bad girl'. All in all, a rather strange name for someone to give his daughter, but again, Jimmy Page – and Charlotte Martin – were kicking against convention, so often being deliberately bad themselves.

Now 27 years old, Page was on the brink of his first maturity, about to make that transition into adulthood that esoteric sources – the sort to which he would pay heed – assert arises from that age for the next four years. How would he manage to transform himself within the Peter Pan-like, perpetually immature and indulged world of rock 'n' roll? Not especially well, time would tell.

His chosen employment was not necessarily in accord with such life changes. The first few months of a child's life are not the easiest of times for a relationship, not least because of all the sleepless nights. So when Page again found himself on tour just a few weeks later, this time in Europe, it may well have come as a sense of relief for the musician.

The relief would be short-lived. On 5 July Led Zeppelin performed in Milan, at the Velodromo Vigorelli, before 15,000 fans. In those days Italian shows were notorious for heavy-handed behaviour by the local police. And this show, in a purpose-built cycling track, was no exception. As soon as Zeppelin hit the stage at 8.30, groups of left-wing radicals in the audience stormed the heavily armed riot police, who responded by firing barrages of tear gas back.

'The promoters ran onstage,' said Page. The group was asked 'to tell the crowd to stop lighting fires. So Robert asked them and suddenly there was smoke by the front of the stage and it was actually tear gas. It was just pandemonium, with nowhere immune from this blasted tear gas, including us.'

Although they endeavoured to complete their set, even when fans climbed onstage to get away from the police, the band eventually came offstage to take refuge in a backstage room. Later, Page claimed to have been 'terribly upset'. 'I couldn't believe we'd been used as the instrument for a political demonstration,' he said.

Led Zeppelin would never play Italy again.

* * *

In the summer of 1971, Roy Harper's *Stormcock* LP was released, his fifth album, on EMI's 'alternative' Harvest label. By now, immensely assisted by the 'Hats Off to (Roy) Harper' tune on Zeppelin's third album, the grizzled, eccentric folkie had become an icon of the counterculture. A powerful outsider record, with its roots in the 1960s Soho folk scene, *Stormcock* featured Jimmy Page on the track 'The Same Old Rock', which clocked in at over 12 minutes. With its heartfelt diatribe against organised religion – something Aleister Crowley would have approved of – Harper recorded his most powerful song ever. It was a triumph, only enhanced by Page's stunningly beautiful, flamenco-like blues solo, the flourishing equal of anything he'd ever recorded, with or without Led Zeppelin. On the record, which sold in only small amounts after Harvest hardly promoted it, Page was credited as 'S. Flavius Mercurius', because of his contractual agreement with Atlantic.

In stark contrast to this, there was another album that deeply offended Page's creative sensibility. The Yardbirds' Anderson Theater show in New York City on their last tour, which Epic Records had recorded, had been rejected by the band for release as a live album because the sound engineer's approach was amateurish. Among the tracks on the LP was the Yardbirds' rendition of 'I'm Confused', which – with additional lyrics – Zeppelin had released as 'Dazed and Confused'.

Now, despite the band's previous objections, Epic Records released the album in May 1971, under the title *Live Yardbirds: Featuring Jimmy Page*. Adding insult to injury, there had been attempts by the label to disguise the unsatisfactory sound with noises from, among other sources, bullfight crowds.

Incensed by Epic's perfidy, Page threatened the label with legal action unless the album was removed from the stores. Epic quickly withdrew it. Page hardly wanted such a substandard representation of his sound available in the US: tickets were already on sale for a further Led Zeppelin American tour, 31 dates set to begin on 19 August.

With no new record in the stores Atlantic were extremely sceptical about the point of their act playing the dates, with some considerable lack of perception deeming it 'professional suicide'. Although the tour had been booked in anticipation of the new record being available, the twist that timing had taken now meant that touring with nothing to promote might well have been the entire point.

The tour was fast-paced, with few days off, putting a strain on Robert Plant's voice. On 19 August, the singer's 23rd birthday, things kicked off in Vancouver, where Peter Grant famously smashed up what he believed to be a recording device. Later, it was learned that it was the local government's equipment, measuring the volume of the Zeppelin performance.

A couple of days later they were down in their favourite US city, Los Angeles, for a Saturday night show at the Forum in Inglewood, some 10 miles down La Cienega Boulevard from where they were holed up in the Hyatt House on Sunset.

When Led Zeppelin played 'Stairway to Heaven' in California for the first time, the capacity crowd responded. 'Not all of the audience stood up. It was about 25 per cent of it, and I thought, Hey, that's pretty good,' said Page. 'They were really moved and I thought, This is wonderful, this is great. This is what we hoped for, that people would be that receptive to our new music.'

Clearly invigorated in LA, the band started the following night's set at the same venue with a run-through of 'Walk Don't Run' by the Ventures, the local instrumental group that had once rivalled the Shadows and the inspiration for Page's first fuzzbox.

The *Cashbox* review of the first show was laudatory – hyperbolic, even: 'They're at it again. I feel weightless after the music's over, escaping from the crowd, riding through the quiet; time and I are strangers, atlas shrugging in the city, remembering how much I enjoy the feeling. And these are only things.

'They call it Rock AND Roll, a fragment of the truth.'

Writing in the *Los Angeles Times*, even the venerated Robert Hilburn was largely positive, if a bit sniffy, about their Forum set: 'I do, strangely, have something nice to say about Led Zeppelin. Not without reservations, mind you, but at least something. Let me explain. There are some rock groups that strike me as so unimportant and uninteresting, both musically and sociologically, that there doesn't seem to be any reason to ever see them again. Deep Purple is an excellent recent example.

'There are other groups, however, that may be depressingly tedious musically, but there is something interesting about their concert – either in an occasional strong piece of music or an ability to create an unusually high degree of audience enthusiasm – that makes you feel another look at the group is justified. Grand Funk – perhaps the clearest current example of low musical quality and high audience response – is an example of this kind of group. Led Zeppelin is another.'

Yet though he was dismissive of their material, Hilburn seemed to get it by the set's end: 'Just when you are ready to dismiss Zeppelin as a group with one lucky song ["Whole Lotta Love"], it begins moving through a number of songs once associated with Elvis Presley: "That's All Right Mama", "Got a Lot o' Livin' to Do" and "A Mess of Blues". And it was sensational. On this 20-minute medley, Zeppelin became an interesting, surging, powerfully effective rock 'n' roll band, totally free of the predictable treadmill they normally employ. On those numbers, Page played a marvellously effective Sun-oriented guitar and Plant rivalled anything Rod Stewart (one of my favourite singers at the moment) and Elvis Presley (favourite singer of the past) have done with "That's All Right Mama".'

Now firmly interwoven into the set was an acoustic section, which introduced another new song, the appropriately titled 'Going to California', as well as the more familiar 'That's the Way' and 'Bron-Y-Aur Stomp'.

Prior to that Saturday night show at the Forum, Miss Pamela had visited Page at the Hyatt. She only saw her former paramour for a brief while, having a chat about Aleister Crowley, before she went to Plant's room. Although the singer confessed his own interest in her, later, in the dressing room at the Forum, he told her, 'Jimmy isn't too happy at home. I know he wants you to be with him.'

After the show, Page climbed into a limousine with Miss Pamela, and they headed for the Whisky, before going back to the Hyatt to spend the night together. 'Jimmy told me tales of Charlotte and little baby Scarlet. They haven't gotten married, and have lots of disagreements,' Miss Pamela wrote in her diary. It was just over four months since the birth of Scarlet Page: was anyone around Page telling him about the inevitable stresses that come with the birth of a child?

Despite Page's pleasant peccadillo in Los Angeles, it appeared that some of the previous spirit of Zeppelin touring America had vanished on this, their seventh tour of the country. 'The incident in Milan had taken a lot out of us,' wrote Richard Cole in *Stairway to Heaven*. 'Once we arrived in America, Zeppelin almost seemed to become reclusive as we moved from city to city, rarely leaving the hotels except for the concerts themselves. Occasionally, Jimmy would venture out to an antique store in New Orleans or Dallas, but those expeditions were more the exception than the rule.'

Although the overt hedonism was less in evidence, it had only disappeared behind literally closed curtains, manifesting in darker forms. In Chicago the promoter received a telephone call: 'Jimmy is going to be shot by someone in the audience tonight.' A similar threat was made in Detroit. Extra security was hired and the local police informed. It was only two years since Charles Manson's Family had killed Sharon Tate and her companions in the Hollywood Hills. Underground culture had thrown up its share of spectres: there seemed to be plenty of dysfunctional, rather frightening characters connected to the American rock 'n' roll circus. For Page the worm had turned; the widely misunderstood Aleister Crowley inscriptions on the third album may not have helped.

The tour ended in Honolulu with a pair of shows on 16 and 17 September and a four-day break on the nearby island of Maui. The wives of the other three members of the group flew out to join them, so Page insisted that the mountaintop mansion rented for the entire group would be for him and himself alone, so as not to cramp his sexual style.

From there they flew to Japan for five dates. Playing two nights at Tokyo's Budokan, they were startled by the hush that descended over the audience as soon as they appeared onstage. 'We weren't used to all of this after coming from America where the whole show people were drinking and smoking joints and going nuts ... But we could have a laugh in Zeppelin. We did enjoy ourselves,' said Page.

When Robert Plant came onstage at the Budokan, however, his lip was partially split. There had been an incident backstage that in another group might have led to its demise. Before the show John Bonham asked the singer to finally settle up over a longstanding debt of £37, a petrol bill the drummer had settled for him. When the singer, whose nickname of 'Percy' was a play on the word 'purse', something he was as reluctant to dip into as his guitarist, yet again tried to sidestep the request, Bonzo lamped him.

An element of self-discipline was rather lacking on this, their first Japanese tour. So great were Led Zeppelin's expenses that, extremely unusually for such a parsimonious outfit, they actually lost money. And the lack of discipline wasn't confined to financial matters.

Disapproving of the choice of music at Tokyo's Byblos club, Bonham pissed on the DJ from an upstairs balcony. Endeavouring to get the almost comatose drummer back to their accommodation at the Hilton, Richard Cole finally gave up, leaving Bonham asleep on the pavement outside the hotel. The pair purchased samurai swords the next day and staged a sword fight in the hotel, wrecking everything that came within their range. After a sleeping John Paul Jones was found in the hotel corridor, Led Zeppelin were banned from the Hilton chain for life.

But a far more egregious example of rock-star bad behaviour took place on the bullet train to their show in Osaka; one that demonstrated the degree of decadence that was seeping everywhere around Led Zeppelin. A pretty Japanese girl called Kanuko, whom Page met in Tokyo, was travelling with them. When the couple disappeared to eat in the train's dining car, salt-of-the-earth John Bonham – always up for a laugh, ho-ho – discovered the girl's handbag. He then took it to the bathroom. When he made his way back to his seat, Bonham gleefully announced to Cole: 'I just shit in her handbag!'

When Kanuko and Page came back from the dining car, she went to the bathroom with her bag. She returned, in tears, ashen.

A furious Page sought in vain for the culprit.

When it came time to return home, Page, Plant and Cole flew to Bangkok, where Page bought a life-size gold, wood and glass Pegasus. Later, the trio visited the city's red-light area, about which Page remarked, 'They must have invented the term "fucking your brains out" here.'

When they moved on to Bombay Page jammed with local musicians, and he, Plant and Cole again visited the city's red-light district. All three of them experienced violent diarrhoea after they asked their driver to take them on a 'locals' experience' – for a meal somewhere he ate regularly.

15

CITY OF ANGELS

Finally the fourth album – *Led Zeppelin IV*, *Zoso*, *Runes* or whatever you liked to call it – had a release date: 7 November in the United States and 18 November in the UK. A mysterious series of ads in the music press, each displaying just one or all of the sigils, had preceded its release.

Jimmy Page was spotted wearing a sweater bearing the Zoso sigil, a gift he received backstage before playing Wembley Empire Pool. Zoso would become comparable to the Rolling Stones' somewhat ugly tongue-and-lip logo. Like Nike's newly minted swoosh, it was a statement of powerful marketing. There is no overstating it: the four Led Zeppelin symbols integrated themselves into popular culture, even being worn as body art.

'All the stopgap titles we throw at the thing are lame: *Led Zeppelin IV*, *[Untitled]*, *Runes*, *Zoso*, *Four Symbols*. In an almost Lovecraftian sense, the album was *nameless*, a thing from beyond, charged with manna,' wrote Erik Davis in his book *Led Zeppelin's Led Zeppelin IV*.

A UK tour began. After an apparently mediocre performance on the opening night at Newcastle's City Hall, followed by shows at Sunderland, Dundee, Ipswich, Plant and Bonham's homeland of Birmingham, and Sheffield, they performed at Wembley's Empire Pool on 20 and 21 November. This pair of London shows was constructed very much as an event, called 'Electric

Magic', featuring support acts Stone the Crows, Bronco and Dundee, as well as circus acts such as dancing pigs, clad in hats and ruffles, a Peter Grant conceit that drew onstage criticism from Robert Plant: 'I expected a bit more from the pigs! Did you? I could have brought some goats.'

The first night at Wembley brought forth a sensational performance from the group, captured in the ecstatic *Melody Maker* review by Roy Hollingworth, a long-time supporter of Zeppelin: 'This was an English band playing like crazy, and enjoying every minute they stood there on stage. They played non-stop for the best part of three hours. Enormous. They played about everything they've ever written. Nothing, just nothing, was spared. This was no job, this was no "gig". It was an event for all. So they get paid a lot of bread, well, people paid that bread, and I reckon they got every penny's worth. It was a great night.'

A bad strain of influenza arrived in Britain that winter, and when Led Zeppelin played Manchester on 24 November, Plant announced onstage: 'Gosh. I think I got that flu that's going about.'

So that the potentially afflicted Plant could take a mid-set breather, Page inserted the wah-wah section from the theme of the movie *Shaft* into 'Dazed and Confused'. Written by Isaac Hayes, the utterly distinctive soundtrack for the hit blaxploitation flick *Shaft* had been a number one US album that year.

By the end of the tour, scheduled for Salisbury, close to Stonehenge, on 15 December, Plant's flu had spread through the rest of the group. The Salisbury date was rescheduled for six days later, when Page would hopefully have recovered from the bug.

Led Zeppelin IV went straight to number one in the UK charts. Jimmy Page breathed a sigh of relief: 'It was probably more painful to get this one out than childbirth itself.' But in America, although it was certified a gold album on the day of its release and was destined to become one of the biggest-selling albums of all time, the record never climbed higher than number two, kept off the top of the charts by Carole King's *Tapestry*.

For once it was *Rolling Stone* who stuck the flag in the summit, via Lenny Kaye. 'It might seem a bit incongruous to say that Led Zeppelin – a band never particularly known for its tendency to understate matters – has produced an album which is remarkable for its low-keyed and tasteful subtlety, but that's just the case here,' he began his finely written review. 'The march of the dinosaurs that broke the ground for their first epic release has apparently vanished.'

And Kaye, who was struck by the sheer variety of the record, saved his real applause until his final paragraph: 'The end of the album is saved for "When the Levee Breaks", strangely credited to all the members of the band plus Memphis Minnie, and it's a dazzler. Basing themselves around one honey of a chord progression, the group constructs an air of tunnel-long depth, full of stunning resolves and a majesty that sets up as a perfect climax. Led Zep have had a lot of imitators over the past few years, but it takes cuts like this to show that most of them have only picked up the style, lacking any real knowledge of the meat underneath.'

So what was going on beneath the façade of the swaggering rock 'n' roller known as Jimmy Page? By now his interest in the occult – by no means strange in that era, of course – was widely known. Any mention of his name would often draw up that two-word response: 'Black magic?'

In Richard Cole's chronicle of his years with Zeppelin, *Stairway to Heaven*, he considered Page's relationship with his muse: 'I had always felt that, more than the others, Jimmy was much too complex an individual to be living for music alone. I knew that his dabbling in the occult continued, although he still kept that side of his life very private.' Although Page would occasionally mention the name of Aleister Crowley, the road manager knew little about the supposed Great Beast.

On assorted occasions, he recalled, Page phoned him to declare himself in the mood 'for shopping for some Crowley artefacts'. 'We'd drive from auction house to rare book showrooms, where Jimmy would buy Crowley manuscripts or other belongings (hats, paintings, clothes).'

When Cole questioned him for some details about Crowley, Page drove the question off to the touchline: '"The guy was really remarkable. Someday we'll talk about it, Richard."'

Needless to say, they never did. 'If the public felt there was a certain mystery surrounding Led Zeppelin, they weren't alone,' Cole concluded. 'As close as I was to them, I felt there was something within Jimmy that he never let anyone see. Particularly when it came to Pagey's preoccupation with Crowley, séances, and black magic, I had a lot of unanswered questions.'

Part of Page's mystery was that he was simultaneously a slightly androgynous boy-man and also carried a rather frightening aura: this was assisted by the atmosphere of menace around Led Zeppelin as a whole. His seeming a little scary was part of the attraction for many of his fans.

Some of Page's more unfortunate character aspects disguised the fact that he was really an extremely evolved human being, and also essentially a nice bloke. For example, there was no doubting the personal loyalty that Page could display. His old friend Jeff Dexter managed America, a trio of expat Yanks who lived in the UK. With their lilting soft-rock sound they had enjoyed huge success globally with their 'A Horse with No Name' single, released the same day as *Led Zeppelin IV*.

But when Dexter was sacked by the band, Page was concerned, as was Peter Grant, who was also well acquainted with the ceaselessly scene-making Dexter. Grant and Dexter had known each other since the days of the celebrated 2i's Coffee Bar on Old Compton Street in Soho. When Dexter became a dancer with Cyril Stapleton's Orchestra, Grant – having been a wrestler himself – suggested Dexter take up the same craft under the moniker the Twisting Wrestler. 'It's all choreography, Jeff. Nothing to do with hurting each other,' Grant promised him. The diminutive Dexter demurred.

Dexter was now managing Isaac Guillory, a uniquely styled American folk singer based in London. To help out their mate, Page and Grant spoke enthusiastically to Atlantic Records about Guillory, and secured him – and his manager – an extremely substantial recording deal with the label.

Perhaps it was a consequence of his shyness in his early years – as well as his damaged family background – that meant Page lacked immediate warmth and was suspicious of outsiders, which was ironic, as that was precisely what he was himself, to a rather extreme degree.

Certainly, with the instant success of *Led Zeppelin IV* he should have felt utterly validated. Even though he always pretended they meant nothing to him, the bad reviews had certainly hurt. Now he even had thorough approval from *Rolling Stone*, whom he had once perceived as an enemy. But he was not so easily won over.

In a little over three years his Led Zeppelin project had become the biggest group in the world. They far outsold, both in terms of records and concert tickets, the Rolling Stones, the only other contender for the title. The fact that the Rolling Stones' albums never sold in large quantities was at that time little known. Yet in achieving his ambition for Zeppelin, Page encountered a similar phenomenon to that which Paul McCartney had found with the Beatles: having reached the absolute zenith of success, he discovered that there was nothing there.

Page was getting into his shit. And, like many other successful rock 'n' rollers before him, he was also going slightly mad from

The James Page Skiffle Group: a 1957 appearance on the BBC's
All Your Own programme, with Jimmy Page just thirteen – in those
days no one knew anyone who had appeared on TV.

Stepping-stones for Jimmy Page: with Carter-Lewis and the
Southerners in 1964; with the Yardbirds in 1966.

Page with his Harmony Sovereign acoustic on the deck of his house in Pangbourne, Berkshire.

Clustered around a Jaguar Mk 2 3.8 for an early Led Zeppelin publicity photo taken outside the Impact Agency offices on Windmill Street, London, December 1968.

Teasing his theremin – or telling it where to get off . . .

The violin bow – or wizard's wand – adding extreme textures to Page's Les Paul during a rendition of 'Dazed and Confused'.

Page would play 'In My Time of Dying' on his Danelectro.

The psychedelic Telecaster used on the first Led Zeppelin album.

Page with his Gibson EDS-1275: along with his sunburst Les Paul Standard, this was the guitar with which he is most associated.

Chasing the dragon? The full 'dragon suit' gets its first
outing at Earls Court, London, in 1975.

The Zoso sweater worn at the Empire Pool shows in London in 1971. Knitted by a girlfriend, it would shrink when Page sweated onstage.

The 'moon' trousers, as worn in *The Song Remains the Same* film.

Heroin chic: an egregiously thin Jimmy Page in his 'poppy suit', on the ill-fated 1977 tour of the United States.

Hanging for the photographer at the Chateau Marmont in Los Angeles in 1969, as America breaks for Led Zeppelin.

Page happy in rehearsals.

Stepping ahead with Richard Cole (left) and Peter Grant (right).

An uncertain feeling? Led Zeppelin ready themselves in 1979 for their first Knebworth 'comeback' date.

Aleister Crowley's Scottish home, Boleskine House, in 1912.
Page would later purchase the property.

Aleister Crowley, the
self-styled Great Beast.

On 31 October 1974, Halloween Night,
Led Zeppelin celebrated the UK launch of
their Swan Song record label with a suitably
unconventional party at Chislehurst
Caves, south-east of London.

The maestro at work: Jimmy Page onstage at Led Zeppelin's
triumphant return to London in May 1975.

the daily pressure. All those arcane books he had read and yet all these prosaic responsibilities with Zeppelin. Attention to detail had always been his thing, to a necessarily obsessive degree: who cared if modern stereo systems were not sufficiently sensitive to pick up the most subtle filigree flourishes he was applying to his recordings? It would linger there in the tune's backstory. But this was all so very wearing, leaving little time for sleep. 'I'm sure people aren't aware of this. I'm sure they think we sit on our arses all day long, but we don't. All I know is I haven't stopped for three years. If it gives you any indication, I haven't had a holiday ever since the group started,' he said the following year.

Of course, the sleeplessness was hardly assisted by the amount of drugs that were now about the group. Industrial quantities of cocaine followed Led Zeppelin wherever they went; one story had a pair of cops turning up backstage at a venue in the southern US and finding Grant seated at a table piled up with what looked like a sizeable chunk of Colombia's annual cocaine production. They began to go through the motions of placing the manager under arrest. Grant glanced at the policemen and picked up a pile of cash, and then proceeded to deal it out: $5,000, $10,000, $15,000 … But to no avail, it seemed, as they continued to read him his rights … $35,000, $40,000, $45,000, $50,000. Finally, the policemen looked at each other and shrugged. One of them leaned over, picked up the cash – and they left. As they stepped out the door, Grant uttered a final line: 'Pleasure doing business with you, gentlemen.'

In early February 1972 Led Zeppelin boarded an Air India flight at London's Heathrow Airport. They flew to Bombay for a four-day break on their way to their first tour of Australia; Peter Grant had secured round-the-world tickets from Air India for only £500 for each traveller. Following a reprise of the sexual shenanigans on their previous visit to Bombay, the musicians spent an afternoon enjoying a camel ride along an Indian beach, which left their bodies sore and battered. Both Page and Plant – especially Robert Plant, in fact – were taken with the notion of imbuing their own work with music from other cultures.

In line with Australia's much-trumpeted tall-poppy view of life – Someone getting above their station? Cut the buggers down to size! – the country's media and forces of law and order had a reputation for meting out harsh justice to visiting celebrities.

And it seemed that an example would be made of Led Zeppelin. They arrived in Perth for their 16 February show at the Subiaco Oval – an outdoors show, as all the dates on this Australasian tour would be – before a crowd of 80,000 people. It was a sensational concert – there was even a stage invasion – and the crowd size was boosted by 300 or so fans who, to the chagrin of the local police, cut their way through fences and gates to get in.

Following the show Led Zeppelin went to a nightclub in the city, where they ended the night banging out classic rock 'n' roll songs together on a tiny stage.

After the group returned to the Scarborough Hotel and put their heads down on their pillows, there came a knocking at their door. It was the police, with warrants to search their rooms, which they duly did. As Led Zeppelin had only just arrived in Australia, they had not even made any drug connections yet. Always a professional despite his severe jet lag, Page was shocked at such incompetence: 'Those stupid arseholes. If they had waited a day or two, we might have had something.' Grant slept through the entire episode, and when he learned of it in the morning, he immediately hired a security team of former police detectives to act as a buffer against any further raids.

Although a thunderstorm delayed their second date, a show in Adelaide, by two days, when it finally happened the local press were ecstatic about the gig, the loudest there ever: 'From the start, all eyes were on brilliant lead guitarist Jimmy Page. His electric guitar work was extraordinary. At one stage, using a bow, he smashed out a string of piercing notes only to end with a run of delicate sitar-sounding music. Thunderous applause followed all his work.'

In Sydney, a city famed for its gay population, they hung out with the transsexuals from a cabaret club called Les Girls. Questions were asked of the four members' sexuality.

In Auckland in New Zealand they played to the largest crowd ever gathered together in the country up to that point. Back in Australia, in Queensland's semi-tropical Brisbane, a version of Dion's 'The Wanderer' was slipped into the 'Whole Lotta Love' medley – for the only time in their career.

Returning home via Bangkok, with the intention of pursuing further sexual possibilities, the musicians were refused entry to Thailand. Their long hair was a no-no. When Robert Plant pointed out that they had been allowed into the country the previous year, they were simply informed that the rules had now changed. Trouble with the forces of law and order in both Australia and Thailand: was someone keeping an eye on them?

Back in the UK in March, Page immediately took the group into rehearsals for the new material he had been working on since January. The rehearsal space was a remote farmhouse in Puddletown, Dorset, arguably the UK's most beautiful county, on the shores of the River Piddle, which came with its own studio, called Jabberwocky.

Eddie Kramer, the engineer from New York's Electric Lady Studios, was flown over to join the group. Despite the success of the fourth album, Andy Johns had been replaced, perhaps as a result of his misguided desire to mix the album in Los Angeles.

Soon, despite the high rental fee demanded by Mick Jagger – £1,000 a week – they were all staying at Stargroves, the Stones singer's country mansion in Hampshire, with the Rolling Stones mobile studio wired up in the grounds.

One of the first tracks recorded, 'The Song Remains the Same', originally titled 'The Plumpton and Worcester Races', was laid down on 18 May. Page used a Fender electric 12-string, with Les Paul overdubs. In the tune there are traces of the highly organised arrangements of Yes, with Page sometimes recalling Steve Howe's six-string flourishes.

Following the successful completion of this epic track, which would become the album opener, at around 5 a.m., Robert Plant had the idea to emulate his idol Ral Donner, who had recorded so many demos for Elvis Presley; he had in mind something in the vein of Donner's 'You Don't Know What You've Got', a hit in 1961.

What transpired was not precisely in Donner's mood, but more like the bluebeat sound Plant had heard at Midlands Mod clubs in the mid-sixties. After Page rapidly constructed a chord sequence, John Paul Jones laid down a ska-style bass line, quickly picked up on drums by John Bonham. Almost immediately this transmogrified into the joyful 'D'yer Mak'er', a clear play on the word 'Jamaica', if the song's rhythm alone did not reveal its origins. Page's guitar playing gives the song an old-fashioned feeling – as though he is from time to time reprising his old hero Hank Marvin's work with the Shadows.

The slow, moody 'Rain Song' was consciously written by Page in response to George Harrison taunting Bonham that Zeppelin were incapable of writing a ballad. 'The Crunge', with its throwaway line 'Can you take me to the bridge?', was more a tribute to James Brown than to the oft-mentioned Otis Redding.

'No Quarter', a melange of cosmic mess and obscure world-music references, had leapt straight from John Paul Jones's keyboard at his home studio in Crowborough in East

Sussex; he had presented the song to the group almost fully formed. Always the quietest and most self-contained member of Led Zeppelin, Jones was the anchor of the unit, always there to assist Page on song arrangements. Jones was a fellow earth sign Capricorn, and Page was always adamant that this created a solid foundation for the quartet.

'Black Country Woman' was recorded out on the lawn at Stargroves. A song that would not appear until the *Physical Graffiti* album, it had Robert Plant's vocals almost interrupted by a jetliner passing overhead. At the singer's insistence, the aircraft's sound was kept on the track.

After just over a week, Page decided that the acoustics at Stargroves were simply not up to scratch, certainly not on a level with those at Headley Grange. Led Zeppelin relocated back to Olympic Sound Studios in West London.

During 1972 a distinct shift occurred in the dynamic of Led Zeppelin, which had up until now been seen as the child of the substantially pedigreed Jimmy Page, the archetypal manifestation of the guitar hero. When the group had started out Robert Plant seemed little more than a nervous, overgrown schoolboy, struggling with all his might to find his place in the group and the world. But in the three and a bit years since, the singer had evolved into the group's dominant presence, both in the eyes of fans and in the media. Invariably bare-chested, his leonine mane kissing his shoulders, rock's golden god – as he was frequently now described – had replaced the apparently moody Page as the visual representation of the group. Prone to all manner of rock star eccentricities – lax timekeeping most certainly one of them – Page had had that nickname 'Led Wallet' bestowed on him by crew-members shaking their heads at his financial tightness. But his singer was no better. Following their Alexandra Palace shows in London at the end of 1972, Plant would offer the entire road crew a single bottle of whisky for Christmas.

It was perhaps inevitable that the singer would replace the guitarist as the visual image of Led Zeppelin. Plant was the man who would stand at the front of the stage and address and embrace the audience. An open individual, he was also happy and at ease both with himself and in his relationship with the media, and the media reciprocated this, respectful of how he was usually ready with an intelligent answer to their questions. The old hippie within him was hard to suppress, and Plant was unquestionably a sensitive soul, yet he was no slouch when it came to self-belief, and he could also be seen as being a little too cocky and rather arrogantly pleased with himself.

He articulated his position to journalist Cliff Jones: 'Page, and Bonham to a degree, were different to me. I reasoned that I could sing about misty mountains and then chip a football into the back of the net on my days off. That felt like the good life to me back then. It wasn't all-consuming for me in the way it was for the others.

'Don't forget that we had no choice but to get caught up in all that hotel-room and drug-binge kind of thing, because it was part of the experience, almost expected. But I always knew there was a time out when I'd get off the bus and come home.'

Back in the US for a summer tour, Page spent time at Electric Lady Studios in New York, tidying up the new record. On Wednesday 14 June 1972, Led Zeppelin played Nassau Coliseum on New York's Long Island. The concert was reviewed by Robert Christgau in *Newsday*: 'Jimmy Page is a highly proficient electric blues guitarist whose expertise is essential to the group's effect, but the star of the show is vocalist Robert Plant.' Christgau also saw through to the heart of the construction of the group's material: 'At some deep level, Led Zeppelin's music is about technology. Philosophically, the band prefers humanity pure and simple, but in practice it must realise its humanity technologically. That seems truer than most good-time pastoral fantasies.'

On the Friday, Catherine James, who had not seen Page since their fling in Los Angeles in 1969, received a surprise phone call. By now she was living with her son Damian in Ridgefield, Connecticut, some 50 or so miles from Manhattan. 'No matter how much time went by, the sound of Jimmy's soft, reticent voice always stopped my heart cold,' she said. 'I hadn't seen him in over two years, but his voice still made my insides stir. He was in New York at the Drake Hotel, and asked if he could come up for the weekend. I thought, "This has to be a dream."'

A couple of hours later Page drew up outside her house in a shining black limousine. 'Jimmy was just as dazzling as the last time we met. He's also the only man who has ever left me at a loss for words. I don't know why, but I always felt slightly shy with him ... I thought I was a bit more self-assured, but the mere sight of him getting out of his limo and strolling up my walk gave me the familiar jitters. Trying to maintain some sense of coolness, I greeted Jimmy like he was a distant cousin. With a quick kiss, I announced, "Damian and I are just off to the market; you're welcome to wait here or come along if you like."

'He said he wanted to go with us, and I showed him how I made the silver Pontiac fly over the dips in the road. We were having a sweet time, and my coolness quickly turned into mush. We had a late-night candlelit dinner and kissed till our lips were swollen.'

They spent the weekend together, going for walks in the woods, listening to Joni Mitchell, kissing and cuddling, everything Catherine James could have dreamt of. 'Jimmy finally said the magic words: "Why don't you come to England?"'

Wouldn't you think Catherine James would have jumped at the idea? But no, she was in a different life now, looking after her son in the country, where she had built a new and satisfying existence for herself. More to the point, on a purely practical level where would Page have lodged her? What would Charlotte Martin's view of this have been, had she learned of it? Was Page reacting to Catherine in this manner because he was in despair over his relationship with Charlotte? Or was this simply a classic example of self-indulgent rock-star philandering?

Whatever it was, Catherine felt she had no choice but to turn down the opportunity. However, she gladly accepted his offer to fly with him to Los Angeles, where Zeppelin were due to play the Forum on 25 June. She arranged child care for Damian and spent a week at the Hyatt House with Page. 'The shows were stunning. The silhouette of Jimmy cloaked in shimmery velvet, moons and stars, and the haunting, abandoned sound of the bow gliding across his guitar were enchantingly sensual. To me, Jimmy was Led Zeppelin, the sorcerer behind the magic; he definitely had it down.

'After my whirlwind week of rock and steamy, romantic sex, I actually looked forward to the sanctuary of my little house, away from the glitz and glamour of Hollywood.'

That show at the Forum was the band at one of their ultimate peaks. Thirty years later, a live recording of the concert, plus further extracts from their Long Beach Arena gig two days later, was released as the sensational *How the West Was Won*, a triple live CD, one of Led Zeppelin's greatest-ever and most representative releases. Page was fully aware of the show's magnificence. 'I think,' he told *The Times* in 2010, 'what we did on … *How the West Was Won* – that 1972 gig – is pretty much a testament of how good it was. It would have been nice to have had a little more visual recordings, but there you go. That's the conundrum of Led Zeppelin!'

Just back from America in July 1972, Jimmy Page once again went into the studio with his friend Roy Harper at Abbey Road. He played electric guitar on two tracks for the *Lifemask* album, 'Bank of the Dead' and 'The Lord's Prayer'.

Page retreated briefly to Boleskine. There he was joined one afternoon by fellow Heston native Ritchie Blackmore, former member of Lord Sutch's Savages, a fertile musical training ground. Blackmore had by now become the powerhouse guitarist with Deep Purple and was also an aficionado of Aleister Crowley; Purple would tour the US only a couple of notches in popularity below Zeppelin.

Blackmore was accompanied to Boleskine by Dick O'Dell, his group's lighting director. O'Dell found the experience 'very interesting and a little scary. The house was spooky – and Gothic, of course. It was a classically rainy, misty, dark Loch Ness day. The house had lots of amazing art, sculpture and weird logos from Jimmy Page's various societies. Including, obviously, pentacles.' That afternoon there was, said O'Dell, an unmistakable element of rivalry between the two gunslinger guitarists: 'Cordial but slightly like two matadors ... I guess Ritchie wanted to see the house. I reckon he was jealous: probably wanted to buy it himself. I always thought Page was much more serious about Crowley, Druidism, Magick, Celtic folklore etc. Blackmore liked the image!'

They had afternoon tea and a couple of joints, before making their excuses and departing.

In October 1972 Page and Plant returned to Bombay in India to investigate the possibility of recording with Indian musicians. The guitarist had been in touch with his friend Ravi Shankar, asking the sitar master to help him in choosing appropriate musicians. The eminent Indian had a think, then he recommended Vijay Raghav Rao, Films Division of India's principal soundtrack composer and arranger. For what would be termed *The Bombay Sessions*, Rao brought in Sultan Khan, a master of the very difficult sarangi, a bowed Indian instrument.

*   *   *

With the recording of the new album complete, there was the not-insignificant matter of the record's sleeve to be designed, which had been something of an issue on the previous two LPs. The most highly regarded design company in London at the time were Hipgnosis; since their design for *A Saucerful of Secrets*, the second album by Pink Floyd, for whom they became designers of choice, Hipgnosis had proven themselves to be on the zeitgeist of contemporary album art. Their work combined the wilfully surreal, sex and satire, playing with the senses in their distortion of convention. After Storm Thorgerson, who founded the company in 1968 with Aubrey Powell, had designed the cover for Douglas Adams's book *The Hitchhiker's Guide to the Galaxy*, the author described him as 'the best album designer in the world'. As well as working with the Floyd, Hipgnosis delivered sleeves for, among others, Free, the Nice, Emerson, Lake and Palmer, and Yes. The previous year, 1971, they had designed the packaging for T. Rex's *Electric Warrior*, the biggest-selling LP in the UK during that 12-month period. (A little-known fact was that in 1970, out of friendship, Page had personally tutored Marc Bolan in the art of playing the electric guitar.)

When Thorgerson was called in for a meeting with Grant, Page and Plant, he was informed that the new Zeppelin album was to be the first to have a title: *Houses of the Holy*. Through his esoteric studies, Page had concluded that human beings were 'houses of the Holy Spirit'.

Despite plenty of evidence in the tone of Hipgnosis's previous album sleeves, the trio had not really appreciated the humour at the heart of much of the design company's work. Page was more than a little surprised when Thorgerson returned with what he claimed was his first rough attempt: a photograph of a tennis court and a tennis racquet. When the mystified guitarist requested an explanation, Thorgerson had a three-word explanation: 'Racquet. Racket. Geddit?' Page asked Thorgerson to leave, although he did concede that the designer had shown 'some balls'. Surprisingly, the band decided to stick with Hipgnosis, and they set up a meeting with Aubrey Powell.

Powell had a rather different concept to his partner for the fifth Led Zeppelin album sleeve: to create an image of children ascending a rocky hill. The idea came from science-fiction writer Arthur C. Clarke's novel *Childhood's End*; the fact that Clarke was later outed as a paedophile lends an awkward subtext to this source material.

In the end only two children, both naked, were involved in the photographic shoot, siblings Stefan and Samantha Gates, their images repeated several times. Page claimed the image symbolised, 'Innocence ... the idea of us being vessels of houses of the holy'. It was only two years since Blind Faith had adorned their first and only album's cover with an image of a nude pre-pubescent girl: how times would change. The inner sleeve of *Houses of the Holy* contained even greater grounds for controversy, depicting one of the children being held aloft in a sacrificial posture.

The ten-day shoot for the sleeve took place on the Giant's Causeway on the north coast of Northern Ireland. When Powell mentioned to Peter Grant that the complex logistics of the expedition might prove very expensive, the Falstaffian manager barked back at him: 'Expensive? We're Led Zeppelin – we don't care about money!'

When it was finally released on 28 March 1973, the complex diversity of material on *Houses of the Holy* again led to baffled reviews. By this time Page knew what he was likely to be reading: 'People still have this preconceived notion of what to expect. But this will be something really new. If you carry on on just one plane, you just repeat yourself.'

* * *

On 4 May 1973 Led Zeppelin were once again on tour in the United States. *Houses of the Holy* had been released six weeks previously and, although it went to number one almost immediately, it would soon find itself sliding into the slipstream of the slowly building juggernaut sales of *Led Zeppelin IV*.

The audience size at the first couple of dates was worthy of Zeppelin's new status as the Biggest Band in the World. An eminence reflected in their use of the *Starship*, a Boeing 720 available to rent for $2,500 per flight hour. They were the first act to use the renovated plane, which came with its own organ as well as bedrooms and bars; the flight attendants were delighted to work aboard, helping themselves to rolled-up $100 bills when the band and their entourage had departed.

Some 50,000 fans came to Atlanta's Fulton County Stadium for the first concert, and 56,800 the next day at Florida's Tampa Stadium, the latter producing gross earnings of $309,000 – not bad for a night's work. The size of the Tampa crowd unquestionably raised the bar for Led Zeppelin, and Peter Grant ordered full-page ads to be taken out in major newspapers across the US advising that the date was the largest attendance for a single performance in history.

'Hello. It seems between us we've done something nobody's ever done before … and that's fantastic,' uttered Robert Plant to the crowd as the show kicked off. But perhaps the majesty of the occasion trammelled the group's chops: parts of the Tampa set were irredeemably sloppy, something Zeppelin – like their great rivals the Rolling Stones – could be more often than they would like to admit.

Two days later, however, journalist Lisa Robinson was transported by what she considered a magical performance in Jacksonville, Florida. 'There were no intermissions, no waiting, no tuning up, no bullshit,' wrote Robinson, who would become tight with Jimmy Page, in the UK's *Disc* magazine. 'Just music. Just gorgeous rock 'n' roll music at its most desperate. The performance was so incredibly timed that you were never completely aware of just exactly when one number started and another began, and the acoustic numbers and the ballads blended in perfectly with the rockers. You couldn't help but beg for more. It was impossible to be a part of that experience and not watch, and listen with a total awe. We don't have bands like this, you know. YOU don't have bands like this ... but you do have Led Zeppelin. And they know what they have. They know the high they can achieve, and they're here again – their album is number one in the country and they're going to go and play everywhere and celebrate rock 'n' roll. God bless them.'

Following their experience in Sydney, Led Zeppelin seemed to have developed a fondness for transvestite bars. In New Orleans, while hanging out in the French Quarter, they spent their time in gay bars. 'The New Orleans drag queens always seemed to be having much more fun than the people we'd meet in straight clubs,' thought Richard Cole. 'We also loved shocking people, and there was no better place to do that than a bar where it was often only us and a few transvestites.'

But not everything ran smoothly on this tour. The 30 May show at Led Zep temple the Forum in Los Angeles was moved to 3 June after Page sprained his hand by leaning on a wire fence at LAX while signing autographs. 'Quite honestly, I don't know why we've had such phenomenal success,' Page told the *Los Angeles Times* during this brief hiatus. 'Perhaps you could relate it to street music and the fact that people feel more of an affinity to Zep's music because it's not constantly hammered down their throats from every direction. All I can say is that whenever we've gone on stage or into the studio, we've always done our best. We've never really been involved in the media, we've never done a TV programme, and air play, of course, is limited because of the fact that we don't record singles.'

'By the end of a tour, everybody is getting pretty much blown out,' Roy Harper, who was the opening act for Led Zeppelin for most of their 1973 US dates, said in 1974. 'I mean you have no idea, you have absolutely no idea, of what the pressures are like. Peter Grant jestfully referred to me as the social worker on the last trip. There's a limit to what human beings can take, and on a cross-country American tour you can watch the gradual disintegration. And when you run into the average hotel jobsworth, you don't actually want to play around with him too much.

'You're going grey, so life gets into a pattern of activity that's inescapable. You reach the ultimate, which is, "What can we do to keep ourselves together?" I've seen cars driven into swimming pools, and walls blown out of hotels with dynamite. But that only happens when you've reached the point of total stress, when you've gone beyond all endurance.'

With its film world and show-business foundations, coupled with its location at the most extreme edge of the Western world, Los Angeles was home to much that was bizarre. This reflected its relatively recent history. During the 1850s the tiny City of Angels had been infamous as one of the most murderous societies in America, where lynching often took the place of legal execution. 'There is no brighter sun ... no country where nature is more lavish of her exuberant fullness,' a local wrote in 1853. 'And yet, with all our natural beauties and advantages, there is no country where human life is of so little account. Men hack one another to pieces with pistols and other cutlery as if God's image were of no more worth than the life of one of the two or three thousand ownerless dogs that prowl about our streets and make night hideous.'

Over a hundred years later, nothing seemed to have changed too much. Many of the city's inhabitants had come in search of fame – though not everybody, by any means – and it was still a wild place. As the 1960s shifted into the next decade, the thinking – sometimes exaggerated by drugs – behind the era's supposed sexual revolution had turned somewhat rancid.

Charles Manson and his family might have had something to do with this.

'You never knew what people were capable of,' said B. P. Fallon, Led Zeppelin's new press agent. 'They'd want me to get a message to Jimmy, and you didn't know whether they were going to pull out a knife or what. So instead I introduced Zeppo to people like Les Petits Bon Bons, who were these wonderful raving young queens from California who'd give Bonzo pictures of their cocks with glitter on them. We went to gay clubs because it was more fun, and simply brought the girls with us.'

In Los Angeles in the first part of the 1970s there was a sense that anything could happen, especially in Hollywood. As well as prime Mexican and Colombian grass, cocaine was readily available. Nestled amidst the head shops peddling pipes, bongs and packets of rolling papers, there was a 'massage parlour' south of Sunset Strip tellingly titled The Institute of Oral Love, a favourite of road crews.

The Los Angeles baby groupies were a further sign of the times, as though summoned by the spirit of the Rolling Stones' 'Stray Cat Blues', with its challenging I-don't-care-if-you're-15-years-old line. Fitted out with easily obtainable fake IDs, these LA girls – often barely into their teens – were often the scions of fractured Beverly Hills showbiz marriages.

Rodney Bingenheimer's English Disco – Rodney's, as it became known – opened in 1972 on Sunset Boulevard, and served Watney's Red Barrel beer on tap, which was imported from England, as was much of the music. The sounds of the Sweet, in particular, sailed out of its doors, but also Gary Glitter, Mud and Suzi Quatro. Bingenheimer had visited the UK in 1971, where he was taken by the first stirrings of glam rock; urged on by David Bowie, he returned to LA the next year determined to make his mark.

'Once inside, everybody's a star,' wrote Richard Cromelin the next year. 'The social rules are simple but rigid: All you want to hear is how fabulous you look, so you tell them how fabulous they look. You talk about how bored you are, coming here night after night, but that there's no place else to go. If you're not jaded there's something wrong ... If you're 18 you're over the hill.'

There were other groupie watering holes – the Whisky a Go Go and the Rainbow Bar and Grill, both on Sunset Strip, while the rooftop pool of the nearby Continental Hyatt House on Sunset was a daytime option – but Rodney's was tailor-made for the needs of visiting rock stars, often British. Although they were wary of their wives and girlfriends seeing photographs of them with the club's female clientele, Led Zeppelin thought Rodney's was a very good idea, which was hardly surprising. Rodney's was a paean to rock-star narcissism, its female assets offered in the pages of *Star* magazine, a kind of house publication that only lasted for five issues before it closed following an onslaught of criticism from a shocked general public. Edition one included an article entitled 'Those Foxy Hollywood High Girls', which revealed the magazine's demographic. The lead feature in that issue – 'Your Very Own Superfox: How You'll Know It's Him' – expressed the philosophy of the baby groupies: 'Foxy Lady, it is written in the stars and in the hearts of every worshipper of the Zodiac, from the inner brooding soul of the Capricorn woman to the deep, easy warmth of the Lady of Sagittarius, that there is a time for her to have her very own SUPERFOX. It is written that the time must come for a girl to move forward and up from the ranks of the shy, blushing Teenybopper, and to express herself as a brave new woman in a brave new world.'

The queen of these brave new women was Sable Starr, who, in the June 1973 edition of *Star*, published when she was 15, revealed that she was 'close friends' with David Bowie, Marc Bolan and some other big names. Spirit's Randy California had taken her virginity when she was just 12. She would eventually run away from home at the age of 16, moving to New York for an inevitably ill-fated relationship with Johnny Thunders after the New York Dolls played in Los Angeles.

Although they liked to think of themselves as muses, most of these girls were little more than trinkets, abused victims. And, as their circumstances dictated, many of them were also hard as nails and capable of being considerably vicious. Jimmy Page would later tell of how one of his girlfriends from that scene had once bitten into a sandwich to discover it contained razor blades. 'I'd be on the road with Hawkwind or whoever, writing for the *NME*, and we'd check into the Hyatt and Zeppelin would be there,' said Mick Farren. 'And the whole place was full of the stinkiest fucking groupies. There was something very unclean about the whole deal. Rod and the Faces sort of kicked it off, but it went to some kind of zenith with Zeppelin … with Zeppelin it just seemed to be running in semen and beer and unpleasantness and old Tampaxes.'

'Something about Zeppelin's energy really altered the *joie de vivre* of the LA rock scene,' said Miss Pamela. 'They thought they could get away with anything – and they could, because everyone wanted to get near them.'

What on earth was going on here with Led Zeppelin – what was the drive behind such behaviour? Clearly it was a power trip: these young girls were not going to tell these guys that they were full of shit. But aren't these guys, our Led Zeppelin rock 'n' roll gods, also chronically immature? Rock 'n' roll often freezes people emotionally at the age they enter it, with their every wish catered for from then on. As Steve Winwood once remarked to me: 'When I left Traffic to become a solo act, I didn't even know how to go to the post office and buy a stamp.' And people who become rock stars are almost always driven by some psychological need, usually deriving from some form of damage that leads them to need the validation of audience acceptance. I asked life coach Nanette Greenblatt about the consequences of this behaviour.

'I agree the young women will not be calling out the behaviour of these guys,' she said. 'The immaturity is linked also to addictions. Finding stuff outside of yourself to prop you up, and make you feel okay. Often inner resources and the creative journey to make the music, write the songs and be on the road, would bring up great highs and proper lows. This takes one psychologically to the edges. Coping with these probably fuelled a lot of dysfunctional behaviours. Those who managed to navigate healthy, connected relationships and friendships sometimes fared better. I think also some people had a calling to express their music. Driven by that urge and unable to contain or understand drives from their conditioning, they could go off the rails. In artists there is a high incidence of seeking and finding religions, occult, sex cults, drugs etc. The creative process can have a devastating effect, especially in the public eye. The public are also fickle. So careers can be unstable. Huge amounts of luxury can feel empty and unfulfilling – all the things that are supposed to make you happy, and they don't, which is confusing. You are adored but you aren't loved for you. It can feel empty. Re-inventing yourself is a challenge. Inspiration can dry up. A kind of numbness can lead to even more extreme behaviours in an attempt to feel alive: the self-harming model, where hurting yourself makes you feel a touch more alive.'

A close contender for LA's number-one groupie was Lori Mattix, Sable Starr's best friend, a mixed-race girl whose photograph, when shown to him by Led Zeppelin press agent B. P. 'Beep' Fallon, appealed to Page to the point of infatuation. He got her phone number from Fallon.

'I got to photograph Lori because she was in my room,' said Beep Fallon. 'Why would I not photograph her? The thing about groupies that's misunderstood is that it was all consensual. The girls were the predators, not the bands. Lori and Sable were very funny, very bright; they wouldn't take any shit from anybody.'

Tall, with a trim frame, her pretty face and large brown eyes framed by cascading chestnut curls, Lori had many admirers, not least David Bowie, to whom she had lost her virginity when she was just 14. But none more so than Jimmy Page. As a Scorpio, she would have made a strong connection with Page's Scorpio rising.

While on the road in Texas he called her: 'Hi, this is Jimmy Page and I wanna meet you.'

'Yeah, sure,' said Lori, assuming it was a prank call and hanging up.

But when Zeppelin hit Los Angeles, Lori and her friends went up to the Hyatt House's rooftop pool, with its views of the Hollywood Hills behind. Page approached her, but she knew that he was still, to an extent, involved with Miss Pamela, who had a reputation for physical intolerance towards anyone trying to get close to him. Addressing him as 'Mr Page', she told him: 'I really can't talk to you.' 'Honey, if you come with me, nobody'll touch you,' he replied.

At Rodney's the next night, Page arrived with Miss Pamela. But when Lori went to the bathroom, he followed her in, she claims. That night was the start of their relationship.

With her tumbling, curly locks, Lori Mattix was, to an extent, a mirror image of Jimmy Page, not unlike Mick and Bianca Jagger. No wonder he loved her so much: she looked just like him. Also, as Jagger had done with other girlfriends, Page styled Lori: 'He was always very conventional and conservative. He wanted me to be such a lady. He used to make me wear long dresses and look gypsy-like.'

What on earth did Lori Mattix's mother think of her pubescent daughter hooking up with a man almost twice her age? Rather like the parents of Priscilla Beaulieu when a suitor called Elvis Presley came calling on their underage daughter, she seemed to go along with it, to all intents and purposes.

'He was a real gentleman,' Lori Mattix told Stephen Davis. 'And she knew that he was a really respectable guy and that he had money and, I mean, what is she gonna say? You know, she knew that I was doing it anyway, so she figures if I'm gonna be doing it, who better with?

'After that first year, Jimmy took me along to all the shows. Sometimes they would dedicate a show to me! And if I wasn't with him, he would call me every day from wherever he was. Especially at the time he was in his prime, 73 to 75, that was the prime of Zeppelin. After that, he got kinda smacked out.'

On 20 July 1973, seven days before the first of three dates at Madison Square Garden that would conclude the US tour, Peter Grant called American-born film director Joe Massot. Page and Grant had long discussed a feature film, almost certainly a documentary, about Led Zeppelin. Peter Whitehead's footage from their 1970 Royal Albert Hall show had been intended as the raw material for it, but at the time it was deemed that the film had been badly lit; this footage would emerge later, in the 2003 release *Led Zeppelin DVD*.

In 1970 Joe Massot, whose film *Wonderwall* featured George Harrison's first soundtrack, had moved into a house in Pangbourne, and he and his wife first became friends with Charlotte Martin, and then Page himself after Charlotte invited them to the boathouse for dinner.

Page invited him to Zeppelin's groundbreaking performance at the Bath Festival, and Massot decided there and then that he would like to film the act. He had made several offers to film Zeppelin since, but Grant always turned him down.

When Page moved to Plumpton he lost touch with Massot. But when the filmmaker saw the scale of the venues the group would be playing in the US he reacquainted himself with Page and pitched an idea for a documentary that would incorporate live performance and more intimate, backstage film. Page liked

the notion and referred him to Richard Cole, who also appreciated the concept of the film, although Cole said that Grant
would have his own ideas. And he did: Grant wanted a better-
known director, one with a first-class pedigree. Yet Massot's
persistence paid off, and finally Grant agreed to the director
filming his act.

So celebratory was the mood on tour that Grant and Page
decided it was time to move ahead with the project and film the
three nights at Madison Square Garden. 'It all started in the
Sheraton Hotel, Boston,' said Grant. 'We'd talked about a film
for years and Jimmy had known Joe Massot was interested – so
we called them and over they came.' It was all very quickly
arranged. Grant declared he would personally finance the movie
and Massot would receive a fee, with all footage being the legal
domain of the act, in the firm hands of Steve Weiss, their
extremely efficient lawyer.

Massot hurriedly assembled a three-camera crew in time for
Led Zeppelin's Baltimore date, on 23 July 1973, and the next
night in Pittsburgh, as a dry-run; it was only the New York
shows that he would actually shoot. These were the last concerts
that the group would play that year. But afterwards, despite
New York filming costs of $85,000, it became clear that there
were plenty of missing elements from the footage. Remarkably,
after three separate performances having been filmed, there was
not a single complete version of 'Whole Lotta Love', Led
Zeppelin's signature song. And there were niggling details that
made things difficult: despite all four members being asked to
wear the same clothes each night, John Paul Jones claimed not
to have received the instructions and wore a different outfit
each time, a cause of considerable continuity problems during
editing. Massot did film some interesting backstage footage,
however, including Peter Grant berating an unofficial-
merchandise seller.

* * *

It was during the second Madison Square Garden show that an extraordinary, and still unsolved, mystery took place at the Drake, Led Zeppelin's New York hotel – glimpses of which ended up in the resulting film's footage.

Richard Cole and lawyer Steve Weiss had placed in the region of $203,000, largely in $100 bills, in a safe-deposit box in the hotel. Why would they have so much cash? The group liked having it on tap, Cole said, so they could always 'buy a guitar in the middle of the night, or a bit of blow'. In fact, Cole would regularly travel with $50,000 in his pocket, prepared for such an occasion. Because they needed to pay the cost of their plane at the end of the tour, they had even more than they usually carried.

The previous night, Cole had opened the safe to take out $8,000 for Page to buy a classic Les Paul guitar, and all the money was there.

As the group were about to leave for the venue for the second night, however, Cole again checked the safe to make sure there was sufficient to pay both Massot's film crew and the fee for the *Starship*.

There was no money there whatsoever. Cole told Grant and Weiss, who were waiting in the lobby, that all their cash had vanished. The frequently irascible Grant simply reacted to the large problem with sangfroid.

Calling the police meant first involving the three men in another task: completely cleaning out each of the group's accommodation of any drug residue, especially cocaine, as it was likely that everyone's rooms would be searched.

Cole was initially the chief suspect in the eyes of the police, and he was given a lie-detector test, which he passed with flying colours.

As the group returned to the hotel from yet another triumphant show, news of the missing money had broken. Grant took it upon himself to grab a camera from the neck of a persistent

New York Post photographer and toss it to the ground. For thus validating his reputation as the most dangerous and volatile manager in the music business, he was immediately arrested for assault and taken downtown to the Tombs. After an hour or so of questioning by the FBI about the theft, he was released without charge. He was never handcuffed, though; the police officer who took him to the station had once drummed with a group supporting the Yardbirds and recognised the manager immediately.

New York photographer Joe Stevens was in the hip Manhattan nightclub Max's Kansas City: 'The joint filled with people from the Zeppelin gig at Madison Square Garden. An hour or so later Page strolls in with their Irish publicist B. P. Fallon. We chatted about the gig and there was general blah-blah. But then someone blurted out to the two about how the newspapers in New York City were making big headlines about Zep's manager Peter Grant arranging to have the previous night's Madison Square Garden take stolen from their hotel's safe. The two laughed. Page said, "It's probably true." Fallon said he was there when the money was deposited, and he saw Grant get a receipt for the money. At that point the conversation changed to an art installation of a crushed auto that had begun to leak transmission fluid onto the nightclub's floor. The Andy Warhol contingent were holding court in the back of the club dining room and neither heard nor experienced any of this.'

In October, back in the UK, Joe Massot set about filming additional fantasy sequences. Almost inevitably, Robert Plant was filmed riding a steed in the role of a medieval knight, with his wife and children by a babbling country brook; John Paul Jones read stories to his kids; John Bonham drove a hot rod and ploughed fields. And Jimmy Page?

Page insisted on being shot on the full moon, on 12 October 1973, on a rocky outcrop behind Boleskine House. In the filmed sequence he climbs upwards until he reaches the top, where he is met by a hooded hermit figure, of the same ilk as in the tarot pack and the gatefold of *Led Zeppelin IV*. The hermit's face then morphs through time, revealing it to be that of an ancient Jimmy Page, an antique Zoso: Page's self-perception, the ancient man of wisdom, essential for spreading his myth and that of Led Zeppelin.

With his purchase of Plumpton Place, Page had set himself up as one of Britain's new aristocrats. But a gentleman with a country estate requires a town house in London, so he set about finding the right one.

The Tower House, at 29 Melbury Road in London's exclusive Holland Park, is a neo-medieval structure built by architect William Burges as a 'palace of art', in the Gothic Revival style. Since his teens, Page had been fascinated by Burges, whose work was interwoven with the Pre-Raphaelite movement.

Dominated by a distinctive cylindrical tower and conical roof, the house was built of red brick. The ground floor had a library, drawing room and dining room, and there were only two bedrooms. Each room had its own theme, such as astrological symbols, butterflies, the ocean. A Grade I listed building, the place felt like high art, as though ordained from above.

Perhaps presciently, the bedroom decoration – exaggerated poppies covering the panels of a bedside cupboard – suggested another of Burges's abiding interests: opium.

The poet John Betjeman, who lived there in the early sixties, had this to say of the house: 'A great brain has made this place. I don't see how anyone can fail to be impressed by its weird beauty ... awed into silence from the force of this Victorian dream of the Middle Ages.'

The actor Richard Harris purchased the house from Lady Jane Turnbull in 1969 for £75,000, gazumping Liberace after learning that the flamboyant American entertainer had yet to put down a deposit. 'It was a strange building and had eerie murals painted on the ceiling ... I sensed evil,' wrote the artist Danny La Rue in his autobiography of a visit to Tower House. Harris claimed the house was haunted by the ghosts of children who had lived in a demolished orphanage formerly on the site – the actor placated them by buying them toys.

A haunted mansion? Just the thing for Jimmy Page. In 1973 he bought Tower House's lease for £300,000, pipping David Bowie, his fellow Capricorn superstar and Crowleyite rival, to the post. 'I was still finding things 20 years after being there – a little beetle on the wall or something like that. It's Burges's attention to detail that is so fascinating,' said Page, for whom detail had always held its own high place, in a 2012 interview.

Some of the detail Page himself brought to Tower House was equally culturally significant, like the rows of velvet suits, neatly hung according to colour. Page has never thrown away a single item of clothing, preserving it all, a further art statement assiduously cared for by dedicated staff who fight the eternal war against moths.

Some ten minutes walk from the house, at 4 Holland Street, just off Kensington Church Street, Page set up his own occult bookshop, the Equinox Booksellers and Publishers, as it was grandly titled. *The Equinox* had been the name of Aleister Crowley's own biannual magazine.

Designed expensively for Page by an architect in the manner of a *fin de siècle* occult lodge, his shop had its share of Art Deco detail and Egyptian motifs, as well as Crowley's birth chart pinned to one wall. He set up the Equinox because he had become frustrated at entering such shops on his travels and never finding what he was looking for. 'There was not one bookshop in London with a good collection of occult books and I was so pissed off not being able to get the books I wanted,' he wrote in his photographic autobiography.

He intended to republish long-out-of-print occult works. The first and only books published by the Equinox Booksellers and

Publishers were *The Book of the Goetia*, personally translated by Aleister Crowley himself, and *Astrology, A Cosmic Science* by Isabel Hickey. But the musician would find the world of esoteric publishing more complex than he had perhaps expected. Mind you, the shop itself would become a focus for aspects of life that Crowley himself might have approved: the consumption of heroin was commonplace. 'They were all busy doing smack in the top room at Equinox,' said Jeff Dexter. 'The initial burst of smack in London came in with Eric [Clapton] and Delaney and Bonnie. And John Lennon.'

'I used to go over there to score,' said John Dunbar, the former husband of Marianne Faithfull.

16

THE KING AND JIMMY PAGE

On 28 October 1973 Led Zeppelin's legendarily substantial contract with Atlantic Records was due for renewal. The band were now responsible for 25 per cent of Atlantic's sales, and Ahmet Ertegun was anxious to retain such a cash cow.

Although already wealthy beyond his wildest dreams, Jimmy Page now saw an opportunity to truly secure his pension. As the Beatles, Rolling Stones and more recently Elton John had done before them, he and Peter Grant decided to form their own record label, something to which the other three Led Zeppelin members each agreed. Unlike the Beatles' and Stones' labels, however, they were insistent that this would not turn into a vanity project: they would sign cutting-edge artists and promote them to success. By setting up their own label through Atlantic, Ertegun and Jerry Wexler's company would essentially become Zeppelin's distributors, although Atlantic remained involved in the marketing.

Grant held a meeting with Ertegun and, after an all-night session between these two music-business *éminences grises*, a deal was finally struck. The Atlantic boss emerged into the dawn light with the line: 'Peter, you've taken me to the cleaners.'

But what would the label be called? There were some predictable suggestions: in addition to Led Zeppelin Records, Stairway, Slag, Slut and Eclipse were mooted, but thankfully dismissed. Then came an odd contender, Swan Song, an idea from Page, a reference to the pair of Australian black swans that roamed freely about his Plumpton residence. Page considered the noise these swans emitted in the moments before their death to be 'one of the most beautiful sounds in the world'. He had played around with the name for a tune he was working on, but instead it became the name of Led Zeppelin's own record company.

As a piece of symbolism, the name 'Swan Song' had considerable resonance, as the ensuing difficult years would prove. The traditional meaning of the phrase is the end of a final act, a last statement before the endgame is arrived at. Was this Page's subconscious means of somehow drawing to an end the subtly ongoing crisis that the entity of Led Zeppelin was creating in the lives of all around it? For if you use Swan Song Records as a chapter marker in the life of the group, it is clear that from then on matters begin to unravel at a frightening pace.

As you would expect from a group whose leader had such a creative aesthetic, the Swan Song logo seemed like high art. It was based around a work by the 19th-century painter William Rimmer, *Evening: Fall of Day*, which Page found in Philippe Jullian's book *Dreamers of Decadence*. Rimmer's painting had been 'improved', to an extent, for the logo: now it appeared to show Icarus falling from his celestial splendour after flying too close to the sun. Later, in an interview with *Mojo* in 2015, Page said: 'If you think about it in relation to the original Led Zeppelin idea of a lead balloon, it's carrying on the original idea of that, isn't it? The idea of the swan song is the dying song of the swan, okay? So there's a parallel.'

The Swan Song label was an almost immediate success, as early as June of 1974. Although Bad Company were signed to Island Records in the UK, elsewhere they were a Swan Song act. Moreover, they were managed by Peter Grant. Clearly a supergroup-in-waiting, Bad Company had Free's impressive blues-wailing singer Paul Rodgers and drummer Simon Kirke;

playing guitar was Mott the Hoople's Mick Ralphs; and on bass was Boz Burrell from King Crimson.

Bad Company's eponymous first album went to number one in the United States and number three in the UK. 'Swan Song was initially a great idea,' said Simon Kirke. 'It had that Island Records vibe, in that it was formed by musicians to look after their musical interests and those of other bands. Of course it was a business and was run as such, but it wasn't a shrine to capitalism by any stretch of the imagination.'

But there were a couple of other acts on Swan Song who did not fare so well. Peter Grant's old friend Maggie Bell, late of club favourites Stone the Crows, was signed up, the intention being to turn her into the UK's Janis Joplin. The first time Bell met Grant, she told him that he reminded her of Orson Welles in *Citizen Kane*. His response? 'Yeah, do you want to be my little Rosebud?'

'He was absolutely enormous but he was a very kind man. I was like a daughter to him, but looking back he didn't really know what to do with me. He managed loads of guys and my career suffered through that.' Maggie Bell's LP *Suicide Sal*, on which Page played guitar – on 'If You Don't Know' and 'Comin' On Strong', a couple of hours' work – was released in 1975. She then moved to New York for a year, recording a pair of albums that Swan Song never released. 'I paid for them,' she said. 'But to this day I don't know what happened to them. I was told they weren't good enough, but believe me they were!' Instead, Maggie Bell ended up working on reception at the Swan Song offices.

The Pretty Things were also signed to Swan Song. One-time rivals to the Rolling Stones on the London R&B circuit, their singer Phil May was friends with Page, who adored their 1964 single 'Rosalyn'. Their 1968 album *S.F. Sorrow*, the first ever concept LP, had been a critical success, but there was a feeling that the group were past their sell-by date. This did not prevent their *Silk Torpedo* album being given a lavish launch in the UK, however. Chislehurst Caves, to the south-east of London, was hired for a Halloween launch party in 1974, one that would go down in rock 'n' roll legend. As Ahmet Ertegun, whose new velvet jacket was sprayed with jelly at the event, once commented: 'Throw a party. And promote the hell out of the party!' With strippers dressed as nuns doing tricks with crosses and candles, Aleister Crowley would have adored the occasion. As everyone grew progressively more drunk and drugged, the party finally wound up with John Bonham and his cronies hurling food at everyone.

Janine Safer, Swan Song's US publicist, had a different point of view to Simon Kirke: 'Swan Song was for and about Led Zeppelin, primarily. To a lesser extent it was about Bad Company. To hardly any extent it was about the Pretty Things. Maggie, though, held a very special place in the pantheon, because Peter loved her and Jimmy loved her. Detective had a brief flurry of activity, but it was a case of Hurry Up and Wait, long months of doing absolutely nothing. No one would hear from Peter and no one would hear from the band.'

Premises were acquired for the label's London headquarters at 484 New Kings Road, in the World's End section of Chelsea, a rundown, scruffy neighbourhood that had always had a criminal subtext. Swan Song's offices were no improvement on the area: beat-up, battered furniture, uncarpeted stairs, more like a squat than the centre of operations for the Biggest Band in the World. Jimmy Page lived in palatial splendour, which he rarely left for 484 New Kings Road: why should they be bothered about what the place resembled? Besides, there was something of an early distressed look about 484 New Kings Road, situated above a branch of the British Legion, which could almost be judged as an anti-aesthetic.

Near Swan Song's HQ was a pricey bar called J Arthur's, favoured by Zeppelin members and Swan Song employees, as well as posh girls and gangsters. The legendary Granny Takes a Trip, from where Page bought some of his most beautiful clothes and which also for a time dispensed heroin to those in the know, was almost next door at number 488 – though the shop would close the year Swan Song moved in. With what in hindsight seems a poetic significance, Malcolm McLaren and Vivienne Westwood had set up their own small fashion emporium, now named Sex, a few hundred yards to the east along the same block. Very soon the Sex Pistols, who would deliver especial antipathy towards Led Zeppelin, would form in that store.

As manager of both Led Zeppelin and Bad Company, and as titular head of Swan Song Records, with a 90-minute train ride in to London from his home near Lewes in Sussex, Peter Grant had his plate full. The pressure would soon start to show, with staff becoming genuinely nervous of the manager's furious tantrums – which increasingly could be diagnosed as cocaine rage.

As though adding to his own mystique, Jimmy Page had resolutely refused to meet Elvis Presley when he saw the King at Las Vegas's International Hotel in 1969 with Miss Pamela. Could he simply have been overawed by the very notion of meeting this idol, the man who had introduced the world to the liberating force of rock 'n' roll?

Again, when the entire group went to see Elvis Presley on Saturday 10 June 1972 at Madison Square Garden, they didn't get to meet him.

On 11 May 1974 this all changed. Page, Robert Plant and John Bonham went to watch Elvis once more, at the venue Led Zeppelin had made their own, the Forum in Los Angeles.

The group were in town for the launch party of Swan Song Records the previous night, thrown at the sumptuous, distinctly pink Beverly Hills Hotel, and the evening had not been without considerable controversy. Page had taken up with Bebe Buell, the girlfriend of Todd Rundgren, the mercurial musician and producer. Inevitably this was to the considerable chagrin and pain of the now 16-year-old Lori Mattix.

Bebe Buell had first met Page the previous year in New York, when she had been introduced to him by her friend Patti D'Arbanville, celebrated in Cat Stevens's 1970 song 'Lady D'Arbanville'. Page had wanted her to come with him to the Plaza Hotel, where he was staying, so they could 'party', with all the euphemism that word contains. But Buell had been preoccupied with returning home to continue an ongoing row she was having with Rundgren – over D'Arbanville, in fact, whom she had found sitting on her boyfriend's knee when she had arrived home earlier.

Later that year, at an Eric Clapton show in Manhattan, Mick Jagger tried to chat her up. Part of his come-on line revolved around warning her off Page: 'You haven't been out with Jimmy Page? You must never date Jimmy Page.' Wouldn't you think these to be the kind of words that would only increase her fascination with the Zeppelin guitarist? Jagger was clearly showing some nervousness about his rock 'n' roll love rival.

At the beginning of May 1974 Buell flew with Rundgren to Los Angeles, checking in at the Hyatt House. After yet another row, Rundgren headed up to San Francisco to play a show, leaving Buell at the Hyatt, along with Rundgren's South American raccoon, almost inevitably named Kundalini, after the primal energy of the coiled female serpent in Hindu philosophy.

In the Hyatt's lobby Buell ran into Kim Fowley and Rodney Bingenheimer, who were there because Led Zeppelin were coming in from the airport 'to host the biggest party of the year for the launch of their Swan Song label. They were the biggest band in the world in 1974.'

Extremely distressed at having been treated badly by Rundgren, she was sobbing to Fowley and Bingenheimer in one of the hotel's elevators when the door opened and Page, Plant and Cole stepped in. They had just arrived at the hotel and were heading for their rooms. 'Jimmy was wearing a pair of dainty black boots, crushed blue-velvet pants, a beautifully ruffled Edwardian shirt, and a velvet jacket worthy of Beau Brummell,' Buell wrote in her book *Rebel Heart*. 'His pale, handsome face was framed by exquisite black ringlets. He looked like Sir Lancelot.'

Page asked Buell if he hadn't met her with Patti D'Arbanville in New York, which she immediately denied, snuffling and running out of the elevator. Page got her room number from Rodney Bingenheimer.

At five the next morning a sleeping Bebe Buell received a phone call. It was Jimmy Page asking her to come up to his suite and have breakfast with him. Playing the sympathy card, he told her he was extremely upset: he had just returned from a session with Joe Walsh, 'playing guitar on a song about his wife and child, who were recently killed in a car accident. Please come and join me for breakfast. I'm very upset and lonely.'

Buell said she would only go up to see him on condition that she could bring Kundalini with her, feeling that the raccoon gave her some edge in the rock 'n' roll eccentricity stakes. Besides, she couldn't leave her on her own. She went up to his suite in her pyjamas, wearing no make-up.

'Come in, darling,' Page said, welcoming her with a bow. 'Would you like some cocaine? Are you hungry? I've got a great idea. Why don't we give this fruit basket to the raccoon and put them both in the bathroom?'

'We proceeded to hang out,' said Buell, 'drinking mimosas, doing some lines, and comparing notes on our current problems.'

When Peter Grant appeared, he questioned Buell as to whether her boyfriend would want to come and shoot Page in the kneecaps. She assured him that Rundgren had better things to do, having effectively dumped her and run off with someone else in San Francisco.

Grant then went to the bathroom, only to discover – to his great surprise – the raccoon. Not only that, but Kundalini had unleashed her primal energy: the bathroom was covered in poo, probably a consequence of all that fruit.

Page was moved to another suite, and he and Bebe Buell finally went to bed together, the musician immediately going down on her: 'He told me I would sleep much better if I had an orgasm; otherwise, the cocaine would keep me awake, and I didn't want any of the Valium he was offering me.'

Not long after falling asleep, they were woken by a frantic Lori Mattix attempting to enter the room: 'I just remember the cacophony of some girl screaming "Jimmy!" outside the door. Then Richard [Cole] suddenly showed up and dragged her off in hysterics.' A couple of hours later they were woken yet again; Buell's room remained unpaid for, and her luggage was about to be removed. Page immediately handed Cole the outstanding $50 for the room. 'Well, Richard, it's very simple,' he said. 'Get the bags and bring them here. She'll be staying with me.' Buell was 'kind of shocked by his presumption, but I was also very happy.'

Then Page told her about the 'lovely party' they would be throwing for Swan Song at the Beverly Hills Hotel, saying, 'I would love you to be my companion for the launch.'

'I became Jimmy's girlfriend for the week,' said Buell. 'I stayed with him and was never far from his side.' Every night they ate at expensive restaurants; during the day they would visit metaphysical bookstores. 'We spent a lot of time in bed … We had a powerful sexual relationship. It was very beautiful. He never tried to have anything but completely straight sex with me, although he had one weird penchant. When he kissed me, he loved to spew his saliva into my mouth. It was odd. I thought of it as his way of coming in my mouth without coming in my mouth. Otherwise, we had the most wholesome sex imaginable ... Jimmy was never violent; he never tried to practise black magic.'

The group leader may never have resorted to physical aggression, but others in the Zeppelin camp were known to throw their considerable weight around. One night Page and Buell went to the Rainbow Bar and Grill to have dinner. 'I noticed that there was a lot of violence surrounding Zeppelin,' she said. 'Somebody came over to our table, and that irritated everyone. Richard Cole hit the guy with his elbow and he fell to the ground, next to his teeth. That was a very disturbing thing for me to witness, because I never thought that violence was part of rock 'n' roll ... But Peter Grant brought the gangster image to the rock 'n' roll scene, and he prospered. Richard and Peter were not to be tangled with. They were rough players.'

There was a public scene as security guards kept Lori Mattix – who had arrived off her head on Quaaludes – away from Page, and therefore Buell, at the Swan Song party. 'And it was made very clear to Lori – who was probably the most beautiful girl in LA and had given herself exclusively to Jimmy from age 14 to 16 – and Miss Pamela that they were history.

'I was very attracted to Jimmy Page,' said Buell. 'He was my type – very dashing, very English, very Renaissance. He had that otherworldly, other-time vibe. If you fantasised about being a princess and having a prince come and sweep you off your feet and take you on horseback to his castle, Jimmy Page was Sir Lancelot. What girl wouldn't enjoy that fantasy, even if it was only for a week?'

The night following the Swan Song party, Buell did not accompany Page to the Forum to watch Elvis Presley.

Towards the end of the show, Elvis asked for the arena's house lights to be switched on so he could take a look at the audience. Beginning his next song, Willie Nelson's 'Funny How Time Slips Away', he suddenly paused and spoke to his band.

'Wait a minute, wait a minute, hold it,' he said, laughing. 'If we can we start together, fellas, because we've got Led Zeppelin out there, and Jimmy Darren, and, uh, a whole bunch of people, and let's try to look like we know what we're doing, whether we do or not … Now, what were we doing?'

Following the concert, Page, Plant, Bonham and Grant were taken to the King's hotel suite, where he was staying with his girlfriend, a recent *Playboy* centrefold. 'We went up to his suite and his girlfriend Ginger was there with just a few other people,' Page said later. 'I can tell you, we were really nervous. When he came to the door, he started doing his famous twitch. You know, he didn't put that on – that was something he really did.'

Although scheduled to visit Elvis for no more than 20 minutes, they ended up being with him for over two hours. John Bonham broke the ice with a classic-car conversation, and later Elvis admitted to his guests that he had never heard any of Zeppelin's songs, other than the inevitable 'Stairway to Heaven'.

What he had heard, however, were scurrilous tales of Zeppelin on the road. Were they true? Elvis wondered.

It was left to tactful Robert Plant to issue a denial: 'Of course not. We're family men. I get the most pleasure out of walking the hotel corridors, singing your songs.'

Plant recalled that 'we all stood in a circle and discussed this whole phenomenon, this lunacy … Elvis was very focused, very different to what you now read.'

Page told the King that Led Zeppelin rarely soundchecked, and that when they did, all Plant wanted to do was sing Elvis songs. Laughing, Elvis asked Plant which of his tunes the singer selected. 'I told him I liked the ones with all the moods, like that great country song "Love Me".' To Elvis's considerable amusement, Plant proceeded to sing his rendition of 'Love Me' to the King of Rock 'n' Roll. Elvis broke up in laughter.

As they left Elvis's suite, extremely happy to have met their hero, they heard a voice behind them. 'So when we were leaving, after a most illuminating and funny 90 minutes with the guy, I was walking down the corridor,' remembered Plant. 'He swung round the door frame, looking quite pleased with himself, and started singing that song: "Treat me like a fool ..." I turned around and did Elvis right back at him. We stood there, singing to each other.'

Led Zeppelin then flew to New York, booking the entire first-class cabin of an American Airlines plane so that the raccoon could fly with them. 'We had a party flying across America at 35,000 feet,' said Bebe Buell.

In Manhattan they checked into the Pierre on Fifth Avenue, and Page had two connecting suites: 'He used one suite for entertaining and the other to live in, because he was fastidious and he didn't like the reek of beer cans and drug paraphernalia, or getting the smell of cigarette smoke on his clothes.'

Not that the lovers confined themselves to their suite all of the time. 'During the days, we went to art galleries and museums, but mostly we went shopping. Jimmy bought great quantities of shirts and jackets; occasionally, he would buy me a dress or a pair of shoes, and he also bought me a wonderful book on the Pre-Raphaelite painter [Edward] Burne-Jones.'

When it came time for Page to return to London, Buell drove out to the airport with him in a limousine. 'He gave me the impression that their relationship [with Charlotte Martin] was souring and he wasn't sure what its future was going to be. He left me dangling, but it was very romantic and he told me he would call me.'

In September 1974 Bebe Buell called Led Zeppelin's London office, asking for Jimmy Page to be informed that she would shortly be arriving in London. Clearly he had not given her his home phone number. What Buell did not mention was that she would be accompanying her boyfriend Todd Rundgren on a promotional tour for his record company, Warner Brothers.

Lodged at the prestigious Savoy Hotel, Buell and Rundgren were sitting down to breakfast when a huge bunch of flowers arrived, accompanied by a card from Page that contained his phone number. Rundgren's response? To take his girlfriend's plate of scrambled eggs and throw them against the wall. Then he delivered a diatribe against Page: 'He's bad. He's evil. He's dark. He's the devil. He's got a woman and a kid. Once he gets tired of you, he'll retire you. Soon you'll be too old for him.' Buell swore to Rundgren that she would never see Page again.

The pair went to Paris and Amsterdam on further promotional work, before returning to London and checking in at the Montcalm Hotel, close by Marble Arch. As soon as Rundgren disappeared for a meeting with publicity guru Derek Taylor, Buell called Page, and he talked her into coming round to see him at Tower House. She had told Rundgren she was meeting some model friends and would link up with him that night at the Speakeasy.

Buell and Page started drinking champagne as soon as she arrived at Tower House, and within 15 minutes they were in bed together. 'In Jimmy's defence,' she wrote, 'he never attempted to use a whip on me, never hurt me sexually, never tried to do anything weird to me … When I hear the legends and myths, I'm always perplexed. I was Guinevere and he was Sir Lancelot, and Todd was King Arthur … And I really thought Jimmy loved me. I thought there was something there.'

She woke up the next day, having missed the Speakeasy. In considerable anguish, she called Derek Taylor, who told her that they had the police looking for her.

Briefly reconciled with Rundgren at the Montcalm, Buell remained in their room as he went to the Warner Brothers offices. Then she called Page, who told her she could only come to his place if she was going to stay there with him. She said she would come for a couple of days. 'Ten minutes after swearing to him that I wouldn't get in touch with Jimmy, I couldn't stop myself. Maybe it was the music. Maybe it was his Satanic Edwardian quality. Maybe it was the medieval Sir Lancelot vibe. I didn't know and I didn't care. I just wanted to be with Jimmy.'

Reluctantly, Rundgren let her stay on in London when he flew back to New York. 'Todd had this theory that Jimmy was evil and he was good. And I was the virgin angel sacrifice in the middle of this duel between the two powers. He felt that Jimmy collected women and that once Jimmy had wooed me away from him and dominated me completely, I would become yesterday's news.'

What did Bebe Buell experience when she once again visited Tower House? 'When I went back to Jimmy, he was a vision in a beautiful white suit. He got an erection, which I couldn't help noticing. He looked at me and said, "See what you do to me? You make me so hard."'

The pair took mescaline and went to bed, where they seemed to spend most of the time. 'When you're tripping, an erection looks even larger than it is; it takes on a whole other dimension,' she said. 'I was afraid to have sex with him for a minute, because I was hallucinating that his penis stretched to the other side of the room. I needed to pull myself together and realise that it was an average-size penis.' That night, still tripping on the mescaline, they went into the Tower House's sizeable garden 'to look for fairies'.

'Jimmy was very sexy. I think that he was having fun, enjoying a very pure exchange with a woman. I was different. Most of the women he knew were wilder and expected the macabre from him. I think if a woman had wanted her ass spanked and her hair pulled, he would gladly have delivered. If a woman had wanted to be beaten with whips, he would have obliged. If a woman wanted a cigarette put out on her chest, he would have done it.'

She described them going out to eat at a high-end Indian restaurant, and how Page would keep people at arm's length when he was in public. 'It was because people didn't know who he was. I think it was because they were genuinely afraid that he was Satan, that he had some sort of evil allure ... Mick Jagger is supposed to be Lucifer, but people never act that way around him. He gets a lot of, "Hey, it's Mick Jagger. Hi!" I never saw that happen to Jimmy Page. Furthermore, unless it was a good-looking girl, Jimmy would act oblivious when someone was having a conversation with him. If some testosterone-driven guy came running up, saying, "Oh my God! You're my hero," he would just look straight ahead and not even acknowledge the person.'

Page asked Buell for her date of birth and drew up her astrological chart. But this reading concerned him: something in it seemed inappropriate for him.

All the same, Page's intentions seemed to be to have Buell live in the house in London while Charlotte and Scarlet remained in Plumpton. 'Of all the men I saw in these years, Jimmy Page was the only one I was seriously considering leaving Todd for.'

In the November 1974 edition of *Playboy*, in which Buell was the centrefold, she was identified as Rundgren's girlfriend. And in the editorial copy that accompanied her nude spread, Mick Jagger was mentioned as a friend who 'called regularly from Montauk'.

'That annoyed Jimmy Page no end,' she said.

However, the *Playboy* spread caused problems for her modelling career. It was suggested she move to London and work there until the heat evaporated in the more puritanical USA. Moreover, Page had started calling again, asking her to come and visit him in London, followed by a cable sent by Peter Grant, requesting her presence in London in November. So she went.

Bebe was supposed to be staying in the flat above Equinox on Holland Street. But Eric, the store's manager, told her that Charlotte and Scarlet would be staying there instead. For, in a touch of Dionysian symmetry, there had been another scandal.

Ron Wood, still a member of the Faces, and his wife Krissy had been to visit Page and Charlotte at Plumpton. After telling her husband she no longer loved him, Krissy Wood became Page's live-in girlfriend for the next 12 or so months. Ron Wood briefly went off with Charlotte, and then Pattie Boyd. When Led Zeppelin played the Nassau Coliseum on 13 and 14 February 1975, Ron Wood joined them each night on guitar for the encore of 'Communication Breakdown'. Earlier, 'Woody', who seemed to live life as though in permanent disbelief and gratitude at the fortunate hand fate had dealt him, had phoned Page. 'How's our bird?' he asked him.

17

COCAINE NIGHTS AND HAUNTED HOUSES

When Kenneth Anger met Jimmy Page he would no doubt have mentioned that, in his youth, just prior to the Second World War, he had seen a Nazi zeppelin prowling the air along the Californian Pacific coast.

Brought up in Los Angeles, an alumnus of Beverly Hills High School, Kenneth Anglemeyer – he altered his name to the simple but telling 'Anger' for reasons of brevity – was turned on to movies by his actor grandmother, a friend of the director Max Reinhardt, and he set up a film society to show little-known European films. Anger was one of the first openly gay directors in Hollywood, and the homoerotic *Fireworks*, made in 1947, was his first film. Later he took his friend Dr Alfred Kinsey, the famous sexologist, to Aleister Crowley's abbey in Sicily, where he spent a summer scraping off whitewash that had been applied to Crowley's paintings after the Great Beast had been expelled under Mussolini's orders.

Anger financed his own films during the latter half of the 1970s through his book *Hollywood Babylon*, a magazine-style tome that recounted many of Hollywood's dirtiest secrets. (When I bought a copy imported from the US in 1975, it was from a small bookshop on Holland Street, only a few yards from Equinox; it seems not unreasonable to assume that Anger himself – who would have been in residence at Tower House at the time, certainly visiting Equinox – could have provided the store with its copies of *Hollywood Babylon*.)

Anger first met Page in 1973 at a Sotheby's auction in London, where they were both bidding for a pornographic manuscript by Aleister Crowley. 'He, of course, had more money than I did,' Anger said later.

Bonding over their fascination with Crowley, Anger accepted Page's invitation to go with him to Boleskine House and exorcise the building of the headless man who had so thoughtlessly been rolling his head about the property. Then Anger asked Page to write the soundtrack for the film he was working on, *Lucifer Rising*.

The two had much in common beyond a love of Crowley, not least a rock-hard core belief in a total extension of consciousness to embrace all possibilities. 'I think that's what you have to keep in mind when you are hearing/looking at Jimmy and Kenneth's work,' Steve Parsons, formerly Snips, the singer with 1970s cult band the Sharks, whom Page would later call on, told me. 'It's an audible/visible extension of a much more involved and complicated process, which includes mental, spiritual and physical reconstruction of the senses.

'Both men have made contact with and seek to "bring down" star beings from the past and the future – Kenneth works in elegant silent gesture and Jimmy utilises thunder and lightning to power his musical machine.

'Our boys did give it a go but, as is mostly the case, it ended in tears. Not sure what Kenneth thinks about *Lucifer Rising* now as he was obviously angry (the clue's in the name) for a long time and, as always, Jimmy keeps his thoughts to himself (probably in another dimension on a finely printed page).'

Extremely iconoclastic, *Lucifer Rising* is based on the theory that the audience will 'get' Anger's redefining the notion of Lucifer – in his terms, the bringer of light, who had essentially been given a bad rap. Set in Egypt, presenting a series of Thelemite rituals, *Lucifer Rising* seems to be about Crowley having *The Book of the Law* dictated to him in Egypt in 1904. Visually stunning, *Lucifer Rising* is a beautiful film, the dream-like substance of Anger's filmmaking providing a sumptuous and rather profound experience, though non-Thelemites may find the film slightly (but only slightly) difficult.

'For me,' says Snips, '*Lucifer Rising* is essentially an optimistic piece concerning renewal through the actions of the primordial mother and father summoning their daughter, Lilith, from the hell worlds below up to the earth plane, where she will greet visitors from space.'

Anger's film had yet to be edited, and with editing equipment installed in Tower House to save the shambles of *The Song Remains the Same*, Page invited Kenneth Anger to his London home to work on the movie. Meanwhile, he promised, he would work on the soundtrack.

The Madison Square Garden shows filmed for *The Song Remains the Same* in July 1973 were the last Led Zeppelin played until 11 January 1975. After the concerts, with all due secrecy, Robert Plant had an operation to remove nodules from his vocal chords – a perennially worrying medical development for untrained singers like Plant. During the 1973 American tour his vocals could be unpredictable to say the least. When Zeppelin played Chicago on 7 July 1973, his voice had seemed utterly shot right from the beginning of the set, and there was similar evidence at several further shows.

Following the operation, Plant was obliged not to speak for three weeks. A further consequence of the procedure was that Led Zeppelin's singer would never again be able to reach the high notes that had been such a feature of his vocal performances. His singing on the soon-to-be-recorded *Physical Graffiti* is different from previous Zeppelin recordings: he sounds more comfortable, controlled and accomplished, with almost as much raw power still present, but rarely hitting those bitch-on-heat wails of earlier days – 'In My Time of Dying' is an exception.

Plant's need for a vocal remedy was indicative of a broader malaise: the group's lifestyle hardly leant itself to disciplined vocal practice. Beginning with the 1972 Japanese tour, on which John Bonham behaved so egregiously, the levels of excess in and around the act had developed to a worrying extent.

The 1973 American tour featured enormous amounts of cocaine: before he performed his 'Moby Dick' drum solo, Bonham would scarf up a handful of coke from a sugar bowl kept by his drum-stool; meanwhile, the other group members would step backstage for their own lines of coke, frequently with the addition of a blowjob. Alcohol was ubiquitous: the drummer was almost permanently drunk; and even Page's booze intake was now a cause for concern. Occasionally heroin was present; nothing like it would become, but it was edging in. And Page, a Capricorn, an astrological sign rather partial to hard drink and drugs, was being pulled into its potentially lethal orbit.

Back in Britain in 1973 he spent some time in his personal archives, tracking down tunes that Zeppelin had recorded over the years but never released. He hoped they would furnish him with sufficient material to ensure that the next Led Zeppelin release, the first on their own label Swan Song, could be a double album. The two-LP set had become a mark of status for all the major players in popular music: the Beatles, Rolling Stones, Bob Dylan, Jimi Hendrix and the Who had all released significant double albums. If the biggest band in the world did not follow suit it could be interpreted as diminishing status. A double record would also bring in substantially more cash for Swan Song, a point that would not have been overlooked by the ever financially cautious guitarist.

'I didn't want it to be a double album with any padding on it,' he told *Rolling Stone*. 'It would be a double album with all character pieces, the way that Led Zeppelin did their music with the sort of ethos of it, if you like, that everything sounded different to everything else.'

Brand-new material would be recorded to complement what he curated. *Led Zeppelin IV*, by far the group's most commercially successful album, had been recorded at Headley Grange. For their sixth LP, Page decided that it should be used once again, and sessions were booked for November 1973.

Then an utterly unexpected crisis arose: John Paul Jones, always the almost unknown face of the group but an essential musical fit, was considering leaving Led Zeppelin. He cited his time away from his family as his principal gripe, and claimed he had been offered the job of choirmaster at Winchester Cathedral. The Headley Grange sessions were abandoned, and Jones was given leave of absence from the group to consider his options. The time booked at Headley Grange was not wasted, however, as Swan Song's premier signing stepped in to record their debut album *Bad Company*.

Jones eventually decided against leaving Led Zeppelin, and recordings for what would become *Physical Graffiti* resumed in mid-January 1974, running for six weeks until the end of February. Ronnie Lane's mobile studio – a cheaper option than the one owned by the Rolling Stones – was employed at Headley Grange, with Ron Nevison as recording engineer.

No one involved with the project particularly wanted to spend their nights at creepy Headley Grange, and everyone instead checked in to the nearby Frensham Pond Hotel – with one abstainer. Page, seemingly at ease wherever spirits roamed, was happy to spend his nights at Headley Grange alone, able to work on ideas until dawn if necessary. (In his fascination with haunted properties, was there an element of showing off – of metaphysical machismo? Jimmy Page, the only one who'd sleep with the spectres? Well, he would, wouldn't he? It could only enhance his four-dimensional image.)

Page had already done plenty of work for *Physical Graffiti* at Plumpton Place. At the top of his Sussex house he had had a multi-track studio installed, where he would work on 'textures'. 'I had the whole of "Ten Years Gone", all of the guitar orchestration, prepared in that house. I came up with "The Wanton Song" and "Sick Again", and I had the whole concept of "Kashmir" basically there,' he told *Rolling Stone*.

But it was the return to Headley Grange that Page found inspiring. 'I knew how we did the drums in the main hall for the fourth album's "When the Levee Breaks". And some numbers would come out of thin air, like for example the way "Rock and Roll" did on the fourth album, and then on *Physical Graffiti*, "Trampled Under Foot", which came out of thin air like that, just starting out of a riff. I was basically musically salivating on the way there.'

Even before setting foot in Headley Grange, the band had three tracks already recorded there while making *Led Zeppelin IV*: 'Boogie with Stu', 'Night Flight' and 'Down by the Seaside', which was heavily influenced by Neil Young's 'Down by the River'. 'Bron-Yr-Aur' had been written for the third album. Plus there was 'Houses of the Holy', the title track for the fifth album, which hadn't fitted the mix of that record's other tunes; 'Black Country Woman', in which Robert Plant sang freely about his sexual relationship with his wife's younger sister, had also been recorded for *Houses of the Holy* in the garden of Stargroves, that plane flying overhead at the beginning of the tune. 'The Rover' too had first been essayed on the *Houses of the Holy* sessions: 'The whole thing about "The Rover" is the whole swagger of it, the whole guitar-attitude swagger. I'm afraid I've got to say it, but it's the sort of thing that is so apparent when you hear "Rumble" by Link Wray – it's just total attitude, isn't it? So that sort of thing, which is sort of probably in my DNA to be honest,' said Page.

The Headley Grange *Physical Graffiti* sessions began with just Page and John Bonham there. Page couldn't wait, he said, 'to get the drums in the hall, to get this big drum sound and then play the riff of ... "Kashmir"'. Originally titled 'Driving to Kashmir', 'Kashmir', a place neither Page nor Plant had ever been, was developed from another piece Page had been working on: 'I had it before going in there [to record]. I had a piece of music that I'd been working on, and just on the tail end of it I had that riff. I thought, "Uh-oh. This is something I really want to try." I couldn't wait to get into Headley Grange with John Bonham and do this.' The song, which he knew had to be built around the drum kit, is 'like a child's riff. Musically, it's a round, like "Frère Jacques", where you can lay things on top of it.' Robert Plant told Page he had some lyrics he had worked on when they had visited Morocco together, although this was well after the entire musical structure had been assembled.

With its epic sweep and shifts of pace, 'In My Time of Dying', which ran to over 11 minutes long, was a close rival to the mighty 'Kashmir' for the greatest track on *Physical Graffiti*. It was a reworking of Blind Willie Johnson's 1927 song 'Jesus Make Up My Dying Bed', itself a version of a traditional gospel song; Bob Dylan had recorded another version of the song. 'There were no edits or drop-ins or overdubs to the version you hear,' said Jimmy Page. 'This is Led Zeppelin just going for it for an 11-minute song with all the changes in it and everything and the musical map that you have to remember when it goes 1-2-3-4, tapes rolling.' At the end of the song, Plant's exultation 'Oh my Jesus' mutates into 'Oh my Gina'. Page expressed his surprise at Plant's daring in so admitting his affair with another rock star's wife.

There was the occasional absurdity. One morning John Bonham arrived with a bag containing 1,500 pills of Mandrax, the UK equivalent of Quaalude. Bonham intended to hide the pills by taping them to the inside of his drum heads, but his plan was flawed: as his drum roadie pointed out to him, Bonham had a Perspex kit. On another occasion, recording stopped while the band led farm animals up to Headley Grange's first floor – an example of 1960s-style 'looning' – while flares were let off. Recording was abandoned for some days after Peppy, one of the roadies, drove Bonham's brand-new BMW 3.0 CSi into a wall. Terrified, Peppy hid in a wardrobe for 36 hours until Bonzo calmed down.

Some of the new material was caught and wrapped on the first take, as both 'Custard Pie', a Zeppelin term for female genitalia, and 'Trampled Under Foot' were, though the latter was subjected to copious overdubs. On the new tune 'Sick Again' Plant seemed at times to be channelling Steve Marriott, as he had on 'Whole Lotta Love'.

Silverhead were an early sleaze-rock outfit, fronted by swaggering vocalist Michael Des Barres, his androgynous look perfectly suited to the dying embers of glam rock. From an eminent British family, Des Barres had been educated at the exclusive Repton School; as a consequence of his love of drama, he was given a part in the 1967 controversial anti-racism film *To Sir, with Love*, starring Sidney Poitier. In 1977 he would marry Miss Pamela Miller, who became Pamela Des Barres. Before that he was extremely close friends with Jimmy Page, an indubitable drug buddy.

The pair first met in the summer of 1974, when B. P. Fallon brought all of Led Zeppelin and Peter Grant to a Silverhead show at a Birmingham club, one of the last gigs that Des Barres's band would play – the group exploding, he said, 'in a cocaine frenzy. Our fan-base was coke-dealers. They got Peter to come and see the band. We were playing this club in Birmingham and there were eleven people in the audience, and four of them were Led Zeppelin.

'I was a really existential bastard and that day I'd eaten so much hash. I was still floating and didn't give a fuck, and loved Jimmy from that one moment when I'd met him.

'At an early age I met Sidney Poitier: I've never met anyone who had that much charisma. So I had the advantage of that. All the same, going back after the gig to Bonzo's farm for a jam in a tiny room, I marvelled at the ease and confidence with which Jimmy would play: what he did was staggering. So that I thoroughly enjoyed.'

He and Page clicked, said Des Barres, 'because I mentioned Rimbaud at the right time. Jimmy is an academic. He would stroll around New York buying books. Pamela would go with him.'

Des Barres found himself invited down to Plumpton Place. 'The real story is that Jimmy is a great artist and Shel Talmy recognised it first. We'd sit around, off our heads, talking about Shel Talmy, playing with a set of tarot cards that Aleister Crowley had not only designed but also owned, Jimmy wearing a cloak that had been Crowley's.

'Led Zeppelin was not necessarily fun for Jimmy: it was colossally hard work. The hugeness, those dark winters, both on tour in the United States and of the soul. You're left with a visual image that incorporates that violin bow and Jimmy Page's hair.'

In August 1974 Led Zeppelin adjourned to Shepperton Studios to restage the Madison Square Garden nights. By now Joe Massot had been taken off the project, replaced by Peter Clifton.

At the very beginning of September, Jimmy Page and Peter Grant flew out to Austin, Texas, for ZZ Top's First Annual Rompin' Stompin' Barn Dance and Bar BQ at the University of Texas Memorial Stadium. Before a 90,000-strong audience, ZZ Top were supported by Santana, Joe Cocker and Bad Company, who were kicking off the event. Bad Company effectively stole the show, Page joining them onstage to play guitar on 'Rock Me Baby'.

Page bonded with the group, especially with singer Paul Rodgers, a pointer to the future. Four days later he joined Bad Company onstage again, on the same number, at the Schaefer Music Festival in Central Park in New York. (With John Paul Jones accompanying him that time, Page would repeat his encore appearance with Bad Company at the end of the year, at their 19 December gig at London's Rainbow.)

On 14 September 1974, Page, along with John Bonham, played with Crosby, Stills, Nash and Young at the after-party of their Wembley Stadium concert; the tunes to which he added his guitar were 'Vampire Blues' and the title track from Neil Young's magnificent new *On the Beach* album. The setting was the extremely upmarket restaurant Quaglino's, which had a small stage on which the musicians could play until the sun came up.

On 16 October 1974 Page recorded a tune he had written entitled 'Scarlet', dedicated to his now two-year-old daughter. Joining him were Keith Richards on guitar and lead vocals, bass player Rick Grech, formerly of Family and Blind Faith, and drummer Bruce Rowland, then with Fairport Convention; original Rolling Stones pianist Ian 'Stu' Stewart also played on the tune. 'It sounded very similar in style and mood to *Blonde on Blonde* tracks,' the Led Zeppelin leader said in an interview with Nick Kent the next year, referencing Bob Dylan's classic double LP; he also defined the song 'a folk ballad with reggae guitars'. The extra-curricular interests of two of the musicians he worked with suggested they were not the healthiest of companions for Page; both Richards and Grech were regular heroin users. And Page was spending more and more time with Richards, linking up with him in Tramp, the high-end nightclub in London's Jermyn Street, and travelling back with him – notwithstanding Page's romance with Krissie Wood – to the Wick, Ron Wood's Richmond house, where the Rolling Stone was hiding out from police raids on his Cheyne Walk home. When Mick Taylor departed the Stones, there were even unlikely rumours that Page might be his replacement. (When Keith Richards was busted for heroin in Canada in 1977, again it was rumoured that, if Richards was imprisoned, Page might deputise for him on tour with the Rolling Stones.)

The time recording 'Scarlet' with Keith Richards, asserted Page in an interview in 1975, was 'great, really good. We stayed up all night and went down to Island Studios, where Keith put some reggae guitars over one section. I just put some solos on it, but it was eight in the morning of the next day before I did that.' Although Page believed that 'Scarlet' might be put out as the B-side of a Rolling Stones single, it never happened. Talk of the track did, however, trigger rumours that Page had recorded a solo album. He resolutely denied it when asked about it the next year by Cameron Crowe for an article he was writing for *Rolling Stone*. 'Chalk that off to Keith Richards's sense of humour,' said Page. 'He took the tapes to Switzerland, and someone found out about them. Keith told people that it was a track from my album. I don't need to do a solo album, and neither does anybody else in the band. The chemistry is such that there's nobody in the background who's so frustrated that he has to bring out his own LPs.' Was this a shot across the bows in the direction of Robert Plant? The singer had recently expressed to Peter Grant his desire to make his own record. But who would play on it? Well, Plant wanted ... Jimmy Page, John Paul Jones and John Bonham. Grant explained the redundancy of such thinking to the vocalist.

For Christmas, Page sent out cards offering 'Thelemic Greetings' from Jimmy, Charlotte and Scarlet. Close friends may have been surprised, given that he was firmly ensconced with Krissie Wood. But then he always was a stickler for the form of convention.

* * *

Physical Graffiti was released on 24 February 1975. It debuted at number one in the album charts in both the US and UK, the first time Led Zeppelin had done this. It stayed there for ten weeks, boosting the sales of the five preceding LPs, which all joined *Physical Graffiti* at various positions in the US charts.

We all had a question about the record: where did the clever title come from? 'Graffiti was appearing, and I imagined something, which was like a physical reaction to it. Since we were in a recording studio, if you're doing a recording, and it's going on the tape, even though its magnetic tape, that's like a graffiti in itself. The music was a physical manifestation.'

Physical Graffiti didn't just sound great; it looked great too. There was a suggestion that the sleeve art was like a more successful version of that on *Led Zeppelin III*. Again, there was the repetition of an almost Advent calendar theme: through the die-cut windows of a pair of tenement buildings were Led Zeppelin members in drag, Peter Grant, the Virgin Mary, Lee Harvey Oswald, King Kong, Neil Armstrong, Judy Garland and the cast of *The Wizard of Oz*, Queen Elizabeth II, Laurel and Hardy, and body-building champion Charles Atlas.

The five-storey buildings on the sleeve had been scouted by designer Peter Corriston at 96 and 98 St Mark's Place in New York's East Village, a rundown location that would soon become extremely hip. The front cover was a daytime shot, while the rear was taken at night. On the inner sleeve, designed by Mike Doud, the song titles were written on closed window shades.

When the record came out Page and Plant were on holiday in the Caribbean, on the island of Dominica, where the local dreads had provided them with ganja and a hallucinogenic jelly fruit. *Physical Graffiti* had been conceived in a heroin haze, the guitarist seeking ways in which to access further portals to his creativity; the day-to-day scenes Jeff Dexter had witnessed at the Equinox bookstore were only a reflection of the existence of its owner. Concerned about his increasing partiality to smack, Page knew he would be unlikely to be able to obtain heroin on Dominica, which was part of its appeal as a holiday destination.

The pair were taking a break in the middle of Led Zeppelin's tenth US tour, on which the band employed a slick stage presentation involving powerful lasers and lighting for the first time. Tucked up in the Plaza Hotel in Manhattan for the nights Zeppelin played Madison Square Garden and Nassau Coliseum, Page complained that his suite was pretentious. 'Something comparable to the Versailles Palace,' he said to Richard Cole.

The roots 'n' culture existence he shared with Plant and the local Dominican dreads was a world he found far more palatable. Page would play *Burnin'*, the second Wailers album on Island Records, in his suite throughout the tour.

The tour restarted in Houston, Texas, three days after *Physical Graffiti*'s release.

At their second night at Long Beach, Plant – also clearly influenced by their Caribbean sojourn – requested that the soundtrack from the classic Jamaican movie *The Harder They Come* be played over the sound system before they went onstage; he personally transported a copy of the record down to the venue, but bad traffic ensured that the band arrived so late that the idea was nixed.

In an endeavour to further broaden Led Zeppelin's market, a public-relations company had been taken on. For the first time ever, Led Zeppelin were on the cover of *Rolling Stone*. Sixteen-year-old reporter Cameron Crowe accompanied the band on the *Starship* to write a lengthy, perceptive article about the band. Plant, now seen very much as the face of Led Zeppelin, was intensely cooperative; Page less so, although he was reasonably forthcoming.

One of his replies was fascinating. When Crowe asked him, 'How much do you believe in yourself?', Page gave a lengthy response: 'I may not believe in myself, but I believe in what I'm doing. I know where I'm going musically. I can see my pattern and I'm going much slower than I thought I'd be going. I can tell how far I ought to be going. I know how to get there, all I've got to do is keep playing … I'm not a guitarist as far as a technician goes, I just pick it up and play it. Technique doesn't come into it. I deal in emotions. It's the harmonic side that's important. That's the side I expected to be much further along on than I am now. That just means to say that I've got to keep at it.'

Danny Goldberg, Led Zeppelin's young public-relations executive, had a brainwave that would potentially give a boost to the band's intellectual credibility. He would link Page and William Burroughs, the legendary Beat writer. Burroughs would interview him for *Crawdaddy* magazine, a New York-based publication that had been described by none other than *Rolling Stone* as 'the first serious publication devoted to rock 'n' roll news and criticism'. Burroughs attended a Zeppelin show at Madison Square Garden, then the pair retired to the author's downtown loft on Franklin Street, where they shared 'two fingers of whiskey'. Burroughs wanted a conversation rather than a more formal question-and-answer session. Both the musician and the writer shared a fondness for heroin, though this was not mentioned in the article, titled 'Led Zeppelin, Jimmy Page and Rock Magic', that Burroughs penned for the June 1975 edition of *Crawdaddy*.

'We started talking over a cup of tea,' wrote Burroughs, 'and found we have friends in common: the real-estate agent who negotiated Jimmy Page's purchase of the Aleister Crowley house on Loch Ness; John Michel, the flying-saucer and pyramid expert; Donald Cammell, who worked on *Performance*; Kenneth Anger, and the Jaggers, Mick and Chris. The subject of magic came up in connection with Aleister Crowley and Kenneth Anger's film *Lucifer Rising*, for which Jimmy Page did the soundtrack.

'Since the word "magic" tends to cause confused thinking, I would like to say exactly what I mean by "magic" and the magical interpretation of so-called reality. The underlying assumption of magic is the assertion of "will" as the primary moving force in this universe – the deep conviction that nothing happens unless somebody or some being wills it to happen. To me this has always seemed self-evident. A chair does not move unless someone moves it. Neither does your physical body, which is composed of much the same materials, move unless you will it to move. Walking across the room is a magical operation. From the viewpoint of magic, no death, no illness, no misfortune, accident, war or riot is accidental. There are no accidents in the world of magic. And will is another word for animate energy. Rock stars are juggling fissionable material that could blow up at any time … I found Jimmy Page equally aware of the risks involved in handling the fissionable material of the mass unconscious.'

Among other things, Page mentioned to Burroughs that on their early US tours, the group would ensure they were never in the country for more than six months, as they would have been eligible for the draft for the Vietnam War.

Much of the interview was less substantial than one might have hoped: interesting yet hardly revelatory. 'We talked about magic and Aleister Crowley,' wrote Burroughs. 'Jimmy said that Crowley has been maligned as a black magician, whereas magic is neither white nor black, good nor bad – it is simply alive with what it is: the real thing, what people really feel and want and are. I pointed out that this "either/or" straitjacket had been imposed by Christianity when all magic became black magic; that scientists took over from the Church, and Western man has been stifled in a non-magical universe known as "the way things are". Rock music can be seen as one attempt to break out of this dead soulless universe and reassert the universe of magic.

'Jimmy told me that Aleister Crowley's house has very good vibes for anyone who is relaxed and receptive.'

Burroughs asked Page his opinion about the 'monster' allegedly lurking in the depths of Loch Ness (Boleskine House sits on the shore of the loch). Page believed that something along those lines did exist. 'I wondered if it could find enough to eat, and thought this unlikely – it's not the improbability but the upkeep on monsters that worries me. Did Aleister Crowley have opinions on the subject? He apparently had not expressed himself.'

Circus magazine had published a one-shot paperback entitled *Robert Plant*, and when Led Zeppelin's tour reached San Diego, Page had words with *Circus* writer Steven Gaines: not to demand a similar tome about himself, but to ensure that there would not be a follow-up book named *Jimmy Page*.

On that 1975 US tour Jimmy Page wore a black silk stage suit, gorgeously embroidered with Chinese dragons, crescent moons and stars. 'Page's look was cosmic Nudie suit, Zen-style rockabilly,' wrote Stephen Davis, on tour with the group.

The night of the San Diego show, Davis sat down with Page in the bar of the Hyatt House and threw a handful of questions the guitarist's way.

'What about the magic thing?' Davis bravely asked.

'Magic is a system of will, and of strength,' came Page's reply, before he effectively sidestepped the question. 'That's what interests me about magic. I can't produce magic, real magic, so what we offer is the illusion of magic – mechanical devices that perform illusions while we play music. And in my own mind, the difference between the illusion and the reality, of the lasers and the theremin and all that, is … hazy. What's a laser beam? Magic, isn't it?'

Davis noted how exhausted Page looked. 'How long are you going to do this?' he asked the musician.

As Page got up to leave, he replied: 'Nothing lasts forever. I'm going to enjoy it while I can.'

Although Page was ostensibly staying at the Hyatt House with Krissie Wood, Lori Mattix had been installed in another suite on a separate floor. And a room had been booked for Bebe Buell, who was expected to arrive imminently. But there were problems with another girl the day before the San Diego show. A woman in her mid-twenties, dressed in a maroon cloak replete with cowl, approached the hotel's front desk in the morning. She was insistent that she needed to speak to Jimmy Page: the guitarist's life was in danger, she said, and she must get a warning to him. Danny Goldberg, who during the course of the tour had been elevated to the position of vice-president of Swan Song, was in his suite, having breakfast with Stephen Davis. He suggested she come up to see him.

Once in Goldberg's room, the girl declared herself to have arrived as an emissary. 'Someone' – she wouldn't say who – had seen some 'bad energy' around Page. And this could manifest the next night in San Diego. Refusing to reveal anything further – she would only tell all that she knew to Page personally – she was finally persuaded to pen a note to Page, which she did in a left-handed scrawl, placing her missive in an envelope and sealing it with her tongue. When she left the room, after one more attempt to see Page, she was angry and slammed the door.

Goldberg then took the unopened envelope and burned it, spreading the ashes before an image of Lord Krishna. He informed Peter Grant of the threat to Page's life, and a further layer of security was added to the San Diego show.

Six months later, when President Gerald Ford visited Sacramento, the California state capital, one 'Squeaky' Fromme, a member of Charles Manson's Family, pointed a gun at the President. A Secret Service agent grabbed the weapon before she could squeeze the trigger. Both Goldberg and Davis felt she looked exactly like the girl who had come up to Goldberg's suite. To this day, Davis believes that the girl so anxious to deliver a 'warning' to Page was Squeaky Fromme.

18

AN ACCIDENT IN EXILE

Led Zeppelin returned to Britain on 10 May 1975, and went straight into rehearsals at Shepperton Studios. Significantly they were about to use up 16 of the 60 days that they would be allowed to spend in the UK during the financial year that had commenced at the beginning of April 1975. For the four members, along with Peter Grant, had decided to be non-resident in their native land in order to avoid paying what they considered punitive tax during a golden financial period for Zeppelin. Their last US tour had earned them $40 million – multiply that by five for a contemporary equivalent figure. And those dates were only the precursors to a set of late-summer stadium shows that would commence in August: dates that would make their take from the late-winter tour they had just completed seem like toy-town money. What they were about to embark on was known as 'tax exile'. Although in the case of Jimmy Page, it could be seen in retrospect as a dangerous exile from his own soul, one that – perhaps more than anything – was fuelled by his dependence on heroin.

But that was to come. For now this was their triumphant homecoming: on 17 May they played the first of five nights at London's Earls Court Exhibition Centre, a cavernous concrete barn that was the largest venue in the capital, holding some 17,000 people. Their American show, involving a vast PA, was airfreighted to Earls Court, along with the equipment to fire their laser beams – which, in the end, would prove somewhat underwhelming. An enormous video screen hovered over the band at the rear of the stage, the first to be used in such a manner in the UK. Production costs were so high that Page later remarked, 'We were so determined to do the same sort of show and more than what we'd been doing in America that in the end we came out of it with just a few hundred pounds over the five days, but it didn't matter because the vibe was so electrifying.'

An acoustic set was built into the show, almost acting the part of an intermission, and during each concert Robert Plant delivered ill-considered criticism of Denis Healey, the Chancellor of the Exchequer, whose punitive taxation measures had been the cause of Led Zeppelin's tax exile. On Sunday 25 May, Plant uttered his final jibe in this vein: 'Thank you, Great Britain, for five glorious days. Thanks for being a great audience, and if you see Denis Healey ... tell him we're gone!' As barely a single member of the band's audience would have suffered similar financial angst, it was hard to feel sympathy for a millionaire rock star bellyaching about the amount of tax he was obliged to pay. Plant's remarks were later held up as an example of dinosaur rock-star thinking, and a justification for the imminent emergence of punk rock, the genesis of which was continuing to develop at Malcolm McLaren and Vivienne Westwood's fashion boutique, just along the street from Swan Song's London HQ: six months later the Sex Pistols would play their very first gig.

On that final Sunday night, an after-show party was thrown backstage at Earls Court, in a sizeable downstairs section. The adored R&B act Dr Feelgood performed, specifically for the edification of Ahmet Ertegun, with whom the Feelgoods hoped to sign a US deal – they eventually went to CBS. The party was a suitably pricey affair, with excellent food and champagne on tap. Plant, John Bonham, John Paul Jones and Peter Grant table-hopped, the quintessence of conviviality. But there was no sign of Page. Finally, at around 4 a.m., the guitarist could be seen gingerly manoeuvring the stairs that led into the party area, accompanied by a slinky Krissie Wood. An etiolated figure, seemingly floating on air, Page hovered down to the event, as though he had little idea of where he was. He seemed utterly out of it.

Led Zeppelin would not perform again in their home country until their Knebworth shows in 1979.

The next day, 26 May, Robert Plant and his family left for Morocco, heading straight to Agadir, the coastal resort in the south of the country. Meanwhile, Jimmy Page flew to New York to work on the material recorded on their 1973 tour, readying it for the soundtrack album that would accompany their much-postponed movie.

Three weeks later the two Led Zeppelin frontmen linked up again, in Marrakech, to attend the city's folk festival. Page was accompanied by Charlotte Martin and Scarlet, who was now four years old. After the festival, they hired a Range Rover and drove a long way south, heading for the town of Taifa, on the edge of the Sahara desert. But the dismal road conditions defeated them before they got there. Moreover, while they were there the Western Sahara War was breaking out over the territorially disputed Spanish Sahara.

Plant had a top-of-the-range recording device with him, and he was intrigued by the possibility of recording rhythms employed by local tribesmen, notably Berbers. But the political environment and transport conditions stymied his ambitions.

After four weeks, they turned the Range Rover around and headed north, catching a boat in Tangier that took them to Gibraltar, from where they drove up through Spain and France to Switzerland. Peter Grant had chosen Montreux, the home of convenient numbered bank accounts, as his tax-exile domicile. It was also the site of Claude Nobs's legendary annual Montreux Jazz Festival. With the rest of the band also in town, they had a meeting about their imminent US tour, due to start at Oakland Coliseum on 23 August; it was agreed they would meet in Paris on 10 August for rehearsals. The four musicians hung out at the jazz festival, which was in full flow.

Plant, however, had developed a taste for sun and sand in Morocco – and he wanted more of it. The Greek island of Rhodes had been recommended to him as a convivial destination by Phil May, singer with the Pretty Things. May had rented a house in Rhodes from Pink Floyd's Roger Waters, and Plant arranged to link up with him there. The Led Zeppelin singer decided to drive there from Montreux with his family; Page followed behind in another vehicle, accompanied by not only Charlotte and Scarlet, but also Shirley – Maureen Plant's sister (she of 'What Is and Should Never Be') – and her husband.

On 3 August Page flew off from Rhodes to Sicily; he was keen to see Aleister Crowley's Abbey of Thelema – little more than a farmhouse, really. It was Kenneth Anger who, having spent that summer cleaning up Crowley's desecrated wall art at the house, had recommended the property to him. The guitarist was considering adding the abbey to his already impressive property portfolio.

On 4 August, beneath the cloudless blue sky of another perfect day on Rhodes, Maureen Plant was driving her husband, their two children Karac and Carmen, as well as Scarlet Page, back from the beach in a rented Austin Mini when she misjudged a bend. The Mini shot off the road and ploughed into a tree, the impact smashing Robert Plant's right ankle and elbow as well as bones in his right leg. As the children in the back of the car screamed in terror, Plant looked over at Maureen: she was bleeding, with a gash in her head. The singer believed his wife to be dead; in fact, she was unconscious, with a broken pelvis and leg, and a fractured skull. Their son Karac had a broken leg, and their daughter Carmen a broken wrist. Only Scarlet, seated between the two Plant children, escaped relatively unscathed, with only a few cuts and bruises. Travelling behind them in another Mini were Charlotte Martin, with Maureen's sister Shirley and her husband. Although they endeavoured to summon help, it took several hours before a fruit truck with a flatbed was commandeered, on which the wounded were transported to the nearest hospital.

Maureen Plant had lost plenty of blood, and hers was a rare blood type. Thank goodness her sister Shirley was with them – she shared the same type – but even so, Maureen needed even more fresh blood than Shirley could give her.

In great distress, that evening Charlotte called Richard Cole in London. Cole immediately went into action. Through the Greek Embassy in London he contacted Dr John Baretta, a Harley Street physician who spoke Greek, and a celebrated orthopaedic surgeon, Dr Mike Lawrence, was also contacted. Both men agreed to fly immediately to Rhodes, but there was a further absurd frustration: Peter Grant was on holiday and uncontactable. And without his say-so, the Swan Song accountants refused to access the funds for a private plane to bring Plant and his family back. Thankfully, Baretta had a vital contact: he was the personal doctor for Sir Robert McAlpine, who owned not only a significant UK construction firm, but also several private jets. One of these, wrote Cole, 'could be turned into a flying ambulance, equipped with special supports for stretchers'.

When the plane took off for a night flight to Rhodes, the aircraft's refrigerator contained eight pints of Maureen's blood type. Arriving at the hospital in Rhodes at 6 a.m., the team were shocked by the sight of cockroaches scurrying about. And there was a further potential problem. 'The police are investigating the accident to see if alcohol or drugs were involved,' the hospital administrator informed the English arrivals. 'Your friends can't leave the country until the police have decided whether they're going to press charges against someone.'

Heeding the advice of Baretta, Cole made the decision to immediately fly the wounded Plant family back to the UK. He rented an ambulance and a pair of station wagons and parked them by a side entrance to the hospital. At 2 in the morning Robert and Maureen Plant – her IV bottle still inserted into her arm and held aloft by Cole – along with Karac and Carmen were whisked away to the local airport.

After refuelling in Rome, the plane was approaching Heathrow Airport at around 11.30 p.m., when all of a sudden it began circling: orders had come in from Peter Grant not to land until after midnight – to ensure the singer did not use up another precious day of his tax-exile status.

The family were transported to Guy's Hospital by London Bridge, where Maureen had an operation and Plant's leg was reset. But he was given a chilling warning by his surgeon: 'You probably won't walk again for six months, maybe more. And there's no guarantee that you'll ever recover completely.'

The US tour booked for late August and September was put on hold, as were planned dates in Europe and the Far East. Everyone involved was aware that Plant's car accident could herald the end of Led Zeppelin.

Bebe Buell spent some of that summer hanging out with Mick Jagger at Montauk in East Hampton, at the end of Long Island. Back in New York City, she one day found herself speaking on the phone to Jimmy Page, who was in London: 'At the end of what seemed like a brief, lighthearted conversation, he told me that he would send me a sign that night at midnight.'

Buell then drove up to Woodstock, where she spent the evening with her girlfriend Jeanne Theis. 'We were sitting in the small dining room when, on the stroke of midnight – I swear – we heard a crash upstairs. It could only have come from the bathroom. Rushing up there, we discovered that the large antique wood-framed oval mirror that had been carefully hung above the sink had been hurled a good ten feet across the room and lay shattered at the edge of the sunken bathtub.' The two girls immediately left the house. And Buell had the property exorcised.

After his operation at Guy's Hospital, with his badly broken leg and ankle reset, Robert Plant was prepared for a lengthy period of convalescence. However, Peter Grant was quick to point out that, if he stayed longer in the UK, his tax-exile status would be in jeopardy, costing him literally millions of pounds.

Once again thanks to a contact of Richard Cole, Plant was flown to the tax-exile island of Jersey, in the English Channel Islands. Page was extremely keen for some effort at work to begin as rapidly as possible. 'The longer we wait,' he told Cole, 'the harder it's gonna be to come back.' 'This could be the end of Led Zeppelin,' said Grant. For his part, Plant drank plenty of beer and regularly played the piano. Confined to a wheelchair, the singer now had a plaster cast extending from the top of his right hip to his toes, and was in considerable physical and mental discomfort; he was also extremely depressed, fearful he might never walk again.

It was decided that, in lieu of their planned dates and any subsequent touring, Led Zeppelin would take their fans to the movies to watch the band onstage. *The Song Remains the Same* would be rush-released, and Led Zeppelin would begin working on a new album as soon as Plant could participate. For now, Page felt they were like 'technological gypsies' in search of a home.

Where would that home be? The answer was relatively straightforward: their favourite American city, Los Angeles.

A pair of houses on the Pacific Ocean beach were rented at the Malibu Colony, one for Page and Plant, and one for Grant. A gated community, the Colony was beloved of A-list movie stars and musicians: Jascha Heifetz, the classical violinist, Robbie Robertson of the Band and Neil Diamond were currently in residence. A gated community with a mile-long beach, part of its appeal was that it was located some 20 miles up the Pacific Coast Highway from the temptations of Hollywood.

But who knew what went on behind closed doors at the Malibu Colony. Certainly some of the stellar neighbours might have been shocked by what transpired at the Page abode. 'We called the house in Malibu "Henry Hall",' Benji Le Fevre, personal assistant to Robert Plant, told Richard Cole; 'Henry' was a euphemism for heroin. There were also large quantities of that Zeppelin staple cocaine, which Plant avidly ingested, even when advised that it might hinder the time it took to recover from his injuries. 'I was the go-between when they were out there in Malibu,' remembered Michael Des Barres. 'The narcotic indulgences were so intense that they really separated these four wonderful beings.'

All the same, Page and Plant did begin to write together, notably on a pair of epics that would open and close the new record that was being developed. Partially written in Morocco that summer, the ironically titled 'Achilles Last Stand' – the Greek hero had suffered a critical leg injury of his own – and 'Tea for One', a fast tune during the LA rehearsals that had significantly slowed down by the time it was recorded.

Notwithstanding his drug interests, Page was resolutely in charge of the new LP, every bit as much as he had been on the very first Led Zeppelin album. *Presence*, as it would come to be titled, was his record, almost a solo album, as he was desperately aware that he needed to save his group. Pay heed to the tonal textures he magics on 'Tea for One', layer after layer, a development from Led Zeppelin's not dissimilar 'Since I've Been Loving You'. By the time John Paul Jones and John Bonham arrived in LA, the songs and arrangements were almost set to go.

And the technological developments employed on the album had risen several levels. As Erik Davis writes of Page: 'By the mid-1970s, he was using digital delays, guitar synthesizers, and a live set-up that included wah-wah, MXR effects, and what he admitted was "total flash": harmoniser, theremin, Echoplex, and the famous violin bow. By pushing the envelope on sound, these gadgets extended the virtuosity associated with the guitar hero into the domain of techno-acoustic experimentation. But these tools also gave Page a way to create the dramatic atmospheres so important to his sense of "light and shade". In particular, Page used electronics to explore what music buffs call timbre; the textural quality of a tone, its sheen, or grain, or colour. Page's timbral flavours define his guitar playing as much as his licks or his blend of acoustic and electric styles.'

But all Robert Plant had was a piece of wood. Employing a walking cane, the singer began to take his first few hesitant steps, finally mustering the nerve to walk up and down the thick sand of the Colony beach every day, gradually strengthening his shattered right leg. To an extent he was also recovering psychologically, heartened by the strength of the new songs and anxious to take them into a recording studio.

The temptations of the Sunset Strip appeared to have lost their appeal for the members of Led Zeppelin. When Cameron Crowe had interviewed the group at length for *Rolling Stone* earlier in the year, Plant had recalled first coming to Los Angeles at the end of 1968: 'Nineteen years old and never been kissed. I remember it well. It's been a long time. Nowadays we're more into staying in our rooms and reading Nietzsche. There was good fun to be had, you know, it's just that in those days there were more people to have good fun with than there are now. The States were much more fun. LA was LA. It's not LA now. LA infested with jaded 12-year-olds is not the LA that I really dug ... it's a shame to see these young chicks bungle their lives away in a flurry and rush to compete with what was in the old days the good-time relationships we had with the GTOs and people like that. When it came to looning, they could give us as much of a looning as we could give them.'

When John Bonham arrived for rehearsals he clearly did not feel that times had shifted, moving into a room at the Hyatt House. There, he moped about being away from his family, and stayed drunk – except when he was snorting smack.

Rousing himself one night to go to the Rainbow Bar and Grill, the drummer pulled up a stool at the bar and ordered 20 black Russians, a powerful cocktail of vodka and Kahlúa. Downing ten of them immediately, he turned around and his eyes met those of Michelle Myer, who worked for Kim Fowley. When she smiled at him – clearly oblivious of his reputation – Bonzo went berserk, staggering over to Myer and punching her full in the face. 'Don't ever look at me that way again,' he barked, returning to the bar and knocking back his remaining ten black Russians. When, on another occasion, he took on the Rainbow's bouncer, he was surprised to discover that the slight fellow was a martial-arts expert who put the drummer on his back in moments.

John Paul Jones was living apart from the other three, sometimes impossible to contact when it came to rehearsing the material at SIR Studios, way down on Sunset Boulevard in Hollywood. 'If you see John Paul Jones, shoot him on sight,' Page half-joked to Danny Goldberg.

Page couldn't find John Paul Jones? It was more like the other way round, on account of Page's unorthodox sleeping habits and time-keeping. Every night, Jones said, he would arrive at SIR, along with Plant and Bonham, to wait and wait and wait. 'I learned all about baseball during that period, as the World Series was on and there was not much else to do but watch it.'

When all four musicians did manage to link up, wrote Stephen Davis in *Hammer of the Gods*, 'the new music was hot. The effort and energy that would have gone into the fall tour went into the new music instead, and Led Zeppelin burned with a rubbery new funk that was taking the band to unexpected destinations. Moroccan white guitar noise dashed with New

Orleans "second-line" rhythms. Time signatures were brutal and labyrinthine. Bonzo was as tough as nails, and Robert was singing in his wheelchair, wiggling inside his cast.'

As is so often the case in southern California, the weather was postcard perfect. Until a storm ravaged the coastline, almost taking away this new temporary home. Always alert to signs and portents, Page interpreted this as an invitation to move elsewhere. Besides, if they remained in the US they would shortly be liable to pay income tax.

After a meeting with Peter Grant, it was decided that they would relocate to Munich in Germany: specifically, to Musicland Studios, which Thin Lizzy had just vacated, having recorded their career-changing *Jailbreak* album there, and which the Rolling Stones were about to enter, to make *Black and Blue*. There was only a short window of 18 days in which to record the new album, and Page appreciated the sense of urgency this would impose on the project.

The musicians stopped off in New York on the way to Germany. From New York, Page and Danny Goldberg flew down to Washington, DC on a Swan Song A&R mission, having been tipped off about a sensational blues guitarist called Bobby Parker. When they found Parker he was playing with an undistinguished group on a nearby army base. Page was called up to the stage to play – badly – on some blues tunes with Parker. Having recorded the set on a cassette player, Page played the inadequate tape to Plant and Bonham. They were both singularly unimpressed. Bobby Parker was not destined to become a Swan Song act.

The band travelled separately to Munich, and Plant, Page and Jones were no doubt pleased that they did not travel with Bonham. Uncontrollably drunk on free champagne on the flight, Bonzo fell asleep and woke to discover he had pissed himself. His first-class seat was soaked with urine, which soon gave off a distinctly unsavoury aroma. Summoning Mick

Hinton, his personal roadie, from his seat in economy, Bonzo changed into a pair of trousers that his assistant always had with him for such an emergency. Then he made Hinton sit in his dripping first-class accommodation, while he moved back to the roadie's seat in economy.

Musicland, which had a strong reputation as one of the best studios in Europe, was situated in the basement of Munich's Arabella Hotel. What especially pleased Page was that it was located in an uninspiring neighbourhood; minimum distractions were required to make that 18-day deadline. There was, however, one principal diversion: heroin, which Page and Bonham were using during the day at the studio, courtesy of Richard Cole, who had located a dealer close to Musicland. Cole was also using smack. 'None of us seemed the worse for it,' considered the road manager.

For Robert Plant the sessions were not easy. From his wheelchair, he felt his vocals were considerably lacking in power; he worried that his voice sounded fatigued. In fact, Plant's hypnotic, shrill singing acted as a fabulous counterpoint to the balanced rhythmic fury of the record. On one occasion he tripped in the studio, falling on his damaged right leg, and the crew were both astonished and impressed with the way Page raced across the room to pick up the singer, who was taken to hospital for tests. All the same, Plant felt he had been hustled into making this record by Page and Grant; it was, he believed, keeping him from being with his wife and kids. Maureen was only slowly recovering from her serious injuries, and Plant was beginning to have serious doubts about the point of remaining in Led Zeppelin. 'I was furious with Page and Peter Grant. I was just furious that I couldn't get back to the woman and the children that I loved. And I was thinking, is all this rock 'n' roll worth anything at all?'

Jimmy Page, for his part, was feeling confident, as though his guitar playing had moved up several levels. As always, he was resolutely in charge of the sessions. At first he would put in 12-hour working days, but by the final week, it was more like 18 hours. And the pressure had its desired effect: both 'Candy Store Rock', a rockabilly tune on which Plant sounded more like his idol Ral Donner than ever, and 'Hots On for Nowhere', were both written in the studio in around an hour.

The thundering *Presence* – almost a forerunner of the punk sounds that would be omnipresent by the end of the year – emphasised the creative relationship in Musicland between Page and Bonham, the drummer's power driving the album from its free-standing epic opener 'Achilles Last Stand', one of the greatest of all Zeppelin tracks, via the snorting, harmonica-enhanced 'Nobody's Fault but Mine' – like *Physical Graffiti*'s 'In My Time of Dying', adapted from another Blind Willie Johnson masterpiece – to its suitably mysterious closing tune, 'Tea for One', with its extraordinary sense of loss and loneliness.

Running out of time to overdub and mix the record, Page called Mick Jagger and explained his predicament. Graciously, the Rolling Stone offered him three days of their time in Musicland.

Working 24-hour days, dropping asleep at the mixing desk for a couple of hours at a time, Page completed the record in this additional window of time, and every single searing guitar overdub was added in just one inspired day. 'I'll tell you about doing all the guitar overdubs to "Achilles Last Stand",' Page told Dave Schulps of *Trouser Press* in 1977. 'There were basically two sections to the song when we rehearsed it. I know John Paul Jones didn't think I could succeed in what I was attempting to do. He said I couldn't do a scale over a certain section, that it just wouldn't work. But it did. What I planned to try and get that epic quality into it, so it wouldn't just sound like two sections repeated, was to give the piece a totally new identity by orchestrating the guitars, which is something I've been into for quite some time. I knew it had to be jolly good, because the number was so long it just couldn't afford to be half-baked. It was all down to me how to do this. I had a lot of it mapped out in my mind, anyway, but to make a long story short, I did all the overdubs in one night ... I thought as far as I can value tying up that kind of emotion as a package and trying to convey it through two speakers, it was fairly successful.'

Richard Cole noted how calm Page was at the end of the final session. 'With some of the earlier albums,' he wrote, 'he would leave the studio feeling pangs of insecurity, convinced that there might have been something else he could have done to make the tracks even better. With *Presence*, however, he seemed perfectly content. Through a frail smile, he told me that not an ounce of energy had gone to waste.' And not an ounce of heroin, either.

Led Zeppelin were still clearing their equipment out of the studio on 2 December 1975 when the Rolling Stones arrived. Page again thanked Mick Jagger for handing him the extra days. When Jagger asked if they had got some songs recorded, the Zeppelin leader informed him that they had completed their album.

The leader of the Rolling Stones, notoriously tardy in the studio, was amazed: 'You've only been here three weeks.'

'That's all we needed,' replied Page, once again getting one over on Jagger.

Critically undervalued at the time, the riff-heavy *Presence* – the first album by the band to feature almost no keyboards – was one of Led Zeppelin's greatest records. 'I think it was just a reflection of the total anxiety and emotion of that period,' said Page. 'There's a hell of a lot of spontaneity about that album. We went in with virtually nothing and everything just came pouring out.'

'The whole testament of the Munich album,' said the guitarist, 'is that it proved once and for all that there is no reason for the group to split up. I can't think of too many groups that have been around as long as we have and still retain that spontaneity. We started screaming in rehearsals and never stopped.'

But the fuel to make *Presence* would exact a considerable cost: both Page and Bonham, not to mention Cole, were now addicted to heroin.

In Los Angeles that December on business relating to *The Song Remains the Same*, Peter Grant questioned Cole about Page, who was also in town. 'Something's different about Jimmy. He acts nervous and jumpy. Something's not right,' said the manager. Page was suffering from heroin-withdrawal symptoms: a runny nose and flu-like aching limbs.

Shortly after, Cole and Page flew back to London together, as the guitarist was anxious to attend Scarlet's Christmas school play. During the journey he turned to Cole: 'Chrissakes, Richard, don't get into this shit.'

Although he well knew what his boss was referring to, Cole asked him what he meant.

'Heroin. I think I'm hooked. It's terrible.'

Cole asked him if he'd tried to stop.

'I've tried, but I can't. It's a real bastard.'

With the recording of the album – though not the mixing – having been completed on Thanksgiving Day, Page's first suggestion for the record's title was 'Thanksgiving'.

When discussions with Hipgnosis over the sleeve began, designer George Hardie declared: 'When I think of the group, I always think of power and force. There's a definite presence there.' Hardie had a notion for an iconic object being displayed on the sleeve; he thought the record should be titled 'Obelisk'. But Page responded to the energy of Hardie's words and felt that 'Presence' was the true title for their new music. Besides, the ambiguities of the word appealed to the musician: Presence meaning – as the designer suggested – charismatic power and force; Presence as 'presents'; Presence as a spectral appearance.

The sleeve was extremely unexpected: an archetypal nuclear family – the husband bearing a resemblance to the actor Jack Nicholson – seated around a table on which was placed a black, obelisk-shaped object. It managed to look both creepy and sinister – as you would expect with Led Zeppelin.

Back in Jersey after Munich, where he had not had a single night out, Robert Plant began to feel relatively energised. Behan's West Park, a nightspot in St Helier, became a regular haunt. On 10 December, along with resident pianist Norman Hale, a former member of the Tornadoes, all of Led Zeppelin played an impromptu rock 'n' roll set; Plant was tucked away on a high stool, almost behind John Bonham.

Later, Page was suitably enigmatic in his explanation of the album sleeve to *Melody Maker*: 'It could be either viewed as past or present. If you look at it, it could be the forties and it could be the seventies. It's got to be viewed in its entirety, otherwise the whole point would be lost. I'm sorry to be elusive on it, but I don't think I should say it's this, that and the other, because it's an ambiguous thing. Photographically it's an ambitious statement, so it's not the right thing to lay down an impression because somebody might have a more illuminating one.'

Under the terms of their tax exile, Led Zeppelin and Peter Grant were permitted to be in the UK for 60 days of that tax year. Returning to their families in England for Christmas had always been factored into their time out of the country, and Plant, Jones and Bonham went back to their relative forms of domestic bliss. Page, who had already been to Los Angeles since the Musicland sessions, flew to New York to do more work on the soundtrack for *The Song Remains the Same*.

In March 1976 *Presence* was finally released. It was the fastest-selling Led Zeppelin LP ever. In the US it shipped to the stores as a platinum album, with over a million copies pre-sold.

In both the US and the UK *Presence* was number one within two weeks. However, without a supporting tour, sales fell off rapidly, and ultimately it was the weakest selling of all Zeppelin records, with some 3.5 million sales.

19

THE KENNETH ANGER CURSE

In 1973 Peter Grant approached Paul Reeves – the fashion designer and taste-maker who became firm friends with Jimmy Page after meeting him on the Yardbirds' last US tour – and asked him to manage the renovation and refurbishment of a mews house he had purchased in London's West End. Money, Grant said, was no object. 'I told him I'd only do it if he didn't come near,' said Reeves.

Involving his pal Jon Wealleans, an architect and artist, as well as friends from the Royal College of Art, Reeves spent almost two years on the project. As Paul Gorman writes in *The Look*, 'Reeves sourced everything from curtain material to cutlery, discovering a talent for interior design and love of beautifully made British furniture and textiles along the way.'

Aware of the frightening reputation of the gargantuan Grant, the pair were extremely nervous when the Zeppelin manager finally arrived in 1975 to view his freshly designed property. As Gorman writes: '"I opened the door and it may be a cliché, but he literally blotted out the sun," laughs Wealleans. Reeves, meanwhile, had prudently put some champagne on ice. "He spent around five minutes looking around, not saying a word," says Reeves. "Then he pronounced, 'I gotta say Paul … it's fucking amazing!' We got the champagne out and a couple of grams of coke and everything was all right!"'

No doubt as part of Led Zeppelin's desire to expand their market, appeal and creative credibility, the Paul Reeves and Jon

Wealleans transformation of Grant's house was featured in both the *Observer* and *Ideal Home* magazines.

At the peak of both Led Zeppelin's and his own success that year, earning enormous acclaim and wealth, Peter Grant – who the next year would be approached by Colonel Tom Parker about a European tour by Elvis Presley – did not appreciate that he too was about to experience a devastating personal crisis. While he was living as a tax exile in a rented house on Long Island, his wife Gloria, a petite former dancer, remained in the UK with their two children at Horselunges Manor, an Elizabethan manor house. Then Gloria left him for another man.

The divorce came close to destroying Grant and, although he eventually – somehow – won custody of their children, there was still the stench of failure about the settlement. And failure was something he was utterly unaccustomed to. Plunged into depression and angst, and perhaps influenced by two of his clients, he began to dabble with heroin.

Tower House, meanwhile, was the site of a mysterious issue for Page. A couple staying at his London home were impersonating the guitarist and Charlotte Martin, and they were summarily expelled from the property. 'That got very ugly,' he said to Nick Kent in the *NME*.

Led Zeppelin spent January 1976 in a freezing New York City, lodged at the Park Lane Hotel on Central Park South. Page was still in the recording studio, editing and adjusting the soundtrack for the perpetually imminent *The Song Remains the Same*.

When he went to Los Angeles to do more work on the film, Page appeared to be in an even worse state than he was in the autumn. Having signed Michael Des Barres's new group Detective to Swan Song for $1 million, Jimmy Page found himself transported from his rental home in Malibu to the Beverly Hills Hotel for what was known in the music business as a 'signing' photograph. Unfortunately, he was rather too relaxed from the smack he had ingested prior to leaving Malibu. So relaxed indeed that it was found impossible to wake him when he arrived at the hotel. The resulting picture showed Page, asleep, surrounded by the perkily awake members of Detective. Afterwards, he blamed his parlous condition on a Valium he had taken.

Detective would become a problem, though largely for themselves. 'They gave us a million dollars: what the fuck do you think is going to happen?' said Des Barres. 'I spent a month getting a snare-drum sound. It was a great band but we didn't have any moral support, sitting around waiting for Jimmy Page to produce us. And when Bonzo owns a fifth of you, there's a problem.'

As a fellow heroin addict, was he concerned about what he could see happening to Jimmy Page? 'I was concerned: for myself. When you're a drug addict you don't care about anybody else. When you're a junkie you don't want to be a junkie. I was annoyed because I couldn't get him into the studio. No, I wasn't worried for him.'

Considering how well acquainted Page was with the works and life of Aleister Crowley, who died a heroin addict, wouldn't the guitarist have felt warned off a relationship with smack?

'It's not that simple,' said Des Barres. 'Jimmy Page's affection for Aleister Crowley was in his ideas of self-liberation. When you get to the hierarchical position that Jimmy found himself in by then, you are at the top of your vision. Jimmy's thoughts were, "I will experiment with life." He emulated something Crowley did, but there are so many more complexities in terms of the narcissism and brilliance of Aleister Crowley.'

The Song Remains the Same was finally released on 20 October 1976. Though the movie had been troubled from the start, the group's enormous cult of fans turned out for the film in their droves. On its initial run it grossed $10 million. So that the music in the film replicated as near as feasible the live sound of the band, Cinema I in Manhattan was equipped at great cost with a quadrophonic sound system for its premiere. Yet, much to Page's chagrin, this was not the case when the film premiered on the West Coast, a screening he and the rest of the band also attended – as they did the London premiere.

Interviewed by Nick Kent in the *NME* the next month, Page admitted the film's defects: '*The Song Remains the Same* is not a great film, but there's no point in making excuses. It's just a reasonably honest statement of where we were at that particular time. It's very difficult for me to watch it now, but I'd like to see it in a year's time just to see how it stands up.'

The Song Remains the Same is flat in tone, shot with little flair, with the sense of a television programme about it. Had no one advised either of the film's directors that the most efficient and efficacious manner in which to convey onstage movement on camera is to shoot from the sides of the stage? The onstage shots are largely unadventurous, and there are often lighting problems. Even Page's hair seems confused: no longer the flowing Pre-Raphaelite locks of yore, but almost a semi-mullet. He even looks a touch jowly. After the godlike perfection in his image from the 1970 Royal Albert Hall gig, he is, at 32 years old, clearly no longer a kid.

In fact, in their performance Led Zeppelin seem very much like they are just doing a job, getting through another gig, firing on maybe only three cylinders. Page even looks slightly confused as to who he is, although that is alleviated by the dramatics – his semi-duck walk, for example – and the magic of the stage and outfits.

The Madison Square Garden performance – cleverly recreated at Shepperton Studios – is intercut with cameos of each of the group, as well as Peter Grant and Richard Cole. It is rather predictable in its self-mythologising; Robert Plant's sword-and-sorcery horseback ride to a castle, followed by a sword fight in which his opponent drops into the moat, makes one think, Yes, of course Plant would see himself like that.

Page's first appearance has him turning to the camera to reveal pink sunglasses, from which pink light pours. That is all the shot is: Page projecting his sinister mystery, an essential part of his package, and a little creepy. There is the scent of panto-mime occultist about it; the use of the red eyes in the film is a complete power trip. But it may also suggest considerable anxi-ety: are his eyes pinned from smack usage? A man fully at ease with himself might not have pulled such a stunt.

Then there is that sequence – filmed at his insistence on a dank, full-moon night – in which he climbs a rocky hill to meet a tarot-like hermit atop the cairn, his face morphing until we appreciate that the hermit is indeed an older Jimmy Page – an interesting self-perception, and commendably accurate where certain aspects of his later life are concerned.

Much later, in 2008, Page discussed this sequence with *Guitar World*. He was thrown a perceptive line: 'I find it interesting that you were choosing to represent yourself as a hermit at a time when you were really quite a public figure.'

'Well, I was hermetic,' replied Page. 'I was involved in the hermetic arts, but I wasn't a recluse. Or maybe I was … The image of the hermit that was used for the artwork on *Led Zeppelin IV* and in the movie actually has its origins in a paint-ing of Christ called *The Light of the World* by the Pre-Raphaelite artist William Holman Hunt. The imagery was later transferred to the Waite tarot deck. My segment was supposed to be the aspirant going to the beacon of truth, which is represented by the hermit and his journey toward it. What I was trying to say through the transformation was that enlightenment can be achieved at any point in time; it just depends on when you want to access it. In other words, you can always see the truth, but do you recognise it when you see it or do you have to reflect back on it later?'

The interviewer brought up the matter of the guitarist's occult studies: 'It may have been subtle, but you weren't really hiding it.'

'I was living it,' replied Page. 'That's all there is to it. It was my life – that fusion of magick and music.'

The *Guitar World* interviewer pointed out how advanced was the Led Zeppelin leader's employment of symbolism, such as the sigils on *Led Zeppelin IV* and the embroidery on his stage clothes, used almost as a form of branding.

'You mean talismanic magick?' Page replied. 'Yes, I knew what I was doing. There's no point in saying much about it, because the more you discuss it, the more eccentric you appear to be. But the fact is – as far as I was concerned – it was working, so I used it. But it's really no different than people who wear ribbons around their wrists: it's a talismanic approach to something. Well, let me amend that: it's not exactly the same thing, but it is in the same realm. I'll leave this subject by saying the four musical elements of Led Zeppelin making a fifth is magick into itself. That's the alchemical process.'

Towards the end of *The Song Remains the Same* a kid is beaten backstage for some unknown sin, a shockingly arrogant moment showing the possibility of darkness within the Led Zeppelin operation. Surely this brief moment had been consciously injected into the film, letting us all know the menace behind the band?

Peter Clifton, who succeeded Joe Massot as director, had been subjected to numerous indignities, including having his house broken into by order of the increasingly paranoid Peter Grant, who was suspicious that the director was secreting away outtakes. Following the end of his relationship with the band, Clifton revealed unalloyed contempt for everyone involved with them: 'The group that comprised Led Zeppelin, whether individually or collectively, were the rudest, most arrogant and inhumane people I ever encountered in my 25 years of filming music. They were all dreadful and behaved appallingly. They were allowed to get away with their horrible behaviour due to their instant commercial success. I can say this with some authority after the ordeal of broken promises and daredevil tactics I put myself through because of my ambition to make the world's most successful rock 'n' roll film. That ambition in 1974 revolved around their co-operation and commitment, which guaranteed the necessary funds. There was no question in my mind that Led Zeppelin were the most enigmatic of all rock bands. They never granted interviews or appeared on TV, never advertised a concert, and yet every one was sold out within hours of the release of tickets. Their popularity lay in myriad reasons: their indisputable talent, their sex appeal and sheer power. The nasty seventies fitted them like an iron glove. It was Jimmy's band and what Jimmy said – or rather what Peter Grant said on Jimmy's behalf – was the way it was.'

In Nick Kent's *NME* interview with Jimmy Page that November 1976, it was revealed that he had returned to Charlotte Martin and their daughter Scarlet from his dalliance with Krissie Wood – 'a more domestically ordered existence', mused Kent. 'Charlotte's been very ill,' said Page. 'But that's something one doesn't need to go into, really, only that ... if you've been with someone for a long time and they get ill, then you immediately have that responsibility ... I don't really need to say anymore.'

'Page,' assessed Kent, 'seems a changed man from the days that seemed to reach their hiatus during the 75 tour of America. Then, the guitarist, at once unattached, was staying up for days and nights on end in some kind of mortal combat with the forces of Nature, pushing virtually everything to the limits and cultivating some potentially bad habits in the process.'

When Kent suggested this, Page informed him that what he witnessed then was nothing compared to the process of making *Presence*: 'That was the ultimate test of that whole ... lifestyle.

I mean, that was 18 hours a day at a real intensity every day. You just plunge in and, I mean, you don't start thinking about three meals a day.'

Page told Kent that following the making and release of *Presence* 'it was a case of sorting out a year's problems in ... say, a month, and not finding the whole process as simple as that. I mean, suddenly I had time to look around, and suddenly I became aware of certain people who'd been taking incredible advantage of me in the year I'd been away.'

As 1976 galloped along, there seemed little respite from the traumas that the last 18 months had brought. And as so often in the esoteric matters to which Jimmy Page was attracted, there was frequently a scintilla of paradox. For example, Aleister Crowley considered cats to be creatures from the underworld, and useful for sacrifices. Yet Page was a cat lover and certainly would not have agreed with Crowley's brutal thinking. Yet in psychological terms, dreams of cats are frequently seen as representative of women, on whom Crowley was even more down than he was towards feline creatures. And this was a sentiment with which Page seemed to be in total agreement: 'Crowley didn't have a very high opinion of women and I don't think he was wrong.'

Meanwhile, there were further, very real problems at Tower House. In the mystical world there is an old adage: two magicians should never meet. And in the second half of 1976 Page found himself embroiled in a battle of wizards. His opponent was Kenneth Anger, and by the end of the year the filmmaker would declare that Page had been 'fired' for failing to complete his work as composer on the soundtrack of *Lucifer Rising*.

Anger decried the guitarist for time-wasting and a lack of dedication to the project, and claimed that Page's personal problems – code for his heroin habit – had made him impossible to work with. Page had supposedly been working on the film for the past three years, but at the point Anger spoke out against him had delivered only 28 minutes of completed tape.

Since their first meeting in 1973, the collaboration between Anger and Page had continued intermittently: Anger was commuting between London and New York, overseeing the publication and distribution of *Hollywood Babylon*, while Page was committed to Led Zeppelin performances and recording.

For some three months Anger had been using the film-editing facilities in the basement of Tower House, chopping down the 17 hours of film he had in the can.

An extraordinary sequence of events unfurled, and Anger apparently became the unwitting victim of a domestic fracas. He was ordered to leave the house by Charlotte Martin. (Later, it was suggested that it was Page's housekeeper, not Martin, who was behind this.)

No reason was given for his eviction, and when Anger returned to the house the next morning to collect his film materials and belongings, he found the door locked and bolted. That afternoon, Anger, unable to reach Page himself, informed Swan Song that the film collaboration was off and that he had fired Page from the project.

The following day Anger was able to recover some of his belongings and the film from the now empty Tower House. Page, who was in town for a friend's funeral, was unavailable for comment, but a spokesperson from Swan Song claimed to be totally mystified by the news that the guitarist had been fired from the *Lucifer* project; he even expressed surprise at the information that Anger was in London at all.

Anger returned once again to Tower House the next day. Now he removed the last of his belongings, as well as artefacts from the film – these included Lucifer's crown, made of paste studded with rhinestones from a dress once worn by Mae West.

'I haven't laid eyes on Jimmy Page since early June,' Anger told me. 'I've been trying to get in contact with him since then:

I've fixed meetings through his office and been stood up half-a-dozen times. I've left messages on his Kafka-esque answering machine. All I've had is promises that the soundtrack is on its way, but nothing's materialised. I've got a fucking film to finish.

'The way he's been behaving is totally contradictory to the teachings of Aleister Crowley and totally contradictory to the ethos of the film. Lucifer is the angel of light and beauty. But the vibes that come off Jimmy are totally alien to that – and to human contact. It's like a bleak lunar landscape.

'By comparison, Lucifer is like a field full of beautiful flowers – although there may be a few bumblebees waiting to sting you if you are not careful. I'm beginning to think Jimmy's dried up as a musician. He's got no themes, no inspiration, no melodies to offer. I'm sure he doesn't have another "Stairway to Heaven", which is his most Luciferian song. *Presence* was very much a downer album. In the first place his commitment to *Lucifer* seemed to be totally serious, and he was very enthusiastic about the project. And he's very into enterprise and hard work. But on the other hand he has this problem dragging him down. He's been acting like Jekyll and Hyde, and I have to have someone who's 100 per cent. This film is my life's work.

'I really don't think he has the zing – the capabilities to do it. If he'd have said he was bored with the project I'd have understood, but he's just strung me along. Now he's no longer on the project; I'm no longer interested in having him.'

The situation was complex, however. According to Anger, Page was never formally employed to compose the soundtrack: 'There was never any discussion about money; the whole idea was that it should be an offering of love. The idea was to go 50/50 on the film's profits and that Jimmy should have all the proceeds from any soundtrack album that came out of it. We never put anything down on paper. We had a gentleman's agreement, which to me is more serious than anything written down by lawyers.'

The subject of *Lucifer Rising*, Anger's most ambitious project to date, was of course the 'fallen angel' of orthodox Christian mythology, who in Anger's film was restored to his Gnostic status as 'the Bringer of Light', an implicit part of Crowley's teachings. No one with a serious interest in metaphysics would have been surprised that such subject matter might attract controversy.

Anger had spent the best part of the previous nine years attempting to complete *Lucifer Rising*, and his difficulties with Page were simply the latest in a catalogue of upsets, misfortunes and disruptions that had stymied the progress of the film. However, until this point Anger's principal problem had been finding someone to take the part of Lucifer.

Following the accidental death of the five-year-old boy originally chosen to play the part, the role was taken by Bobby Beausoleil, a former guitarist with the group Love. But Beausoleil was fired from the movie after a prolonged altercation with Anger, and he left, taking most of the completed film with him. Two years later, after he fell under the spell of Charles Manson, Beausoleil was sentenced to death – commuted to life imprisonment – for the murder of Gary Hinman.

With the little footage remaining from the Beausoleil episode, Kenneth Anger shaped another film, *Invocation of My Demon Brother*, with a synthesiser soundtrack by Mick Jagger. The Rolling Stone was evidently taken with Anger's work, and indeed the filmmaker claimed it was their conversations that inspired Jagger to write 'Sympathy for the Devil'. Jagger agreed to take the part of Lucifer, but he backed out before shooting began, apparently fearing that the Satanic aura he had once sought to cultivate was becoming too tangible for comfort. His brother Chris took his place, but an on-set row with Anger led to his dismissal. Eventually, a Middlesbrough steel worker named Leslie Huggins was recruited for the part, and with Marianne Faithfull and Donald Cammell (co-director of the epochal *Performance*, and son of a biographer and friend of Crowley) also taking principal roles, filming began.

In 1976, having fired Page, Anger continued editing the film, hoping to meet a Christmas deadline. He was looking for another musician to write the soundtrack. 'I'm seriously questioning whether to use a musician from the rock world,' Anger told me in the *NME*'s Carnaby Street offices. 'It seems like most of today's rock music is savage, deliberate bad taste. It's not optimistic, constructive or even fun anymore. I'm certainly jaded with the rock-superstar syndrome. They're like renaissance bandits. Who needs those people?' The director would not come anywhere near to meeting his self-imposed Christmas 1976 deadline, though a single shot of Page would make it into the finished film.

As for the soundtrack, Anger eventually decided to let Bobby Beausoleil do it from prison in the late 1970s. The CD was released in 2004 – as Beausoleil continued to languish behind bars.

When I asked if he felt vindictive towards Page, Anger declared: 'You bet I do. I'm not a Christian, turn the other cheek kind.' He allowed a thin smile. 'In fact, I'm all ready to throw a Kenneth Anger curse …'

Persistent attempts at the time to contact Swan Song for a statement from or on behalf of Page were met with silence. Not even a 'no comment'.

The 'Kenneth Anger curse', however, was no idle threat. Almost 30 years later, a still-angry Anger confirmed that he had indeed followed through with it. 'He was a multi-millionaire miser,' he said. 'He and Charlotte, they had so many servants, yet they would never offer me a cup of tea or a sandwich. Which is such a mistake on their part because I put the curse of King Midas on them. If you're greedy and just amass gold you'll get an illness. So I turned her and Jimmy Page into statues of gold.'

Page was utterly dismissive of this. He told me later that this 'curse' consisted of newspaper cuttings underlined in red ink that Anger sent to him. 'It was quite pathetic, actually. *Lucifer Rising* was going to be a masterpiece, but he didn't manage to pull it off.'

All the same, it cannot be overlooked that from this point on, Led Zeppelin's nosedive was inexorable. Now mired in heroin addiction and alcoholism, Jimmy Page's days of greatest creativity with the group were behind him. What lay in the future for Led Zeppelin was remorseless tragedy and death, followed by an eventual phoenix-like rebirth for its principal player.

20

FACE TO FACE

In February of 1977, an absolutely pivotal year for Jimmy Page and Led Zeppelin, I secured an interview with him for an American magazine called *Gig*.

In the UK, due to the sudden emergence of punk, a cultural shift was underway. In December 1976, Led Zeppelin began rehearsals for an American tour scheduled to begin on 27 February 1977. By January 1977 they were ensconced at Emerson, Lake and Palmer's Manticore Studios at the bottom of Fulham's North End Road. Two months previously I had been to Fulham Town Hall, only a few yards away, to see the Clash, one of the inspirational new punk acts that had sprung up in the UK during 1976. The only time I would ever come again to Manticore would be 18 months later, to watch the Clash – by then risen considerably in status – play a secret pre-tour warm-up gig at the ELP establishment.

So there was a cultural and poetic twist to Led Zeppelin rehearsing at the studio of another rock behemoth for a tour that would be the utter antithesis of punk. This was Zeppelin's most massive tour ever of America, 51 shows in 30 cities, largely playing stadiums, and naturally the band stood to earn a colossal fortune. For example, for the date in Pontiac, Michigan, Led Zeppelin would pack in an audience of 76,229 devotees and earn $900,000. 'The big business nature of the band has always been more of a hazard than anything else,' said Page. 'One day you're just playing guitar and the next day there's a knock on the door and you realise you're in the realms of high finance. It's very heavy.'

If the speed and attitude with which the first Led Zeppelin album had been recorded was thoroughly in the spirit of punk, which it really was, it is unsurprising that – traduced as the four musicians may have been by Year Zero attacks on them as the very worst examples of irrelevant dinosaur rock – they found immediate empathy with this iconoclastic new form.

At the urging of their former publicist B. P. Fallon, who was now working on the new, sort-of-punk Stiff Records releases, Page and Robert Plant went along with Beep to Covent Garden's Roxy club on 13 January 1977 to watch the Damned, who were supporting – an example of punk's almost perverse egalitarianism: the Damned had released the first UK punk single and already had an album out (on Stiff, which afforded Fallon dual loyalties) – Eater, famous on the punk scene largely for their 13-year-old drummer. 'I was aware there was a bit of nudging going on from the audience when they saw us in there,' said Page. 'But we felt very comfortable. And when the Damned kicked off … it was absolutely fantastic. You felt this wall of sound almost pressing down on you.'

Page and Plant loved the Damned's high-speed, slightly bonkers set, and on the subsequent US tour Page would irritate the more reactionary elements of the Zeppelin entourage with his insistence on repeatedly playing the Damned's first album, *Damned Damned Damned*. Guests at the Plaza Hotel in Manhattan would complain about the volume at which he was playing the LP in his suite.

'I was standing onstage at the Roxy Club,' said Captain Sensible, the Damned's bass player, 'and I saw two hippies standing at the back. I thought, "What are they doing here?" Then I looked a bit closer, and it was Jimmy Page and Robert Plant.'

'I was at the bar talking to Jimmy Page and Robert Plant,' said Glen Matlock, bass player with the Sex Pistols.

'Everybody was winding everybody up. "What are they doing down here?"'

Four days later, Plant returned to the Roxy, this time accompanied by John Bonham. Desmond Coy, on the door, told Plant to go to the back of the queue. And charged him full admission. At the bar, he noted, the Zeppelin members were asking for receipts, for considerably larger amounts than they had paid. Again, the Damned were playing, this time supported by Eater and the Boys. After the Damned's brief set, according to Glen Matlock, 'John Bonham was onstage going, "What is this? We play for four fucking hours! Get the band up there without that Mouse Scabies and I'll play drums!" He was really pissed.'

'Bonham was carried out,' said the Damned's guitarist Brian James. 'He was out of his head, drinking vodka all night. It was cool that these geezers were willing to chance their arms down there with no security.'

These visits by three-quarters of Led Zeppelin to punk's Mecca earned them considerable column inches in the next week's music press, with pictures of Page and Plant at the Roxy.

There was a pretty, rather stylish and classy girl at Swan Song who showed me in to a broad room furnished with a pair of opposing couches for my *Gig* interview with Jimmy Page. I liked the girl and we smiled at each other as she left. 'She's lovely, isn't she?' said Page. Then, surprisingly, almost sadly, dispensing with any expectation of his acting out the role of *droit de seigneur*, 'But nobody knows her story.' (Well, you and your cohorts could always engage her in conversation, I thought.)

I had been asked by the Swan Song office, to whom I had pitched the idea of an interview with Page, to come to Manticore; I was to accompany my friend Pennie Smith, the *NME* photographer who had been commissioned to shoot some snaps of Led Zeppelin in rehearsals. It was a brief connection – they were not actually playing when we arrived – and I felt I was being checked out. But there was none of Zeppelin's legendary horribleness to the press: everyone seemed in good spirits and rather nice, even the allegedly terrifying John Bonham. Robert Plant flirted with Pennie; he was immediately tactile with her, almost as if he felt obliged to act this way as part of his job as Sex God. Worryingly, however, he seemed slightly lopsided, as though putting weight on his left leg to alleviate the stress on his damaged right limb. Page was off to one side, smiling but largely silent.

Ultimately, the first 12 dates of this US tour would be cancelled thanks to Plant suffering from laryngitis. A singer unable to sing on what were essentially comeback dates? Sounded psychosomatic to me ...

By the way, at this time I had heard only vague rumours of Page's problems with heroin. Anyway, this is what I wrote for my *Gig* piece in February 1977:

> The overriding first impression that emanates from both Led Zeppelin's music and the legendary self-isolation the band and its entourage maintains is one of *power*. Something akin to a mega-sized armour-plated rhinoceros moving relentlessly – and often, one suspects, humourlessly – through contemporary rock music.
>
> In what seemed initially to be thoroughly in keeping with this assumed tradition, it soon became apparent that endeavouring to be placed in an 'Interview Situation' with Jimmy Page would not prove to be the easiest journalistic task I had ever undertaken. Indeed, there were moments when scoring this interview seemed to be taking on all the elements of a parody of The Quest for the Rap with the Big Name Rock Star.
>
> Negotiations commenced at the end of November last year. They were consummated in the second week of

February at Swan Song's offices on London's Kings Road. In the interim, Page had cancelled two scheduled appointments, though we had actually met on one of these occasions. There had been a further meeting at Emerson, Lake and Palmer's converted cinema rehearsal studios, where Zeppelin was rehearsing for their first tour since Robert Plant sustained severe injuries in a car smash on the Greek island of Rhodes in the summer of '75.

Almost predictably, when the interview did actually take place, six days before the band was due to fly out to Texas (where the first dates would be postponed because of Plant's laryngitis, though that's another story), Page revealed none of the superstar arrogance or aggression one might expect, talking at length of Led Zeppelin with an almost religious fervour.

We also discussed his fascination with the occult and, in particular, with the self-styled 'Great Beast', Aleister Crowley (whose former Scottish home, Boleskine House, Page now owns), and his related interests in ecological matters. The guitarist seemed more content and at ease when dealing with these subjects than when talking about the band; though by the time they were raised he had warmed to the task of being interviewed.

For the first 15 minutes of the interview he sat on the edge of a couch, huddled over and shivering into the cup of tea he was holding in both hands. His speech was frequently little more audible than a whisper. Indeed, he seemed so fragile and it appeared to be such an exhausting emotional effort to talk about Led Zeppelin, the impression remained that it might completely upset his thought pattern – or he might actually call off the interview – if he were asked to speak up.

Later on in the interview I would look up from my notebook and see Jimmy Page lying back on the couch and looking at me through his legs. Or stretched out with both eyes firmly shut and a hand stuffed down the crotch of his frayed jeans as he delivered his semi-audible soliloquy.

Notwithstanding an acute bronchial cough that punctuated his speech, he chain-smoked throughout the interview ...

His eyes were ringed with the kind of wrinkles that some would describe as laugh lines and others might attribute to the effects of constant nervous tension. In fact, in the autumn of last year Page spent some time as an in-patient at an exclusive health farm near London. This was supposedly to recuperate from the effects of having become dangerously underweight. Now, though, as he told me in his soft accentless Home Counties voice, 'I just needed to get away for a while and see things from a different perspective. There was nothing sinister. I needed to get into a regular pattern. A regular schedule. And it seems to be working.'

'What sort of ... uh ... line do you want to take on this?' he asked me with what seemed to be a slight edge of suspicion.

I summarised the majority of my questions. After that, he seemed a little more comfortable: 'Okay. Well, fire away. You can always edit out what you don't want.'

Okay, then. So how have the rehearsals been? Pretty rigorous?
'The rehearsals started a month before Christmas and with the Christmas period off we've been working consistently ever since. They've been going well. *Really* well.

'Of course, the first task was to clean off the rust which is obviously going to set in after 18 months without being on stage ... Although we recorded *Presence* some 14 months ago it's not quite the same because a tour is a concentrated series of dates. We'll have three days on and one day off. And we have like a three and a half hour concert to contend with.

'Consequently there was a stamina aspect involved apart from anything else. Plus the constant dilemma that appears from tour to tour about the repertoire as such. What to drop, what not to drop … Which is always a great problem when you've seen everything go down really, *really* well for its own merit, for its own *vibe*, so to speak, and the atmosphere that that particular number's portrayed and evoked. As has been the intention.

'As far as our playing goes, the way it ended up was everyone was just a hundred per cent confident and really bursting to go.'

Have you dropped any numbers that were in the last live set?
'We've dropped a few things. But nothing of great importance. None of the epic things but …'

What have you added?
'Stuff from the new LP. "Candy Store Rock", "Achilles", "Nobody's Fault but Mine" … We've also added "Ten Years Gone", a number we never did in the past. It offered such a challenge as far as the guitars went. It's really my baby because I worked it out note for note at home. At one point there were *nine* guitars going to present all the harmonies so obviously we lack some of that. But nevertheless the overall *feeling* of the number comes across. And comes across very well.

'And we're doing "The Battle of Evermore" which I think [laughs] is a very sort of noble challenge really. We'll probably get applause for the sheer guts of the thing rather than anything else.

'But they're coming off good. All of them.'

So it's all happening okay, then, as far as live …
'Yeah.'

Do you get very apprehensive about going back on the road?
'Well, obviously when you haven't played a concentrated
tour for two years ... well, it goes on for months. And
obviously you've got to take into account the fatigue aspect
and all this sort of thing.

'But I'm pretty confident. Everyone's confident. As far as
the playing goes there's no problems at all. We've got such a
variety in there – oh, "Babe, I'm Gonna Leave You" is another
number that we've been doing ... pedal steel guitar instead of
the usual. So it sounds pretty different from the original.

'It's very interesting. And yet we've obviously kept in there
all the key epics: "Achilles", "Kashmir", "Stairway" ... things
like that.

'But the most amazing thing, really, is that we started nine
years ago putting out albums, albums which have been
constantly subject to change as far as content goes, to the
point where we stuck our necks out only because that's the
material that we've got when it comes to the time of
recording. But rather than stick to the previous formula and
work stuff around it we've just stuck to our guns. And
because of that we've got a wide variety of material ...

'But nevertheless it's marvellous to think that after what is
basically a two year break – even though the film's come out
– to hit the top of all these polls [a reference to Zeppelin
having swept the boards of various assorted music
publication polls throughout the world] is really quite
stunning, really quite ... *awe*-inspiring. A confidence boost
beyond all measure, you know, to realise you're still thought
of as being really contemporary instead of a ... [laughs]
nostalgia-band, shall we say.

'Not that I ever thought we'd become a nostalgia band
because we've got too much up our sleeves to fall into that
bracket. Nevertheless, it's nice to be reassured. In the
warmest possible way.'

You obviously feel as strongly about the band now as ever.
'Yes [very decisively]. And I feel very strongly about the
timeless quality of the songs too. I think that's where it's at ...
That's probably why we're so critical about their
construction when we start putting them together. So you
don't just rest on the obvious sort of clichés that were around
in '72.

    'I mean, it's so easy to sit there and jam a soul riff and to
make a song out of a soul riff.'

*The reaction that I have to Led Zeppelin's music – and I
know I'm not unique in this – is unlike what I get from any
other band. On first hearing a new Zeppelin record it often
seems to slightly grate. There are usually edges to it which
you have to grow to understand. Also, whenever I haven't
played any of the records for a couple of months I'll put them
on and immediately get a colossal rush.*

    *There's something there – something indefinable unless
you accept that it's just down to the chemistry of the four
members – that suggests the band contains the true essence of
rock 'n' roll.*
'Well, *inventive* rock 'n' roll ... it's got the root which is in all
rock 'n' roll ... the earthiness. But it's also got all the other
facets that, shall we say, musicians of today have been able to
get. You know, finger style, folk areas and things like that.
And traces of jazz. Generally the three strong areas. Which is
so important.'

*And also whether it's in the hard rock or the acoustic side
there's also this enigmatic sense of power and strength. Yet
many people still look on you as just a heavy metal band.*
'Well, they did. I think it's dawned on them now that we are
a band that's going to be subject to change all the time. Like
it or loathe it.

'But the most encouraging thing about that is that when an LP is announced the advance orders are so great that it seems they automatically assume there is going to be a certain overriding quality to it. Which is really reassuring because that's what we've been going for. Which again related to that lasting quality. Which one can only *hope* for.

'One can say – and it sounds pretentious – but it's the test of time which shows it.'

So was that your idea of the band when you first conceived it after the Yardbirds ended? That it should have incredibly strong quality and inventiveness?
'*Definitely*. Yeah. I mean, the first album has got the catalyst for so much. You know, the blues and the sort of step off from that. And the working together between Robert and myself and the acoustic work and the way you can stretch an acoustic number … you know, keep the dramatic quality there. Which is, after all, the atmosphere that you're trying to convey. And trying to, you know, develop the mystery. Just really because the whole aspect of what's going to come round the corner as far as writing goes is the dark element, the mysterious element. You just don't know what's coming. So many good things have come out of that that it would be criminal to interrupt a sort of alchemical process like that. And we're aware of that and we wish to play forever.

'And I hope that's still there. I think it is.'

How do you feel about Presence?
'I think it's the most important album myself. In many respects. Because of the amount of time it took to do. Working up against a deadline it took three weeks: the tracks took about a week. Then we had a slight break in the middle when Robert fell over and he thought his leg had gone again. Then we started again and continued.

'And it was pretty much up to me because after that the group really left it to me. Which is really an honour after so long to have that sort of trust; that they know you're not going to sort of *mess it up*, and don't mind if you embellish the thing or whatever ... Because some of those tracks changed immensely by the time all the overdubs and effects had gone on.

'Although it may not be the best track on the album "Royal Orleans" ... the first verse of that is as it was. As a riff. After that you hear all these guitars coming in [hums guitar parts]. And that's the sort of thing which I can do to change the whole mood of how a number comes out.'

So when you did Physical Graffiti, *for example, you'd work in the same way whereby you'd just be left alone to produce the tracks?*
'Yeah. Pretty much. There'll be the tracks and then Robert will come in and do his vocal parts and sometimes Jones will come in and do a little synthesiser work on the tracks. But usually it's down to me and [laughs] I'm quite happy with that.

'As I say, it's an honour to have that sort of relationship with the band.

'The time spent on *Physical Graffiti* was really because of work that came in between time and there was the problem of studio availability. We just couldn't get in.

'And there was the new material which related to that point and I wanted it to have a sort of chronological touch about it. And that's why there are all those tracks that go way, way back and reflect the development of the band. And then you have the apex of "Kashmir".'

What do you feel in retrospect about The Song Remains the Same *film?*

'Well, I think the film's successful in so much as it is a frozen celluloid statement of an evening.

'And the soundtrack as such … [pause] I wouldn't call it a live album because we've got so much live stuff in the bag going back to '69 at the Albert Hall. We've got some *fabulous* live stuff. And, it wasn't necessarily the *best* live material we had but it was the live material that went with the footage so it had to be used. So, you know, it wasn't like A Magic Night. But it wasn't a poor night. It was an honest sort of mediocre night.

'You know, I've always thought of the band as being reasonably consistent as far as the concerts go. I think we always start off *shaky* and it's at the end when the whole thing builds. Which we build up between ourselves. We build up the – I don't know what you might call it – the ESP aspects of it where when you do start jamming and entering areas which are open to free form and you start coming across the different rhythms and you might just *stop* it and start and *stop*. And use some shock tactics.

'A lot of that is just off the cuff, you see. And that's where everybody's really working. You can just anticipate what's coming. And a lot of bands don't manage to be able to do that … a lot of larger bands anyway. They play it safe with everything just about note for note perfect apart from some change in the solo or something.

'But they don't let the solos go on for a long time on purpose so they can really get their teeth into improvising and showing what can really be done.

'And consequently you hear a number one year and so much has changed from a few years before. Because there is that quality.

'Again *Presence* by the way ... We really *needed* that as a band that has been together for such a long time to prove to ourselves that ... You know, we've always spoken of the instant chemistry and how the band get together and start jamming and within those jams, riffs come out. And it doesn't take long before you've got the framework of a song which often gets reviewed but nevertheless it's there from the inception.

'Whereas you do hear stories of big bands that get together for two or three weeks and they can't get anything together. There's like two or three different strong frameworks every rehearsal. And that sort of three week thing proved that it can be done.

'Mind you, there was a helluva lot of emotional anxiety and frustration related to that as well. You know, the uncertainty of Robert's position and one thing and another ... And the way that the band really stuck together during this whole thing because of the loyalty between the band and each other. And that was the emotional release of getting it all out.

'That's why it's an important album to me. Because it reflects all the spontaneous aspects.'

How did you personally react when you heard about Robert's car smash? What were your immediate reactions?
'Well, I was shattered. [profound concern in his voice] I'd been with Robert the day before and I'd just left to go to Sicily. And I was in Sicily when I heard the news.'

So did you hear what state he was in or did you just get garbled reports?
'No, I just heard that he was hurt very seriously. A doctor had to come out from London immediately and put him on a plane because the medical facilities there were so impossible.'

Was there any time when you thought, 'Well, what happens if he doesn't get better or if he dies? What happens to the future of the band?'

'Well, I've always felt – and this has been discussed – that no matter what happened, provided he could still play and sing, and even if we could only make albums, that we'd go on forever.

'Just really because the whole aspect of what's going to come round the corner as far as writing goes is the dark element, the mysterious element. You just don't know what's coming. So many good things have come out of that that it would be criminal to interrupt a sort of alchemical process like that. And we're aware of that and we wish to play forever.

'There's a lot of important work to be done yet anyway. It's only just started.'

You're obviously very confident of the future of the band now. Have you always been so?
'Yeah.'

Never any doubts at all?
'No, no, no.'

But there does seem to be a contradiction in that you're so into the music …
'It's the all important thing, yeah.'

But at the same time Led Zeppelin is a colossal business empire.
'Well, that's just one of those things that happened to snowball up behind us really. But nevertheless the music *is* the most important thing. If we'd been conscious of trying to sustain a particular sort of market then we'd have stuck to a

formula. Which is a terribly dangerous thing. When you know you're going through changes it obviously reflects on your music – lyrics, especially. If you try and suppress that, then you get into trouble. If you suppress it for the sake of a formula.

'But then that's *our* philosophy of what we're up to and other people have a different way of looking at it.

'But it's only the test of time which can lay down the importance of what you're doing. You see, there's been so much flak directed towards us. I knew that it would take a time before a proper perspective was reached about what we were really doing. The fourth album probably being the first milestone in that respect, even though the third should have been.

'When the third LP came out, Crosby, Stills, Nash and Young had just toured. They'd done an acoustic set followed by an electric set. And, of course, our third album having more predominant acoustic work on it then the reviews related it to Crosby, Stills, Nash and Young and said, 'Well, obviously they've been influenced by them.' And missed the point altogether. They forgot that we'd used acoustic guitars very heavily on the first album. Not quite so much on the second but it was there.

'And, you know, after we'd been on the road after the second album had been released we really wanted to have a rest, and consequently sitting around a log fire in Wales you don't put up a 200-watt Marshall set-up but you get your acoustic guitars. Consequently acoustic numbers came out.

'And if they've got a validity you owe it to yourself to lay them down.'

Oh, incidentally, I've always felt that John Paul Jones's
situation within the band was exceptionally important,
especially in the way he seems to cloak a lot of the changes.
Do you not feel that he's underrated?
'Underrated? Well, quite possibly. Yeah, as far as a bass
player relative to a rhythm section. Yeah.

   'But as far as the writing goes everybody has an equal
share of coming forth with the ideas they've got. But it
always seems to end up with myself when it comes to most of
it. And I think Robert and I are sort of very sympathetic to
the sort of loony vibe because we've always been working
together.'

Yeah, there is a sense of you and Robert as the Terrible Duo,
the Inseparables …
'Yeah. Yeah. But it's not to the point of a Jagger–Richards
thing where nobody else gets a look in. It isn't a cut-off
situation. It's just developed from the early days where, say,
Jonesy may come up with one riff for one section and Bonzo
the same whereas I'll probably come up with the whole
framework. Or piece together all those little bits and pieces.'

How is Robert standing up to the stagework?
'Fine. Fine. He's been rehearsing ten hours a day. Ten hours
on the trot.'

I understand that a changed Robert Plant who has taken to
reading Nietzsche on plane journeys has emerged since the
accident. I know that you were ill for about nine months
prior to joining the Yardbirds and I've heard you're supposed
to have spent much of that time reading. Was that when your
interest in the occult began?
[Fifteen second pause] 'My interest in the occult started when
I was about 15.'

*Do you agree that whereas Western society tends to see
occult matters as a very dark – a very black – thing, it is, in
fact, a very light and enlightening thing?*
'Well, there has been a major revival, a spiritual revival,
throughout the world and it reflects all over the place. Not
just within the West.

'And there's a great interest in the Celtic mysteries and the
Dark Ages and the areas where a lot of these truths were just
erased for the sake of the Church, you know. But I'm quite
fascinated by these things.'

*So obviously the folkie Traditional English side of Zeppelin
all emanates from one logical area of interest, no?*
'Yeah. Well, a man's a product of his environment. It depends
how much he wants to educate himself in that framework.
You know, in relationship to his craft. There should be no
boundaries, so just carry on as far as you can and do it.'

Page, of course, is an ardent aficionado of occultist and
magician Aleister Crowley (1875–1947). Indeed, the guitarist
owns Equinox, an occult bookshop situated off London's
Kensington High Street, which has a large section devoted to
Crowley's works as well as having his birth chart pinned to
one wall. And, as already mentioned, Page spends most of his
time on British shores at the home that Crowley once owned,
Boleskin House. [This wasn't actually true – although I didn't
appreciate this at the time.]

Not unexpectedly, such matters are beginning to arouse
the interests of the more sensational end of the British
press. In fact, only a few weeks ago a *National
Enquirer*-like weekly magazine featured an aerial photograph
of the house on its cover along with details of collapsing
staircases and the appropriate 'Dark Man of Pop' blurb
about Page.

'Well,' says the guitarist, 'they should have gone into the history of the house and Crowley would've come out like a shining angel compared with what else went on.

'I mean, it's had a history of suicides and con tricks. Plus the site of the house is on the site of a church and a graveyard, and the church was burnt down by an arsonist with the whole congregation in it. So the actual foundations of the house are built on hallowed ground.

'But I'm not really interested in going on about Crowley in so much as, say, Pete Townshend does about Meher Baba. I'm not interested in trying to turn anybody on in any way whatsoever. You know, there are a thousand paths and they can choose their own.

'All I know is that it's a system that works … [laughs] Although, of course, there's not much point in following a system that *doesn't* work.'

But what about the hassles you've had with Kenneth Anger? (Page wrote the score for filmmaker occultist, and author of Hollywood Babylon, *Kenneth Anger's imminent film,* Lucifer Rising, *but was turned down by Anger towards the end of last year and replaced by none other than Mansonite Bobby Beausoleil. Since then Anger has denounced Page on every possible occasion.)*

'I think it's more the problems he's had with himself. All I know is that at the end of the film I promised him – as I had before – the loan of a three-speed projector which makes the editing so much easier. I said to him, "Well, it's just going to be your own time invested." And I also told him that he must put the music on after he put the footage together so I was just waiting for him to contact me, really. He had other music that I'd done instead of the stuff that I'd delivered which he said he wanted to use. Nevertheless, I still needed to hear from him. And I never heard anything.'

Didn't he come down here and stick things onto the door of this record company?
'Oh, that was his curse. That was *pathetic*. His curse amounted to sending letters to people. Silly letters saying "Bugger off, Page" and this sort of thing.

'How can you take that sort of thing seriously? [Sounds quite deeply disappointed]. A man you had thought to be a genuine occultist and it turns out to be just ... *theatre*. It's a shame, really.'

Although it's quite acceptable these days, do you wish your occult interests weren't known about?
'I just don't want it rammed down people's throats as though I'm saying it's the be-all and end-all and the only way you'll be able to put things together. I'm not saying that at all. You might go off and study the Gurdjieff system and be equally ...

'But what I can relate to is Crowley's system of self-liberation. In which repression is the greatest work of sin. It's like being in a job when you want to be doing something else. That's the area where the true will should come forward. And when you've discovered your true will you should just forge ahead like a steam train. If you put all your energies into it there's no doubt you'll succeed. Because that's your true will. It may take a little while to work out what that is, but when you discover it, it's all there.

'You know, when you realise what it is you're supposed to be here for. I mean, everyone's got a talent for something. Not necessarily artistic but whatever you care to say. And it's just a process of self-liberation. I mean, I just find his writings to be *twentieth century*. As a lot of the others weren't.

'And there's really nothing more to say than that. I find him quite a curious, highly enigmatic character. Consequently I enjoy my researches into him. But it doesn't want to be blown out of all proportion, though, because that would be … silly, you know. I'm just another artist, too.'

Yeah, it's an interest in all things occult and, as you said, all things English or, rather, of Albion. And that's just one area, right?
'Mmmmm.'

Uhh … Returning to the music for a moment, do you feel any great responsibility in your position as one of the ruling triumvirate of rock 'n' roll along with the Stones and the Who? Do you feel any great responsibility towards rock 'n' roll?
'Well, I've always felt a commitment, shall we say? Because I got into it because I was so turned on by the sounds that I heard when I was really young and I just wanted to be involved in it. It was just something thrilling that could send chills up your spine.'

Presumably your parents told you you'd grow out of it …
'No, actually they were very encouraging. They may not have understood a lot of what I was doing but nevertheless they had enough confidence that I knew what I was doing; that I wasn't just [laughs] a nut or something …'

Do you and the other three members of Zeppelin see much of each other socially?
'Not that much. But we do. We don't live in each other's pockets so it's always a great joy to see each other again.'

Do you by any chance find the rock 'n' roll lifestyle a strain in any way?
'What side of it?'

*Well, and, taking into account your stay at the health farm,
the irregularities of the hours, for example?*
'Well, that taxes you physically.'

And inevitably, therefore, it must tax your mental powers …
'Well, in a way, yes. Except that when I'm very tired I can do
my best writing. You know, late at night because there's
nothing to distract you and all those day-to-day problems have
gone. And I can just start concentrating on the guitar and get
lost within it and I find that all these things are coming out.'

*But there are those who bemoan rock 'n' roll as being vastly
uneconomic in terms of both financial and human terms,
especially human terms …*
'But the willpower gets you through. And the adrenaline and
the feedback from the audience at live concerts – which is
maybe what we've been missing – is the thing that charges
you up like a battery.'

You really enjoy playing on stage, do you?
'Oh yeah.'

You don't prefer recording from playing live or …
'Both. And things have been out of balance in that respect.
And one knows something's missing and gets edgy about it.
But it's not until you play again – when you rehearse – that
you know what it is.

'Of course, a lot of it has been done by Robert's recovery.
And certainly not even wanting to breathe a word of the
subject of a tour until nature had dictated her terms and
things became good.

'But then there is that bond between us that gives enough
confidence to just wait and see. Not just go off making solo
albums or kicking with others, as they do.

'There's incredible dedication in what we're doing. Be that rightly or wrongly. Subjectively, that's just the way it is. That's the way it's got to be. There's nothing complacent about things. The minute you start not criticising what you're doing then you're in trouble.

'And if you start thinking everything you're doing is a masterpiece [laughs] then you're in trouble.'

21

THE RULES OF ENGAGEMENT

Ten days before Led Zeppelin's 1977 tour of the US was scheduled to begin, the *Starship* developed a serious mechanical problem: during a flight one of its engines had come close to falling off, and the plane had been grounded at Long Beach Airport. Aware that the four Zeppelin musicians were always nervous of airborne transport – none more so than Jimmy Page – Richard Cole never mentioned this small difficulty and simply lined up another private 720 jetliner, *Caesar's Chariot*, owned by the Las Vegas casino Caesars Palace. *Caesar's Chariot* was almost identical to the *Starship*, although it lacked the Thomas organ on which John Paul Jones had regularly led his fellow passengers in archetypal London pub sing-songs.

The postponed tour finally kicked off on April Fool's Day 1977, in Texas, at the Dallas Memorial Auditorium, followed two days later by a show in Oklahoma City at the Myriad. But these two dates, at which Led Zeppelin seemed extremely rusty, even lacking in confidence, with Page playing solos in the wrong key, were like warm-up shows for the first residency dates on this, their eleventh tour of the US; as Stephen Davis points out in *Hammer of the Gods*, 11 was Aleister Crowley's favourite number, the reason he added the letter 'k' to the word magic. At Chicago Stadium – a misnomer, as it was only arena-sized, holding audiences of around 16,000 – Led Zeppelin were set to play four shows, with a one-day break in the middle.

What was already becoming evident was that Page was in a permanent altered state. And it wasn't bringing out the best in him. 'I showed up on the third date at the start of the tour,' said Jack Kalmes, the head of Showco, the production company for the tour. 'The mood was ugly and there had been a buzz in the PA and Jimmy had come over and thrown a trash can over one of the main techs.'

On another occasion, in another location, Page spat in the face of a technician midway through the acoustic set, before a crowd of 50,000.

Could Page's diet – or lack of it – have had anything to do with his unsociable frame of mind? 'I prefer to eat liquid food,' he claimed. 'Something like a banana daiquiri, which I can put powdered vitamin in. I'm not really into solid foods very much. I know I'll never turn down some alcohol, so a banana daiquiri, with all the food protein, is the answer.'

How was Robert Plant adapting to stage performance after such a disastrous accident and long lay-off? Not too well. Apart from when he was sitting during the acoustic segment, he would stand for the three-hour sets; sometimes he would literally be carried off the stage at the end of the show. His damaged right foot was considerably inflamed; much of the time the singer was in a state of semi-pain, constantly consuming painkillers administered by the doctor travelling full-time with Led Zeppelin, a Harvard graduate who had been on tour with other rock bands, notably the Rolling Stones on their 1972 US tour.

But Plant wasn't the only one in the group who needed to be physically assisted around the stage. By the time Led Zeppelin began their six-night stretch at the Forum in Los Angeles, Page would be physically hoisted onto the performing platform by Richard Cole – and carried off later. The doctor accused Page of stealing Quaaludes from his supply. The guitarist's response? To threaten to fire him: 'Accusing me? Who the fuck does he think is paying his salary?'

The doctor was not always able to help his patients. On the third Chicago date Page seemed even more out of sorts than usual, playing the intro to 'Since I've Been Loving You' while the other band members were beginning 'Nobody's Fault but Mine'; trying to play on a single-neck guitar what he required his double-neck for; during 'Ten Years Gone', the sixth number, he actually passed out, although nodded out might be the more accurate way to describe it. 'Jimmy has got a bout of gastro-enteritis, which isn't helped by firecrackers' – a reference to the artillery barrage of firecrackers that rained on the stage – 'so we've gotta take a five-minute break,' declared Plant. Page was in no condition to return to the stage and, after some time, Richard Cole came out onstage. 'Jimmy does not want to do a half-hearted show tonight,' he told the audience, advising them to hang on to their tickets, as the concert would be rescheduled.

Led Zeppelin, who once had only Cole with them, now had a large entourage. As well as his own personal roadie, each band member also had his own assistant; Page had Rick Hobbs, his butler and chauffeur from London. And Cole brought in, as special minder to Peter Grant, handsome John Bindon, whose favourite party trick – which had allegedly impressed Princess Margaret, supposedly a lover – was to hang a row of pint mugs on his enormous dick. Bindon was also a very dangerous man. But Grant needed someone with him; enormously depressed by the explosion of his marriage and dabbling with the heroin that seemed omnipresent on the tour – even the crew were using – Zeppelin's manager was no longer the life and soul of the party.

'I told one of our roadies that to me this seemed like the beginning of the end for the band,' wrote Cole, who was himself using smack. 'The soul that had driven Zeppelin since 1968 just seemed to have weakened, and drugs played too much of a role in everyone's life.'

'There were bodyguards everywhere, and that was a real big sea change from 75 to 77. There was just a cloud that seemed to hang over everybody,' recalled *Creem* journalist Jaan Uhelszki.

By 10 April, Led Zeppelin had wrestled themselves into delivering their first fully successful performance of the tour, at their fourth show in Chicago. 'Jimmy was feeling ill last night, but it was only a false pregnancy, so that's all right,' Plant told the audience. Answering a local radio station's suggestion that drugs and drink may have been behind the guitarist's mysterious collapse the previous day, the singer defended him to the audience: 'Mr Page neither smokes, drinks, takes women or does anything like that, so we want an apology tomorrow and a crate of alcohol!'

Plant's argument was somewhat reduced by Page's rather curious appearance that night: he was clothed in a Nazi storm trooper's uniform, a cap upon his head and jackboots on his feet and spindly legs – he might have been in the Sex Pistols. Similarly strange were the rooms of his suite at Chicago's Ambassador East Hotel: the curtains were perpetually drawn, electric light was forbidden and candles gently fluttered.

Late on the night of 7 April he entertained journalist Lisa Robinson there. When she inquired about the band's feral reputation, he gave a four-word reply: 'We haven't really stopped.' When asked about the myriad rumours that sat about Led Zeppelin, Page simply replied, 'I must have had a good time.' His soft voice, she noted, was 'slurred'. Robinson came to the conclusion that he was 'either very tired, or very stoned'.

People were genuinely concerned about his appearance. When *Trouser Press* writer Dave Schulps, scheduled to conduct a much-delayed interview with Page, first saw him on *Caesar's Chariot*, he was surprised: 'At first sight I was struck by how extremely frail he appeared, escorted by a bodyguard who seemed almost to be propping him up.'

There were tales of Page having to be pushed through airports in a wheelchair. When I asked him about this two years later, he vehemently denied the suggestion: 'I may have done that for a laugh – not seriously. No, no. That wasn't happening at all.'

When interviewed by *Guitar Player* magazine's Steve Rosen, who flew with the band, Page expressed the concern he had felt when the first dates needed to be cancelled: 'We had done our rehearsals, and we were really on top, really in tip-top form. Then Robert caught laryngitis and we had to postpone a lot of dates and reshuffle them, and I didn't touch a guitar for five weeks. I got a bit panicky about that – after two years off the road that's a lot to think about.'

Rosen later revealed the written rules of engagement for journalists permitted on the band's plane:

1. Never talk to anyone in the band unless they first talk to you.
2. Do not make any sort of eye contact with John Bonham. This is for your own safety.
3. Do not talk to Peter Grant or Richard Cole – for any reason.
4. Keep your cassette player turned off at all times unless conducting an interview.
5. Never ask questions about anything other than music.
6. Most importantly, understand this – the band will read what is written about them. The band does not like the press nor do they trust them.

Later on the tour, John Paul Jones learned that, eight years previously, Rosen had unfavourably compared Led Zeppelin to the Jeff Beck Group. The suddenly, irrationally furious bass player demanded that Rosen hand over all his cassette tapes.

The chucking of cherry bombs onto the stage had become like the dark antithesis of the jelly beans peppering the Beatles

12 years before. In Louisville, Kentucky, a lobbed bottle hit Page's guitar: he and the other musicians momentarily quit the stage, but soon returned.

But it was not all angst and moodiness. On 28 April in Cleveland, Ohio, there was a magical performance where everything gelled. And the enormous show at the Pontiac Silverdome was similarly inspiring.

Following it Plant, Jones and Bonham returned to their families in the UK for a two-week break in the schedule. And Page? He flew direct to Cairo, lodging himself at the luxurious Mena House Hotel, adjacent to the Great Pyramid. Cairo, of course, was where *The Book of the Law*, the foundation of Thelemite thinking, had been dictated to Aleister Crowley by an outerworld entity.

On 12 May 1977 Page was back in London. He and the other members of Led Zeppelin, along with Peter Grant, were at the Grosvenor House Hotel in Park Lane for the annual Ivor Novello Awards: they were presented with the 1977 award for Outstanding Contribution to British Music.

A week later they were on a plane to the United States for the second leg of their American tour. It kicked off in Birmingham, Alabama, at the Coliseum, where Jimmy included a snatch of 'Dixie' in a guitar solo.

When the band played in Maryland, adjacent to Washington, DC, Peter Grant invited a number of Soviet diplomats to the show, having already dined with them at the Russian Embassy. Grant had arranged for John Paul Jones to slip a section of Rachmaninoff's Variations into his set-piece solo during 'No Quarter'. The Soviet officials were delighted. As was Peter Grant: his ambition was for Zeppelin to play in Moscow.

But everywhere there seemed – appropriately enough for that year of change that was 1977 – near-anarchy from the fans. All around them on that final American tour, the dystopian, anarchic future promised by the very nature of Led Zeppelin, which had long lain dormant, appeared to have risen out of its primordial slime. On the tour's first leg there had been over a hundred arrests when a thousand fans tried to break into the Cincinnati Riverfront Coliseum; during a second show at the venue a youth fell from high up on a gantry and died.

On 21 May in Texas, a state that held almost as much empathy and adoration for Zeppelin as southern California, the band played the Houston Summit Arena; forty people were arrested and over half a million dollars' worth of damage was caused in the city after a post-show audience riot.

A fortnight later there was far greater mayhem. In Tampa, Florida, always prone to the eccentric extremities of its subtropical climate, there was a flash flood 20 minutes into Led Zeppelin's set.

This show had already earned a difficult reputation: on the day that tickets had gone on sale, Zeppelin fans, tiring of waiting in line, had gone on a rampage of destruction, stealing food from stands, tearing up offices and ripping out seats. To control this outbreak, a SWAT team had been brought in from Miami.

The Tampa date was an outdoor event, before an audience of 70,000. Peter Grant, unusually for him but perhaps unsurprising considering his depressed and drugged frame of mind, had neglected to note that the contract with the promoters contained a 'rain or shine' clause; in other words, whatever the weather the show must go on. Since Leslie Harvey, Maggie Bell's guitarist in Stone the Crows, had been electrocuted onstage at Swansea Top Rank after touching an unearthed microphone with wet hands, Grant had been ever alert to the dangers of untrammelled electric force. He was always insistent that the outdoor venues Led Zeppelin played, such as the one at Tampa Stadium, must have the stage covered by a solid metal roof.

Again, this last edict had been overlooked at Tampa by the promoters; there was only a canvas awning above the stage, already overloaded with water from earlier rainfall. When the tropical storm broke 20 minutes into Zeppelin's set, their manager immediately pulled the band offstage, ending the concert. The 'rain or shine' clause meant the event could not be rescheduled for the following day. On learning this, a major riot broke out among the audience, who were chanting, 'We want Zeppelin! We want Zeppelin!' As the roadies began to dismantle the equipment, bottles rained down on them. Fans even attacked other fans.

Waiting outside the stadium were 40 cops in full riot gear, most of whom were extremely unsympathetic to the ever-controversial notion of Led Zeppelin and their fans. Now they swung into action, quite literally, racing into the venue and bringing their billy clubs down on the fans' heads, who fought back with fists and any weapon they could find, as a full-scale insurrection appeared to be taking place.

It was a shocking scene: 60 fans were taken to hospital, along with 12 police officers. The next day, at Grant's hectoring insistence, the promoters placed a full-page advertisement in the local newspaper accepting full responsibility for the disastrous show, absolving Led Zeppelin of any blame – which was theoretically correct.

The next dates, in the relative civilisation of New York City, were punctuated by further firecracker attacks: when one hit Page on the hand while he was onstage, he returned to the dressing room for five minutes. He returned when it was apparent that he had not suffered any injury. But these six nights at Madison Square Garden also restored a considerable measure of triumph to the tour. Page proved himself to be the guitar god for which he was revered, delivering blistering solos and performances that were of the very highest order. Always aware of the value of prestigious venues, it is almost certainly no coincidence that, after a number of creaky shows in the American provinces, he rose to exhibit the full majesty of his status in New York City.

The Madison Square Garden shows allowed Led Zeppelin to briefly become social fixtures on the Manhattan scene: Page hung out with Keith Richards and Ron Wood, visiting Trax disco with them; and John Bonham's fondness for throwing television sets and sundry furniture off his balcony led to the band being ejected from the Plaza Hotel – for ever. Robert Plant purchased a new Lincoln Mark VI, which he immediately had shipped back to the UK.

When Led Zeppelin left New York for California, Page was so out of it that he had to be virtually carried onto *Caesar's Chariot*. The party checked into the Beverly Hilton in Los Angeles, once again eschewing the pleasures of the Hyatt House. There was an English woman living in the city called Pennie who was friends with Plant and his personal tour manager Benji LeFevre. Jimmy Page, she was led to believe by the singer, was in a bad state during that tour because of drugs. For the seven nights at the Forum in Los Angeles no one would really see him until he emerged from his hotel room to go to the gig, where his playing would still be sensational. 'I was there all seven nights at the Forum and I can tell you that nobody slept,' said Michael Des Barres. 'Every evening Jimmy was carried onstage by Richard Cole and carried off.'

Benji LeFevre would add 'sound tricks' to Plant's vocals with an electric harmoniser that permitted him to sing with himself. Then Page would perform a virtuoso guitar performance that could last for up to an hour, and for which the fans would go crazy; during such soloing Plant would sigh, 'Jimmy, oh Jimmy!' However, Plant and LeFevre would refer to this as 'Jimmy Page's Comedy Hour'. A sign of insurrection in the camp? An indication perhaps of the 'lack of camaraderie' that Richard Cole claimed was prevalent on Led Zeppelin's eleventh American tour? It was rare, Cole noted, for the individual band members to spend time with each other: 'When we did socialise, streaks of hostility or maliciousness towards other members of the group sometimes surfaced.'

Although Page might have appeared to be missing in action, apart from when he was onstage, he was in fact right at the centre of the action. In his suitably murkily lit suite, he gave a few interviews and trawled through tour photographer Neal Preston's concert slides, anxious not to let out into the public domain any pictures in which his now slightly protruding belly was visible.

When she finally gained admission to Page's suite, *Creem*'s Jaan Uhelszki found herself in one of the most extraordinary interviews of her life: 'I'd been on the road with them for over a week and couldn't get him to agree to an interview. Finally, on the last day of the tour, he agreed to an audience on the condition that the publicist had to be there. I agreed, but didn't realise the implication until I began asking my questions. Jimmy stipulated that I must first ask the publicist my question and then she relay the question to him – even though we all spoke the same language and I was sitting a mere six feet from him. This went on for about an hour, and was so odd, and rather humiliating.'

By now Miss Pamela had married Michael Des Barres; in a nice twist, the ceremony had taken place in the back garden of Catherine James's house in Laurel Canyon. 'We saw a lot of Zeppelin, and they were not aging gracefully, except for Robert, who still had his shoulders thrown back,' Pamela Des Barres wrote of these Forum dates. 'Jimmy wore a Third Reich costume, made the Heil Hitler! gesture, and had to be propped up by two flunkies at all times. I saw him take 20 minutes to crawl across the room to get to a black bag full of pills. He kept toppling over, and everyone else in the room pretended not to notice. Or maybe they really didn't notice.'

There was a three-week break after the Los Angeles dates. Again, the rest of the group flew back to England. Again, Page flew to Cairo.

On 17 July 1977 the third leg of Led Zeppelin's epic tour of the US began in Seattle, before 62,000 people. It was only an average show. 'It was a night of pot, pills and popcorn with the popcorn coming in a close third to the other two,' wrote the *Seattle Post-Intelligencer*. 'But overall, the Led Zeppelin concert at the Kingdome came off without too much trouble. There were several arrests, lots of dope and booze smuggled in – either under coats or inside bodies – and some very sick kids from drinking too much. Plant promised that the 1977 tour would be "blood, thunder and the hammer of the gods". A squad of paramedics was geared up for the blood and everybody else was geared up for the blood and thunder part.'

If Seattle had been just average, the next gig, three days later, at Arizona State University Activity Center Arena in Tempe, was claimed to be 'a strong contender for their worst ever show'. After the concert began, an hour late with no explanation given, Page seemed utterly off his head. He fluffed intros, going into 'Black Mountain Side' for ten seconds before shifting into 'Kashmir', leaving the rest of the baffled group to catch up. Utterly static and seemingly uninspired throughout the set, he was thrown onto his back by one of the flash-pot explosions at the climax of 'Achilles Last Stand'. 'Moby Dick' was dropped, the set concluded with 'Stairway to Heaven' and there was no encore.

Three days later Led Zeppelin and their considerable entourage boarded *Caesar's Chariot* and flew to San Francisco for two dates just across the bay, in Oakland, California. Then they would fly to New Orleans.

The first Oakland show, of course, was the one at which Bill Graham's employee Jim Matzorkis was attacked and beaten by John Bonham, Peter Grant and John Bindon. Thoroughly egregious, it was the moment when all of Led Zeppelin's legendary inhumane treatment of lesser beings fully came under global exposure in all its shocking dysfunctionalism. 'I wasn't there, but I do know it was nothing really heavy. Certainly nothing heavier than I'd witnessed out front during the concert,' Page said to me in 1979 about the Oakland assaults.

On receiving the devastating news of the death of his five-year-old son Karac, Robert Plant immediately flew back to London that night, Tuesday 26 July, accompanied by John Bonham and Richard Cole; the last seven dates of Led Zeppelin's tour were summarily cancelled. *Caesar's Chariot* was not licensed for travel outside the US and Atlantic Records had lent their corporate jet to President Jimmy Carter; Cole booked the three of them onto a flight from New Orleans to Newark, and then first-class seats on a British Airways plane to London. At Heathrow, Cole had arranged for a private jet to immediately whisk them up to Birmingham Airport. Plant never broke down, but tears were frequently visible on his face. 'Karac was the apple of Robert's eye. They idolised one another,' said Plant's father, who met his son at Birmingham Airport. 'All this success and fame,' his father added. 'What is it worth? It doesn't mean very much when you compare it to the love of a family.'

Did Richard Cole have time during that unhappy flight back to London to ponder on what had happened in Oakland? He, John Bonham, Peter Grant and John Bindon had been arrested and charged with assault. They were on $250 bail each, and awaiting trial.

With the assistance of his old friend Bonham, Plant withdrew into himself, alone with Maureen and Carmen. He gave up all drugs, cancelling them out of his life in an instant. But he did drink so much beer that by the next spring he considered himself to be obese. By then Maureen was pregnant.

What still seems utterly extraordinary, a certain sign of the complete collapse of the flimsiest moral structure or humanity within Led Zeppelin, as though they didn't give a fuck, was that neither Jimmy Page, John Paul Jones nor Peter Grant – who was probably still blaming Bill Graham for Karac Plant's death – attended the poor boy's funeral, held in the first week of August. What on earth was each of them thinking? Were they so consumed by rock-star narcissism that they were simply unable to view life from Robert Plant's point of view and see that he would certainly need their support? Or – certainly in the case of Page and Grant – were they simply so out of it on smack and downers and booze that their thinking was utterly befuddled? A bit of each, one might feel. It was a big mistake, not least in the eyes of Plant.

'Shortly after Karac died,' said Joe Jammer, 'I bumped into Robert and Maureen outside of Swan Song. He was getting into a Jaguar. And he says to me, "Stay away from Jimmy. Stay away from Jimmy. He's evil, he's evil. It's his fault that Karac is dead." And Maureen is crying her eyes out. And I'm standing there going, "Oh, it's Jimmy's fault?" And then they were gone.'

With the UK media more concerned with the seemingly unstoppable upwards surge of punk rock, the summer months of 1977 were a strange time: it felt as though the old order was being utterly overturned – Jimmy Page's world of Pre-Raphaelite whimsy seemed rather outdated and irrelevant. On 16 August, Elvis Presley, the King of Rock 'n' Roll, who had so inspired both Page and Plant to become musicians, died of a heart attack at the age of 42 while seated on the toilet. In September 1977, hurrying back from the pub in his Jensen Interceptor, John Bonham ran out of road near his home and ended up in a ditch, breaking two ribs in the process; abandoning his vehicle, he struggled home on foot before police arrived.

In the mythology of the street Led Zeppelin's tragic fall was interpreted as a perhaps deserved response to the group's gargantuan ambitions, aspirations that had been driven by Page's supposed obsession with the occult. Rumours now surfaced of that deal having been done with the Devil to ensure Zeppelin's success when the band first formed; of the blood sacrifice in which Page, Plant and Bonham had participated, but which John Paul Jones had stepped back from. In the subsequent reading of this, following one further large tragedy, the proof was declared to be in Jones emerging from his time with Led Zeppelin apparently unscathed.

Zeppelin biographer Mick Wall claimed that the distance Plant felt from the rest of the group, apart from loyal, supportive Bonham, was profound; that Page, Jones and Grant's non-appearance at Karac's funeral created a rift that never truly healed. 'Until then, Robert was still in thrall to Jimmy and what he had created with Zeppelin. After that incident, Jimmy no longer held the same mystique for Robert,' Wall remarked in 2011. 'It was also the beginning of Robert having much more power over what the band did or didn't do next. He truly no longer cared and therefore was ready to walk at any point if they didn't fit in with him. And that's the way it remains to this day.'

For his part, Plant was considering giving up singing altogether; he enrolled on a course to become a teacher of the Rudolf Steiner method of education.

Page, however, was intent on keeping the Led Zeppelin flag flying. On 5 September 1977 he went with Atlantic Records UK boss Phil Carson to the annual WEA Records convention, held that year at the Metropole Hotel in Brighton, not far from Plumpton Place. As the evening wore on, the guitarist found himself onstage in a loose jam with the soon-to-be celebrated British composer and musician John Altman, who was on piano, along with Carson on bass. They played 'an instrumental blues which went on for at least 30 minutes – Jimmy kept apologising for losing his place. And there was a more up-tempo number also,' recalled Altman. Towards the end of the set a Warner employee took off all her clothes and writhed on top of Altman's piano – at which point, as he would do at Rodney's in LA in such circumstances, Page made himself scarce. Altman was at the convention to play sax with a pack of the first wave of British rockers, including Vince Eager, Marty Wilde and Wee Willie Harris, who all witnessed Page's guitar efforts. 'Jimmy was pretty out of it, I have to say,' thought Altman.

Although he was only performing in front of an invited audience – at what would later be defined as a 'corporate event' – Page was displaying himself in the best way he knew how. Much was being written and spoken about Plant having twice fallen victim to 'the Led Zeppelin curse'; not perhaps that initiated by Kenneth Anger, but a more nebulous business, a product of Page's endless dabblings with darkness. The Led Zeppelin leader was only too aware of such supposition. Mired, however, in addictions to heroin, cocaine, downers and alcohol, he was floating only inches above a black slab of depression generated by his own confusion about the cause of recent occurrences, including the all-consuming madness of the feral audiences on that last US tour. Why had everything become so crazy? Was he responsible for it? Even though he refused ever to acknowledge it in any interview form, he would have to have been very gone indeed not to have considered this. Maybe he was.

After Page and Grant had a meeting in which each was adamant that their singer be left to nurse his pain for as long as necessary, the guitarist declared that he would take a holiday, in Guadeloupe in the French Caribbean, with Charlotte Martin and Scarlet. When Page suggested that Richard Cole accompany them, he revealed a double purpose: the holiday would be an endeavour to get 'clean', as heroin would be impossible to score in Guadeloupe.

'It means about two weeks without heroin, but with plenty of white rum,' he told Cole, revealing his intention to mollify heroin withdrawal on the island by getting drunk on powerful overproof rum; it sounded like Page had been taking drug-dependency advice from Keith Richards, who famously substituted cocaine and vodka for heroin.

Page and Cole duly drank their way through the holiday. You wonder what Charlotte Martin and Scarlet thought to this. Despite their essentially successful efforts to kick their addictions, both Page and Cole returned to junk when they came back from the Caribbean. 'I had heard that Pagey got back into heroin before long, but because I didn't see him for a while, I had no way of knowing for sure. When the band re-formed the following year, however, he seemed as immersed in smack as I was,' wrote Cole. In fact, Cole confessed that within two days of his return he was back on the gear. And his level of alcohol consumption had increased, it would seem, exponentially: Cole went to Peter Grant's home straight from the airport, drinking 40 cans of beer as Grant debriefed him over the condition of their star asset.

No one in Led Zeppelin was doing anything of note, which gave plenty of opportunity for those so inclined to do very bad drugs. Normally Page would have been eager to seize such free time for ceaseless studio liberation, the science lab of his great art, working out new creations. But apart from allegedly going through Led Zeppelin live material from 1969 for a potential live album, which never materialised, he seemed to do very little. There were some press interviews that he really only undertook to deny the persistent reports that Led Zeppelin were over. And there was that other unrelenting rumour: that he would replace Keith Richards in the Rolling Stones if the Stone received the seven-year prison sentence he was facing in Canada for large-scale heroin possession. That one junkie would be replaced by another never seemed to be factored into this increasingly well-lit fantasy.

Yes, Jimmy Page is into junk. But it's not that at all. Why is he doing the junk? On the one hand because of the colossal pressures of being the biggest rock star in the world (though Robert Plant is a strong rival for that position), but also because, in his Pre-Raphaelite vision, he really wants to see what life's possibilities are. As Michael Des Barres says, he's in a position to do so. And he wants to see what it feels like.

You just can't come down: after the shows Page's adrenaline is firing so fast on the buzz of the never-guaranteed achievement – and its accomplished success – and the fiery love of the audience that it is impossible to even consider going to bed. Life – the endless party! – has now just started. Get high, that's the first edict. Because otherwise you might succumb to the nights of sleep you've missed. Get high. And get going, whatever it is: sexual, narcotic, intellectual or a bit of all of them, which is the best, clearly the most interesting, as Aleister Crowley would have prescribed. But Jimmy Page doesn't have this anymore. He is at home, exhausted. It has all finally caught up with him. He is drained beyond all belief, even without Plant's terrible difficulties. Where can he replenish his energies? Smack is the anaesthetist, but not the route, as the paucity of material for the next album demonstrated. But that was a little in the future.

In the spring of 1978 Roy Harper gave an interview to a farming magazine. Much of the interview concerned the sheep he kept on his farm. But he also mentioned that he had been working on the words for new Led Zeppelin material with Jimmy Page. Considering himself also to be a farmer, Robert Plant subscribed to the same publication. And he was outraged by what he read. Brimming with anger, the singer phoned Page, who denied the story. Yet it seemed to be a creative connection, and accordingly Page conversed with Peter Grant.

In May 1978 Grant booked several days at Clearwell Castle, which Bad Company had already used; on the Welsh border, it was not far from Plant's home. As seemed obligatory with properties associated with Page, the neo-Gothic edifice was haunted, this time by a female ghost with a penchant for singing lullabies to her spectral child; for added effect she would employ a music box. For some time the four musicians played and jammed, but there was almost none of the requisite magic. Page was urging the others on, insisting that it was time for Led Zeppelin to resume business. 'Robert, however, wasn't so sure,' wrote Richard Cole. 'He knew that once the band got back into motion, there would be no turning back. And he wasn't convinced that he was ready, that music was as important to him now as it had been before Karac's death.' Several times during those Clearwater Castle sessions Plant declared that he would never again sing 'Stairway to Heaven'.

A couple of months later, the singer got in touch with an outfit local to him fetchingly named the Turd Burglars. In a small church hall in Worcestershire, Robert Plant essayed a handful of songs with them, including the rock 'n' roll classic 'Blue Suede Shoes'. In August, while holidaying in Ibiza, he went to the club Amnesia with Dr Feelgood, a sometimes magnificent R&B outfit who peppered their own material with such classics as 'Riot in Cell Block Number 9' and who had played at Led Zeppelin's after-show party at Earls Court; Plant joined in on their repertoire. A few weeks later he appeared onstage in Birmingham with Dave Edmunds, who had been signed to Swan Song; the Zeppelin singer worked out on material similar to that played with the Feelgoods.

During the summer of 1978, Peter Grant, who was only 43 years old, suffered a minor heart attack. He was advised to utterly change his lifestyle: to give up alcohol and drugs, and to change his diet in order to lose some of his considerable weight, which had shot up to 28 stone. The coronary thrombosis perhaps could have been predicted: as well as his main source of income potentially drying up, the manager had been involved in that bitter divorce battle over the custody of his children, which he had won. Moreover, he had spent much of the time since the Oakland debacle involved in the legal fall-out.

At the court case in Oakland, six months after the event, Grant, John Bindon, Richard Cole and John Bonham had filed a joint plea of *nolo contendere* (a Californian legal byway that effectively means 'I will not plead guilty'); found guilty all the same, they each were fined and given suspended prison sentences. Grant was heard to remark that 'the biggest mistake I ever made was employing John Bindon'. (Later that year John Bindon would kill Johnny Darke in a knife fight near Putney Bridge, further along the New Kings Road from Swan Song. This stabbing was allegedly a hit, the bankrupt Bindon having been offered £10,000 to murder Darke. Badly wounded himself, Bindon managed to escape to Ireland, where he had an operation. At his trial for manslaughter the next year, he was somehow found not guilty, assisted considerably by the character-witness statement of the actor Bob Hoskins. John Bindon would die in 1993 of an AIDS-related illness.)

The four Led Zeppelin members only met again in September 1978, at Cole's wedding, a joint ceremony with Simon Kirke, the drummer with Bad Company. Wary of his potential response, no one mentioned to Plant that Led Zeppelin might now come back together.

Finally it was felt that sufficient time had passed so that Led Zeppelin could enter a recording studio. But where? Certainly not in the UK. There were considerable tax advantages to be enjoyed by British musicians who chose not to record in their home country.

Time was booked at Polar Studios in Stockholm, from 14 November to 21 December 1978. It was perhaps not the best time of year to visit Sweden, which was bitterly cold and snowbound when Led Zeppelin arrived the day before the sessions began. Polar, which had only opened in May that year, was owned by Björn Ulvaeus and Benny Andersson from Abba; keen to popularise their venture with overseas artists, they gave Led Zeppelin free time at their studio. Mr Led Wallet jumped at the idea.

The four musicians had been rehearsing new material for six weeks at Eazy Hire in north London, much of which had come from John Paul Jones, aware that someone needed to be in the driving seat. During the Eazy Hire sessions, Jimmy Page brought in a Gizmotron, a bowing gadget for the guitar invented by 10cc's Kevin Godley and Lol Creme. Page adored it, and used it extensively on the moody introduction to 'In the Evening'.

For the Polar Studios sessions, Led Zeppelin would fly to Stockholm each Monday lunchtime, returning on an evening flight to London the next Friday night. Yet Page was clearly not match fit. Frequently he would arrive at the studio – as Jones put it – 'two days late', as would John Bonham, half the band in thrall to what Kenneth Anger called 'the white lady': Richard Cole had found a connection close to the studio. On the other hand Jones and Robert Plant would turn up at ten o'clock each morning, fresh-faced and eager for work. They would lay down their parts, which Page would take back at the weekend to Plumpton Place, where he would add his own sounds. The tracks would sound utterly different when they returned to Polar. (Down at Plumpton, Page was even known to jam in the village pub, the Half Moon. 'I remember being in JP's house where he got his first home studio,' said Joe Jammer. 'It was for Charlotte's birthday: me, Jimmy, Jeff Beck, Eric with Pattie Boyd, Ronnie Wood and John Paul Jones, and in the kitchen he had a giant picture of the Sex Pistols. He took me up to the top of the house in the country and showed me his first ever studio. Lots of equipment. He wanted knobs made of Bakelite. He played me his first composition in this studio, and it was the chorus from Handel's *Messiah*, which he did himself. But it ain't funky. I brought a whole load of James Brown albums to play. He warned me of the future: "There's a new movement coming called digitalisation." He said, "Resist it as much as you can." He said it will be good for editing and for mixing, but it will be no good for recording. Always record analogue and always mix and edit digitally.')

Although Page would later claim that this last Led Zeppelin album, which would be tellingly titled *In Through the Out Door*, was somewhat lightweight, he needed to shoulder most of the blame: his smacked-out lack of vision was the major contributory factor. Jones and Plant were only too aware of Page's condition, as well as Bonham's, and simply seized the reins. After all, didn't someone have to?

Although Page would still be credited as 'producer', all such work on *In Through the Out Door* was essentially done by Jones, with Plant also a force. Frozen in his heroin addiction, Page had minimal input. Over the years Jones had accumulated plenty of material that not had been used by Led Zeppelin. And he had lately acquired a Yamaha GX-1 synthesiser – a harbinger of the electronically dominated sounds of the imminent eighties – whose sound washes he applied rather too lavishly to the project, although in so doing he invented what would soon become clichés. So the new sound that Led Zeppelin displayed on *In Through the Out Door* could be interpreted as their being ahead of the cutting edge. Or it could be viewed as a somewhat desperate effort to release some new product and shore up the foundations of an increasingly dysfunctional outfit in which, with the exception of Jones, all the other players were in one way or another exceptionally vulnerable – including their manager, who seemed never to be at Swan Song and was almost uncontactable. Swan Song indeed seemed especially dormant: both the Pretty Things and Detective had broken up, and it was now that Maggie Bell was reduced to manning the reception desk at the company's offices.

The rockabilly 'Hot Dog' somehow set the tone: the fourth of the seven songs on the record, it was like an Elvis Presley outtake, momentarily appealing but instantly forgettable; in the US it would be released as an unsuccessful single. There was one great track: the opener 'In the Evening', moody, Moroccan and misty with the sound of meditative contemplation. In the tradition of Zeppelin's epic set-piece tunes like 'Kashmir' or 'Achilles Last Stand', it was the album's standout track, running to almost seven minutes.

Jones and Plant wrote 'All My Love', the album's other significant song, with no input at all from Page. Clearly a tribute to Karac, Plant's vocals are almost heartbreaking in their intensity. Later Page was dismissive of 'All My Love': 'I could just imagine people doing the wave and all of that ... I wouldn't have wanted to pursue that direction in the future.' His cold assessment of the song seemed rather to miss its point.

'I'm Gonna Crawl', which closed the LP, was an archetypal Zeppelin blues lament. 'On this album,' wrote Stephen Davis, 'where he seemed to have run out of ideas, Jimmy Page turned back to the blues for solace, and his solo seemed to cry with abject remorse.'

It couldn't be denied – there was something desperate about *In Through the Out Door*. Yet one creative act by the still-grieving Plant and his wife had been successful: on 21 January 1979 Maureen gave birth to a son, Logan Romero Plant.

22

BONZO'S LAST STAND

In his *Rolling Stone* review of *In Through the Out Door*, Charles M. Young, who had written the magazine's first article about UK punk, argued that Jimmy Page's diminished creativity had left Robert Plant with a lack of strong material to work with; somewhat unsympathetically in the circumstances, he also condemned Plant's lyrics as inane. In *Melody Maker* Chris Bohn asserted that Zeppelin were 'totally out of touch' and 'displaying the first intimations of mortality'. By contrast, Nick Kent, in the much more punk hard-line *NME*, found the LP in no way an 'epitaph', seeing its 'potential points of departure' as being worthy of further plays.

All the same, *In Through the Out Door* was number one after only two weeks in the US, and sold 6 million copies; in the UK it was similarly number one, shifting 300,000 units.

With a new album about to be released, on 15 August 1979, what would any act do? They would endeavour to promote it with live shows, the umbilical link between 'product' out in the marketplace and the touring circuit.

Having somewhat recovered from his coronary, Peter Grant started to put out feelers. Rather than announce a tour, he wanted Led Zeppelin to come back – for a 'comeback', as show-biz parlance would have it, was essentially what this would be, a career salvation operation – with an enormous staged event, not dissimilar to Bob Dylan's surprise return to the stage at the 1969 Isle of Wight Festival after his motorbike accident.

Grant started to talk to his old friend Freddy Bannister, who had staged the Bath Festival of Blues and Progressive Music, which had been such a memorable triumph for Led Zeppelin in 1970, their true UK breakthrough point. Since 1974 Bannister had held annual one-day festivals at Knebworth House, in Hertfordshire, 30 miles north of London. These always involved one stellar name, with a strong bill of supporting acts. The first event featured the Allman Brothers, with support from – among others – Van Morrison, Tim Buckley and the Sensational Alex Harvey Band. Indeed, before Grant settled on Earls Court, it had been mooted that Led Zeppelin would be the headline act at Knebworth in 1975. Part of Bannister's ethos was to give his audiences the best possible value for money by keeping tickets at as low a price as possible.

In May it was announced that Led Zeppelin would play an outdoor concert at Knebworth House on 4 August 1979. Freddy Bannister had balked at the idea at first: Grant was demanding a cool £1 million for two shows, on successive Saturdays. There was no question that the event would be a success. Yet from the off the atmosphere of excess about everything connected to it seemed utterly contradictory to the prevailing do-it-yourself mood of punk. The paradoxically puritanical United States of America is endlessly attracted to prestige: the excess that Zeppelin purveyed – money, power, arrogance – was how megastars were expected to behave. It didn't go down so well in the UK.

Offered the opportunity to interview 'Pagey' to promote the Knebworth dates, I willingly accepted. My article was published in the 4 August 1979 edition of the *NME*, the day of the first Knebworth show. I had interviewed Page eight days previously, on a late Friday afternoon. It was given the title – not chosen by me – of 'Smiling Men with Bad Reputations'. Here it is:

Of all the old superfart bands it is certainly Led Zeppelin who have been and still are the most reviled by the New Wave.

Whatever jerk-off socialite absurdities Jagger may have got himself into, the Rolling Stones have at least always had one of the prime punk archetypes in Keith Richards. The Who, meanwhile, have the ever-perceptive Townshend, a man who appears to have gone through something of a personal rejuvenation that seems to be a direct result of his encounters with Punk.

For whatever reasons, though, the manner in which Led Zeppelin have consistently presented themselves has made the band's name synonymous with gratuitous excess. Even the almost equally guilty Pink Floyd have at least had the decency and sensitivity not to quit these shores just for the sake of saving money.

Don't sell your soul for silver and gold, as Lee Perry once said. If rock 'n' roll is essentially an all-encompassing roots culture, then obviously any musician who isolates himself away in some anal-retentive tax-exile lifestyle is neither responding to his obligations nor in harmony with those roots. Also, his initial purpose and motivation must be doubted.

The Clash's Paul Simonon summed up pretty well the total lack of respect that the new bands feel towards Zeppelin. 'Led Zeppelin??? I don't need to hear the music – all I have to do is look at one of their album covers and I feel like throwing up!'

In some ways part of the reason for the venomous loathing directed at the band is not just because they've let themselves down, but also because you know damn well that Jimmy Page at least – like many of the new Punk icons a former art student – certainly knows better.

'I've read about many records which are supposed to have turned me on to play rock 'n' roll,' the guitarist told *Trouser*

Press in September 1977, 'but it was "Baby Let's Play House" by Presley … I heard that record and I wanted to be part of it; I knew something was going on. I heard the acoustic guitar, slap bass and electric guitar – three instruments and a voice – and they generated so much energy I had to be part of it. That's when I started.'

Yet, in the same way that the death of the original, classic rock 'n' roll punk the previous month to the publication of that article could have been seen as a serious warning of the false paths and box canyons into which Babylon could misroute rock 'n' rollers, it also appeared at the time that perhaps the whole mighty edifice which Led Zeppelin had created itself to be was starting to crumble away as inevitably as the Malibu Beach Colony will one day slide into the Pacific Ocean.

By the middle of the year when the two sevens clashed, the belief that the whole Led Zeppelin operation had got it all more than a little bit wrong appeared to be backed up by concrete facts. The band appeared to be in a state of crisis. In artistic terms they seemed to have reached an absolute nadir. Following the turgid *Presence* LP released in the spring of the previous year there'd then been, six months later, the critically lambasted *The Song Remains the Same* film and double soundtrack album. Even this emphasis on double records – two out of the three LPs the band had put out since they'd formed their own Swan Song label had been two-record sets when none had been released before – suggested attempts to milk their market for all it was worth while fighting a rear-guard action to forestall an inevitable end.

Perhaps more to the point, though, a general atmosphere of personal doom and gloom appeared to surround the once invincible Zeppelin. From the outset the lengthy US tour undertaken by the outfit in the spring of '77 seemed ill-fated.

It was to have been the band's first live work since 1975 when vocalist Robert Plant had been severely injured in a car smash on the Greek island of Rhodes during a year of British tax exile. It was ominous then that the first dates were cancelled when Plant developed a throat infection.

Jimmy Page himself was also believed not to be in a good state, an assumption fuelled by the news that the full-time services of a doctor were being employed to care for the guitar hero. Now Page denies that the medic was there to look after him alone – 'We had a doctor to look after all of us, period. It was a bloody long tour' – with the same ease that he dismisses reports of his having been wheeled around between gigs in a wheelchair – 'I may have done that for a laugh – not seriously. No, no. That wasn't happening at all.'

In addition, manager Peter Grant was said to be severely depressed following a divorce. Matters appeared to reach what seemed to be an inevitably unpleasant culmination when, following a Bill Graham-promoted San Francisco gig, one of the promoter's security men was badly beaten up by Grant, drummer John Bonham and one John Bindon, a Zeppelin employee.

If some form of near tragedy during the tour had seemed unavoidable, however, it was yet to wreak its worst toll. This happened some two weeks later when Robert Plant's five-year-old son died of a sudden mystery virus infection and the tour was abandoned while the grief-stricken singer flew home.

Now, of course, all these incidents may be seen as random happenings, as the chance intervention of fate. However, if you believe that you create your own fate and that human beings do not exist in isolation from one another and from the universe but are part of a far greater, interacting scheme in which actions and activities of the past create those of the future, then all this begins to look rather different.

Certainly, Jimmy Page's interests in the occult suggest that he should believe in such a cosmic overview. Indeed, there are those who would claim that it is solely down to Page's interests in these matters that such a tragic atmosphere has surrounded Led Zeppelin in its latter years. Personally, though, I don't think that Jimmy Page has inked a pact with Satan. To think like that is mere superstition and that's taking into account certain rumours which have floated about the music business the past 18 months or so that there are even certain members of the Zeppelin entourage themselves who lay blame for these assorted misfortunes on Page's fascination with Aleister Crowley.

When it comes down to it, though, I don't really think that there's been some clear-cut metaphysical holy war of good and evil waged on the rock 'n' roll boards the band has been treading the past ten years. In fact, it's probably that outside interest which has kept the guitarist's head relatively together during the most successful years of the band. The occult, after all, is concerned with knowledge and plumbing one's own mystic depths for certain truths that are beneficial to the whole of humanity. Yes, of course, it can be used in a malevolent manner, but to view all occult activity as the work of the Devil is a red herring laid down by Babylon and therefore is the work of the tricky Devil himself.

I think, though, that Jimmy Page is very confused. His confusion doesn't spring from his occult interests but, I feel, from the very nature of Led Zeppelin itself and his position with regard to the band of which he is indubitably the leader. Indeed, when we met in Swan Song's London office on the hottest day of the year, it became glaringly obvious that Jimmy Page was totally comfortable and, at times, positively exhilarated when talking about these extra-curricular activities.

It was noticeable, however, that when the conversation changed to the subject of his band he appeared frequently to find eye contact exceptionally awkward. Now, it's quite possible to blame that on the fact that in the isolated, self-enclosed existence in which Jimmy Page dwells he probably doesn't have that much verbal interchange with people outside his own sphere. Also, like many musicians who are far more at ease when living out their fantasies onstage, he may well be slightly nervous. Mind you, although a hermetic, fairly newsless lifestyle is part of the whole Led Zeppelin problem anyway, Page's behaviour does suggest that he is not always totally convinced by his arguments – and Page is adept in the art of being a media salesman for his band while at the same time revealing little about himself; check how many times the word 'Knebworth' gets mentioned in this piece.

It's the very nature of Led Zeppelin itself that is the problem. Let's not mince words, it's always been regarded as a 'heavy' operation. There has been a slightly odd vibe about it.

Now, of course, part of the nature of rock 'n' roll is the manner in which it allows people involved with it to live out their childhood Cowboy and Indian fantasies. So I don't know whether Peter Grant really is a figure from the fringes of the underworld or whether he just enjoys people thinking that he is. I suppose it doesn't really matter (though in a way it does) because I've no doubt, as Page himself comments later on, that certain of the behind-the-scenes music industry figures with whom he has to deal, particularly in the States, actually are dodgy characters. So maybe it gives him an edge over them. (Unless they're also all just living out their fantasies – in which case it all gets a bit complicated and self-perpetuating, and a bit pointless too.)

'The whole point of the bit in *The Song Remains the Same* film,' Page tells me when I ask him about this, 'where Peter plays a gangster, was just to send up all that and show how it was just a joke anyway.'

Nevertheless, I counter, there was the slight problem with the security guy in San Francisco. There's certainly concern in his voice when he replies, 'I didn't see it, you know, so I can't say exactly what happened. There were no million-dollar lawsuits put out on me, y'know.

'But,' he continues, 'you must remember that Bill Graham has a very heavy reputation, that all his security people have a reputation for heaviness. As for Peter ... Well, he's a very big guy and, if people are coming up to him all the time and calling him a bastard and telling him to piss off to his face, then he's probably going to react accordingly.'

Alright, fair enough. But let's not forget that John Bindon is currently in Brixton either awaiting or serving a sentence for a subsequently committed manslaughter [in fact, John Bindon would soon be acquitted] – an incident which wasn't connected in any way with Led Zeppelin. Once again, judging from his reply to being reminded of this, there's no doubt that this genuinely troubles Page, much more out of real concern for Bindon, I feel, than for any unhappiness about him being linked with Zeppelin. It's a pity I forgot at the time, but I'd like to have also got his reaction to Nick Kent's claim that John Bonham once threw a drink over the hapless writer for a negative review.

But that's by the by, I suppose. It seems more important to tell the guitarist that, whether he's aware of this or not, an oft-expressed opinion on Led Zeppelin has been that the problems Robert Plant has faced have been something of a karmic backlash that Plant, as the most accessible and open band member, has had directed towards him.

Page seems very shocked by this. 'I don't think that's so,' he replies slowly, almost as though slightly dazed, 'if what we were doing was really evil then ... then I suppose we'd just put out lots of records and try and make loads of money … I hope that's not so.'

Sometime about the middle of last Friday morning I'd had a call from the Swan Song press office. Could I arrive maybe an hour before the interview was due to begin? That way I could be given an earful of the new Zep waxing. I can't pretend the idea exactly thrilled me to the bones, especially in the light of the last studio album, *Presence*, which I find utterly unenjoyable. If I felt the same way about the new, as yet untitled, LP, it could mean a chilly start to an interview.

By lunchtime, however, this potentially awkward situation had been resolved by Jimmy Page himself. A further phone call passed on the information that the guitarist felt it pointless for me to hear the record as it was, apparently, 'a separate entity' – from what I'm not certain. Obviously it did cross my mind that maybe he was thinking the same way as myself and saw little gain in the songs being numbered some time before the record was even released.

Perhaps predictably, when the record did come to be mentioned he was full of enthusiasm for it. The titles of the new numbers are: Side 1 – 'In the Evening', 'South Bound Suarez', 'Hot Dog'; Side 2 – 'Carouselambra', 'All My Love', 'I'm Gonna Crawl'. The Knebworth bashes will feature 'at least two songs from the new album plus several numbers from previous LPs that haven't been performed live in the past. What can I say?'

I was also asked for some idea of the sort of questions I'd be asking. As I was at that time deciding on these for myself I couldn't really help out there. Besides, would this not have detracted from the natural spontaneity of the occasion? I was, however, informed that questions about the death of Plant's son and about Aleister Crowley were strictly taboo. This did not augur particularly well, especially when, while waiting for the assistant-editor chap from the *Melody Maker* to finish his rap with Jim, photographer Adrian Boot emerged from that session to inform Pennie and me that Page was 'doing a Chuck Berry' and ignoring most of Michael Watts's questions. The guitarist was also apparently none too happy about Boot's snapping needs.

In the event, of course, Page gave Pennie plenty of pix-taking time prior to our encounter. Also, as far as my interview went, Page and I just started talking conversationally (but not before he made a rapid attempt to flog Knebworth) rather than adhering to any strict question and answer form. This situation lasted for much of the interview.

Page was drinking pints of lager from a straight plastic glass and chain-smoking Marlboros. So was I. It was probably down to a combination of the booze and the hot weather, but the conversation quickly became very speedy. Maybe we were also blocked on the carbon-monoxide fumes wafting in through the open window from the early evening rush-hour traffic three floors below on the Kings Road.

What with the roar of London Transport Roadmasters stopping just past the offices and the constant rumble of jets on their way to Heathrow overhead, it was often hard for either of us to make out what the other was saying. Though his enunciation is very clear indeed, Jimmy Page's soft Surrey accent – the family business is Page Motors in Epsom [Not so!] – makes him perhaps the most quietly spoken interviewee I've ever come across. Even so, I was pleased that he didn't pull the slumped-out whispering wimp number that I'm told is one of his favourite interview techniques. Not once, I think, did he lean back on the couch on which he was seated next to the window.

No doubt exacerbated by the booze intake – Jim is fond of the odd tipple, I'm told – perspiration poured off of his forehead in large drops, frequently lodging for a few moments in his close-to-shoulder-length hair. Coupled with the collarless striped white shirt he wore, he didn't look very different at all from when in the late sixties he laid down the ground rules for the classic Pre-Raphaelite, faintly androgynous British rock star. He actually looked younger than when I'd encountered him a couple of years back. Only the lines around his sometimes troubled eyes gave any indication of age.

The Selling of Knebworth began right from the very outset. I don't think you really like doing interviews, do you, I ask?

'Well [laughs], it depends. I don't mind if the questions are alright.'

You look incredibly well.

'Well, I was looking forward to … to Knebworth, actually. We've done a lot of rehearsing and checked things out. We've actually been down there and worked things out relative to the actual site.'

It must seem odd with it being such a long time since you've played onstage …

'Well, it did at first … But then again it's like a natural amphitheatre, so I should imagine it's actually quite a good gig to be at. I went to Blackbushe, but that was a bit of a sea of bodies. But it was great to see Dylan.'

Phew, that was close. The Zim to the rescue. At least we can talk about Bob Dylan for a while. This might be handy. Maybe if I mention to Jim that I met Dylan last year when he went to an Alton Ellis gig at the 100 Club and that he told me how he preferred the vibe in England to that in the States, and also in Germany from where he'd just returned, then we can get onto this matter of Punk and the New Wave without too much discomfort.

Instead, though, Page mentions his surprise that Dylan had played in Nuremburg. 'I couldn't believe him doing that.

They played the place where they had all the big rallies. He must have come out of there feeling very strange. I know I would and I'm not even Jewish.'

He hasn't heard of Dylan's conversion to Christianity. 'Oh, that's very interesting. Especially after that Nuremburg thing. When did that happen? Quite recently?'

Oh, about six months or so ago, I think.

'We met his mum once, actually,' Page tells me. 'It was about the third tour and we were in Miami, and this typical Miami woman comes up with the spectacles and tinted hair bit and she says, "Oh, I hear you're a group. My son's a singer. You've probably heard of him – Bobby Dylan. He's a good lad."

'The strangest thing she said of all was that he always goes back to his … you know, the school turn-out when they got their degrees and things. He always goes back to that … Which is obviously a side of Dylan that many people would be actually shocked about. He's probably very orthodox in some areas where you expect him to be very bizarre and anarchistic.'

Logically, I suppose, the matter of meeting Dylan at a reggae gig leads to discussion of matters Rastafarian. Jimmy Page is far more au fait with it than I would have expected.

'Yeah, it's very interesting: the Lost Tribe of Israel and all that. It was at the time when Haile Selassie died that I wondered "What's going to happen now?" Because there is this big thing that he's invincible and that he would never die but obviously,' he chuckles, 'he could give up his bodily form if he wanted to, that was the loophole.

'But it is fascinating.'

We talk about Egypt for a minute or two. Page's trip to Cairo had, indeed, been the subject of some quite splendid rumours. On the first leg, I think it was, of that last ill-fated Led Zeppelin US tour it was said that one night he'd been watching TV when the screen became filled with flashing lines. Immediately, so the tale went, he cancelled the next dates and flew off to Egypt. The conversation didn't lead into my mentioning that and, besides, I'm fairly certain I once read a fairly thorough refutation by the guitarist of that story.

Thoughts of Cairo seem to make Page feel very happy. 'I didn't want to come home,' he smiles, 'it was so good. I didn't go for long enough, though. I went at the end of an American tour and with every day I was there family ties in England were pulling more strongly. I just thought, "Oh, I'll be back soon," and haven't made it yet. I'd certainly like to see the Valley of the Kings near Luxor.

'I haven't been to many Arab countries, but I've been to Morocco and there and in other hot countries there's this constant hubbub, but in Egypt it's just so tranquil. It really is quite an experience. Let alone the pyramids.'

Equinox, the Kensington occult book shop that Page owned and which specialised in the works of Aleister Crowley, is closed these days. The lease expired and, besides, 'It obviously wasn't going to run the way it should without some drastic business changes and I didn't really want to have to agree to all that. I basically just wanted the shop to be the nucleus, that's all.'

His interests in the occult haven't in any way diminished, however. 'I'm still very interested. I still read a lot of literature on it.'

I mention that last time I'd gone past Equinox a small sticker that someone had placed on the door had attracted my attention. 'For the real truth about the changes in the Church of Rome,' it had read, 'write to the following address.' The name and address of a priest in Mexico was given. We talk about the Rasta belief that it was at the Pope's insistence that Mussolini invaded Ethiopia in order to prevent Haile Selassie organising the Christian Church in such a way that would have reduced the Catholic Church to the second largest Christian Church in the world.

'I know the Pope definitely blessed the bombers going to Ethiopia,' says Page. 'That's a fact. My lady went to the Vatican. She said it's like Fort Knox, a completely separate state. A highly guarded treasury. And they have all these links with suspect organisations …

'The whole image of the Pope being borne around St Peter's on a throne doesn't even bear thinking about. They had some programme on TV about the Vatican and they got through to one of the heads of the business division. And he was asked if it wouldn't be an act of faith to give all this wealth away – if your faith was sufficiently high and strong then obviously this wouldn't really affect the church. But he was dumbstruck. So obviously,' he laughs, 'he didn't have the faith.'

Jimmy Page has had some involvement with the community politics up in Scotland where he owns Crowley's former home, Boleskine, on the shores of Loch Ness. After, against much opposition on the local council, a harbour wall utilising raw materials had been built under the guidance of the local job recreation scheme, Page, largely as a result of previous similar activities within the community, was involved in the final unveiling ceremony. The local Labour man, he said, jumped on the platform at this event in a predictable attempt to make political mileage.

'I just got up and said, "I'm not here for any political reasons whatsoever but just from my own endeavours as an untrained musician. And it's just sheer determination that's been employed here against a good 80 per cent of the council who wished them to have no encouragement whatsoever."'

One is not particularly surprised that the politician appeared to milk the event for his personal aggrandisement;

it is the nature of such a breed of people to behave in that manner, no matter what political party they belong to. It does seem interesting for a moment, though, that, when I inquire as to whether the council members were operating in a truly reactionary manner, Page seems a little uncomfortable when he realises that I regard 'Reactionary' as being synonymous with 'Tory'.

Maybe that's by the by. Page has, after all, been involved up there in other battles with officialdom. 'The Hydro board in Scotland were putting in this scheme which wasn't of benefit to anyone except for a small percentage of local labourers – although, in fact, most of them were being brought in from places like Manchester and Liverpool.

'What it was going to do was pump power at peak times to the South. It wasn't going to benefit the Scots at all. And for this they were going to put pylons up all over the place and mess up the loch. There were no pylons there whatsoever before. And I just didn't think it was on. For them, of course it was purely a financial investment. It was really a revelation to see how these things go on. So corrupt.

'But we managed to force a public inquiry whereby it was put under the Secretary of State. They really put you through it at those things. It's like a court of law. They try and throw so much mud at you. Although it does seem that in London these days if they're pulling down buildings to put up new ones they are trying to keep the old facades. It makes it much more palatable. At least you don't get things like that too much,' he waves in the direction of the World's End council-housing project.

'But,' he continues, 'so often people just get apathetic and think there's nothing they can do. At least sometimes you can uncover a bit of unsavoury business that's going on. I do really care about these things. I don't particularly go around doing a load of public campaigning, but both those things were there on my doorstep. On the other hand it can help if it is on your doorstep because it gives your protest much more credibility.'

By now I'm feeling a bit confused by Page. I rather like him. Even though I have the reservation that when he pointed out of the window at the housing development he was perhaps more concerned with aesthetic niceties than with the bureaucratic contempt and condescension with which it is decided that human beings should have to live in such monstrosities, it still seems that his spirit is very definitely in the right direction. Yet how is this compatible with the lumbering dinosaur that his rock band has become?

Well, Jimmy Page is essentially a conservative person. He is also a Conservative person. A Capricorn, he has much of the rather hidebound love of tradition and status that can be a characteristic of that sign. He could do with a bit of overstanding of things. He voted Tory at the last election, he says. 'Not just for lighter taxes – I just couldn't vote Labour. They actually stated that they wanted to nationalise the media – so what possible criticism of them would you be able to have?'

Although I believe all politicians of whatever creed to be largely self-seeking egotists, I point out that, as the City already has effective control of both Fleet Street and ITV, then the Tories already control the media. Page doesn't seem that convinced.

He voted Tory at the previous election too, he tells me. 'I voted Conservative then because I believed in Heath. And I still believe that Edward Heath was a very honest man. He was too honest to be a politician. But I suppose that's politics.'

Actually, I'm not surprised Page rates Heath, a man who was certainly superior to the deplorable Thatcher. Page has much of that same laissez-faire mercantilist attitude to life that Heath favoured. The only problem with espousing that particular political philosophy is that it can permit you to piss on a lot of people in the name of freedom. I'm not suggesting that Page necessarily behaves in such a manner, of course. A better clue to his attitude to such matters comes in the same series of *Trouser Press* articles from which I took the Presley quotation.

He's talking about the song 'Hats Off to (Roy) Harper', on the third Zeppelin album:

'[Harper's] *Stormcock* was a fabulous album which didn't sell anything. Also, they wouldn't release his albums in America for quite a long time. For that I just thought, "Well, hats off to you." As far as I'm concerned, though, hats off to anybody who does what they think is right and refuses to sell out.'

In the light of this quote, and another, more ambivalent one relating to the New Wave, I ask him if he'd ever in younger days inclined more to anarchy.

'Well,' he replies with due deliberation, 'anarchy's alright if you can see where you're going afterwards. Although I don't see any point in destroying things just for the sake of it. It's the easiest way out. It's hard to have an optimistic goal and strive towards it – that's really hard work. But, yes, anarchy can certainly be an answer to a situation if there's no other answer.'

Quite understandably the Establishment always presents anarchy as being very negative when, in fact, it's more concerned with a positive spirit ...

'It's difficult,' Page nods. 'At the time when Hitler came into power in Germany during the thirties, he appeared to be stabilising the economy and giving people more work and was emerging as a very patriarchal figure. The Germans felt that everything was going to be alright. Yet underneath was this fundamental plan – be it evil or whatever.

'And at the time when Hitler came in there'd been a form of anarchy existing. So, yes, you just have to see at the end of the day what's really gone down.'

And so, boys and girls, we come to that section of the interview when we talk to Jimmy Page about New Wave music. Even though he seems to consider Dire Straits a New Wave band, Page is perfectly aware that there are punk bands and punk bands who aren't really punk bands. He has heard the Clash and appears to rather like them. He warms very much to the mention of Ian Dury. 'Yeah, he really imparts such a great feeling, doesn't he? Makes you feel so good. That was certainly the first thing that struck me about New Wave music – that it was sheer adrenaline pouring out. Real energy just tearing to get out.'

But how did the beat group Led Zeppelin relate to it? They were presumably aware of what was going on. I remember Page and Plant going down to the Roxy to check out the Damned once.

'We were aware of it,' he nods, 'but it's not … I mean, music is like a 360-degree circle from which some people may drop out to let others come in. And there are obvious examples of that – say, the feeling that Free generated and which was replaced by Bad Company. Also, the raw blues, going back to the early Fleetwood Mac days. Well, now you have George Thorogood. And Herman's Hermits are replaced by the Bay City Rollers.

'Bands like us and – I hate to say it but … the Floyd … we're off in our own little bits. It's always open for anybody who's really raw and earthy and who makes sheer rock 'n' roll music. Even though much of the New Wave had the political content … I mean, the Damned – I was absolutely amazed by the power that was coming out of them. Though they didn't really fit into the New Wave movement as such.

'Nevertheless, there are categories. But it's all relative; anyone who plays good music and is expressing themselves with an instrument or on vocals has got something to say. It just depends whether you can relate to them or not. And that also depends on whether your musical tastes are narrow or very broad.'

And certainly from what you're saying you would claim to be able to relate to New Wave …

'But I can also relate to classical music – and you wouldn't find them saying that …'

Oh, don't count on it. I think you'd be very surprised.

'Oh … well … good … well, they ought to.'

I think if you went round to the places of a few punk musicians you'd be very surprised by the width of listening material you'd come across.

But equally, and I think this must be said, of all the old fart bands, certainly Led Zeppelin, for whatever reasons, are the most loathed.

'Really????' Jimmy Page sounds quite startled.

'Fraid so …

'We-e-elll …' he pauses for several moments, '… people write to us, you know, and a lot of younger people who I'd never have expected to have got into us have said that they got really fired up by the energy of New Wave bands – and they still like New Wave bands – but they got interested in the actual musical content and wanted to go one step further which is how they discovered bands like us …

'And … uhh … I'm not sure whether that's going to last or not,' he laughs, not altogether confidently, 'but it's quite good if you can keep turning people on.'

Didn't you ever worry, though, over the past months while you were making the new record and planning the Knebworth thingy that it might be like throwing a party for which no one turns up?

'Yeah,' he laughs again, more confidently this time, 'but no – because when we'd finished our album I knew at the time that it didn't matter if it didn't come out for nine months afterwards because I knew that I could rely on the fact that Led Zeppelin hadn't dated – the actual identity of the band is still there. There's a fresh approach which can still give it an edge.

'I had my reservations at one point about playing a date like Knebworth. But in the end it all went hand in hand with the LP. When that was finished I did actually stop and take a breath, and I thought, "No, it's alright. We've moved on sufficiently to be able to see the next horizon."

'We're not sounding complacent, I hope. There's a lot of hard work still to come, obviously. It's not like we've felt we had to change the music to relate to any of the developments that have been going on. There's no tracks with disco beats or anything. But I think some of the numbers are some of the most immediate we've done anyway.

'Like I say, it's not a new musical form but there is still something very fresh about it.'

But, prior to doing it, were you not perhaps apprehensive? I'm not talking about how you'd do in the States, where obviously you're still going to sell loads of records. Presumably it still does mean something to be respected in your own country …

'No, sure. We were concerned about it being good. And we were pleased to hear that the actual environmental area of the stage was good. But if the playing hadn't been feeling right, I would've worried. But that feels alright so I'm pretty sure it'll be good …'

But I wasn't really talking about Led Zeppelin to Play Gig Shock Horror. I was actually wondering whether maybe you were concerned you might make this platter and no one would buy it in Blighty …

'Well, we were worrying about too many other things at the time. I was worried more about whether we were still going to gel. Having felt something special towards the band for that amount of time and still wanting that feeling to be there without … without being quite sure it would be. But then we got together a few times to play and could see that it still was … well, it was a very good feeling.

'The LP really is a bit of a by-product. To me Knebworth is far more important … Because people can buy the LP and we won't see how they're reacting to it. But,' he laughs, 'I will at Knebworth. The LP's a frozen statement which can be always referred to, but Knebworth's going to be different.'

Do you actually see much of each other?

'No, not really.'

Robert Plant and John Bonham don't live in London, do they? They live up in the Midlands, yeah?

'Yeah, they live pretty close to each other. No, I mean, we don't have monthly get-togethers for the sake of it.'

Now look, you've been involved in community politics up in Scotland, but should it necessarily stop there? For whatever reasons, Knebworth is a huge gig. But a couple of weeks back the Clash – who are quite a big band these days; their last LP entered the charts at number two – did a couple of gigs for orphans. Have you ever thought of doing something like that?

'We did that – about the third year of the band. And we got fucked for it. Previously we'd played places like Manchester Free Trade Hall and the Albert Hall and we'd had all these letters saying, "Why do they let their fans down? Why don't they play the clubs any more?"

'So we said, "Yeah, let's play clubs!" And it was chaos because people couldn't get in. So the next barrage was, "Why are they so selfish doing small clubs?" So the supply-and-demand thing becomes a problem. So from then on we were faced with a sort of dilemma. But then again it became a challenge to see if we could try and make it work on a large scale.

'Don't get me wrong. I'm the first to admit it can get too large, but something like Knebworth can be a challenge because you know it's worked in the past. But we couldn't do that. We tried – when we'd done the LP, we were trying to work out where we could get in and play. But then we thought, "Are we running away from something?" And we weren't.

'It was almost like denying what you were. And you've got to be true to yourself.'

Hmmmm ...

'I know what you mean, but it just gets impossible to do unless you play four weeks at the Marquee.'

But you're supposed to be a rock 'n' roll band. Why don't you just play? Look, it's not that hard: the Clash did two dates at the Notre Dame off Leicester Square. It wasn't publicised – only by word of mouth. They played new songs, tried out new sets, made money for charity. So it obviously is feasible ...

'I'll give you an example of a band that I don't think could play the Marquee: Status Quo.'

What an odd thing to say. I'd rather have hoped that Page would consider Zeppelin to have a slightly different awareness to the dandruffy riffers. But of course, I counter, they could play it if it wasn't announced as such ...

This is ignored. 'And I know they've played Wembley – so, if 15 per cent of those people tried to get in, it would be chaos. So you see the problem.'

Not really.

My next question is interrelated with a lot of things we're talking about – just how important is the institution of the music business to you? Do you feel that Led Zeppelin is part of the great corporate conglomerate?

'Obviously. Yeah. But to them you're only a matrix number. We sweat the songs out, though.'

But is it down to just letting the shareholders have bigger dividends? You're a musician, right? I think that's what you feel you are …

'Yeah, but don't you see that we're only as good as whatever we come up with? Say we didn't put out another LP … Well, we've probably done really well for our record company but, if we did that, they'd probably come right down on us. I think it's probably really ruthless behind the scenes. It comes down to things like Kinney owning car parks and things.'

You imply, I suggest to Page, you don't care about the record company. But, by acceding to those demands to play those huge venues – and in a way they're just perpetuating the whole thing …

'I see what you mean – though I'm not sure you see what I mean. The problem is trying to supply the demand of the people who want to see you. You can only gauge that. I mean, it is a rather nice feeling deciding on this huge date and not being quite certain that there's enough demand and then finding you can play a second one the same size.

'Anyway, at this point in time we just want to get back into playing music. And we will be doing other dates. I don't know where: not necessarily in England. We've been talking about playing Ibiza – Just getting in there and playing. Just so we've got a chance of trying out new ideas and new riffs and arrangements and songs.'

So do you not think that Led Zeppelin has become part of some huge thing that's got totally out of hand?

'Well, if it has it certainly won't in the future because we'll be playing places like Ibiza.'

Was there a stage that you reached with Led Zeppelin when it became important just to make money?

'No. Never. No, because we've been our own worst enemies over that. But you wouldn't see it like that now. But at the time we put out our fourth LP we had the worst reviews of anybody. And to put out an untitled LP at that time was considered professional suicide. It probably doesn't seem it now. But then …'

Are you very materialistic?

'Well, I dunno. Yeah, I suppose I am a bit. But on the other hand, even though I have material possessions, the most important things are books, studios and records. If I had to get up and run that's what I'd try and take,' he laughs.

Do you think that you personally have perhaps unavoidably become caught up in the Whole Great Sell?

'I don't think I have. No, no. I haven't. Otherwise I wouldn't have opened up a book shop. I'd have opened a boutique or something where I could really make money. Equinox was never designed to make lots of money but just to tick over so it could publish books.'

Do you think people have ever taken advantage of your having such desires?

'Quite probably. Yes,' he replies in a certain tone.

But you're a reasonably happy human being?

'Well,' he seems momentarily uncertain now, 'as happy as the next one.' Then he gives a spirited chuckle. 'I think I'm pretty fortunate in that I'm able to do what I'm best at. It's a pretty fortunate position to be doing what you really want to do and turning people on.'

But you've made tapes with people like Keith Richards. Obviously you must have wanted to make records with other people …

'Yeah, I did. But in the end it comes down to playing with the people who I really like to play with.'

Jim now tells me that he must leave in a few minutes as he has to meet Charlotte, the lady with whom he lives and by

whom he has an eight-year-old daughter, Scarlet. This is
unfortunate. We were just getting going, it seemed to me. It's
a pity also that interviews with members of Led Zeppelin are
inevitably set in the anonymous Swan Song offices, thus
providing writers, and therefore readers, with little
comprehension as to how the band members actually live.
Even the Stones seem to have woken up to the fact that both
journalist and band benefit from less clinically set-up
situations. But I suppose that's all part of the Led Zeppelin
problem anyway.

There were many other things I'd like to have asked Page:
what have he and the other three band members done for the
last 18 months or so, for example? Whose records has Page
been playing recently? Why doesn't Swan Song sign any hot
new acts?

As it is, though, I only have time to touch on some of the
more, uhh, 'controversial' topics that are raised in the first
section of this piece.

A large part of the original strength of Led Zeppelin surely
stemmed from the energies and ideas Page derived from his
lengthy session work in the sixties. Now, though, it seems
that all that has been exhausted and there is little new
creative input to replace it. Page's views on the music
business show a startling lack of original thought and clarity.
Mainly, though, they suggest, as I mentioned earlier,
confusion. And it's by perpetrating that state of chaos and
confusion that the music business is able to persist in its
Babylonian and fatuous desire to be part of the vast
dehumanised, cynical corporate state. Grrrrr …

On the other hand, compared with certain of his
contemporaries, maybe he's not faring too badly. I ask him if
he feels isolated and cut-off. He claims not to feel that now,
though admits to having been in a pretty weird state round
about the time of the band's fourth LP.

'Of course,' he adds, 'it can do very odd things to you, the whole guitar hero bit. Look at Eric Clapton. Peter Green ... Well, that's the obvious example. Jimmy Page: well, I don't think I'm doing too badly,' he laughs, with a fair amount of confidence.

Who would be the support acts for Led Zeppelin at Knebworth? Ian Dury and the Blockheads were approached, but adamantly refused to associate themselves with what they considered to be a Babylonian event. In fairness, it was only Ian Dury himself, egged on by aide-de-camp Kosmo Vinyl, who considered taking up such an offer to be morally and philosophically unsound – even when the fee dangled in front of them rose and rose to £140,000. (The rest of the Blockheads were allegedly extremely miffed at missing out on their share of such a sizeable lump sum.)

In the end, it was Keith Richards and Ron Wood's New Barbarians, Todd Rundgren's Utopia, Chas and Dave, Fairport Convention, Southside Johnny and the Asbury Dukes, and the Marshall Tucker Band. Not a bad bill.

There had been a trio of tunes left off *In Through the Out Door*: 'Ozone Baby', 'Wearing and Tearing' and 'Darlene'. Jimmy Page had the unconsummated idea of releasing them as an EP before the Knebworth show.

Despite Peter Grant's claims that a quarter of a million people attended the pair of shows, the reality was more prosaic: 104,000 on the first date; a mere 40,000 on 11 August.

Yet it was the first Zeppelin show in the UK in four years and the anticipation was infectious. Backstage there was a sprinkling of the new punk icons, paradoxically still in awe of the majesty and glamour of Led Zeppelin: Sex Pistol Steve Jones, Mick Jones of the Clash, Tony James of Generation X and Chrissie Hynde. And in Grant's special enclosure, a reminder of the true power behind the group, was Ahmet

Ertegun. Equally significantly, so was James Page, Jimmy's father.

Just before Zeppelin went onstage, the writer Mick Brown, reporting on the event for the *Sunday Times*, noticed something rather curious: 'Jimmy Page was carried to the stage on a stretcher.' Page was wearing a narrow-lapelled jacket and a Slim Jim tie; instead of making him look hip, it was more like an avuncular relative trying to show how hip he was. Onstage, he seemed to have a lit Marlboro permanently nailed to his lips. In an open polka-dot shirt and dark-grey cord trousers Robert Plant looked more convincing, until you observed the deep worry lines etched into his once-angelic face. In a clear effort at looking 'relevant', all of Led Zeppelin had had haircuts: Plant's semi-mullet hardly helped. It only made them look like successful men in their thirties – precisely what they were.

Perhaps Page required the stretcher because he was crippled by anxiety. Flown in by helicopter, the band were trembling with nerves, almost unable to speak: to them it seemed their future depended on this first Knebworth show. There had been a pair of warm-up dates in Copenhagen, and on 2 August the band had inspected the site at Knebworth. Page had arrived in Richard Cole's pokey Austin-Healey 3000, its top down on the warm summer evening, which irritated him when the wind dishevelled his hair. In beautiful Knebworth House itself he inspected artefacts left behind by Sir Edward Bulwer-Lytton, the 19th-century bestselling author and occultist whose ideas had been taken up by the theosophist Helena Blavatsky, an acquaintance of Aleister Crowley. Thus intellectually fortified, Page and Peter Grant retired to a back room for more conventional stimulation.

For the concert itself, Led Zeppelin's American PA had been flown in, 100,000 watts of audio power, plus a 600,000-watt lighting system, their American laser network and the video screens. Onstage there were five guitars lined up for Page, plus

John Paul Jones's white grand piano, synthesised Mellotron and clavinet.

Somehow Robert Plant had been persuaded to perform 'Stairway to Heaven'. In fact, the set was essentially the same as on that last, fateful American tour, with the addition of 'In the Evening' and 'Hot Dog'.

Although Page had arrived in a chopper with Charlotte Martin by his side, he was seen backstage after the show with Krissie Wood; they looked, thought Lisa Robinson, 'totally out of it'.

But the shows also revealed that, back playing the emperor once again, Peter Grant was at his egregious worst; again on cocaine, he was exhibiting extreme signs of the paranoia the drug could create. On the morning of 4 August Richard Cole received Grant's orders to insist that Freddy Bannister waive any film rights to the Zeppelin shows. Still smarting from *The Song Remains the Same*'s creative failure, Grant had hired Mike Mansfield, the director of ITV's successful *Supersonic* pop show, to film the entire concert, using 12 cameras, for a projected film release. In such circumstances the promoter might reasonably expect a measure of financial recompense from any consequential film. Instead, Cole informed Bannister that Grant would give him 5 pence for all rights. Cole warned him that, the mood the manager was in, it would be advisable to accept the offer. Finally, Bannister agreed, on the basis that any subsequent legal case he brought against Zeppelin would be bolstered by the derisory, insulting offer Grant had made.

Following the show Grant pulled another stunt: based on his estimate that a quarter of a million people had been at the concert – more than double the actual amount – he demanded immediate payment for both shows.

Distressed, Freddy Bannister and his wife and business partner Wendy drove down to Grant's home, Horselunges, the next day. They encountered a scene in which Grant acted like an archetypal evil business manager in a Hollywood gangster film.

When Wendy Bannister protested against Grant's audience figures and demand for immediate payment, Zeppelin's manager brandished his fist in her face and said: 'Don't you get smart with me.'

The next day a black-suited American, like a Mafia hitman from central casting, turned up at their home, accompanied by a man who claimed to be a former Metropolitan Police super-intendent. Freddy Bannister came to the conclusion that both were private detectives. The pair claimed to have seen aerial photographs of the 4 August show that proved once and for all that 250,000 people had been at the gig.

Twenty-four hours later Grant visited the Bannisters. Oddly, he claimed to be willing to reduce his act's fee for the next concert. With the proviso that his own people would man the entrance gates.

By now utterly sick of the enterprise, Freddy Bannister agreed. And Peter Grant came face to face with the truth: that only 40,000 people came to that second show, moody with rainfall and bad vibes from the New Barbarians, themselves demanding their payment upfront. The awful reality – that Led Zeppelin appeared on the slide, perhaps past their sell-by date – only served to make Grant even more belligerent: four weeks after the second Knebworth show, the American private detective, if that was what he was, insisted on another meeting between Grant and Freddy and Wendy Bannister at the Dorchester Hotel on London's Park Lane. Grant demanded that Freddy Bannister sign a prewritten letter absolving all blame for any resulting brouhaha from Peter Grant and Led Zeppelin. The US court cases the previous year had left all involved, including John Bonham, with the possibility that US visas might not be granted to them; therefore Grant wanted to stop any discussion of their heavy-handed, aggressive behaviour at Knebworth.

'So why did we retire abruptly? In a word – fear. Peter Grant was in such a terrible state, both mentally and physically, we thought he was on his way out and would be delighted to take us with him,' said Freddy Bannister in his book *There Must Be a Better Way*. In 1982, Tredoar, Freddy and Wendy Bannister's concert-promotion company, was forced into liquidation by their financial disputes with Led Zeppelin.

So many things about Knebworth were a bad vibe. So many things about Led Zeppelin had become a bad vibe.

'Under pressure from the new wave of rock 'n' rollers, one of Britain's longest established bands chose to fight back in 1979,' opened *Melody Maker*'s press release about that year's poll results. *Melody Maker*'s readers voted *In Through the Out Door* the best album of 1979. Moreover, Led Zeppelin or its members won seven of the twenty categories in the poll: as well as the album's success, they also won Band of the Year, Top Live Act and Top Composers; Robert Plant succeeded Yes's Jon Anderson as Top Male Singer, and Jimmy Page supplanted Yes's Steve Howe as Top Guitarist. He also replaced Genesis and David Hentschell as Top Producer, an irony unlikely to have been lost to John Paul Jones.

But Jimmy Page was missing when the rest of the group turned up at London's Waldorf Hotel with Peter Grant to be presented with their gongs. The story given out was that Page was on holiday in Barbados, but that was not the case. The guitarist, however, was not lying in some smacked-out reverie in one of his impressive properties. Rather, he was in Sussex, giving evidence at an inquest. A friend of his, a local photographer and designer named Philip Hale, who was 26, had died at a party at Plumpton Place on 24 October 1979. Though the cause of death was given as 'vomit inhalation', significant levels of cocaine were found in Hale's blood.

At the end of 1979 Page moved out of Plumpton Place, his friend's death the principal factor. He moved into Old Mill House in Clewer, Windsor, not too far from Heston, where he was first brought up; as was the case with most of his properties, with the exception of Tower House, his new home was close to water, the River Thames in this case, soothing for the watery aspect of his Scorpio rising. The three-storey residence, which he purchased from the actor Michael Caine, cost Page £900,000, and the guitarist also owned a nearby studio, the Sol, in Cookham.

Then suddenly, in the summer of 1980, Led Zeppelin were on tour again, in Europe: Switzerland, Germany, Austria, Holland and Belgium; dates in France were cancelled by Page. They were playing smaller venues, each with a capacity of around 3,500. There had been a month of rehearsals at the Rainbow in north London, and at the New Victoria Theatre in central London. Robert Plant had expressed grave doubts about playing again in the US. The intention of these shows, running from 17 June to 8 July, was to rekindle enthusiasm within the group, and hopefully get the singer in the frame of mind to cross the Atlantic. Just in case, Peter Grant had booked a two-legged US tour, to begin on 17 October running until 15 November 1980.

For these European dates everything was stripped down. Endless guitar solos were dispensed with: the set now opened with 'Train Kept A-Rollin'', the first number Led Zeppelin ever played together, in that Gerrard Street rehearsal space; it had not been played since 2 September 1970, in Oakland of all places. The acoustic songs were ditched, and an abbreviated version of the Knebworth set was performed. Richard Cole was temporarily relieved of his duties, his smack problem not considered a good influence on Page and John Bonham, both struggling with their own habits. Those who encountered Page on this tour were shocked by his appearance: the wafer-thin limbs; the junkie pallor and pinned eyes; the chipped and rotting teeth and gums, a sure sign of heavy heroin and cocaine use. 'It was incredibly sad to see him in such a state,' wrote Marc Roberty, 'and ultimately the band having reached these low depths.' There simply seemed no enthusiasm there whatsoever. All four members seemed chastened from their collective Led Zeppelin experience, as though parts of them had not survived.

In Vienna, Page was hit in the eye by a firecracker. When he returned to the stage, he played the introductory moments of 'Deutschland über alles', before heading into 'Stairway to Heaven'.

The next night, 27 June 1980, Page stepped up to the mike in Nuremburg to declare that two members of the band were not feeling well. A quarter of an hour later Bonham collapsed. The cause of his illness? Eating too many bananas, came the official response from the Zeppelin camp.

Three nights later the Frankfurt show was one of the best of the tour. A magical version of Barrett Strong's 'Money (That's What I Want)' was played as an encore, with Atlantic Records boss Phil Carson on bass. An interesting choice of song, of course.

Peter Grant confirmed that Led Zeppelin would indeed be playing the US tour. This may have been an even bigger mistake than hiring John Bindon.

The last thing John 'Bonzo' Bonham wanted to do was leave his family – he always hated doing this – and tread the US boards. Especially as there were rumours of civil lawsuits lurking from the Oakland debacle.

His drinking remained ferocious – essentially, Bonham was always drunk. He had supposedly stopped using heroin, though some cast scorn on this. He was certainly using Motival, an antidepressant.

On 24 September 1980 Bonham was picked up at his home by Rex King, who had replaced Richard Cole on the European tour. King was driving Bonham to Page's new home, Old Mill House. En route, the drummer insisted on stopping at a pub; he drank four quaduple vodkas with orange juice, and ate a couple of sandwiches. During rehearsals at Page's practice studio at his house, Bonham continued to drink vodka. He became so inebriated he could hardly play.

When rehearsals ended Bonham kept on drinking. By 11 p.m. he was so drunk he passed out on the sofa. He was helped to bed and laid on his side.

Page's assistant looked in on Bonham at eight o'clock the next morning. The drummer was sleeping soundly; the feeling was that he should be left alone to sleep off his heavy intake of booze.

When he didn't appear by the afternoon, Benji LeFevre, Robert Plant's assistant, went into his bedroom with John Paul Jones at 1.45 to chivvy the drummer along. But Bonham's face was blue, he had no pulse and he was cold. He was dead, at the age of 32. The cause of death: inhalation of vomit.

On 4 December 1980 Led Zeppelin put out a statement through the Swan Song office: 'The loss of our dear friend, and the deep sense of harmony felt by ourselves and our manager, have led us to decide that we could not continue as we were.'

Led Zeppelin to split?

Yes: they just had.

23

THE HERMIT

With the death of John Bonham, Jimmy Page's great art project of Led Zeppelin had effectively ended. Now he – and the rest of the group and manager Peter Grant – were on the creative comedown that inevitably follows the conclusion of such work. And the greater it has been, the larger the comedown always is. So when you have been at the helm of the biggest group in the world, what you experience is almost unparalleled. No one you know can fully empathise with your state of mind. Page had been out there on his own for so long, enjoying the freedom his natural desire for solitude brought him. But where could he now turn? He plunged into acute depression, which his increasing reliance on heroin and alcohol did little to alleviate.

After the demise of Led Zeppelin, the group – like such other UK symbols of the early 1970s as Prime Minister Edward Heath or Morris Marinas – felt almost immeasurably and immediately out of date. Its dungeons and dragons world had almost instantly evaporated.

You can of course trace back the commencement of this comedown to 1975 and Robert Plant's terrible car accident, at the start of his Saturn return. But that was the time that heroin started to catch up with the lives of Page, John Bonham, Peter Grant and Richard Cole; the lonely days Page spent working on *Presence* made it more of a solo album for him than anything that the band had delivered. The desperation of 1975 had made an exponential leap in 1977 with the full horror of the Oakland incident and the utter tragedy of Karac Plant's death three days later.

When Nick Kent asked Page in 2003 whether he regretted becoming so dependent on heroin and cocaine, the Zeppelin leader was unrepentant: 'I don't regret it at all, because when we needed to be really focused, I was really focused. That's it ... You've got to be on top of it.'

Jimmy Page was a broken man. And he only plunged into smack even more deeply. It was a terrible time for him. 'My life was Led Zeppelin,' he told Kent. 'I lived and breathed Led Zeppelin. When I wasn't touring, I was at home writing music for the group. I could hear John's drumming. I could hear Robert ... and John Paul. It was a total obsession for me. And suddenly ... it was all over.'

He was in deep mourning for John Bonham. He thought that he might never play the guitar again, especially after his Gibson Les Paul went missing shortly after the drummer's death. 'It seemed like an omen,' said Page. 'If I even looked at a guitar, it would remind me of a dear friend I had just lost.'

Peter Grant was equally devastated, also plunging into depression, which manifested in a kind of clinical ennui. Richard Cole, meanwhile, was in prison in Rome, awaiting trial for cocaine possession (he would eventually be acquitted). Told that one of Led Zeppelin had died, he immediately thought, 'Poor Jimmy!' He was even more shocked to learn that the death was of his old mucker Bonzo.

Assorted drummers had contacted Peter Grant almost straightaway after Bonzo's death. On 7 November Jimmy Page, Robert Plant and John Paul Jones went down to Jersey in the Channel Islands to consider their options. They were unanimous in their decision. Returning to London they held a meeting with Grant in a suite at the Savoy Hotel. 'They told me,' said the manager, 'that without Bonzo there was no desire on their part to carry on. It could never be the same again. I was relieved. That was exactly the way I felt.'

Soon there was an offer, conveyed by Peter Grant. Chris Squire and Alan White, respectively the bass player and drummer with Yes, a pair of excellent musicians, suggested linking up with Page and Plant in what was once quaintly known as a 'supergroup', to be named XYZ (Ex-Yes and Zeppelin ... ho-hum). Page had a couple of meetings with the Yes men, but decided against it. Plant had dismissed the idea as soon as he heard of it.

To all intents and purposes, both Page and Grant became recluses. Years later, Malcolm McLaren, who had managed the Sex Pistols, endeavoured unsuccessfully to make a film about Grant's life. At the time McLaren wrote: 'Grant needed the camaraderie of hard, dangerous men who gave him a sense of power. The harder they were, the tougher he felt, and only then was his desire for control satisfied. It all fell apart when Grant aped the lifestyle of Jimmy Page, who then ostracised his biggest fan.'

Robert Plant's instinct was that he needed to work his way out of this predicament. Linking up with his old mates from home, guitarist Robbie Blunt – who had played with the Steve Gibbons Band, revered in their native Midlands – and bass player Andy Silvester, he put together the Honeydrippers, essentially a covers group playing old R&B; he based himself, some thought, on his old hero Ral Donner. Starting off with a show at Keele University on 3 March 1981, the Honeydrippers played 15 shows, finishing in June, although Plant insisted that his name must never appear on any promotional material for the band. His stint with them got him back on his feet and performing again, and he began to put his assorted tragedies to one side. Besides, ever since the car crash on Rhodes in 1975, Plant had been conflicted over what he was doing in Led Zeppelin. Always the frontispiece – the front office, really – of Led Zeppelin, he had seemed the most susceptible to any strange energies bouncing back at the band.

But recovery for Jimmy Page was far slower. Help came from an unexpected quarter: film director Michael Winner, his direct neighbour in Holland Park. Considering how Page had adorned his existence with seemingly effortless good taste, it was perhaps not the prestigious product with which he would have liked to be associated. But all the same, writing the blues-based soundtrack for Winner's *Death Wish II*, a Los Angeles-set revenge thriller starring Charles Bronson, at least temporarily aroused his creativity.

Though Winner could quite literally have approached Page over the garden wall, he instead contacted Peter Grant – not that easy a task. At the time Page was on holiday on a narrowboat on the River Thames. He was uncontactable, and Winner's deadline had been eaten into by the time he actually received the director's request, in August 1981, giving him a cut-off date of six weeks.

It was almost surprising that Page had managed to get out of his home and onto a boat. At this point he had been a virtual recluse for almost a year: he didn't return phone calls and wouldn't connect with any old friends. Visitors to Tower House, there to see Charlotte Martin and Scarlet, would catch glimpses of him upstairs, clad in a dressing gown, like a spectral character in a Gothic novel; for weeks at a time he wouldn't leave the property. There were tales of Charlotte Martin welcoming fans who had travelled from far away and would ring the doorbell on the off-chance of it being opened. She was known to order them take-away food, and let them have a peek around the basement studio. Was this the source of high-quality bootlegs of rare Zeppelin material that later appeared?

'I'd lived next door to Jimmy for many years,' said Winner to *Uncut* magazine in 2008. 'It was a very bad time for him – the drummer had died, and he was in a very inactive period. Peter Grant and I made arrangements for Jimmy to do the *Death Wish II* score, for which he wasn't actually paid, because Grant wanted to restore Jimmy back to creativity. Jimmy rang the doorbell, and I thought if the wind blew he'd fall over. He saw the film, we spotted where the music was to go, and then he said to me, "I'm going to my studio. I don't want you anywhere near me, I'm going to do it all on my own." My editing staff said this is bloody dangerous! Anyway, we gave him the film, we gave him the timings and he did it all on his own.'

Michael Winner at least got Page working. Perhaps the guitarist was inspired by how badly the soundtrack to *Lucifer Rising* had turned out and wanted to rectify that rare failure. At his studio in Sonning, Page produced a series of pieces relevant to the film. There was 'Prelude', essentially a complete steal of Frédéric Chopin's Prelude No. 3 in G, the great Polish composer's patriotic piano-playing replicated on Page's electric guitar. 'In the Evening' transmogrified into 'Who's to Blame', the main theme song for *Death Wish II*, sung by Chris Farlowe, who had almost been given the vocalist role in Led Zeppelin. 'City Sirens' was soft rock, and there was the psychedelic 'A Shadow in the City'. 'The Release' was a chase sequence: a succession of droning sounds that would have made Kenneth Anger proud. Every one of the 12 tracks was credited only to Jimmy Page. 'Everything hit the button totally!' said Winner. 'I've never seen a more professional score in my life.'

The soundtrack record was released on 15 February 1982 on the barely functioning Swan Song. Label boss Peter Grant wouldn't answer his phone; the drawbridge at Horselunges had been raised.

While Page was working on the *Death Wish II* soundtrack, Robert Plant took *Pictures at Eleven*, his first solo album, recorded at the legendary Rockfield Studios in Monmouth, down to Old Mill House, where John Bonham had died. Plant had produced the record himself, and he and Robbie Blunt had written all the tracks, with keyboard and synthesiser player Jezz Woodroffe co-writing three of the songs – though Plant balked at signing the joint publishing deal with his co-writers that he had allegedly promised, leading to a general bitterness. All the same, the singer wanted his old mentor to be the first to hear it. 'Well, ah, I thought you could have done something a little better than that, old chap,' said Page, with that dismissiveness that often couches jealousy.

'So I said, "Well, thank you." And yet again, I was just the singer of the songs.'

'It was very emotional,' Plant later reflected on that visit to Old Mill House. 'We just sat there and I sort of had my hand on his knee. We were just sitting through it together. He knew that I'd gone, that I was off on my own with the aid of other people and just forging ahead, and all I wanted was for him to do the same.'

Released on 28 June 1982 on Swan Song, *Pictures at Eleven* was the label's last substantial seller, reaching number five in the US album charts and number 2 in the UK.

Although living out his tarot-card archetype of the Hermit, the *Death Wish II* soundtrack seemed to have urged Jimmy Page out of an unproductive existence: *Coda*, a ragbag of impressive Led Zeppelin outtakes, was released on 19 November 1982. 'Coda was released, basically, because there was so much bootleg stuff out. We thought, "Well, if there's that much interest, then we may as well put the rest of our studio stuff out,"' said Page.

Coda made number four in the UK and number six in the US *Billboard* charts, where it sold over a million copies. The record kicked off with Ben E. King's 'We're Gonna Groove', which featured on so many of the early live shows. Incorrectly listed on the original release as having been recorded at Morgan Studios in north-west London in June 1969, the recording was actually taken from the celebrated live show at the Royal Albert Hall in January 1970; the tune had opened the concert. The audience applause was removed and – this was the work actually done at Morgan Studios – Page added guitar parts to it. A live version of Willie Dixon's 'I Can't Quit You Baby' also came from the Royal Albert Hall show, with blistering, searing guitar playing from Page. The steaming 'Walter's Walk' came from the *Houses of the Holy* sessions. The acoustic 'Poor Tom' had been made for *Led Zeppelin III*. There were a trio of tunes recorded for *In Through the Out Door*: 'Ozone Baby', 'Darlene' and 'Wearing and Tearing'. 'Bonzo's Montreux', intended as a tribute to John Bonham, had been recorded in Switzerland in 1976, a steel pan added into the mix. The punky 'Wearing and Tearing' closed *Coda*, stripped-down, grungy rock 'n' roll, a reference to the very first Led Zeppelin album with its raw, garage-band feel. 'They were good tracks. A lot of it was recorded around the time punk was really happening ... basically there wasn't a lot of Zeppelin tracks that didn't go out. We used everything,' said John Paul Jones.

Meanwhile, Page sat at home, doing very little and – above and beyond his problems with heroin – stuck in a miasma of depression, naked and vulnerable. A month before the release of *Coda*, there had been yet another problem; matters were unravelling at some speed of knots.

On Tuesday 5 October 1982 Page was given a conditional discharge for cocaine possession. He had been searched by a policeman near the Swan Song offices on the Kings Road, and 198 milligrams of cocaine was discovered in his coat pocket. He claimed he had found the drug on a mantelpiece at his house during a party and had removed it to prevent anyone taking it. He had also lied that he bought it for £20 from a man he met in the street. But then he said he had made up that story on the

spur of the moment. His defence was essentially based on mone-
tarist thinking. Claiming that his client was putting together a
new group and was about to tour Japan and the United States,
his QC John Matthews pointed out that a harsh sentence 'would
result in the loss of not thousands but millions of pounds during
the next few years'. The implication clearly was that it would
be the UK taxation system missing out, and not just Page
himself. Zeppelin Star Wins Freedom, said the *Daily Star*'s
headline the next day.

The cocaine bust can only have added to the stress of being
Jimmy Page. At home things were no better. By the end of 1982
his 13-year relationship with Charlotte Martin had finally fallen
apart. Even if you are a rock superstar you do not escape the
pain of a broken partnership; again, Page found solace in
heroin.

In the summer of 1982 there had been a reforming of the
Yardbirds, involving Jim McCarty, Chris Dreja and Paul
Samwell-Smith. At a party at Jeff Beck's Kent house, Page
expressed his irritation that no one had asked him to take part
in it. Of course, the reason no one had asked him to play was
that they all assumed it was utterly inconceivable; the extent
to which Page had become an almost Howard Hughes-like
recluse was well known in London, as were his addictions. Ian
Stewart, the Rolling Stones keyboard player, was at the party,
having a conversation with Jeff Beck about an imminent
ARMS (Action into Research for Multiple Sclerosis) charity
show to raise money for Ronnie Lane, the much-loved Small
Faces and Faces bass player who had multiple sclerosis. 'So at
this party,' said Stewart, 'while I was discussing the Ronnie
Lane benefit with Jeff, Jimmy came up and he said, "Nobody
ever asked me to play. Why can't I play on it?" So we said,
"Step this way."'

At the charity show, at the Royal Albert Hall on 20 September
1983, many in the cast and crew were shocked by Page's appear-

ance and his inability to put a coherent sentence together. 'He was so pale, so thin, like a walking skeleton. It was obvious he was still deeply into the heroin at the time,' said his friend Dave Dickson. It didn't help his nervous frame of mind that while he was at the Royal Albert Hall soundcheck, his illegally parked car was towed away.

Yet appearing alongside his old Yardbirds chums Eric Clapton and Jeff Beck, the first time all three of them had ever played together, Page delivered extremely serviceable versions of 'Who's to Blame' and 'City Sirens', from the *Death Wish II* soundtrack, and an instrumental version of – what else? – 'Stairway to Heaven'. From the Royal Box he was watched by Prince Charles and Princess Diana.

The Royal Albert Hall show proved such a success that further dates were set up in the US, nine in total. Page played on all of them – a courageous return to the performing stage. 'He's probably one of the bravest among us – he's really putting himself on the line,' said Kenney Jones.

For the nine American ARMS shows, Page played several numbers, including his version of Chopin's Prelude. On 'City Sirens' and 'Who's to Blame' he performed with Steve Winwood; and that hoary old chestnut 'Stairway to Heaven' was again included. The shows ended with three nights at San Francisco's Cow Palace, from 1 to 3 December 1983.

'Page's set was a triumph of style over substance,' wrote Kurt Loder in *Rolling Stone* of a Cow Palace gig. 'A small white spot opened up on the right of the stage, and suddenly, there he was: cigarette pasted to his lip, a cascade of black curls tumbling down over his eyes – the very picture of wrecked rock-star elegance. First, he removed his long white scarf – to resounding applause, of course – then the various rings on both his hands, and then he rolled up his sleeves and set to work. Had he played not a note, the audience would have been with him anyway. But he picked up his black Telecaster and, leaning back in classic

Zep fashion, proceeded to dig into "Prelude", a haunting instrumental piece from the soundtrack of *Death Wish II*, which Page scored.'

After two more numbers Page brought on Paul Rodgers, the Free and Bad Company singer. Together they performed a song that was a work in progress to be titled either Midnight Moonlight or Bird on the Wing. 'This piece was, to put it tersely, a rambling disaster,' wrote Loder. 'It was followed by a supremely flaky *instrumental* rendition of the epochal "Stairway to Heaven", toward the thrash-crazed end of which Beck and Clapton strolled out and attempted, as best they could, to join in. Page appeared to be on another planet.'

Loder, who had considerable access, remarked that there seemed to be moments of tension between Clapton and Page, noting that Clapton had long ago kicked his own heroin habit, while Page was clearly still imprisoned in his own. When Loder asked Clapton how he perceived both Page and Beck, the guitarist's response was ambiguous: 'I think their characters have become very clear – have become compounded.' Loder described how, after each show, the assorted musicians would mingle. But Page would step into a black van and be driven straight back to his hotel.

Ian Stewart expressed his fondness for Page to Kurt Loder: 'This tour has got him moving again, and I hope he can find something to do after this. It's a shame that he just sits at home and does nothing. He seems to miss John Bonham very much; but at the same time, I think he'd like to play. It's just that ... maybe nobody asked him for two or three years; I don't know. Jimmy's pretty laid back, really. He's still very interested in music. He's always coming up with obscure things, like classical things and Bulgarian folk things. We had a big natter the other night about Django Reinhardt guitar solos. So the interest is still there; he just needs a bit of motivation.'

Loder concluded his article with an assessment of the three former Yardbirds guitarists; he defined Page as 'the sensitive space case'.

24

MIDDLE-AGED GUITAR GOD

On 9 January 1984 Jimmy Page turned 40, not something that was easy to admit for someone who had been a god to 'the kids'. It is an age that often brings a measure of concern to people: is half my life over? Whereas the younger Robert Plant had seemed to harness time to his advantage, for Page it increasingly appeared to bring adversity. He needed an ally. And hanging out with Paul Rodgers had given him an idea.

For those aware of London gangland terminology, the name of the group they formed together – the Firm – was like a throwback to the thuggish world of Peter Grant and John Bindon; it was a term employed for the groups of football hooligans who would travel England causing mayhem. The name alone seemed like an implicit threat: buy our record or we'll send round the boys! Yet no blame for the name can be attributed to Jimmy Page or Paul Rodgers: 'the Firm' was the idea of drummer Chris Slade, formerly of Uriah Heep. On bass and keyboard was Tony Franklin, who had worked with Roy Harper, with whom Page had played a low-key show at the Cambridge Folk Festival in the summer of 1984, as well as several other unpublicised appearances elsewhere with his eccentric friend.

This included a spot of fell-walking for the pair of them, an endeavour to publicise *Whatever Happened to Jugula?*, Harper's upcoming album; *The Old Grey Whistle Test*, BBC TV's weekly 'serious' popular-music programme, filmed Harper and Page performing on the side of a mountain in the Lake District in August. They had worked together on *Whatever Happened to Jugula?*, Harper's new album, which would be released in March 1985; although Page had played on several of Harper's records, *Whatever Happened to Jugula?* was the first he had worked on in its entirety. At one point it was mooted that the record would be credited to 'Harper and Page'. Rather coyly knowing, the album at first had the working title of 'Rizla'.

At their first late-evening meeting with the pair, in their Ambleside hotel, Mark Ellen, the show's presenter, and Trevor Dann, his producer, noted that there were two modes of operation: one motored by 'red tackle', which involved replenishing the assorted goblets of expensive red wine; and the other driven by 'white tackle', where one of the acolytes would empty a packet of cocaine onto the dining table, to be duly hoovered up by Page and Harper. Especially of interest to the pair of BBC men was that 'the 40-year-old guitarist of Led Zeppelin was on a blind date with a girl of 18'. Harper had played a show the previous evening in Leeds, picking up a 19-year-old. A mate of his was coming up from London, he said: had she a friend who might want to join them? She had, and the friend was now Page's temporary paramour.

When Trevor Dann mentioned that the film crew would be arriving at eight the next day, Page assumed he meant eight in the evening. When Dann said he was going to bed and would see the pair at breakfast, Page looked horrified. 'He'd assumed Trevor had meant eight in the evening. So had Harper ... They looked tight-lipped and ashen-faced,' wrote Ellen in *Rock Stars Stole My Life*. 'There was an awkward, head-scratching silence while two men who'd never risen before the crack of noon pondered their fate. "Tell you what," Page decided. "We'll just have to stay up all night."'

Needless to say, it was several hours after breakfast that first Harper, and then Page appeared. 'Page stumbled out and joined the fray,' declared Mark Ellen, 'cutting the most dissolute figure imaginable, his teenage pal padding along beside him ... The very sight of them seemed to scream debauchery.'

Harper had ordained that the interview would be conducted in the ruins of the Roman fort of Galava. When Page was asked why this location was necessary, he gave a stony, all-knowing reply: 'The vibes, man.'

After several hours of driving through the Lake District's steep countryside, however, the Roman fort of Galava remained as elusive as it had been when they set off from their hotel. The film crew came to the rescue, suggesting nearby Side Pike, where there was a pretty hillside, for the interview.

It got worse. When Trevor Dann asked for the promised live performance, he received not a tune from the new record, but a 12-minute version of 'Same Old Rock', a 13-year-old Harper tune. The chain-smoking Page, wearing riding boots, a battered leather flying jacket and a long white silk scarf, strummed along, effectively backing up his friend. As though wary of the power of the camera, Page consistently looked in the opposite direction to it as he played. When the cameraman managed to get a head-and-shoulders shot of him, he looked pretty great, his face framed by his tumbling hair. At times during the interview he was also extremely honest. Speaking of John Bonham's passing, he admitted that 'I didn't pick up a guitar for 18 months. I was frightened to even look at it. When I did I found I couldn't even change a chord.'

And he also admitted that he had been rehearsing for ten days with Paul Rodgers. As yet this project lacked a name, although he joked that they would be called 'the MacGregors', 'because that was the rebel clan'.

Perched on this pile of rock, Page and Harper then proceeded to utterly dismiss almost all contemporary music, Harper repeatedly showing his contempt for Frankie Goes to Hollywood by wittily referring to them as 'Bannock Goes to Frankieburn'.

Page rather ill-advisedly dismissed the notion of acts employing computers: 'It's still verses and choruses like it was in 1960, and with all the technology they've got and all the outspoken statements they make, I think they ought to come up with something special. They all sound the same to me.' As he did very often, he dismissed new acts as being like 'Herman's Hermits'; Page himself had played sessions on several hits by Peter Noone's hugely successful Manchester act. But for some reason Herman's Hermits, whose records John Paul Jones had often arranged, were a real bête noire to the guitarist. Page and Harper seemed to be entirely from another age.

As the interview wound to a close, Page and his girlfriend wandered off into some adjacent shrubbery. 'What a great TV moment,' Trevor Dann told me. 'If only we could have used the shot of Page taking a slash while his teenage girlfriend held his knob.'

Bad Company had released six albums, with a sales trajectory that was increasingly dwindling. In 1982, following the release of their *Rough Diamonds* album, they broke up. Among other matters, they now had an absentee manager in Peter Grant, who had looked after their career from the beginning.

Grant, however, had negotiated Robert Plant's five-album deal with Atlantic. Jimmy Page was so miffed by this that he asked Phil Carson to watch over his career; Carson negotiated his deal for the Firm with Geffen Records.

Page already had Paul Rodgers in mind as someone to work with. 'I tried to get together with Paul earlier, but it was difficult because he was doing a solo LP,' he later told Ultimate Classic Rock. 'But when the ARMS charity shows came up in America, Paul came with us. Stevie Winwood – who sang in London – had pulled out. So we went to the States and had a very good tour, singing songs like "Bird on the Wing", which we did on the album. At the end of the tour I asked if he fancied carrying on and doing something else, because I really love his singing. He's such a brilliant singer. If I do a guitar solo I have to warm up and do three takes. He does it in one take. Note perfect. No problem! He's an amazing man.'

Page admitted to *Creem* magazine that the period immediately following Led Zeppelin had been extremely difficult for him: 'After the split, I just didn't know what to do. I lived in a total vacuum. I didn't know what I was doing. In the end, I went to Bali and just thought about things. And I wasn't sitting on the beach because it was the rainy season! I sat in my room thinking. Then I thought, Dammit, I'm going to do the Firm and see if it works. At my time of life I should just do what I enjoy.'

Rather in opposition to what he said on *The Old Grey Whistle Test*, Page was thoroughly aware, he told *Creem*, of the passing of time and trends in popular music. 'Yes, I *am* a musician of the sixties and seventies,' he told *Creem*. 'I got fired by the music of Chuck Berry and Elvis Presley. I was hit by so much energy from their records. But every five years people get fired by the music they hear and want to become part of it. So now, I'm past middle age. But what do you do when you get to middle age? There was no one for me to look up to who said, "This is what you do next." I read in the music press that after 30 you are fucked. But I'm not, and there's a lot more for me to do.'

Just over two years after his first coke bust, Page was in court again for cocaine possession. The story went that he had attempted to withdraw money out of a bank by Victoria railway station to buy a birthday present for his mother. The cashier doubted that he was the real Jimmy Page, partially because of his curious behaviour: at one point he was said to have fallen over in the bank. A passing constable was called over, who searched Page and found a packet of 'Charlie' in his coat pocket. Initially Page claimed that he had lent the garment to a friend, and this unnamed person must have placed the drug in it. On 5 November 1984 Page was fined £450 at Marylebone Magistrates Court for possessing cocaine. He admitted the offence.

The silver lining in this cloud was that, although he was still snorting coke, Page was no longer addicted to heroin. As he had done on his holiday in Guadeloupe with Charlotte, Scarlet and Richard Cole, he first attempted to come off heroin by dousing himself in copious amounts of alcohol and cocaine, the Keith Richards cure. Later, he would claim that withdrawal had not been too onerous, taking only four days. Which seems unlikely, junkie machismo. In fact, according to Lori Mattix, Page had taken another tip from Keith Richards: he had gone to a clinic in Switzerland and had his blood changed; with his veins bulging with clean blood, he was off the smack.

The Firm's first, eponymously titled album, released on 11 February 1985, was a Top 20 record in both the UK and the USA. The final track, the nine-minute-long 'Midnight Moonlight', was a reworking of 'Swan Song', a tune left off *Physical Graffiti*. For the Firm's shows Page even disinterred 'Dazed and Confused', his set-piece Zeppelin speciality. Although they had a slight funk feel, the Firm's records never really rose above average, burdened by a lugubrious, plodding, slightly ponderous feel. Yet there was sparkling guitar all over them from Page, and the Firm were a strong live attraction. They played over 70 dates in total, Page revisiting and selling out such Zeppelin power-points as Madison Square Garden, the Los Angeles Forum and Wembley Arena. But the second album, 1986's *Mean Business*, did less good business, and Page broke up the band; later he claimed it was never intended for the Firm to last for more than a pair of records.

* * *

For a Fourth of July concert in 1985, Jimmy Page, ever in search of creative rehabilitation, joined the Beach Boys onstage in Washington, DC. Jeff Foskett, the Beach Boys' guitarist, was given the task of showing Page the key for each Beach Boys song. John Stamos, a 21-year-old actor friend of Foskett, was there as the guitar hero was taught how to play the songs. 'We're in this hotel and we go up to the penthouse suite and there's cases everywhere ... and I thought it was guitars everywhere. He had like whips and devil shit,' said Stamos. 'He immediately offered us a shot of Jack Daniel's.' While Foskett was otherwise occupied, Page asked the actor which key certain songs were in. Stamos's uncertain responses brought out the guitarist's displeasure: '"I can't fucking solo in E flat!" Jimmy was yelling at me.

'There were a couple of acoustic guitars, and he grabbed one and put it in my hands and said, "All right – what are we doing?" I said, "Uh, I think you're playing 'Barbara Ann', right?" He said, "Right. What key?" I told him it was in F sharp, and he said, "I don't like to solo in F sharp. Why is it in F sharp?" I was like, "I don't know, man!" "Fun, Fun, Fun" was in E flat, and he didn't like that key, either. So I'm sitting there, showing Jimmy Page how to play these three-chord songs. I'm, like, 21 years old. I could barely play guitar and had no business teaching him anything!'

The next day there was a reprise of the Washington, DC show in Philadelphia. When gaga fans near the front of the stage flashed the newly fashionable devil's horns symbols with their fingers, a recently developed sign of approbation among heavy metal fans, the not entirely drug-free Page became paranoid. 'I think they're hexing me!' he said. John Stamos had to talk him down: 'No, no, it's a good thing!'

* * *

A week later something extremely unexpected happened: Led Zeppelin got back together.

On 13 July 1985 at JFK Stadium in Philadelphia, the American leg of the Live Aid concert was held. An unavoidable irony of the event for the three surviving Led Zeppelin members was that it was promoted by Bill Graham, Led Zeppelin's personal nemesis. With a pair of drummers – Chic's masterful Tony Thompson and an under-rehearsed Phil Collins – Page, Plant and Jones played 'Rock and Roll', 'Whole Lotta Love' and 'Stairway to Heaven'. It was not a good performance: Plant's voice was hoarse and Page was unable to hear what he was playing thanks to problems with his monitors; and both the drummers were out of sync. Predictably, their appearance was greeted with hysterical approval from the 90,000-strong audience – people were in tears trying to call them back for at least 15 minutes – and from television viewers across the planet. But it was a distinctly disappointing return to the stage for the three Zeppelin members. 'My main memories, really, were of totally panic,' said Page.

The three musicians had come together by accident. Page, with the Firm, and Plant had both been touring the US. The plan was for the two of them to play together as the Honeydrippers. When Jones learned of this, he pushed his way into the line-up. This meant that there was almost no time for rehearsals, however, and by this time Paul Martinez, who was in Plant's band, had been confirmed as bass player. The only slot for Jones to fill was on keyboard. Later, a considerably displeased Jones told *Classic Rock*'s Dave Ling, 'It was Plant again, you see. Basically, I had to say to them, "If it's Zeppelin and you're going to be doing Zeppelin songs, hi, I'm still here and I wouldn't mind being a part of it … I elbowed my way in. It's all about Robert and what he wants.'

Plant, who for so much of his time in Led Zeppelin had very distinctly been the sorcerer's apprentice, clearly now considered himself a fully fledged sorcerer. Where did that leave Page? Well, he was still ready to give it another go. At Meadowlands in New Jersey, ten days after Live Aid, he appeared at Plant's concert, joining in on the Elvis Presley classic 'Mean Woman Blues' and Roy Head's 'Treat Her Right'. Plant's adoration of such rock 'n' roll evergreens had stood him in good stead. At the beginning of the year his cover of Phil Phillips's 'Sea of Love' had reached number three in the *Billboard* charts. It was taken from an extended EP, *The Honeydrippers: Volume One*, a collection of five R&B songs; the other tunes were Wynonie Harris's 'I Get a Thrill', Ray Charles's 'I Got a Woman', Mose Allison's 'Young Boy Blues' and Roy Brown's 'Rockin' at Midnight'. The production of the record was credited to 'Nugetre', Ertegun spelled backwards. The producer, of course, was really Ahmet Ertegun; but the sound of the record, with its Latin flavour and sumptuous strings of a type with which Ben E. King had been well acquainted, might have been by Ertegun's former employee and Page's mentor Bert Berns.

Following the Meadowlands show, Page and Plant agreed to meet up and have 'a cup of tea'. And they would bring Jones along too.

When they assembled in January 1986 for the two weeks booked in a village hall in the historic spa town of Bath, it was not only the bass player who joined Page and Plant: Tony Thompson was flown in from New York. As the drummer with the superb Chic, Thompson was an extremely good idea, one you suspect may have come more from Plant's relentlessly modernist thinking than from Page.

The first day of rehearsals went relatively well. 'I don't know if Jimmy was quite into it, but it was good,' Jones told Zeppelin chronicler Dave Lewis. Again, it was Robert Plant who seemed to desire to hold the reins. He would become irritated that Page, slightly drunk most of the time, would take so long to set up and get into playing.

One evening, when Tony Thompson was returning home from the pub in a minicab, the driver misjudged a bend, finishing up in someone's basement. Thompson was hospitalised. Which completely freaked out Plant; memories of former car crashes swam vividly before him, and he took this as a bad portent. Perhaps affected by contemporary visions of hipness, Plant – whose Big Hair look was decidedly unhip – was struggling with the relevance of what they were doing. As Jones explained to Dave Lewis: 'What I recall is Robert and I getting drunk in the hotel and Robert questioning what we were doing. He was saying nobody wants to hear that old stuff again and I said, "Everybody is waiting for it to happen." It just fell apart from then – I suppose it came down to Robert wanting to pursue his solo career at the expense of anything else.'

There is something unpleasant in Jones's response, which seems small-minded and petty, almost the kind of sniggering that roadie Glen Colson had observed in Zeppelin dressing rooms. It hardly seems the most charitable or measured view of Plant's feelings: the man still limped from his 1975 car crash; and if he hadn't been on tour with Led Zeppelin in 1977 he might somehow have been able to prevent the death of his son Karac.

'One of the roadies then played drums,' Plant told *Rolling Stone*'s David Fricke. 'He was quite good, too, but the whole thing dematerialised. Jimmy had to change the battery of his wah-wah pedal every one and a half songs. And I said, "I'm going home." Jonesy asked why. "Because I can't put up with this and I don't need the money." For it to succeed in Bath, I would need to have been far more patient than I have been for years. It wasn't to be.'

Plant made his excuses and left the rehearsals for good. Unlike Sam Peckinpah's ageing bad men in *The Wild Bunch*, the old gang could not be gathered together again for one last raid. Certainly not for now, anyway.

Several of the biggest promoters in the world were anxious to learn of Led Zeppelin reforming. In the mid-1980s Ron Delsener, who had booked memorable gigs by the Beatles, Bob Dylan and David Bowie, was probably the biggest promoter on the US East Coast. Delsener had become friends with Kosmo Vinyl, whose role with the Clash and Ian Dury was similar to that of B. P. Fallon with Led Zeppelin: vibes merchant. It was Vinyl who had urged Ian Dury that it was ideologically unsound for him to support Zeppelin at Knebworth. 'I'd ask Ron, "Who would you put on to make money?" He would reply, "If I could put Led Zeppelin on in a giant stadium until they couldn't play anymore." But that storm-trooper swagger was getting a bit tired when they were doing it.'

There were intimations of a continuing friendship, no matter how difficult, between Page and Plant, those two ultimate rock 'n' roll warhorses. In the autumn of 1987, Plant was ensconced in Studio One of Marcus Music in Kensington Gardens Square, West London. He was recording the album that would be known as *Now and Zen* – not a bad cosmic jokey title. Andy Priest, who was working on the front desk, recalled a time when 'Jimmy Page turned up to surprise him and so I directed Jimmy to the studio. After a few hours he came out and asked me to call him a cab. I asked where he was going to. He said, "Windsor." I was about to finish my shift so I said, "If you can wait a few minutes I'll be able to give you a lift. I'm going near there, so you might as well save yourself a few bob." Happy to accept my offer, he got in the passenger seat of my old rattling Triumph 1500 and I set off. On the M4 motorway I stopped at Heston Services for petrol and, while I was filling up, he went to the kiosk and very kindly paid the bill. We spent the rest of the journey talking about music until I dropped him off at his gate. I went on to play bass for a reformed Sham 69, but that's another story.'

*   *   *

Jimmy Page met Patricia Ecker on 25 April 1986, on the Firm's second US tour, when she served him in a French restaurant in New Orleans. Ecker was a 24-year-old model who was working as a waitress. Blonde and beautiful, she bore a certain resemblance to Charlotte Martin. For Page, in thrall to his emotions often more than he would like, and certainly responding to his vulnerable heart's need for succour, it was love at first sight: Pat was 18 years younger than him. When the tour ended, she came back to London with him. New Orleans, voodoo central: for Robert Plant a city that brought him news of utter tragedy; for Page a place that brought him love and re-birth. The poetry of such Led Zeppelin paradoxes is apparently infinite. And food for meditation.

Pat Ecker was soon pregnant: their son James Patrick Page – following a tradition in the Page family of first sons taking that name – was born on 26 April 1988. She and Jimmy married.

The birth of a child brings fresh luck, they say. And not too long after that failed reunion in Bath, and the birth of James, Led Zeppelin did come formally together.

On 14 May 1988 Atlantic Records held its 40th anniversary show at Madison Square Garden. At the time Plant was touring the USA, promoting his *Now and Zen* album. Ahmet Ertegun personally asked Plant, who continued to be released through Atlantic, to play the event. But he also asked all concerned if Led Zeppelin could reunite to close the evening. Amazingly, they agreed. Even though Plant appeared to be constantly closing off such a possibility, there was a side of him clearly still open to the Zeppelin journey, a journey that seemed increasingly one of the soul. And, all things considered, who would be surprised by that?

The Atlantic Records 40th Anniversary Concert was broadcast live in the US on a simulcast between FM radio and HBO television, an enormous promotion. Plant performed a well-rehearsed, well-received solo set, following Crosby, Stills and

Nash, the Bee Gees and Yes. But the night before the show Plant and Page had had words about Led Zeppelin's concert-closing act: the singer had wanted to use his new drummer, Chris Blackwell (no relation to the Island Records boss); but Page was adamant that Jason Bonham be employed, arguing, not unreasonably, for a Zeppelin bloodline continuance. Also, Plant had refused to perform 'Stairway to Heaven', although – again – he changed his mind under pressure from Page.

'Well, that was awful,' Page said to Mick Wall. He told him that Plant 'came together with Jason, Jonesy and me in New York, where we were rehearsing, and started singing "Over the Hills and Far Away". And it sounded really brilliant, actually. Then we rehearsed "Stairway" and that sounded great, too. Then the day before the show he called me up that evening and said, "I'm not going to sing it." I said, "What are you talking about? You're not gonna sing 'Stairway'? But that's exactly the one thing that everybody expects to hear us do!" He said, "I don't wanna do that!"'

They performed 'Kashmir', with its broody opening chords, 'Heartbreaker', 'Whole Lotta Love', 'Misty Mountain Hop' and – of course – 'Stairway to Heaven'. The time-honoured view of the show is that it was a shambles. Yet it is easily available on YouTube, and watching its full 32 minutes, it is eminently clear that this was not the case. Moreover, everyone seemed very happy after the performance. It seems a measure of the full extent to which the tide of popularity had receded for Led Zeppelin that such dismissiveness has become the established currency of how this show was. Especially in comparison with some of their performances on the fated 1977 tour, it really wasn't a disaster at all. But there was something else hovering over the participants. 'I had a strong feeling that the way the Atlantic thing went put a Zeppelin reunion on the back burner for him,' said Doug Boyle, Plant's guitarist. 'Before it I thought there might have been something happening a couple of years down the line. I don't know what went down but that gig was a very tense time between Robert and Jimmy.

'I think there was a part of Robert that missed Jimmy an awful lot. He'd often say to me, "Jimmy would have done this" or "Jimmy would have done that" … The two of them are like brothers. There's something very, very deep there.'

Although certainly not evident during their time onstage at Madison Square Garden, the psychic tussle between Page and Plant over 'Stairway' the previous day had depleted the guitarist. Afterwards, he told Mick Wall, 'I didn't really sleep that night. I was jetlagged anyway because my son had just been born in England and I'd left within a few days of that. And I was really on a roll from that, you know, the high that you're into after the birth of a child. And all of a sudden, I plunged to the ground! Like, what the hell am I doing here?'

On 19 June 1988 an eagerly anticipated event occurred in the life of Jimmy Page and his fans. It was one that could have been of significant consequence in the history of popular music. It should have been a major musical statement, placing him on a par with his friend Eric Clapton, whose solo albums regularly sold in the region of four million copies. Such a record would have reinflated his legend, stating his clear pole position among British blues guitarists. Unfortunately, this did not prove to be the case.

The album *Outrider*, the supposed first step in Page's solo career, was released four and a half weeks after the profile-rising venture of the Atlantic Anniversary Concert.

Even the title was curious, feeling inappropriate, sounding like a character from the then popular *Mad Max* films' dystopian anarchism; it seemed ill-thought out, but revealing. Was this how Page now perceived himself, riding one of the outer cosmic asteroids? It could equally have been titled, more accurately, as Outsider. Extremely uneven, *Outrider* seemed further evidence

of Page's seemingly inexorable decline during the 1980s, a fall
in personal standards to which the very existence of the Firm
appeared to attest.

But what are the positives? At first Page had intended to
make a double album. But demo tapes of many songs disappeared when he had what he described as a 'domestic' situation
in a house he had temporarily vacated. 'It was totally different
to this stuff,' he told Bud Scoppa in *Guitar World*, describing
how at that stage all the missing material was acoustic. 'There
were two tapes, actually, that had a lot of stuff – it was like a
compilation of stuff – I don't know if they're ever gonna resurface. And if they do, well, they'll be heard anyway, won't they?'

So what did Page do after the demo tapes went missing?
Without any tunes written whatsoever, he simply went into his
own Sol Studio and started recording. How it turned out was
how it turned out.

He was clearly rejuvenated by his new relationship with Pat
Ecker. The nine-tune record, with all music except for one track
solely credited to Jimmy Page, was recorded in early 1987, after
he returned to the UK with her; the trio of vocalists supplied
their own lyrics. 'The Only One' was the closest to a Zeppelin
tune, notably because it had Robert Plant on vocals, the sole
track – aptly, a cock-rock extravaganza – on which his former
protégé featured. Elsewhere, the singing was handled by John
Miles, who had had a number one hit in the UK with 'Music' in
1976, and by Page's old mate Chris Farlowe. The use of three
vocalists was an indication of Page's perception of what he was
providing: a showcase for his own guitar playing, arranging and
producing. Using a pair of 24-track desks, flipping sounds
across and between the two of them, there would sometimes be
as many as 30 guitar parts on a number; the Page Guitar Army
on manoeuvres.

Jason Bonham, Bonzo's 22-year-old son, was on drums and
percussion, except for two tracks, 'Liquid Mercury' and

'Emerald Eyes', on which Barriemore Barlow, a former Jethro Tull member who had played most recently with Plant, took over these duties. And who would replace John Paul Jones? As he had with vocalists, Page required three bass players: Durban Laverde on 'Wanna Make Love', 'Writes of Winter' and Leon Russell's 'Hummingbird', the only cover; Felix Krish on 'The Only One', 'Liquid Mercury', 'Emerald Eyes', 'Prison Blues' and 'Blues Anthem'; and Tony Franklin, from the Firm, on 'Wasting My Time', the first song recorded and the album opener. Sometimes you felt that Page could have fared better with Jones's consummate arranging skills.

The material wasn't too bad, but it also wasn't that great. Out of the nine songs there were three instrumentals: 'Writes of Winter', with its flavour of Thin Lizzy at the peak of their ringing twin-guitar supremacy, a Grammy-nominated track; 'Liquid Mercury', which was underwhelming and a little boring, like a sketch of something unfinished; and 'Emerald Eyes', which you felt was intended as a stand-alone 'White Summer' sort of number, replete with raucous, fuzzed guitar, but that never hit the transcendent heights at which it appeared to be aimed.

The smoky 'Prison Blues', with the earthy vocals and salacious words of Chris Farlowe, was in the great Zeppelin tradition of dirty blues, as was 'Blues Anthem'. Yet wasn't that part of the problem? *Outrider* sounded as though it could have been made in the late sixties or early seventies. In other words, it was rather out of date. It feels terrible to say this, but Page's first effort at artistic redemption was a disappointing failure. If anyone felt that the accusations of musical dinosaur had been unfairly directed his way, the lukewarm reviews of *Outrider* spelt out the truth. 'A bizarrely dated-sounding effort, *Outrider* is mostly British blues rock at its most mediocre,' wrote Lynn Van Matre in the *Chicago Tribune*. The disc was a damp squib, scraping 500,000 sales worldwide.

Page's view of the media and its participating players also seemed not to have shifted one jot. Interviewing him at the Four Seasons Hotel in Los Angeles, Bud Scoppa, a former *Rolling Stone* writer, noted in his *Guitar Player* article: 'The one aspect of the man that seemed in keeping with his reputation was a surliness that lurked ominously just below the surface of his demeanour – a sort of Loch Ness Monster of latent hostility.' Scoppa also observed that when there came a knock on the door of Page's ritzy suite, a bellman stood there bearing a gift: a paper bag displaying the Burger King insignia. Page then brought his burger and fries to the interview table. Liberated from his heroin and cocaine diet, he had fleshed out, his body thickening, his face almost a little jowly; a fast-food diet would do that to you. But so would coming off smack.

On 21 June 1988, two days after the release of *Outrider*, Jamie Kitman, the manager of They Might Be Giants, was at New Orleans Airport, waiting to board a flight to New York. A man in a wheelchair was pushed to the front of the queue for the plane. He had a blanket over his knees and on top of it sat a tabby cat. It was Page. Much to his distress, the cat was taken from him for the duration of the flight. Then he was gingerly helped up the steps to the first-class lounge.

During the flight Kitman stepped forward from coach into the first-class lounge. He found Page, looking unwell. He briefly introduced himself and placed a cassette of the They Might Be Giants album on his tray table. 'Jimmy stared at it, as though it might hurt him,' said Kitman, who made his excuses and returned to his seat in coach.

Kitman's experience on that flight seemed like a spectral vision of everything one feared for Jimmy Page.

The reviews for *Outrider*'s live tour were no better than those the record itself received. It kicked off on 2 September 1988 at the Miami Arena in Florida, and after 15 dates, including those

Zeppelin strongholds Texas and Los Angeles, it hit Chicago, another favourite town for Page's former group.

Though acknowledging the extremities of satisfaction felt by the audience at Chicago's UIC Pavilion, David Silverman, writing in the *Chicago Tribune*, criticised John Miles's vocals and attitude: 'Rough like broken glass, but not nearly as sharp, Miles plugged his way through the set with little emotion or enthusiasm.' He added: 'Without Plant's vocals and the unique Zeppelin sound, it was a hollow reminiscence. At times, Page seemed too alone on stage, working through material that appeared as distant to him as the band's past. The result was a cold reminder that what once was Zeppelin is now distant history.'

As well as almost all the *Outrider* material, Page and his group played new versions of 'Custard Pie' and 'Over the Hills and Far Away'. The Yardbirds/Zeppelin rearrangement of the great 'Train Kept A-Rollin'' was also featured as the penultimate number, before the predictably enormous and ecstatic audience response to the inevitable 'Stairway to Heaven', the set closer.

David Silverman didn't even mention that as well as Jason Bonham and Miles on stage, Page's touring band was rounded off by bassist Durban Laverde.

'The result was an evening that was successful for Page as a solo artist and for Bonham's excellent drum work. But the attempt to build a band around Page's immense and unique talent came up short,' concluded the journalist. 'The merging of old Page and new Bonham was the only bit of magic that could be squeezed from the show.'

On 10 January 1990 Jon Bon Jovi introduced Page during a Bon Jovi show at London's Hammersmith Odeon: emerging from the wings, the guitarist performed what by now had become his old standby of 'Train Kept A-Rollin'', and – wow! – the stunning solo from his session work on Joe Cocker's 'With a Little Help from My Friends'.

At the 1990 Monsters of Rock Festival at Castle Donington, Page joined Aerosmith onstage before 70,000 people. He jammed with the revived act's guitarists, Joe Perry and Brad Whitford, on 'Train Kept A-Rollin''. Three days later, he played with them again, before 300 people, at the Marquee Club, performing not only 'Train' but also 'I Ain't Got You' and 'Think About It', old Yardbirds tunes. 'Aerosmith are a great band, a really good band to play with,' said Page. Then he led the Boston rockers into 'Immigrant Song', the Marquee exploding with emotion.

Led Zeppelin themselves seemed to have become a wedding and parties outfit. In November 1989 Page, Robert Plant and John Paul Jones attended the 21st-birthday celebration of Carmen Plant, the singer's daughter, on the Welsh border. Alcohol duly down the hatch, they played together on 'Misty Mountain Hop' and 'Trampled Under Foot', among other tunes, a set of over half an hour. Then, on 28 April 1990, all three once again were together, playing with Jason Bonham at his wedding in Bewdley, Worcestershire. This time they played a different set of tunes: 'Bring It on Home', 'Sick Again', 'Custard Pie' and 'Rock and Roll'.

On 30 June 1990 Page joined Plant for his performance at Knebworth House. It was a star-studded bill, including Pink Floyd, Eric Clapton, Elton John and Paul McCartney, among other major names. It had been rumoured for some days that both Page and Jones would join their old spar onstage. Although Jones was a no-show, Page most certainly was there, playing 'Rock and Roll', 'Going to California', 'Wearing and Tearing' (from *Coda*), 'Misty Mountain Hop' and 'Immigrant Song' with Plant. A sense of Led Zeppelin getting back together was building.

In September 1990 a Zeppelin compilation of sorts was released. It was a four-CD set entitled *The Led Zeppelin Boxed Set*, a substantial bestseller, making the US Top 20. In the late

1980s all of Led Zeppelin's material had been released for the first time on compact disc. Yet they had been derived not from re-equalised master tapes, but from sound-generation tapes equalised for the original vinyl releases; this angered Jimmy Page, always keen – as we would come to see – that the legacy of Led Zeppelin was as perfectly accurate as feasible. 'They even cut off the cough at the end of "In My Time of Dying",' he complained later to *Guitar World*. He personally supervised the remastering process, spending a week in May 1990 at New York's Sterling Studios, upgrading the analogue tapes to digital standard.

'My awareness was re-heightened when we were remastering the material to do that CD box set in 1990,' said Page, 20 years later. 'When you hear it all, song after song, you realise what a textbook it is for musicians who are coming along, and that's so great. The whole thing is about passing it on, because that's how it was done for me when I was learning from all those old blues and rockabilly records. It's all part of how this cultural phenomenon keeps moving on. I think everyone carries the flame on.'

Heightening the mystery, the boxed-set sleeve bore an image of a crop circle, upon which was cast the shadow of a Zeppelin airship, highly effective and pleasantly ironic in the self-belief of its omniscience.

Four months later, in the slipstream of the success of *The Led Zeppelin Boxed Set*, the three surviving members met up to consider the possibility of getting back together for a tour. Jason Bonham was not invited to the meeting: Plant was urging the others to consider Mike Bordin, the drummer with the hip Faith No More, as replacement for Bonzo. His pair of old spars would not go along with this, which set Plant off on a departure from the idea before it had even begun.

By now Page had sold his studio the Sol, which had been a going financial concern throughout the last ten years. Elton John had made a pair of albums there; and in 1989 Jeff Beck had recorded *Guitar Shop* at the studio, a comeback album of sorts. The next year Page sold Boleskine House; some claimed that his interest in Aleister Crowley had considerably diminished.

Page set about making a new solo album. But his record company, Geffen, urged him instead to team up with another of their artists: David Coverdale, the former Deep Purple vocalist who had subsequently established himself in the album charts with his group Whitesnake. On paper it didn't seem too good an idea. Whitesnake were a kind of Led Zeppelin-lite, Coverdale a sort of Robert Plant imitator. The idea appeared quintessentially naff. Yet that was precisely what Page needed. But he wanted to meet Coverdale first, to check his 'character'. Clearly Coverdale passed the test.

After sessions in Vancouver, Miami, New York and Abbey Road in London, the album, to be titled *Coverdale/Page*, was completed by the spring of 1992, and finally released on 15 March 1993. Robert Plant sneered at the very notion of Page working with, as he put it, 'David Coverversion'. (According to Guy Pratt, who played bass on the subsequent tour, Coverdale retorted, 'I'll challenge him to a shout-off any time you like.' 'Missing the point,' said Pratt, 'that we'd had to take most of the Zeppelin songs down about two and a half notes, because no one but Plant can get up there.')

Yet the record charged up the charts: number five in the USA and number four in the UK. It was considerably assisted in its course by the heavy rotation on MTV of 'Pride and Joy', number one in the *Billboard* album track rock chart for six weeks.

But the project then stalled, following a Japanese tour. Dates had been set up for American shows, but were cancelled, supposedly due to poor ticket sales. 'It was originally meant to be an American and European tour,' said Pratt, 'but it was booked as arenas and the ticket sales just weren't there. So it was to be played in theatres instead. Jimmy was happy with that but David Coverdale considered his place in the firmament to be arenas. So Coverdale considered he would be seen to be downsizing. So we did these rehearsals, did nothing for six months, and then went to Japan.'

During the two-week Japanese tour Page did not look too good, overweight and clad in bulky waistcoats and big ties. Hardly the once-beautiful Prince of Darkness. Of this former image Pratt felt he had a perspective: 'It is potentially one of the most clever pieces of PR management ever. The guy is basically just a collector. But if you recast him as the devil, it's kind of genius.'

But although Page's marriage was falling apart at the time, he seemed to enjoy himself during the tour, no longer retreating to the seclusion of his hotel room following a show – he was drinking alcohol but seemed drug-free. Almost within hours of arriving in Japan the entourage had acquainted themselves with a set of local strippers, as though this was their on-the-road modus operandi, and in Tokyo Page met a pair of Israeli girls whom he found most entertaining.

However, Page now had something he wanted to do far, far more: he was going to work again with Robert Plant.

The singer's solo career was faltering. His most recent album, *Fate of Nations*, had barely scraped the US Top 40 albums. And he had been distinctly unpleased to find himself on a European tour opening for Lenny Kravitz, who was heavily influenced by Led Zeppelin. Moreover, the subsequent development confirmed what Guy Pratt had felt during the dates with David Coverdale: 'Jimmy Page just can't get over Percy Plant.'

25

THE SORCERER'S APPRENTICE

Plant had been asked to appear on MTV's *Unplugged* show, an occasional series featuring classic artists playing acoustic sets that had first aired in 1989. And then Jimmy Page was pulled in to the performance. Once again it seemed he was being drawn along by the influence of his old guitar chum and neighbour Eric Clapton: Slowhand's recording of his 1992 MTV *Unplugged* show had been released as an album that sold 26 million copies, the biggest-selling live album ever.

Bill Curbishley, who had been managing Plant since the 1980s, contacted Page shortly before his Japanese tour with David Coverdale. 'I had a call from Robert's management to pop in and see Robert in Boston on the way to LA to rehearse,' remembered Page. 'Robert said, "I've been approached by MTV to do an *Unplugged* and I'd really like to do it with you." So I said okay. It gave us a chance to revisit some numbers and use that same picture with a very, very different frame.'

'By that time I didn't feel like I was even a rock singer anymore,' said Plant. 'Then I was approached by MTV to do an *Unplugged* session. But I knew that I couldn't be seen to be holding the flag for the Zeppelin legacy on TV. Then mysteriously Jimmy turned up at a gig I was playing in Boston and it was like those difficult last days of Led Zep had vanished. We had this understanding again without doing or saying anything. We talked about the MTV thing and decided to see where we could take it.'

But there was a notable absentee: John Paul Jones, who was touring with Diamanda Galás, was not invited to this party, a cause of considerable upset for him. At a subsequent press conference, the pair were asked where was the bass player. 'Just parking the car,' came a bitchy response from Plant. When the first Page/Plant record emerged, given the title *No Quarter*, Jones was even more miffed, claiming that the fact that the title track existed at all was almost entirely down to him.

In March 1994 Page and Plant were tucked away at the Depot, a rehearsal space in London's King's Cross. They started off by playing along to North African-inspired drum loops provided by Martin Meissonnier, a French music producer of considerable ability; Plant then brought in the drummer and bass player from his own band, Michael Lee and Charlie Jones, the latter also by now his son-in-law.

On 17 April Page and Plant, along with Lee and Jones, played at Buxton Opera House at a memorial concert for the late Alexis Korner, who had been such an inspiration and support for Plant. Among the songs they played were 'Baby Please Don't Go', 'I Can't Quit You Baby' and 'Train Kept A-Rollin''.

Then they went into an upstairs room at the King's Head on Fulham High Street, a pub-rock venue back in the days of nearby Swan Song, and only a hundred yards from what was once Manticore, where they had rehearsed for the 1977 Zeppelin US tour.

Plant had been inspired by Peter Gabriel's work on the soundtrack to Martin Scorsese's *The Last Temptation of Christ*, filtering North African music and talent through Western perceptions. Accordingly, Hossam Ramzy, an Egyptian percussionist and composer who worked with Gabriel on the film, joined them in Fulham. Plant also took on Ed Shearmur, a soundtrack composer and arranger. The pair, the singer informed them, would be responsible for creating the required blend of Western folk-rock and traditional Arabic and Indian music. Led

Zeppelin's songs were about to be savagely reinterpreted and brought up to date, as befitted the pair of now middle-aged rockers.

The equivalent of a baptism by fire, Plant ordained that he and Page would set to work straightaway with these two new collaborators on probably the hardest of the Zeppelin tunes to be restructured; though philosophically it was also the most ready, potentially extremely malleable: 'Kashmir'.

Through his Indian family connections Plant brought in Najma Akhtar, an award-winning, English-born singer of Indian descent with a voice that was almost celestial. 'Robert was very much in control of the whole enterprise and what he said went,' she told Paul Rees. 'He originally sent me three songs to listen to and I remember Jimmy suggesting to him that I should sing on all of them. Robert said no, just "The Battle of Evermore". Jimmy tried to ask why not, but I only did the one.

'Generally I think Robert is the key-holder in their relationship. Both of them are extremely intelligent and knowledgeable about different kinds of music, but they're otherwise very different people. Robert interacted with me more. He was the taskmaster. Jimmy seemed shy and very reserved. There was a lot of tension between them, both artistically and also personally.'

Part of this tension was over Plant's insistence that they would not play 'Stairway to Heaven'. In order to keep the project going, Page, who had turned 50 that January, needed to subjugate himself to Plant, something that would not even have crossed his mind to do 25 years earlier. He sat in a corner of the rehearsal space watching, listening, absorbing. Always aware and highly intelligent, Page was only too appreciative of the classic circumstances they found themselves in, the student overpowering his teacher.

That July, along with an Egyptian orchestra and an English string section, they rehearsed at Wembley for a week.

Early in August they travelled down to Plant's beloved Morocco, where a traditional Gnaoua band had been enlisted. Learning of this, you couldn't help but recall something William Burroughs had said of Moroccan musicians to Page when they met in 1975: 'Their music is definitely used for magical purposes. For example, the Gnaoua music is to drive out evil spirits and Joujouka music is invoking the God Pan. Musicians there are all magicians, quite consciously.' So, you may wonder, by involving Gnaoua musicians was Plant consciously or unconsciously doing some psychic soul-cleansing?

With so many pre-filmed sequences planned, Page and Plant's was to be an unusual twist on the established *Unplugged* format. With the cameras rolling during the day in Jemaa el-Fna, the Square of the Dead, in Marrakesh, they performed a pair of new acoustic songs: the beautiful 'City Don't Cry' and 'Wah Wah', a considerable stretch away from previous Zep material. That evening, again with a full film crew, they played another new tune, 'Yallah' (also known, curiously, as 'The Truth Explodes'), even steamier and moodier than the other two songs; they played to Martin Meissonnier's loop, kicking off with a crunching power chord from Page that could have come from a grunge act like Nirvana. 'Wah Wah' was also performed again. The mystery and mystique, the sense of wandering into the unknown that had always couched Led Zeppelin, was there again. Again there was an element of smoke and mirrors. Michi Nakao had been employed as the shoot's make-up artist. Her brief was not easy: Page desired that not a glimpse of his grey hair appear on film; at the same time he would not accept any dye in it. From time to time she would be obliged to 'smooth' back the guitarist's hair, her hand concealing the black stain she had secreted. At the end of the shoot, as an act of gratitude – unaware of her sleight-of-hand subterfuge – Page gifted her with a leather icon of a local deity.

On 16 August, on a Welsh mountainside, they were filmed performing a new version of 'No Quarter'. The next day, nearby, they shot and recorded 'Gallows Pole', 'Nobody's Fault but Mine' and 'When the Levee Breaks'.

On 25 and 26 August they were at a London television studio, filming the on-set sequences for *Unplugged*; the next month was spent mixing the show and the forthcoming album. On 12 October 1994, *Unledded*, as it had become titled, was broadcast on MTV in the US. It got the highest viewing figures of any show aired under the *Unplugged* brand. By now a world tour had been booked for Page and Plant, a half of Led Zeppelin tour; they spent November rehearsing for it.

The album *No Quarter: Jimmy Page and Robert Plant Unledded* went on sale on 14 October 1994. The next week it entered the US album charts at number four, its highest position, going on to sell over a million copies in America alone; in the UK it only hit number seven, but sold over 100,000 copies.

Page and Plant knew that this was a golden opportunity, a chance to revive their former glory, maybe the last for these ageing rock 'n' roll gunslingers. They pulled out all the stops; drawing upon their mutual love of Indian and Arabic music, they truly scored: *No Quarter* is a stunningly great record. By then world music may have already peaked, during the second half of the 1980s. But few of Zep's original audience would have had too much awareness of this. And the result was grown-up, very intelligent music, even if much of it was Led Zeppelin reinterpretations.

One important consequence of *No Quarter*, and Page and Plant's assiduously creative work together, was to commence the restoration of Jimmy Page in the eyes of the world's music fans. That tide that had been out for so long – with the widespread perception of him as a casualty, a wasted junkie and dark-arts practitioner, an image only enhanced by the Firm and his work with David Coverdale – was beginning to flow once again towards the shore. As he learned, through necessity, to let go of his Capricorn love of control and hand it over to Robert Plant, something wonderful happened for him.

On 12 January 1995 the pair, plus John Paul Jones, were at the Waldorf Astoria Hotel in New York, as Led Zeppelin were inducted into the Rock and Roll Hall of Fame. 'Thanks to my friends for finally remembering my telephone number,' uttered Jones with understated sarcasm. The three of them, along with Jason Bonham, played with Joe Perry and Steven Tyler from Aerosmith on 'For Your Love', 'Train Kept A-Rollin'', 'Bring It on Home' and 'Baby Please Don't Go'. Then, accompanied by Neil Young, they played 'When the Levee Breaks'. Neil Young wrote the song 'Downtown' about this experience, which was included on his *Mirror Ball* album, released that summer.

The Page and Plant *No Quarter* world tour kicked off on 26 February 1995, 22 days after Page had played with the Black Crowes in Paris, joining in on that old warhorse 'Shake Your Money Maker'. You sensed this endeavour was not only to raise his profile, but also to get match fit for the upcoming tour. And to have some fun: in early 1995 Page and his wife Patricia Ecker had split up, and would finally divorce. Then she went home to her native New Orleans with their son James.

The 51-year-old Page had already started a new relationship, with Jimena Gomez-Paratcha, a 23-year-old San Franciscan activist with Argentinean parents. Her first name, of course, was a Latin version of his own. Page appeared to have two, classically opposite female archetypes: statuesque movie-star-like blondes, like Charlotte Martin and Patricia Ecker, and sultry, dark-haired sirens, in the manner of Lori Mattix and, now, Jimena Gomez-Paratcha. They all had one thing in common, however: they were invariably young. 'You can have sex with anyone these days, whatever sex,' said Steve Parsons, the former singer with the Sharks. 'But the big taboo remains older men with younger women. I think that's subconsciously why Jimmy does it, because he knows how it winds people up. He has always liked to be a rebel.'

The pair had met in Rio de Janeiro in Brazil when he was doing promotion for the upcoming *No Quarter* tour. Jimena was working as a community worker with local street children. Moved by the plight of these homeless kids, Page – assisted by Jimena – established a shelter, Casa Jimmy. Soon she would assist him further, bearing a new family for the musician: Zofia Jade, who was born in 1997, and Ashen Josan, who arrived two years later. Jana, Jimena's daughter from an earlier relationship, was also taken under Page's wing.

The Page/Plant world tour was an enormous undertaking; it started with 47 dates in the US, on 26 February 1995 in Pensacola, Florida. On 31 March Page and Plant played the Palace, Auburn Hills, Michigan. A 23-year-old man rushed the stage to make an attempt on Page's life. Demons surrounding Page had driven him to it, he claimed. Some things never died down.

Then there were 27 dates in Europe, including a triumphant appearance on the Pyramid Stage at Glastonbury Festival, its bohemian milieu perfect for the pair's spirited melange of exotic influences. Plus, after an eight-week break following their Wembley shows in London on 25 and 26 July 1995, another 22 in the US and Mexico, concluding with a pair of shows at Madison Square Garden. Peter Grant was invited to the Wembley dates, and Plant paid tribute to him from the stage. There was an irony here: for all Grant's efforts at reaping the maximum financial rewards for his clients, the *No Quarter* tour – one of the biggest earners of the year – brought in even more cash than any set of dates by the full Zeppelin line-up. More importantly, it was a colossal creative triumph. 'It was heroic to take something like that around the world,' Page told Charles Shaar Murray in *Mojo*, 'because it was using two orchestras: one Western, one Arab orchestra, with a hurdy-gurdy. It was great going around the world to turn people on to sounds they hadn't heard. It wasn't an easy thing to do, but it was worth it.'

During the tour – why break the habit of a lifetime? – Page remained very much the rock 'n' roll recluse, tucked away in his hotel room most of the time. Nigel Eaton, their hurdy-gurdy player, thought he was 'one of those loner types at school that never went out ... He was always very nice to me, but he was much more intense and I was warier of him.' Page may have been off drugs, but he was drinking a great deal, with Plant's mates complaining that his boozing was adversely affecting his performances. Plant, meanwhile, began a relationship with Najma Akhtar, who sang on selected dates.

According to photographer Ross Halfin: 'I found that tour really unpleasant. It was sort of Jimmy's camp, which was his guitar tech and me, and then Robert and everyone else. You were made to feel as if you shouldn't be there. Admittedly, Jimmy was drinking a lot by the end of it so he was hard work.

'The two of them did seem to get on for the most part, though. Robert used to call Jimmy "Jimbob" all the time to try and annoy him but Jimmy would just ignore it. Jimmy had also wanted John Paul Jones to be there but Robert wouldn't have it. Jimmy was as much to blame for that situation because he gave in to it.'

On 21 November 1995 Peter Grant died from a heart attack; he was 60 years old. His funeral took place the next month, at St Peter and St Paul's Church in the possibly aptly named village of Hellingly in East Sussex, where Grant's mansion Horselunges was located; he had long since moved to Eastbourne. Jimmy Page, Robert Plant and John Paul Jones were in attendance, along with Jeff Beck, Bad Company, Phil Carson and even Denny Laine, the father of Catherine James's son, who by now had a child with Peter Grant's daughter Helen. And which song was played as they departed the church? Vera Lynn's 'We'll Meet Again', the controversial manager having requested the voice of Britain's wartime songbird.

At the wake, held nearby, Page was the first to leave, the door slamming shut behind him as he walked out, now with only memories of his close friend and confidante, the man directly responsible for recognising his great talent and facilitating what became the biggest group in the world. Page issued a terse statement: 'Peter was a tower of strength as a business partner and a friend. I will miss him and my heart goes out to his family.'

The year before his death, Grant had read Bill Graham's autobiography, which contained a graphic account of that shocking night in 1977 at Oakland Coliseum. Grant had supposedly broken down and cried, a final release.

In the new year, 1996, there were Page and Plant shows in South America, Japan and Australia. The very last date of the *No Quarter* tour took place on 30 November at the Mumbai Sports Complex in India, their ambition to play on the subcontinent finally realised.

While Page/Plant were in Sydney, Australia, at the end of February 1996, Jeff Buckley played a sensational show in the city to a fantastic crowd response, remembered his friend, the producer Jack McKeever. Buckley believed it to be one of the best shows he had ever done. Immediately after, he was exhausted and dripping with perspiration. In his dressing room he put a white towel over his head, soaking up the sweat that was running down his face and neck. Suddenly he felt someone come into the room. This person picked him up and danced around the room with him, holding him above the ground. 'That was fantastic. You are fantastic. You are the best thing in the last 20 years. Can I produce your next album?' It was Jimmy Page. Jeff Buckley was an enormous Led Zeppelin fan; the group had influenced him more than anything else. He was utterly knocked out by Page's response. Yet he turned down the production offer, feeling it would not be entirely appropriate.

The next year, 11 November 1997 saw the release of Led Zeppelin's *BBC Sessions*. Page had compiled and mastered the tapes, setting standards for quality control on subsequent reissues from which he would never deviate. In the United States, Zeppelin's sales heartland, *BBC Sessions* was a number 12 album.

What would Page/Plant do next? What any other musicians in their position would do: they made another record, *Walking into Clarksdale*, its title inspired by the legendary crossroads in Clarksdale, Mississippi, where blues legend Robert Johnson allegedly sold his soul to the devil in return for his talent. Equally allegedly, Robert Plant was said to have carried a pouch of earth scraped from that very crossroads with him at all times.

At the singer's suggestion they brought in Steve Albini as producer. Once again, a sign of his maturing years perhaps, Jimmy Page relinquished control: he apparently no longer needed to be in charge of production. Albini was the grunge wunderkind, a crucial figure in independent record production, who had produced – among countless other successful albums – Nirvana's 13-million-selling *In Utero*, with its unutterably bare and dirty sound. Albini was a very good decision.

Walking into Clarksdale was recorded at Abbey Road in London, again with Charlie Jones on bass and Michael Lee on drums and percussion. Page and Plant ditched the idea of working with orchestras or arcane instrumentation again. 'The most obvious thing for us to do,' said Page, 'was for us to go back to the four-piece unit that we knew best and always worked for us. A lot of people thought we were going to carry on with that big extravaganza … but for us it was important to come to terms with the songs.'

Walking into Clarksdale is another sensational album, on a par with *No Quarter*. It is a really great rock 'n' roll record, with a worldbeat spirit, characterised by Plant's semi-ululating African vocal punctuations. When it was released on 21 April 1998, *Walking into Clarksdale* was extremely, and bafflingly, critically underrated. Still, it made number eight in the US album charts and number three in the UK.

For the first time since tunes like *Led Zeppelin II*'s 'Thank You', Page was playing on a record that often sounded like it was made by a late 1960s garage band. It feels like it was how Page always wanted it to be: tight but loose. At times it is like the driving, screaming early 1990s live work of Neil Young; Page's guitar work is relentless, joyous. 'House of Love', the almost teenage penultimate track, sounded like all that time playing with the Johnny Burnette Trio's master song had rubbed off. A key tune was the sensational 'Most High', which won Page and Plant the Grammy Award for Best Hard Rock Performance in 1999; number one in the *Billboard* Mainstream Rock chart in May 1998, it made the Top 30 in the UK, bringing a first ever appearance on *Top of the Pops* for Page; time – or pragmatism – had mellowed him.

In the early months of 1998, Page and Plant, along with Lee and Jones, undertook a tour of countries formerly in the Eastern Bloc. They played Croatia, Hungary, the Czech Republic, Poland, Romania and Bulgaria. Renting a car, Page and Plant drove from show to show, studying how these countries were adapting to breaking free fom Communist rule. They ended up with a show in Istanbul in Turkey. Page declared that he would next be travelling to Egypt, to visit the tombs of the pharaohs – something he had already done three times during that last Led Zeppelin tour in 1977, of course.

A month before the release of *Walking into Clarksdale*, Page and Plant announced the dates for a US summer tour. The Walking into Everywhere tour was set to begin on 19 May, at

Pensacola, Florida, just like the *No Quarter* tour. There were 27 dates listed, concluding at New York's Madison Square Garden on 16 July. 'I would expect Page and Plant to do quite well,' commented Gary Bongiovanni, editor of the US concert-industry trade paper *Pollstar*. 'Certainly if you look at the popularity that somebody like Ozzy Osbourne has maintained, you gotta believe that there's still an audience for hard-rock music. Page and Plant are certainly not overexposed. They haven't been touring every year. There should be significant demand for them.' After a break there would be another set of dates, taking in the pair's beloved West Coast of America, followed by further shows in Europe.

Before the tour began, Warner Brothers' film division, in tandem with Bill Curbishley, who now managed both Page and Plant, had green-lit a biopic to be made about Led Zeppelin. Accordingly, Brian Helgeland, who that year had won an Academy Award for his superb adaptation of James Elroy's *L.A. Confidential*, was hired. Helgeland certainly seemed the correct choice: he had moved to Los Angeles because he had been inspired by Zeppelin's 'Going to California'.

Given access to the pair of principal players, Helgeland was at Madison Square Garden and a show on Long Island. Plant, however, refused to cooperate. 'There was something going on between him and Jimmy Page, but also Plant seemed to be having some relationship breakup difficulty,' said Helgeland.

Yet Page, presumably always anxious to secure a positive legacy for his Led Zeppelin art project, could not have been more helpful. Chatting backstage, Helgeland found him utterly charming. 'Then his wife Jimena arrived holding baby Zofia. She put her in Jimmy's arms. He carried on talking to me, a Marlboro Lite stuffed in the corner of his mouth. As he spoke I could tell what was going to happen. Suddenly the long pile of ash that had built up on his cigarette descends ... to fall on the top of Zofia's forehead. Jimmy carried on talking: I'm not sure he noticed.'

Plant's stance led to Warner Brothers abandoning the projected Led Zeppelin movie. Moreover, the singer then told Page that he was not interested in making another record with him. He no longer wanted, he told Paul Rees, to continue what seemed to have become a religious observation of Led Zeppelin at their concerts. 'I needed to go off and do something that was the very antithesis of playing huge buildings in places like Mannheim in Germany to people who wanted Led Zeppelin and the two of us were the nearest thing they could get to it.'

The fact is, though, that Page and Plant had carried on for five years and 200 gigs, not bad going for something that had sprung from a simple request for a single appearance on MTV *Unplugged*. 'I wanted to keep working,' Page told Nick Kent. 'But Robert wouldn't hear of it.' He confessed that he had been hoping to bring John Paul Jones in with the pair of them: 'But it was hard enough getting two of us together, let alone three.'

Jimena Page had organised an event at London's plush Café de Paris on 27 July 1999 for a pair of charities: the ABC (Action for Brazilian Children) Trust, which she and her new husband had founded, and SCREAM (Supporting Children through Re-Education and Music). Page played with the Black Crowes, with whom he was already very taken, as well as with Aerosmith's Steven Tyler and Joe Perry; Michael Lee was on drums and Guy Pratt, who had toured with him on the Coverdale/Page project, on bass.

When Plant proved utterly resistant to Page's entreaties to continue their work together, the guitarist became angered. He called up his mates in the funky, Faces-like – with a smidgen of Allman Brothers – Black Crowes. 'Let's do something together,' he said. The Black Crowes were also Small Faces-like, with singer Chris Robinson's Steve Marriott-clone voice reminding you how Zeppelin might have sounded if Page had secured his original choice for vocalist. You can hear this especially on their interpretation of 'Shapes of Things', the Yardbirds classic they perform on *Live at the Greek: Excess All Areas*; Robinson also has a flavour of Rod Stewart about his tonsils, as though he has been listening to the Jeff Beck version of the song on *Truth*.

Bill Curbishley, who managed the Who as well as Page, set up a tour that would feature both acts; night by night they would alternate between the Black Crowes and the Who to close the show. The tour started on 24 June 1999 in Chicago, ending in Albuquerque, New Mexico, on 12 August. The second leg of the tour was cancelled, the 55-year-old Page suffering from a back injury: nothing to do with his osteopath's specialty earner of wearing his guitar almost down by his knees? It resumed on 9 October 1999 in East Rutherford, New Jersey. On 12 October Page and the Black Crowes played the first of a three-night engagement at Manhattan's Roseland Ballroom: Page's archetypal rock 'n' roll tresses had been trimmed, exposing his ears for the first time in over 30 years, accentuating a jawline we had hardly seen before; his body had thickened considerably. On 18 and 19 October they performed at the Greek Theatre in Los Angeles, an outdoor arena on the edge of the Hollywood Hills.

Live at the Greek: Excess All Areas was the live double-album artefact of these shows. What was extraordinary was that it was initially released only on the internet, on 29 February 2000. Page could get in a dig at an old rival over this: 'Everyone gives David Bowie the credit for having gone on the internet with his *Hours* album,' he said. 'But he just put it up there for two weeks or something. It was more publicity than anything else. But here we've gone and done it for real.'

On 4 July that year it was released as a physical entity on TVT Records. Page bigged up the project. 'Anyone can have a crack at a Zeppelin song and plenty do,' he told Mick Wall. 'But to do it properly, especially when someone who partially created these songs is standing there, well, it can't have been easy. But the Black Crowes did it, and with their own identity intact too.'

But not all involved were as enthusiastic. 'I didn't really have that much fun doing it,' complained Chris Robinson to *Classic Rock*. 'It was all right, and Jimmy's a phenomenal guitarist, but to me it was just a job. I'm not a big fan of Robert Plant's lyrics or his singing, so that part of it was a little boring for me.'

Although the Black Crowes played a handful of their own tunes, punctuating what was essentially a Led Zeppelin tribute set, for copyright reasons they were withheld from the *Live at the Greek* release.

Still, *Live at the Greek* sold over half a million copies in the US, earning a gold album for all concerned. According to *Guitar World* magazine, Jimmy Page's playing on *Live at the Greek* 'reaches levels of fire and fury that it hasn't attained in years'. 'It's very musical, isn't it?' said Page of the project. 'The Crowes are really known for jamming and adlibbing. And that's what I've been doing ever since I've been playing. So it's complementary. And I know people respect the fact that there are musicians trying every night to put themselves right on the edge.'

Despite Page falling out with Plant over his refusal to continue in the Page/Plant combination act, the pair together attended a screening of *Almost Famous*, Cameron Crowe's film based on his experience of going on the road with Zeppelin for his *Rolling Stone* cover story. When the film was released on 13 September 1999, it was revealed that there were four Led Zeppelin tunes on the soundtrack. Plant also had fuelled rumours by stating that he and Page had been in a recording studio and that they would be working together in 2000. More to the point, Page was promising a second solo album, a rather belated follow-up to 1988's *Outrider*.

But now it seemed that Page was entering another phase of his life – and his relationship with Led Zeppelin. Apart from one very significant event, from now on he would largely be dedicated to curating. On 26 May 2003 *How the West Was Won* – a triple-CD live celebration of Zeppelin's shows at the Forum in Los Angeles and Long Beach Arena, on 25 and 27 June 1972 respectively – was released. Around 150 minutes long, it was one of the finest Led Zeppelin records ever released, a sensational encapsulation of the four-piece at the peak of their playing, power and performance; it included an over-25-minute version of 'Dazed and Confused' and a 23-minute 'Whole Lotta Love' extravaganza featuring Wanda Jackson's 'Let's Have a Party', Rick Nelson's 'Hello Mary Lou', John Lee Hooker's 'Boogie Chillen'' and Howlin' Wolf's 'Going Down Slow'.

Page had found the tapes of these two Southern Californian shows, and remembered how the performances were close to breathtaking. 'I'd always wanted to capture what we were doing in LA as we always played at our optimum there. I have memories of that place that somehow just bring something out of you, whether it was the Yardbirds or Zeppelin. LA is always fantastic, so I hope I haven't jinxed myself with that. Each member of the band was playing at their best during those performances and giving like 150 per cent. And when the four of us were playing like that, we combined to make a fifth element. That was the magic, the intangible,' Page told *Guitarist* in 2003. A magnificent, truly representative live album had always been absent from the Zep canon: now that had been remedied. Over 20 years since Led Zeppelin had ceased to exist, *How the West Was Won* entered the US album charts at number one.

The same day that *How the West Was Won* hit the shops, a second iconic release provided this fresh presentation of Zeppelin's live power with a quantum leap. *Led Zeppelin DVD* featured not only the 1970 Royal Albert Hall gig (after which he met Charlotte Martin), but also the 1979 Knebworth shows; footage from the Earls Court concerts; the original film of the Madison Square Garden dates for *The Song Remains the Same*;

footage of a live 'Dazed and Confused' for *Supershow*; plus such snapshots as their performance on Danish TV in 1969 and assorted press conferences and videos. *DVD* and *How the West Was Won* were so detailed that they were almost academic curations in their attention to detail, doctorate studies in Led Zeppelin. For Page it was that amount of detail that was always crucial. 'We wanted something that would trace the journey of Led Zeppelin. In that context, it's a truly historical document,' said the Zeppelin Godfather.

'We were never really part of the pop scene,' he added in an official statement to accompany the releases, repeating the old rap. 'It was never what Led Zeppelin was supposed to be about. Our thing was playing live. In that sense, Zeppelin was very much an underground band. The fact that it became as successful as it did was something that was almost out of our control. We actually shunned commercialism, which is why so little official footage of the band has ever been seen before.'

For the next three years the *Led Zeppelin DVD* would remain the bestselling music DVD in the United States; ultimately it was the biggest-selling music DVD globally ever. This pair of releases returned Led Zeppelin very much to the public's attention. (As though part of a time capsule, I bought my copy at Tower Records on Sunset …)

But the greatest purpose – the reformation of Led Zeppelin – again was avoided, with only one person responsible for this failure. A short US summer tour had been provisionally booked for 2003. More interested in promoting the no doubt coincidental release of his compilation, *Sixty Six to Timbuktu*, Robert Plant stepped back from this immensely financially rewarding possibility. Plant would also ultimately nix a pair of Madison Square Garden shows pencilled in for 2005 to commemorate the twenty-fifth anniversary of John Bonham's passing; the vocalist couldn't decide whether or not it was a good idea. On the other hand, Plant was said to have literally gone down on his knees in front of John Paul Jones to beg his forgiveness for the sneaky, sarcastic comments he'd flung the bass player's way at the beginning of the Page and Plant exercise.

On Monday 28 February 2005 Page, Eric Clapton and Jeff Beck had been invited to Buckingham Palace for a reception honouring the UK's music industry. Also present were Jeannette Lee, managing director of Rough Trade Records, and Mick Jones of the Clash, who were old friends from the days of punk rock. Seeing the triumvirate of heavy-guitar friends, Lee insisted to Mick Jones that they cross the floor to them and introduce themselves. These guitar gods were not taking themselves too seriously. 'We still think we're the kids rehearsing in his mum's garage,' Beck pointed to Page, who smiled quietly.

When Her Majesty Queen Elizabeth II was formally introduced to the Led Zeppelin megastar, she only had one question: 'Are you a guitarist too?' Page simply nodded.

Towards the end of the year, on Wednesday 14 December 2005, Page was back at Buckingham Palace. He was received by the Queen as an Officer of the Order of the British Empire – in other words, he had been granted an OBE. Was this for his sterling work as one of the pagan overlords who conquered the United States of America, bringing immeasurable quantities of American dollars into the UK economy? No, it was for something far more important: Page was awarded an OBE for his work with impoverished Brazilian children; not only had he set up a safe house, benefitting over 300 children, but he had also provided medical and psychological backup, as well as food, clothing and employment training. 'I think when you're faced with a plight that's inescapable, and there's something you can do about it, you hope you can make a difference,' he said mildly.

On 29 October 2006 Ahmet Ertegun, who had founded Atlantic Records and remained its boss, was present at a Rolling Stones benefit concert for the Clinton Foundation. The show was at

New York City's Beacon Theatre; former president Bill Clinton was in attendance. Backstage prior to the show, the 83-year-old Ertegun fell, badly banging his head on the concrete floor. Taken straight to hospital, his condition appeared stable. But it soon deteriorated. When Led Zeppelin were inducted into the UK Music Hall of Fame on 14 November 2006, Page, the only Zeppelin member who could be bothered to turn up, made an official announcement about Ertegun's plight. Shortly after, Ertegun slipped into a coma: he died on 14 December 2006.

A tribute concert for Ertegun, a much-loved and revered figure in the music business, was announced for 26 November 2007 at the O2 Arena in London. The proceeds would go to the Ahmet Ertegun Education Fund, which provided university scholarships.

On 12 September 2007 promoter Harvey Goldsmith announced at a press conference that the bill-topping act at this event would be the three surviving members of Led Zeppelin, joined by Jason Bonham on drums. Tickets were priced at £125, and were sold through a lottery website. Such was the demand that the website crashed almost straightaway. Goldsmith had already predicted that the concert would create the 'largest demand for one show in history': he claimed that over 20 million people tried to buy one of the available 18,000 tickets. When a pair were officially auctioned for the BBC's annual Children in Need appeal, they sold for a staggering £83,000.

Later, Page commented: 'I knew it was going to sell out quickly, but the tidal wave of euphoria that preceded the gig – the anticipation – went beyond what I could possibly have imagined. We'd had a few shambolic appearances in the past, like Live Aid, so if we were ever going to come back together, we were going to do it properly and stand up and be counted.' Each member of Led Zeppelin was only given ten free tickets. When someone tried to blag one from Page, he laughed, 'Impossible: I've had four wives.'

As seemed rather like a Led Zeppelin cavalier tradition, it was almost predictable that the show, announced on 1 November, suddenly seemed to be arbitrarily moved to 10 December. Yet again, apparently, Page had suffered an injury; he had fractured the little finger on his left hand in 'a gardening accident'. Unfortunate for those from all over the globe who had booked plane tickets and hotels in London for the original date of the show. The ulterior motive suspected behind Page's 'medical issue' was – yet again – a problem with Robert Plant.

With only a month to go before the 26 November date there had come a sudden, almost poetic shift in the circumstances of the band. At 59, the relative youngster of the three original members, Plant appeared to be an archetypal example of the sorcerer's apprentice. Having initially received instruction from the occultist magus who was Page, Plant was the only Led Zeppelin member to have carved out a successful solo career since the demise of the group in 1980.

Plant had recorded a new album with the bluegrass-country singer Alison Krauss, *Raising Sand*. Released on 23 October 2007 to resounding critical acclaim, in its first week *Raising Sand* sold 112,000 copies, entering the US album charts at number two; it would eventually reach the number one album slot in the USA, following a Grammy award for Album of the Year. Plant had been extremely busy promoting the album, in both the USA and Europe, and had had little time to rehearse for the Ahmet Ertegun benefit, which Page insisted had to be note-perfect.

Suspicions were raised: was this a devious, arrogant ruse to secure further rehearsal time? Were matters not proceeding according to plan? Was this a symptom of acute nervousness on the part of the guitarist? Or of power games within the dynamic of Led Zeppelin? Probably all these elements were there. But the last was the most overriding.

Though the response to *Raising Sand* almost certainly benefited from publicity from the O2 date, Plant was suddenly in what seemed an unassailable place of power. The focus of attention had shifted to the singer – the dynamic weighted in Plant's favour ever since Led Zeppelin split up now reaching its apogee.

By so arbitrarily and suddenly moving the date of the concert, the event acquired some of the mouldy scent of the archetypal shoddy treatment of Led Zeppelin fans. It also seemed clear that fear was more likely the motivating factor here. When the four musicians finally got together at rehearsals Plant laid down his stipulations. He insisted that the set not be too 'heavy metal' – thus ruling out 'Immigrant Song' and, to Page's distress, 'Achilles Last Stand' – though he did concede to performing the cheesily ubiquitous 'Stairway to Heaven', but only if it was demoted to a nondescript slot midway through the set, and not employed as a grandstanding finale. Also, he was adamant that there should be no free-flowing, extended jams: they had to know precisely what they were doing, replicating the sound on the records.

Plant was now running the Led Zeppelin show – perhaps, as Peter Grant had felt, something he had always wanted to do: in 1993 Grant had told Dave Lewis, the Zeppelin archivist, 'You've got to realise Robert always wanted to be the boss of the band anyway. He finally got his own way.' And in this particular instance, Robert Plant may have had a subconscious cause behind his martinet-like approach: he was genuinely upset that, having given early copies of *Raising Sand* to Page and John Paul Jones, neither sought to comment on the singer's new record. Shortly after the O2 concert, Page ran into another musician. 'That cunt!' he declared. 'That cunt put his record out at exactly the same time we were due to play the show! Fucker!'

All the same, apart from the atrocious sound for the first five numbers, the O2 show was sensational: tight, punchy and unrelenting, with almost none of the group's previously characteristic improvisation; indeed, at only just over two hours long, the set was somewhat unrepresentative of their former epic performances.

Beginning at the beginning with 'Good Times Bad Times', track one off their first album, they charged into 16 of their most classic songs, including 'Stairway', 'Whole Lotta Love', 'Kashmir' and 'Rock and Roll'. For most of the set they stood close together, clustered around Jason Bonham's drum kit, as though it were the altar in the church of Led Zeppelin; and, speaking of religious symbolism, Page still had the Zoso sigil on his amps.

Yet there were signs of nerves. Especially in the now silvery tressed Page – he came on wearing sunglasses – whose playing at first seemed rusty, as though a curious irony was about to be unleashed and the group's founder prove to be the weak link in this reunion. But by 'Black Dog', the third song in the set, Page had mastered himself and his guitar work, and the awesome power and majesty of the music was undiminished. 'There is a kind of loud serenity about Led Zeppelin's set,' wrote the *New York Times* of this hard-rock triumph.

'A band who, implausibly, sound once again like the greatest rock band in the world,' considered *Uncut* magazine. 'For the time being, at least, Led Zeppelin's legend has the happy ending it always deserved.'

But that happy ending would not endure. For immediately following the gig there arose the inevitable question: would there be more dates? Page now appeared revitalised. A month short of his 64th birthday at the O2 date, he had hoped that the concert would be the precursor to a worldwide Led Zeppelin tour. All he wanted to do, it seemed, was to continue playing shows with Led Zeppelin. And Jones and Jason Bonham were equally eager to continue the O2 triumph. The hold-out, however, was Plant, now committed to a lengthy tour to promote *Raising Sand*. Indeed, so adamant was Plant in his refusal to comply with Page's desires that it had the tang of a rebellious son working against his father's wishes.

And this attitude of estrangement continued when work commenced on the DVD of the O2 show. Page and Plant were so intransigent and unable to compromise in the construction of the film that it would take almost five years from the time of the concert before the DVD and live album were released. Whereas Page was insistent on re-recording musical sections that he considered flawed, Plant was equally immovable in his demand that the film should reflect the exact sound that the audience experienced.

Page would send Plant what he considered to be a completed filmed version of the concert, only to find when it was returned to him that all his changes had been removed. Then he would repeat them, return his master copy to Plant, and once again they would be taken off. And so it continued.

When the film was finally released on 17 October 2012, it was apparent that Plant had had his way: *Celebration Day*, which received enormous critical acclaim, was an aural facsimile of the O2 event.

Celebration Day rapidly sold half a million copies, making it the highest-selling DVD of 2012; before the year was out the CD of the show had sold 1.8 million copies. To enjoy such success late in life, as though a continuation of one of those quasi-mythical battles that his life had become during the existence of Led Zeppelin, Page had been obliged to concede defeat to his own once-young apprentice.

26

PHOENIX RISING

Without a singer, Jimmy Page's plan to spend 2008 on a worldwide Zeppelin tour appeared to be scuppered. Steven Tyler briefly tried out as vocalist, before making the catastrophic strategic error of suggesting that Page, Jones and Jason Bonham try out their chops on some Aerosmith material. For this sin he was allegedly sent packing.

On 24 August 2008 Page performed 'Whole Lotta Love' with Leona Lewis at the closing ceremony of the Beijing Olympics. Standing beside a London double-decker bus, Page considered himself part of a patriotic effort to plug the London Olympics, to be held in four years time. 'We put so much into Beijing, but weren't helped by the Chinese giving us next-to-no practise time,' he said. Guy Pratt played bass on the recording, made prior to the event: 'We recorded it in Olympic Studios in the original studio with all the original amps,' he recalled. 'It was amazing. It has this big orchestral arrangement. The actual song seemed a bit shorter than I remembered. Then I realised that we had left off the final verse: I suppose that for Leona Lewis there simply was no female equivalent of a "backdoor man".

'I had a show on Planet Rock at the time. I said something to the effect of: "Oh, by the way, when you hear Jimmy Page closing the Olympics, that's me playing bass on 'Whole Lotta Love'." Jimmy loved it that I'd revealed that, which I should have kept quiet about, because he can't wait for an excuse to be upset with you. I went to a book launch where I knew he was going to be. And it was, "Well, we're not talking to you, are we?" And he made me tap dance.

'Last time I saw Jimmy was in Earls Court. He was having dinner at the Troubador. This time he was so lovely and friendly. He says, "Don't be a stranger. Don't be a stranger." And I said, "Jimmy, I've got nine phone numbers for you and none of them work."'

Less than a year on from the O2 event, there was a tragedy. Michael Lee, who had played percussion on the Page and Plant *Unledded* sessions and was one of the backing musicians on their 1995–96 world tour, suddenly died after a seizure, aged only 39. Lee had been co-credited as a songwriter on all 12 tracks on the *Walking into Clarksdale* album. Page, who liked Lee and had been considering him as a potential member of any musical unit he put together, was reportedly devastated.

In March 2012 Page finally released an album entitled *Lucifer Rising and Other Sound Tracks*, the music he had fallen out with Kenneth Anger over. Although Page finally had completed the music, up to then it had rarely been heard.

Page went back to what, like a garden-shed hobby, he had been doing now for years: curating the Led Zeppelin legacy. Over the ensuing years, all the Zeppelin material was released in so-called Deluxe Editions, including out-takes and live cuts that had been previously unavailable.

'The curating thing is part of a magician's work,' said Steve 'Snips' Parsons. In August 2010 he ran into Page in curious circumstances. While out in London's West End, he overheard a familiar voice saying: 'Oh, I always take them to *The Mousetrap*.' Page was explaining to photographer Ross Halfin how he entertained visitors from overseas, citing London's longest-running play, an Agatha Christie potboiler, as the destination he would choose for them. As Snips in the Sharks, Parsons had been a powerful, soulful vocalist. Just the kind of person Page was looking for, especially as Parsons also considered himself a Thelemite.

The pair had a meeting. Page quizzed Snips about movie-soundtrack work, which Parsons had been involved in for almost 30 years: Page regretted he hadn't done more. For *Death Wish II* he had been pissed off that Michael Winner wouldn't pay for a stereo mix: his soundtrack is only in mono. 'I was only with him for a short time,' said Snips. 'Clearly I didn't pass the test.' He had always had his own reservations about the two of them getting together. 'Two magicians should never meet,' Parsons had thought to himself, citing a mantra-like adage of those involved in the supposed dark arts.

With his own interests in Aleister Crowley's work, Parsons had considerable insight into Page's approach to life in his twilight years. 'Jimmy Page is relating to the work done many years ago. Jimmy is always tweaking things. Led Zeppelin may have been relatively brief, but things have to be done after-wards. For occultists they make these big connections and moments, opening their minds, and it takes a long time to work this stuff out. Kenneth Anger even now works on his films, re-edits sometimes appearing.

'Like Jimmy Page, Austin Osman Spare disappeared for a long time. He was found living in squalor, but then there was something of a redemption.

'A certain thing must go on, that is not of a normal milieu. Magicians don't cherish memories; they use them to make something happen.

'And where was Jimmy Page from the end of Led Zeppelin until relatively recently? Not necessarily here, in all senses of the word. When he was working in the Firm and with David Coverdale, I don't think he was really with us. But Jimmy Page is certainly back with us now.'

On 15 January 2010 Page announced that he would perform at April's Show of Peace Concert in Beijing. Meanwhile, the

United Nations' Pathways to Peace took the opportunity to recognise the Led Zeppelin guitarist by presenting him with its first-ever award.

'We've been asked to give awards over the years but never have done so until this day,' said Michael Johnson, a representative of the organisation. 'We're doing this because musicians have a global impact on the world, and we also know that people who use their name and fame for peace building need to be honoured.'

A clearly touched Page responded modestly: 'Although this award has my name on it, this is a tribute to the power of music and its positive effect. Music has been the most powerful language to reach the hearts of people around the world. During my career, I've experienced the connection and harmony that music can bring.'

In September 2010 'a photographic autobiography' and 'a career in pictures', to use Page's words to describe the project, was published by Genesis Publications, whose speciality was high-end exclusivity. *Zoso: Jimmy Page by Jimmy Page*, as the tome was titled, was released in a limited edition of 2,500 copies, each individually signed by him. Totalling 512 pages, with over 700 rare or unique images, his book retailed at the extremely pricey £425.

Maybe I missed this in the reviews of his book, but I saw no mention of the fact that the cover image of Page is almost identical in composition and facial expression to the most familiar image of Aleister Crowley, the one that adorns his autobiography *The Confessions of Aleister Crowley*. I think we are being told something.

Whatever, the photographic book was a revealing work, emphasised by the early shot of the author in a choirboy's cassock, looking as though butter wouldn't melt in his mouth, bearing the caption, 'It might get loud ...'

Although clearly a testament to rigorous, highly selective picture editing, *Zoso* – yes, here he comes again! – was a rather magnificent and impressive tome. Canny as ever, Page had only given Genesis the first rights to the book; when it was reprinted, still under the Genesis imprint in 2014, he allegedly earned every penny from this second publication, which retailed at the more reasonable price of £40. Undertaking a lengthy book-signing tour of the United States, Page surprised purchasers when his signature turned out to come from a rubber stamp that, in an almost Warhol-like manner, he carried with him. Inviting a rather older Lori Mattix to the Los Angeles launch, Page somewhat surprised his former girlfriend when he sighed, 'Oh, Lori: we were so young then.' To which she replied, 'Well, I was!'

On 3 June 2011 Donovan played an evening at London's Royal Albert Hall dedicated to his 1966 *Sunshine Superman* album. For the title track Page appeared onstage with his guitar, playing along with his old mate Donovan; Jimmy looked considerably animated, as though he was having a terrific time, a palpable empathy between himself and Donovan. At a party in the Gore hotel after the performance, Page, his silver hair tied back in a ponytail, looked troubled when I suggested to him that it would have been terrific if he had played more of the set. 'I'm so rusty,' he said. 'It was all I could do to just do what I did.'

Just over a year later, on 21 June 2012, he was a guest at the launch party for Paul Gorman's biography of Tommy Roberts, Page's old friend who had started the shop Mr Freedom. The crowded event was at Roberts's retro-furniture shop Two Columbia Road in Hackney. I introduced the Led Zeppelin main man to Tapper Zukie, the legendary Jamaican deejay: both seemed as puzzled as the other as to who exactly they were meeting.

* * *

On an early morning in March 2016 I found myself at Christie's, the art auction house in London. I was there with a friend who, like Page, had an interest in the art of Austin Osman Spare, several of whose paintings were for sale.

In addition to my mate, there were several other potential buyers. Yet every time a certain price was realised, the auctioneer would declare that there had been a phone bid for a higher amount. Each of the paintings was bought by this anonymous devotee. My friend and I looked at each other ironically: we suspected we knew who this faceless buyer was.

After the auctions, my mate suggested having lunch at the nearby Chelsea Arts Club. Arriving, we went up to the bar, to be served by a statuesque, pretty red-haired girl. Suddenly I appreciated who this was: Scarlett Sabet, the new love of Jimmy Page's life, according to the *Daily Mail*. Another Scarlet, Page's first daughter, had also worked behind that same bar.

In 2015 director Adam McKay's film *The Big Short* was ready to be released. An extremely clever and impressive movie about the subprime-mortgages scandal of the first decade of the 21st century, *The Big Short* would win an Academy Award for Best Adapted Screenplay. The film had a lot going for it. Apart from a wonderful script and direction – it would also be nominated for Best Picture at the Oscars – it had an impressive cast: Brad Pitt, Christian Bale and Ryan Gosling.

But to complete it, Adam McKay needed something more to give *The Big Short* that final touch. He wanted to include Led Zeppelin's 'When the Levee Breaks' on the soundtrack, to play as the end credits rolled. And – crucially – he wished to have the song as part of the film's trailer. 'We cut the trailer and put in the Zeppelin song,' said McKay, 'and it's not only one of the greatest songs of all time, but it drives you through the trailer. But then we were told we might not be able to get the rights.'

Led Zeppelin were known to be difficult over the use of their songs in films. But, shown a copy of *The Big Short* and its trailer, Robert Plant and John Paul Jones immediately agreed, as did John Bonham's estate. There was only one hold out. And that was because no one could find him. 'What do you mean you can't find Jimmy Page?' the director said. 'I was told he has a new girlfriend, and I guess they were off having a good time ...'

Page had fallen so far off the radar that Adam McKay considered postponing the trailer premiere, something he was extremely reluctant to do: in Hollywood such action can lead to rumours about problems with a film's production.

'We finally heard that he was in some pub out in the English countryside,' said McKay. 'So an assistant drove two hours to get to the pub, breaking every speed limit, goes into the pub and puts a computer in front of Jimmy Page so he can look at the trailer and say either yes we can use the song or no. Then at like 1.55 a.m. or something I got the email that he said yes.'

But this saga did not end there. Page had one condition for also using the song in the end credits of the film. 'He said we can't edit the song. He told us he didn't like how they cut up his songs in movies.'

This presented a further problem: before Robert Plant even opens his mouth, 'When the Levee Breaks' has 84 seconds of instrumental music. McKay decided to open the music before the credits actually roll, subsuming the instrumental in New York traffic noise, so that the moment the credits begin, Plant's voice comes in. 'That was the crazy thing,' said McKay. 'That was a pure accident. It just happened to lay out perfectly when the credits begin.' Carl Jung, of whose philosophy Page was fully aware, would have told McKay that in such situations there is no such thing as an accident or coincidence.

The woman Page had been ensconced with while McKay so anxiously sought him out was the same Scarlett Sabet who had served me at the Chelsea Arts Club. More than 40 years younger than Page, and of Iranian-French descent, she is a poet and actor. Page met her when she gave a poetry reading at the Troubadour in London's Earls Court. The couple were photographed by the *Daily Mail* as they left the Kensington branch of Nando's, the fast-food chicken restaurant where they had celebrated his 71st birthday in 2015. 'Scarlett has been very good for Jimmy,' commented a friend. You feel certain that part of his attraction to Sabet was her first name, recalling how Aleister Crowley always gave his girlfriends the nickname 'Scarlet Woman'. Page no doubt required female company: Patricia, his mother, for whom he had bought a property in Berkshire, had passed away that year.

As might be expected, the populist *Daily Mail* was extremely pleased also to be able to run stories of an alleged feud between the Led Zeppelin stalwart and Robbie Williams, the enormously successful former member of Take That. In 2013 Williams had purchased the home of Michael Winner after the film director's death. Now Williams was desirous of improving the property by building a basement extension, complete with recording studio and swimming pool.

Page was appalled. Concerned that Williams's prospective development might destabilise the foundations of Tower House, he unsuccessfully attempted to prevent the planned building works, the local council rejecting his concerns in 2015. In May 2017 he won a pyrrhic victory of sorts: Williams's building firm was fined £5,000 for making construction noise outside of permitted working hours, something of an irony considering Led Zeppelin's penchant for noise pollution.

But in August 2017 there was a further brouhaha. While being interviewed by an Italian radio station, Williams spoke off air about his difficulties with Page, comparing his behaviour to a 'mental illness'; these comments were then posted on the radio station's Facebook page. Williams was obliged to issue a somewhat grovelling apology: 'I would like to offer my sincere apologies to Jimmy Page, my neighbour, for my comments made before Christmas about him in relation to my recent building works, in which I likened alleged behaviour on his part to suffering from a mental illness.

'Jimmy Page has explained to me that certain specific factual assertions which I made were in fact not true and I am happy to accept what Jimmy Page says.

'I understand why Jimmy Page will have found my comments offensive and I apologise for any hurt that they have caused him and his family as a result.

'I did not intend my comments – which, so far as I am concerned, were made privately – ever to be published.'

As a consequence, the rift between the two rockers was said to have healed.

Rather in the manner of the Clash's Mick Jones, who can be seen on his regular perambulations around Notting Hill, Jimmy Page is frequently sighted in neighbouring Kensington. Page visited Jones's Rock 'n' Roll Public Library on the Portobello Road, an exhibition of the Clash guitarist's immense pop-art archive. 'You've got even more stuff than me,' he declared, amazed. Page also has an enormous collection of memorabilia of all types, especially pop-culture artefacts, including old records, particularly rockabilly – he is a regular visitor at Reading's Sunday Record Fair, where he is considered simply as an exceptionally congenial regular customer, always convivial unless a certain subject is brought up. He also favours a work-ing-men's café in the Earls Court area.

On 24 June 2016 Led Zeppelin partially resolved an issue that had hung over the group since May 2014, when Mark Andes, the bass player with Spirit, had filed legal papers in an endeavour to prevent 'Stairway to Heaven' being rereleased on *Led Zeppelin IV* without Spirit's Randy California, who had passed away in 1997, being co-credited as a writer. 'Stairway to Heaven''s descending chord sequence intro, Andes claimed, was taken directly from Randy California's instrumental tune 'Taurus', which appeared on the first Spirit album.

If it could be proven that Page and Plant had essentially nicked parts of 'Stairway', it would be a landmark moment in the history of popular music. The most-listened-to record ever on American radio, 'Stairway to Heaven' had earned over $562 million by 2008.

All three surviving members of Zeppelin attended the court case. Page was the first member to take the stand, and he drew attention to the influence of 'Chim Chim Cher-ee', from *Mary Poppins*, on 'Stairway'. But he also claimed that he had never heard 'Taurus' until 2014. A music expert stated in court that the chord progressions in both 'Stairway to Heaven' and 'Taurus' had first appeared over 300 years previously.

Half an hour after retiring, having listened to both 'Stairway to Heaven' and 'Taurus', the jury reached its verdict: 'there was no substantial similarity in the extrinsic elements of "Taurus" and "Stairway to Heaven".'

Page and Plant jointly issued a statement: 'We are grateful for the jury's conscientious service and pleased that it has ruled in our favour, putting to rest questions about the origins of "Stairway to Heaven" and confirming what we have known for 45 years. We appreciate our fans' support, and look forward to putting this legal matter behind us.' Apart from that professionally worded declaration, there seemed little sign of amity between the pair.

On 18 May 2017 came shocking news: Chris Cornell, the singer with Soundgarden and Audioslave, had hanged himself. The handsome, highly intelligent Cornell had long suffered from depression, exacerbated by drug dependencies he seemed to have conquered. His solo album *Euphoria Morning* had included a tune entitled 'Wave Goodbye', a tribute to his late friend Jeff Buckley. In its tribute to Cornell, the *Los Angeles*

Times compared him favourably to Robert Plant. This was a quality of which Jimmy Page was eminently aware.

Page had become friends with Cornell. When he toured his book in the United States, he was interviewed by Cornell onstage in the beautiful art deco theatre in Los Angeles' Ace Hotel. With selected images from the book projected onto a screen, Page regaled the audience with tales of both Zeppelin and his earlier life.

At the end of 2015 Page had announced that he would be releasing a new album and touring with a brand new line-up in the coming year. He knew who the vocalist would be: Chris Cornell. Even though, as with so many matters associated with him, the project was put on hold, Jimmy Page was determined that his musical future would be intertwined with Cornell.

When he performed Cornell would include such Zeppelin numbers as 'Immigrant Song' and 'Tangerine'. The last song he ever played live, at a show in Detroit, Michigan, was Zeppelin's 'In My Time of Dying', with its lines 'In my time of dying, I want nobody to mourn/All I want for you to do is take my body home'.

'RIP Chris Cornell. Incredibly Talented. Incredibly Young. Incredibly Missed,' tweeted Page.

On 23 October 2017, as many a venerable elder statesmen had before him, Page made an appearance at the Oxford Union, topping the bill of speakers that Michaelmas term; his silver hair, usually so neatly tied back, now billowed fluffily around his head, making him look precisely like an eccentric professor; Page always had that precise attention to detail in his appearance.

He revealed that in his time playing with the beat poet Royston Ellis, around 1960, he had previously appeared at the Oxford Union: 'I was accompanying him on guitar for a couple of his poems.' Page also recalled the occasion he had accompanied Jeff Beck to that Yardbirds show at the university when Keith Relf freaked out existentially on stage, causing Paul Samwell-Smith to storm out of the group, leaving the way for Page to join.

Then a member of the audience asked him a pertinent question: what was Page's most cherished memory of being in Led Zeppelin with regards to the lifestyle and the 1970s experience?

'Well, I was creating an art form,' he replied. 'That's what I was doing. I mean, I was, from day one I was developing a whole persona, but I was living it. It wasn't anything that was false or sham. I was living it every inch of the way. And that was the determination of it, because I was so committed to the whole aspect of writing new music and presenting views on music that other people hadn't really got to yet. I mean, they probably would do, but to be able to do that, I just really … each and every one of us in that band, as I said, it was a communion and that was just something which was such a buzz to be playing in a band like that and certainly a band that, initially from *Led Zeppelin I*, I knew exactly the whole of the textures that I wanted to present to people so that they would go, "Wow, that's really interesting. I haven't heard so many things approached in one go." Just the ethos of keep moving and moving and moving forward with these ideas. That was just intoxicating.'

In the way that Page chose to disport himself during Led Zeppelin's supremacy there certainly are disagreeable elements: how he manifested the group's pre-eminence and the image he chose to display to his audience. As time progressed, culminating in the debacle of the cathartic July 1977 Oakland shows, he seemed increasingly less in control of not only his act, but also of himself. Three or four years earlier in that decade the very mention of Jimmy Page's name could induce in some the kind of frissons of fear that suggested the villain of a Gothic horror novel. Yet by the summer of 1977 the behemoth of Led Zeppelin, his sacred art project, until then the decade's biggest and most influential band, had set about consuming itself.

An artist accustomed to living amid inspiring dreams and apparitions, Page's addictions to drink and drugs clearly began to dam up such outlets. And during the next decade his output, and his appearance, would certainly suggest someone missing in action, not only from his audience but also from himself. As high as he had been, so low would he fall.

There is a music-business adage that 20 years is the period before a formerly great act, having fallen off the radar, is reappraised and restored to its previous legend. In fact, despite the weak output of the Firm, the *Outrider* album and the project with David Coverdale, Jimmy Page's period in the wilderness was relatively brief. By the mid-nineties his work with Robert Plant, beginning with the *Unledded* MTV show, had restored him to heights that were almost at the level of Led Zeppelin. To hell with any talk of backstage angst or bad vibes between Page and Plant; it had not been that great with Led Zeppelin. And by the new century – and even before the 2007 Led Zeppelin one-show reunion – his deliverance seemed complete: no longer the feared figure of rock 'n' roll sword and sorcery myth, Page has emerged as the most revered and respected of all classic rock artists. Despite all the odds, Jimmy Page has become the greatest national treasure of British popular music.

SOURCES

Among the seemingly countless books I have consulted, the following have proved especially invaluable:

Baker, Phil. *Austin Osman Spare: The Life and Legend of London's Lost Artist* (Strange Attractor Press, 2012)

Berbergal, Peter. *Season of the Witch: How the Occult Saved Rock and Roll* (Tarcher, 2015)

Bordowitz, Hank (editor). *Led Zeppelin on Led Zeppelin: Interviews and Encounters* (Omnibus Press, 2015)

Boyd, Jenny with George-Warren, Holly. *It's Not Only Rock 'n' Roll* (John Blake Publishing, 2013)

Buell, Bebe with Bockris, Victor. *Rebel Heart: An American Rock 'n' Roll Journey* (St. Martin's Press, 2001)

Calef, Scott (editor). *Led Zeppelin and Philosophy: All Will Be Revealed* (Open Court, 2009)

Case, George. *Jimmy Page: Magus Musician Man: An Unauthorised Biography* (Backbeat Books, 2009)

Case, George. *Led Zeppelin FAQ* (Backbeat Books, 2011)

Cole, Richard with Trubo, Richard. *Stairway to Heaven: Led Zeppelin Uncensored* (HarperCollins, 1992)

Crowley, Aleister. *The Confessions of Aleister Crowley* (Penguin, 1989)

Crowley, Aleister. *Magick* (Red Wheel/Weiser, 1998)

Crowley, Aleister. *The Diary of a Drug Fiend* (Weiser Books, 2010)

Crowley, Aleister. *The Book of the Law* (Createspace Independent Publishing Platform, 2011)

Davis, Erik. *Led Zeppelin's Led Zeppelin IV* (Bloomsbury Continuum, 2005)

Davis, Stephen. *Hammer of the Gods: Led Zeppelin Unauthorised* (William Morrow & Co., 1985)

Davis, Stephen. *LZ-'75: The Lost Chronicles of Led Zeppelin's 1975 American Tour* (Gotham Books, 2010)

Des Barres, Pamela. *I'm with the Band: Confessions of a Groupie* (Helter Skelter Publishing, 2003)

Des Barres, Pamela. *Take Another Little Piece of My Heart: A Groupie Grows Up* (Chicago Review Press, 2008)

Ellen, Mark. *Rock Stars Stole My Life!* (Coronet, 2015)

Ellis, Royston. *The Big Beat Scene* (Music Mentor Books, 2010)

Faragher, John Mack. *Eternity Street: Violence and Justice in Frontier Los Angeles* (W. W. Norton & Company, 2016)

Gillett, Charlie. *Making Tracks: Atlantic Records and the Growth of a Multi-Billion-Dollar Industry* (Panther/ Granada Publishing, 1975)

Goldberg, Danny. *Bumping into Geniuses: My Life Inside the Rock and Roll Business* (Penguin, 2010)

Graham, Bill and Greenfield, Robert. *Bill Graham Presents: My Life Inside Rock and Out* (Da Capo Press, 2004)

Greenfield, Robert. *The Last Sultan: The Life and Times of Ahmet Ertegun* (Simon & Schuster, 2012)

Guralnick, Peter. *Sweet Soul Music: Rhythm and Blues and the Southern Dream of Freedom* (Canongate, 2002)

Hoskyns, Barney. *Trampled Under Foot: The Power and Excess of Led Zeppelin* (Faber & Faber, 2012)

James, Catherine. *Dandelion: Memoir of a Free Spirit* (St. Martin's Press, 2007)

Johns, Glyn. *Sound Man* (Penguin, 2014)

Lewis, Dave. *The Complete Guide to the Music of Led Zeppelin* (Omnibus Press, 1994)

Lewis, Dave. *Led Zeppelin: The Concert File* (Omnibus Press, 1997)

Lewis, Dave. *Led Zeppelin: A Celebration* (Omnibus Press, 2003)

Mathers, S. Liddell MacGregor. *The Key of Solomon the King* (Createspace Independent Publishing Platform, 2010)

May, Betty. *Tiger Woman: My Story* (Gerald Duckworth & Co. Ltd, 2014)

Napier-Bell, Simon. *Black Vinyl White Powder* (Ebury Press, 2002)

Napier-Bell, Simon. *You Don't Have to Say You Love Me* (Ebury Press, 2005)

Page, Jimmy. *Jimmy Page by Jimmy Page* (Genesis Publications, 2014)

Power, Martin. *Hot Wired Guitar: The Life of Jeff Beck* (Omnibus Press, 2012)

Power, Martin. *No Quarter: The Three Lives of Jimmy Page* (Omnibus Press, 2016)

Pratt, Guy. *My Bass and Other Animals* (Orion, 2007)

Preston, Neal. *Led Zeppelin: A Photographic Collection* (Vision On Publishing, 2002)

Rees, Paul. *Robert Plant: A Life* (HarperCollins, 2014)

Roberty, Marc. *Led Zeppelin Day by Day* (Backbeat Books, 2016)

Selvin, Joel. *Here Comes the Night: The Dark Soul of Bert Berns and the Dirty Business of Rhythm and Blues* (Counterpoint, 2014)

Shapiro, Harry. *Alexis Korner: The Biography* (Bloomsbury Publishing, 1996)

Tolinski, Brad. *Light and Shade: Conversations with Jimmy Page* (Ebury Press, 2012)

Townshend, Pete. *Who I Am* (HarperCollins, 2012)

Wall, Mick. *When Giants Walked the Earth: A Biography of Led Zeppelin* (Orion, 2008)

Welch, Chris. *Peter Grant: The Man Who Led Zeppelin* (Omnibus Press, 2002)

Welch, Morgana. *Hollywood Diaries* (Xlibris, 2007)

Williams, David. *The First Time We Met the Blues* (Music Mentor Books, 2009)

Wolman, Baron. *Groupies and Other Electric Ladies* (ACC Editions, 2016)

Wyman, Bill. *Stone Alone* (Viking, 1990)

Yorke, Ritchie. *Led Zeppelin: Led to Gold 1967–1989* (Rock n Roo, 2015)

Zanetta, Tony. *Stardust: The David Bowie Story* (McGraw-Hill, 1986)

ACKNOWLEDGEMENTS

Three years ago I was in Los Angeles, staying at the apartment of my son Alex. On the morning I was due to return to London I woke early, then briefly fell asleep again. I had a dream. 'Write the Jimmy Page book!' I was told. I'd had the dream in LA, the archetypal Led Zeppelin town. It all seemed to make sense to me. So I decided to listen to what I'd been told.

And during the writing of *Jimmy Page: The Definitive Biography* I listened to words of wisdom from many people, including John Altman, Dave Ambrose, Wayne Bardell, Jonathan Barnett, Michael Des Barres, Dave Berry, Chris Blackwell, John Bold, Mick Brown, Tony Busson, Roy Carr, JC Carroll, Chris Charlesworth, Glen Colson, Trevor Dann, Chalkie Davies, Jeff Dexter, Trevor Dolby, John Dunbar, Rick Elgood, Mark Ellen, Tony Fletcher, Paul Gorman, Nanette Greenblatt, Billy Harrison, Brian Helgeland, Henry Scott Irvine, Joe Jammer, Brixton Key, Jamie Kitman, Jeanette Lee, Nick Logan, Jackie McAuley, Jack McKeever, Alex Masucci, Lori Mattix, Julian Moseley, Michi Nakao, Simon Napier-Bell, Suzette Newman, Dick O'Dell, Steve 'Snips' Parsons, Mark Plummer, Guy Pratt, Andy Priest, David Robson, Jon Savage, Tim Spicer, Joe Stevens, Kosmo Vinyl, Mick Wall, Michael Watts, Chris Welch, Richard Williams, Bruno Wizard and the great Rod Wyatt.

To these and many others I am heartfully grateful. And I am especially indebted to Becky Thomas, my agent, and to the wonderful Natalie Jerome, who commissioned this book, and the equally fantastic Jack Fogg, who then guided it to its destiny, along with the splendid editing of Steve Burdett.

Another exotic location also played a part in the writing of *Jimmy Page: The Definitive Biography*. Flat-out exhausted at one point, I knew I badly needed a break. But instead it was clear that I had to keep writing, otherwise the book would not be completed. In the end, I had some great aid: Chris Blackwell, who has helped with this book, lent me a cottage at GoldenEye, the Jamaican estate he owns at which Ian Fleming wrote the James Bond books. So for a month I would get up early, write (hoping to pick up some Fleming vibes) until mid-afternoon, and then swim my knackeredness away. Give serious thanks ...

INDEX